Women and Social Change

Feminist Activism in Canada

D0143794

Women and Social Change

Feminist Activism in Canada

Edited by
Jeri Dawn Wine and Janice L. Ristock

James Lorimer and Company, Publishers
Toronto, 1991

Canadian Cataloguing in Publication Data

Main entry under title:
Women and social change

ISBN 1-55028-358-8 (bound) ISBN 1-55028-356-1 (pbk.)

1. Feminism - Canada. 2. Women in politics - Canada. 3. Women - Canada - Social conditions.

I. Wine, Jeri Dawn. II. Ristock, Janice L. (Janice Lynn)

HQ1453.W65 1991   305.42'0971   C90-095418-6

Cover photo: International Women's Day Demonstration in Toronto, Canapress, 1988.

James Lorimer & Company, Publishers
Egerton Ryerson Memorial Building
35 Britain Street
Toronto, Ont M5A 1R7

Printed and bound in Canada
5 4 3 2 93 94 95

Contents

Preface

As editors of the present volume, our primary goal has been to affirm and strengthen the links that exist between feminists in the academic and non-academic communities. We consider it important that the false division between feminists in these communities be further bridged in order to foster a climate for future feminist social change. The present book was conceived in an effort to strengthen the relations between the two communities by providing feminist models of social change, examples of successful organizing efforts on the part of activists in both the academic and non-academic communities, and feminist teaching methods intended to foster feminists social change.

The idea for this volume arose from our own frustrations in trying to find a Canadian collection of material that documented women's experiences and struggles in their community organizing. Jeri Wine was teaching a graduate course at the Ontario Institute for Studies in Education (OISE) on feminist community activism. She was aware of the lack of Canadian sources. The only materials available were in Canadian women's movement periodicals and in unpublished movement documents. Janice Ristock was a PhD candidate at OISE researching feminist collectives. Through her research she became aware of the tendency of women's groups to repeat the same process when addressing orgazinational difficulties. Our awareness of the lack of easily accessible Canadian women's material on social change efforts, combined with our knowledge of and involvement in many feminist groups, led to the development of this volume. This book, in many ways, represents a synthesis of our academic and political commitments.

The organization of the volume reflects our goals of producing useful learning and teaching materials on the Canadian women's movement. The first section presents frameworks and strategies that are representative of feminist activism in the Canadian context. These chapters reflect the Canadian political environment, as well as theoretical and practical links with the global women's movement. The second section contains chapters on specific organizing efforts and forms. Though the content and the format of these chapters vary considerably, they are all at a descriptive level that conveys the specific nature of the feminist activism they discuss in order that they may be used as feminist organizing tools, as texts in feminist studies classrooms, and as historical records. The final section consists of contributions that describe feminist innovations in linking theory with practice. In traditional male-centred thought the contributions of academics are seen as providing theory while activists carry out practice. The work described in these chapters bridges the male-defined distinctions between theory and practice, academy and community. It includes discussions of a unique Canadian national umbrella organization that brings together feminists whose primary locations are either the academic or non-academic community, a university based structure which allows feminists in the non-academic community access to resources fostering activist goals and descriptions of feminist research and teaching designed to bridge academic/non-academic barriers.

This book has taken us more than two years to complete. We began with a great deal of euphoria as we gathered exciting contributions for the volume. We had to maintain the energy and commitment to the book and to each other, in spite of numerous obstacles. We also had to work to maintain communication with the contributors to this volume. We would like to thank all of the contributors for their patience with this project. Their commitment and hard work was often tested when we asked them to re-write or edit sections of their contributions and to keep to timelines. We think that the book is strong because of the quality of the contributions and the diversity of the contributors.

We also wish to thank the people at James Lorimer and Company for their guidance bringing this edited collection to fruition.

We especially want to thank our friends and families for their support and encouragement about this book. They have helped us believe in this book when the work seemed endless and have listened and talked with us about our ideas for this work. Jeri would particularly like to express her gratitude to

Anneke Steenbeek, for her ongoing support. Janice would like to thank Natalie Zlodre, Margo Rivera and Rebecca Sugarman for their continued support.

We also want to thank one another for persevering despite many obstacles. Not only have we completed this book together, but we have maintained a friendship and increased our commitment to working for social change.

Jeri Dawn Wine
Janice L. Ristock

Introduction

Feminist Activism in Canada

Jeri Dawn Wine and Janice L. Ristock

The contemporary women's movement has been a potent force for social change in Canadian society for more than two decades. Change has been elicited at all levels of government — federal, provincial, and municipal — in the institutions and regulations affecting women's lives. Women are in the paid workforce in ever greater numbers, and are entering previously male-dominated occupations with greater frequency. Feminist activism has succeeded in changing public understanding of male violence against women and girls, and providing services to many female victims. Women have organized to elicit changes in educational practices and materials at every level of the educational system as a result of the feminist recognition that, traditionally, education has fostered male power and control. Feminists have created a network of organizations, publications, book stores, presses, and small businesses. Perhaps the most impressive impact of the movement is the massive shift in the consciousness of the Canadian public in terms of affirmation of women's right to equality, including reproductive freedom, equal treatment in the workplace, and freedom from violence (Adamson, Briskin & McPhail, 1988).

The effects of Canadian feminist activism are evident in legislative, constitutional, and judicial landmarks at the national level, in areas as diverse as the winning of our Equal Rights Amendment, clause 28(b) of the Constitution (Kome, 1983); the 1988 Supreme Court ruling supporting women's right to access to abortion (Van Wagner 1988); change in the blatantly misogynous Indian Act granting native women the same treaty rights as native men (Silman and the women of Tobique Reserve 1987; see also Bear, Chapter 11); recognition of the prevalence of violence against women reflected in changes in the federal government's official positions on wife battering (MacLeod 1980 and 1987), child sexual abuse (Cole 1987) and sexual assault (the Bill C-127 Working Group 1983); and recognition of the necessity for affirmative action to insure women's equal treatment in the workplace (Bill C-62, passed in 1986). These feminist successes at the national level have been parallelled by achievements at the local community and provincial levels. Every feminist success has been achieved with the labour and commitment of countless women in communities across Canada, and each one requires constant vigilance to maintain, as made clear by the recent (May, 1990) Conservative government's regressive federal legislation recriminalizing abortion, which was defeated in the Senate on January 31, 1991.

The contemporary movement is often labelled the "second wave" women's movement in recognition of the important work accomplished in "first wave" feminism in the late-nineteenth and early-twentieth centuries when basic human rights for women — voting and property rights — were won. Though building on the basics provided by the "first wave" movement, the contemporary movement has been more sweeping in its demands and successes.

The accomplishments of the movement are impressive, though the changes in the material circumstances of women's lives have not been as extensive as those for which feminist activists have aimed. Poverty remains a predominantly female experience in Canada, with women earning little more than half of men's earnings, nearly half of female-headed households, most disabled women, and single elderly women living below the poverty line (National Council on Welfare 1988; Doucette, Chapter 12).

Women are highly subject to male violence, in intimate relationships in the home, as well as from acquaintances and strangers outside the home. Women remain almost solely responsible for emotional and physical care-taking in families, resulting in a double workday for women with families who are in the paid work force. Women are under-represented in governmental and other institutional authority structures. Our reproductive rights are not firmly established, as reflected by the recent attempt to re-criminalize of abortion, and women's widely varying access to abortion across the country. Our right to live as lesbians is still in question as federal human rights legislation protecting lesbians and gays lags behind political promises. In spite of our efforts to effect changes in education, educational institutions and practices are still largely under male control and producing male-centered knowledge, with the exception of feminist enclaves such as university women's studies programs.

The institutionalized or public face of feminism has been shaped largely by the interests of middle-class white feminists, while the concerns of women more marginalized from the centres of power have been surfacing in recent years in the grassroots activism of poor and working-class women, lesbians (Stone, Chapter 13), Native women (Bear, Chapter 11), immigrant women (Ng, Chapter 10), women of colour, disabled women (Doucette, Chapter 12), elderly women, and rural women (Haley, Chapter 9 and Miles, Chapter 3). Though most Canadian women espouse agreement with the various aims of the movement, it is typically with the preface "I'm not a feminist, but ... "

Clearly, the women's movement has been a potent force for change in Canadian society, as its many accomplishments attest, yet there is considerable work to be done. Fortunately, in spite of the media's wistful proclamations that "the women's movement is dead" or that "this is the post-feminist era," the movement is still very much vital and alive. It is represented in feminist activism in communities in every Canadian province and in national organizations, activism that reflects the diverse class, ethnic and linguistic identities and concerns of Canadian women, and the diverse geographic and demographic characteristics of their communities, as well as the uniquely Canadian political climate.

In the present volume, our goals are to provide accounts of some of the directions, strategies and actions of the contemporary Canadian women's movement. There have been excellent accounts of the movement, the most comprehensive being Adamson, Briskin and McPhail's (1988) recent broad historical overview. We wished to provide in-depth descriptions of particular features of the current movement that may serve as teaching and learning materials. Our intention is that these chapters will be used by feminist activists, both in the community and in academia, who wish to learn from our history.

The perspective we have taken as editors is a "nonaligned" (Bunch 1987) or "integrative" (Miles, Chapter 3) approach to feminism, emphasizing commonalities among the aims of feminists of differing political orientations, such as liberal, radical, socialist, and seeking to establish feminism as a politic in its own right, rather than a derivative of male political thought.

It is our belief that the accomplishments and directions of the contemporary movement have been a result of coalesced efforts among feminists of differing political strands. The focus of the volume is on feminist practice though some of the contributors address some of the important theoretical differences among activists in Canada. These theoretical positions and related practices do not fit neatly into the categories most frequently used of liberal, radical and socialist strands of feminism.

The contributors to the volume are feminists active in the Canadian women's movement whose chapters are based on their experiences and analyses. Our intention was to include contributions from across Canada representing women's concerns in various strata of Canadian society. These contributors describe feminist frameworks and strategies for social change, activist efforts by feminists at the local, provincial and national levels, as well as efforts to link theory and practice through organizational forms, research and teaching that simultaneously embrace feminist activism and theory. The volume deals primarily with the anglophone Canadian women's movement. Though the Québécois women's movement articulates with the anglophone movement in many ways, it has had an independent and vital history.

The Contemporary Canadian Women's Movement

The radical activism that permeated North America in the sixties provided a climate for the development of feminist concerns — activism that included the civil rights and anti-Vietnam war movements in the U.S., and the peace and New

Left student movements in Canada. The Voice of Women, an early precursor of the women's movement, was organized in 1960. It was a national organization that initially addressed peace issues, though it soon took up other causes of particular concern to women.

A major landmark of the movement was the Royal Commission on the Status of Women (RCSW), headed by Florence Bird. The RCSW was created by the federal government in 1967, in response to the pressures of the Committee for Equality of Women in Canada, a group comprised largely of white, middle-class professional women. The recommendations of the report, completed in 1970, have served as a blueprint for the public face of feminism in Canada. The value of the report and the direction it has provided in the movement is debated among feminists. Those whose goals include a more radical transformation of society have been frustrated by RCSW's alignment with liberal tradition, rather than more directly challenging societal power structures (Adamson et al. 1988). The report's recommendations are surprisingly comprehensive and progressive, considering its date of publication and the fact that it is a government-sponsored report. Though many of the feminists who had organized to demand the establishment of the royal commission had expected that the federal government would assume ownership of the recommendations and move quickly to implement them, many of the issues have yet to be addressed in any fashion by the government.

The most immediate effect of the RCSW report was the creation of official spokespersons and bodies in the federal and provincial governments intended to deal with women's concerns. In the more radical and left-wing feminists' view, however, the purposes of the governments' actions were primarily to contain and re-direct the movement. These posts and bodies ranged from the Minister Responsible for the Status of Women in the federal cabinet and the Canadian Advisory Council on the Status of Women at the federal level, to the provincial Status of Women committees and corresponding cabinet ministers. There has been considerable criticism of the provincial committees, yet in some cases their work has been clearly feminist and supportive of the movement. Chapters 6 and 7 refer to the work of provincial committees in Saskatchewan and Manitoba where they have been particularly effective at coalition-building among diverse groups of women.

Leah and Ruecker (Chapter 6) describe the work of the Saskatchewan Action Committee on the Status of Women (SAC), in building a coalition representing a wide spectrum of women's groups and organizations in the province. The coalition was explicitly constructed to protest provincial government cutbacks to women's groups and projects. In the past, SAC has also refused government funding when it was believed that the funding would compromise feminist principles. Often the concerns of women in the sparsely populated North receive little attention in the movement. Graveline, Fitzpatrick, and Mark (Chapter 7) discuss coalition-building around the concerns of women (primarily non-native women) in northern Manitoba, work initiated by northern members of the Manitoba Action Committee on the Status of Women.

One of the early government departments created in 1972, the Women's Program of the Department of the Secretary of State, has served as an important source of funding for women's movement activism, though it has moved from being staffed by committed feminists to staffing primarily by government bureaucrats (Findlay 1987 & 1988; Schreader 1990). This change accompanied a generally more conservative trend in the Canadian political climate in the eighties, including a federal Progressive Conservative government that is quite unresponsive to feminist concerns, and an organized right-wing movement. The best known representative of that movement is R.E.A.L. (Realistic, Equal, Active and for Life) Women, a conservative, pro-life group opposed to virtually every aim of the women's movement.

The nature of the feminist movement in Canada can be described as somewhat contradictory since it has been shaped by two poles: feminist aims that involve restructuring society in opposition to the very close links that exist between the movement and the state. The movement-state links are a result, in large part, of two related factors, the first being the RCSW report and its sequelae, the second, that much of the movement has been state funded.

Institutionalized and disengaged feminist activism

Briskin (Chapter 1, also see Adamson, et al. 1988; and Findlay 1988) distinguishes between the institutionalized or mainstream face of feminism, and disengaged or grassroots organizing. The former is represented by feminist efforts to work within and to influence the institutional arrangements of the Canadian state through lobbying for changes in legislative and judicial decisions, engaging in electoral politics and similar activities. The latter refers to more autonomous women's community-based grassroots activism that resists connection to state influence. Briskin notes that a total commitment to one or the other pole can limit the accomplishments of the movement. In Canadian feminist activism these terms frequently represent emphases rather than separate poles. Often the efforts of Canadian feminist activists represent a sometimes unwieldy and unsatisfactory synthesis of the two.

Vickers (Chapter 4) describes the Canadian political climate as one of "radical liberalism," which is partly the result of the presence of a recognized left-wing political party. According to Vickers, Canadians have a history of peaceful pressure and lobbying for response from the Canadian government, accompanied by a belief in that responsiveness. In the feminist movement this "radical liberalism" is a synthesis of institutional and grassroots organizing and is reflected in the frequency with which women's movement groups and organizations in Canada, even the most radical, seek and receive funding from government bodies (however inadequate the funding and compromising to movement ideals).

Feminist Organizational Forms and Processes

Vickers suggests that national umbrella organizations, coalitions representing the interests of diverse and widely dispersed women's groups, have been particularly appropriate to the Canadian feminist movement, in view of Canada's large area and relatively small population. In general, coalitions are a frequently utilized organizational form in Canadian feminist activism. In contrast, many feminists, particularly radical feminists, consider the small face-to-face group that operates on an egalitarian, collective model to most fully reflect feminist process. It has proven difficult for feminists to meld the structure and procedures associated with the former with the participatory democratic values inherent in the latter, though the national umbrella organizations and other women's coalitions have often done a reasonably good job of melding institutional and grassroots politics.

The Committee for Equality of Women in Canada (CEW) which lobbied in 1967 for the Royal Commission became the Ad Hoc Committee on the Status of Women when the RCSW report was produced in 1970. The Ad Hoc Committee was formed expressly to lobby the government to implement the recommendations of the report; it evolved into the National Action Committee on the Status of Women (NAC). When first formed the Ad Hoc Committee represented 15 groups, many of them professional and mainstream women's groups. In 1988, NAC had grown to represent 570 member groups and organizations (Riggs & Tyler 1988). Vickers estimates that there are a total of some 2500 feminist organizations of one sort or another in Canada, but those that are members of NAC represent the full spectrum, from radical grassroots feminist groups to women's caucuses in political parties.

"The challenge for NAC in the years to follow (its creation) was to become a coalition that would truly represent the variety and range of the women's movement in Canada" (Adamson, et al. 1988, 53). There is considerable difference of opinion on the extent to which NAC has been able to meet this challenge as an organization, but there can be no denying that it is a feminist organization unique to the Canadian political climate. Though occasionally characterized as parallel to the National Organization of Women (NOW) in the U.S., there is little similarity. NOW is a self-consciously liberal feminist organization, representing only itself and lacking formal connections with other women's organizations. In contrast, NAC has sought to represent the entire Canadian women's movement, an audacious, perhaps impossible, but worthy feminist aim.

NAC is criticized for functioning in a primarily reactive fashion to the legislation and actions of the federal government, and for being focused on lobbying rather than on a proactive creation of feminist politics. It has also come under considerable attack for its lack of attention to feminist process in its organization, procedures and functioning, as more groups representing women who are not relatively privileged, white and middle class have joined in recent years. Chapters 4 and 5 of this volume deal directly with this debate. Vickers makes a strong case for the necessity of a representative democratic process in a national feminist organization, and recommends broadening our understanding of the nature of feminist process, a position supported by Briskin (Chapter 1). Greaves questions the realization in NAC of a genuinely feminist democratic process fully representing the concerns of member groups or the wide regional base of the organization, and makes suggestions for organizational and procedural changes to address these concerns. The frequency with which NAC is mentioned in contributions in this volume underscores its importance in the Canadian feminist political milieu.

The Canadian Research Institute for the Advancement of Women (CRIAW) is another national feminist umbrella group that was created in the mid-seventies as a coalition of feminist activists, whose primary locations were both in the community and in academia. The major aims of CRIAW are to encourage, coordinate and disseminate research on women's experience in Canada. Christiansen-Ruffman (Chapter 14) discusses the aims and accomplishments of this unique Canadian organization in some detail. CRIAW has cross-country representation and there has been considerable effort over the years to insure francophone participation.

State funding. Both NAC and CRIAW, like many other Canadian women's movement groups and organizations, rely heavily on funding from the Secretary of State Women's Program; this reliance has been a source of strength, as well as an area of vulnerability. The operating budgets of both organizations have been cut by 15 to 20 percent in each of the last two years by the federal government. In the most recent spate of cuts in May 1990, funding was also cut to all other national feminist groups, to Quebec provincial feminist groups and was eliminated entirely for feminist publications. Funding to women's centres across Canada was also eliminated, but was restored for a single year in response to massive protests across the country. Clearly, the Progressive Conservative govern-

ment is determined to reduce, if not sever, the close relationship between the women's movement and the state. In view
of the fact that the cuts were accompanied by similarly massive
cuts to the Native movement, it's likely that the government
is attempting to eliminate from the public arena voices critical
of its actions. These governmental reactions attest to the effectiveness of the women's movement as well as to its vulnerability.

Feminists in the United States and Britain have been more
wary about ties with the state, and have been active in seeking
funding sources that do not obligate them to follow
bureaucratic directives and expose them to pressure to refor-
mulate their feminist ideology and goals. There are, certainly,
advantages to an autonomous feminist movement that is not
tied to and dependent on the state (Adamson, et al. 1988;
Findlay 1987 and 1988; Ng, Walker, and Muller 1990). Janice
Ristock's discussion of feminist social service collectives
(Chapter 2) indicates some of the contradictions and tensions
involved for feminists attempting to maintain an egalitarian
organization working for social change when that organization is state-funded and, to some extent, state-controlled. The
collectives that she has researched are primarily ones active in
providing social services to women who have been the victims
of violence.

The issues involved in the ties between the movement and
the state as represented by state funding are complex ones.
Many of the achievements of Canadian feminist activism
would not exist had such funding not been available; and
meeting women's needs is now (however inadequately) entrenched in governmental bureaucracies. Many feminists
strongly believe the movement is as entitled to state money as
is government bureaucracy or the corporate sector. On the
other hand, movement ideals have been compromised: feminists working in state-funded organizations have found themselves involved in meeting the terms of government contracts
(which often do not correspond to the aims of their activism),
spending much of their time seeking funding, taking valuable
time and energy from work necessary to the movement, and
policing themselves and other feminists in terms consistent

with bureaucratic directives in order to insure continued funding.

Feminist process. The search for organizational structures and processes that reflect feminist values and goals is a theme that echoes throughout the volume. Feminists have critiqued patriarchal organizational models for the extent to which power, leadership, decision-making and expertise are embedded in a rigid, hierarchical authority structure (e.g., Ferguson 1984). However, there is controversy among feminists regarding the possibility of developing organizational models that clearly reflect feminist values of inclusion and non-hierarchical structure, that are enduring and that *work*, and that allow us to reach feminist goals in a reasonable time frame. As discussed above, Vickers and Briskin question the norms for feminist process derived from the collective practice of small face-to-face homogeneous feminist groups, in their application to large, heterogeneous national organizations, such as NAC. Greaves, on the other hand, makes interesting suggestions for the functioning of NAC that accommodate to its size, while allowing for inclusion and a more horizontal structure.

Ristock (Chapter 2) has examined small, localized feminist social services that function on a collective model, the model most often considered to be particularly reflective of "feminist process." These collectives operate according to an egalitarian organizational structure, with a consensus decision-making process. She notes the difficulties described by women in these collectives with the lack of clear structure and accountability, pressure for conformity and concealed leadership. She describes innovative organizational experiments some collectives are carrying out to address these problems. She concludes that there is no single structure or mode of functioning, even in small face-to-face groups, that is ideally feminist in nature. She makes a plea for feminists to move beyond simplistic either/or thinking in this area and encourages further analysis and experimentation with organizational forms and processes.

In practice, a number of organizational forms are described throughout the volume and are used throughout the movement. For example, Reddin (Chapter 8) describes a variety of types of feminist organizations in one small community, Prince Edward Island. Canadian feminist activists have used structures that are appropriate to particular circumstances and problems, while attempting to give voice to all of the women involved. It's important for feminists to address explicitly and inventively the issues of organizational structure and process in feminist organizations of differing sizes, purposes, compositions, and stages of development. The early simplistic dichotomous feminist beliefs that hierarchical structure (indeed, often defined structure of any sort) was invariably masculinist and therefore unacceptable, and only collectivist structures of a particular kind could be feminist, are neither adequate nor descriptive of the complexities of the movement.

Women's Diversity and the Canadian Women's Movement

In its first decade the goals and actions of the Canadian women's movement were shaped by white middle-class feminists, whose understandings of the nature of oppression were shaped by their own experiences. Though the various documents of the movement, beginning with the Royal Commission report, have addressed race and class, these concerns have been additions to the core concerns which were constructed around the experiences of white, middle-class women — they have not been integral to feminists' understandings of the nature and purposes of the movement. In the late 1970s and 1980s, white Canadian feminists have become acutely aware of women's diversity, as have feminists in other countries, and of the failure of some of our early understandings of feminist aims to centrally address the concerns of the women most marginal to the power structures of Canadian society. White feminists are having to come to terms with the racism, classism, heterosexism, ageism, and 'ablebodiedism' of the movement and of ourselves.

Black women's writings and activism, both in the U.S. and Canada, have been particularly instrumental in initiating these changes (see Stasiulis, 1987 for review). Their work has made it clear that black women are likely to experience racism as more oppressive than sexism. The history of black peoples' slavery in North America and its virulent racist sequelae have had a more powerful effect on the day-to-day lives of black women than has the sexism of black men or of society at large. They have challenged white feminists to recognize that the feminism they have constructed has little to do with the lives of black women.

The activist work of Native women to change section 12(b) of the Indian Act, and its denial of treaty rights to Native women who married non-Native men (Bear, Chapter 11) has also been instructive to white feminists. That battle was fought almost entirely by Native women, though women's movement organizations provided some support. Again, Native women typically state that they experience racism as being more powerful in its effects on their lives than is sexism. Though aboriginal organizations controlled by Native men did not, for the most part, support the battle to change Section 12(b), many Native women, like many black women, feel that it is important in their work against racism in Canadian society to maintain solidarity with the men who share their experience.

Immigrant women have also challenged white women's understandings of feminism (Ng, Chapter 10). As Ng notes, the very category, "immigrant women," is itself a racist creation, since only women who are either non-white, poor or non-English speaking are likely to be labelled in this fashion (*see also* Bannerji, 1987). The lives of immigrant women are circumscribed in ways that have no precedent in white, middle-class Canadian women's experience, e.g., as sponsored immigrants they lack access to training in English as a second language, or to government support in the labour market. Canadian immigration policies have been and are, frankly, racist, affecting the experiences of immigrants from differing countries in different ways. Ng discusses the activism of immigrant women in which she has been involved in three Canadian provinces.

Though lesbians have been very active in the movement since its inception the statements and actions of the organized movement have, for the most part, been oddly silent regarding lesbian experience and oppression. It's likely that the close relationship between the movement and the state in Canada has helped to insure this silence in order to avoid jeopardizing other movement goals. The present Progressive Conservative government has given good cause for such caution, with the Secretary of State Women's Program's homophobic policy of refusing funding to "those organizations, projects and recipients whose primary purpose is to promote a view on sexual orientation" (Fairness in Funding report 1987, 15). The organized far right and the conservative trend of the eighties has provided a milieu which contributes to the silencing of lesbians. Stone (Chapter 13) discusses the activism of a Toronto-based lesbian group, Lesbians Against the Right, who organized in the early eighties to fight the homophobia of the organized right.

Disabled women pose another great challenge to the women's movement. The movement, until recently, has been quite blind to its 'ablebodiedism' — its assumption that all women are essentially ablebodied. Conferences and other events, feminist book stores, as well as feminist social services have often been inaccessible to disabled women. Moreover, until recently the demands of the movement have not taken into account the needs of disabled women. However, the activism of disabled women is bringing results. Sign language interpretation for the deaf at feminist events, and more accesibility to feminist services are steps along the way that the movement has to travel to fully address the concerns of disabled women. As Doucette notes (Chapter 12) the vast majority of disabled women in Canada are severely impoverished and are particularly vulnerable to violence. She describes the creation of the DisAbled Women's Network (DAWN), a cross-Canada organization, young and struggling for survival, that has carried out important networking and has successfully challenged women's movement organizations.

Other groupings that have been neglected by the organized women's movement are elderly women and rural women. Haley (Chapter 9) describes the organizations that farm women have themselves created that represent their particular concerns, some of them clearly representing the institutional face of feminism, others that are grassroots organizations whose mandates are more centrally representative of women's concerns. As Miles (Chapter 3) notes, the female culture that tends to be solidly present among rural women is a firm basis on which to build feminist activism.

The task of bringing the concerns of these diverse groups of women to the centre of the organized women's movement is an enormous one. To date, their activism has been largely centered within particular groupings and focused on each group's particular needs and concerns — a form of politics Briskin (Chapter 1) describes as "identity politics" — presently many are insisting that their interests be represented more centrally in the movement. The International Women's Day Coalition in Toronto has been among the most successful movement activities in making central the voices of women of colour and working-class women (Egan 1987; Egan, Gardner & Persad 1988). The national organizations and feminist coalitions are becoming more unwieldy as these groups of women whose voices have previously been silenced or marginalized, clamour to be heard and to be centrally represented. The hurdles to be crossed to achieve the goal of integrating the diverse voices and needs of Canadian women in these organizations are difficult ones. There appears to be firm commitment on the part of feminists presently involved in these organizations and coalitions to insure that the voices and concerns of the diversity of Canadian women are represented. It is likely that two of the most important forces to shape the movement in the nineties will be the precarious relationship between the movement and the state, and the necessity of representing the diversity of women's experience.

Feminism in Education

One of the most important accomplishments of the contemporary North American women's movement, which marks it as different from the "first wave" women's movement of the late-nineteenth and early-twentieth centuries, is the recognition of the necessity for transformative change in educational institutions and practices. The history of the Canadian women's movement and the development of feminist influence in Canadian higher education are tightly interwoven. There has been exciting feminist work at every level of the educational system; its effects are most identifiable at the level of post-secondary education. Early in the second-wave movement feminists in Canada and the U.S. recognized that knowledge is male-centred and male-controlled, and that academia is an important site of knowledge production and control. Both the male-centered nature and content of knowledge, and the authoritarian, hierarchical structure of higher education were seen as in need of transformation (e.g., Rich 1975).

The feminist transformation process is a slow and agonizing one, in the sense of changing the academy as a whole; but the success of one of its central features cannot be denied — the establishment of women's studies courses in universities and community colleges across Canada. Feminist academics began to teach women's studies courses simultaneously in a number of institutions across Canada and the U.S. in the years 1969 to 1971. At first, these efforts by feminists were spontaneous and uncoordinated; though information networks and organizations soon developed. At present, most anglophone Canadian universities have some representation of women's studies, from a few courses to full-degree programs, as Brodribb (1987) has recently documented. She warns feminists to avoid becoming complacent about our accomplishments in academia. Feminist academics are often in precarious non-tenured positions and many women's studies programs have no full-time staff. The widespread presence of women's studies courses and programs suggests that they are here to stay, though vigilance and continued activism within academia is required to insure their survival.

In Canada, feminist academics have created a number of organizations representing the interests of feminists within their academic disciplines, for example, the Section on Women and Psychology of the Canadian Psychological Association and the Status of Women Committee of the Canadian Sociology and Anthropology Association (*see* Drakich & Maticka-Tyndale, Chapter 15). The national organization that represents feminist academics' interests is the Canadian Women's Studies Association. The Canadian Research Institute for the Advancement of Women, an express purpose of which is to link academic and community feminist activists, has a large membership of academic feminists (*see* Christiansen-Ruffman, Chapter 14).

Feminist academics have also been active in changing the nature of established academic disciplinary organizations in North America, with particular effectiveness in the social sciences and humanities — those disciplines in which there is the largest concentration of women (Spender, 1981). These efforts have involved such changes as disciplinary support for affirmative action programs in faculty recruitment, change in journal editorial policies, increased attention to gender issues in journals, conference programs and disciplinary coursework. Drakich and Maticka-Tyndale (Chapter 15) provide a case study account of the work of feminist activists in the Canadian Sociology and Anthropology Association.

Feminist academics have been concerned to do more than "add women and stir" (Bunch 1987). Feminist research and teaching methods are innovative and radical, involving an intense focus on and legitimization of women's experience. They include conscious efforts to break down power hierarchies in the classroom, with an express intention to make women's perspective central and continuous, by bridging theory and practice in concert with a conscious linkage with feminist efforts toward change in the world outside of academia. Prindiville (Chapter 18) and Wine, (Chapter 19) describe feminist teaching efforts designed to honour women's perspectives, and to foster women's activism.

Feminist academics have been active in developing approaches to research that are non-exploitative of the women researched; indeed, in feminist action research it is the concerns of the research participants that shape the work. Messing (Chapter 17) describes a unique program of action research guided by feminist consciousness that has been helpful in addressing the working conditions of women in female-dominated occupations. Feminists have been innovative in creating strategies and structures for empowering women in the community; for example, Bishop, Manicom and Morissey describe in Chapter 16 a university-based organizational structure designed to link women in the community and in academia.

Most Canadian academic feminists have been active in the feminist movement outside of academia (Eichler, 1990), as well as engaging in activism to establish and maintain women's studies in the academy; while many community activists look to academic feminism to provide theory for and documentation of their work, and frequently seek credentials through women's studies programs. Christiansen-Ruffman (Chapter

14) and Bishop, Manicom and Morissey (Chapter 16) discuss some of the tensions between academic and community feminists, noting that community activists sometimes resent the relatively stable, high incomes and resources available to academic feminists, though both are considerably lower than that available to men in similar positions. Women in the community sometimes object to feminist scholars "using" them for research, re-interpreting their experiences in inaccessible academic language, and gaining academic credibility through such use. In some cases there is real cause for such concern, yet there are more commonalities than differences between the aims of feminism in the academy and in the community. And it is feminist, woman-centered documentation of women's experiences and activism, if made accessible, that makes it possible for feminists to learn from our history and to avoid reinventing the wheel each time we engage in activism.

Jeri Dawn Wine
Janice L. Ristock

Section I

Frameworks and Strategies for Social Change

Introduction

This section presents perspectives on models and strategies of feminist organizing, offering frameworks for understanding the variety of issues — theoretical, organizational and strategic — that are facing women in the struggle toward feminist social change. The chapters reflect some of the controversies among feminist theorists and strategists with regard to these issues, and include analysis of feminist activism in such diverse settings as the National Action Committee on the Status of Women, the rural community of Antigonish, Nova Scotia, and small, feminist social service collectives. The contributions meld theory and practice, creating perspectives on feminist praxis that reflect the unique Canadian socio-political milieu.

There are marked theoretical differences among these contributors, differences that do not sort neatly into the frequently used categories of liberal, radical and socialist feminism. Linda Briskin (Chapter 1) writes from a socialist feminist perspective, but presents a model for the analysis of feminist activism that moves beyond the boundaries of socialist feminism. The model addresses two poles of feminist activism: *disengagement*, which is based on a critique of the system while operating outside of it and attempting to create alternative structures, and *mainstreaming*, which relates more directly to the system while attempting to address the majority of the population. She sees dangers in exclusive reliance on either pole, suggesting that exclusive reliance on disengagement is likely to lead to marginalization, while reliance on mainstreaming can lead to institutionalization and co-optation of the movement. She critiques liberal feminism for too much reliance on mainstreaming, with particular concern that the public face of feminism in Canada has become institutionalized. She critiques radical feminism for too great an emphasis on disengagement, and is particularly critical of the norms for "feminist process" which have evolved from radical feminism, norms for egalitarian functioning and consensus decision-making based on interaction in small, homogeneous, face-to-face groups. She calls for a creative integration of the disengagement-main-streaming poles in Canadian feminist activism.

Vickers (Chapter 4) rejects the label of "liberal feminist" for those Canadian feminists engaged in the kind of "mainstreaming" activism described by Briskin. She sees the Canadian political environment as having fostered a political position of "radical liberalism" which has resulted in a rather unified movement (at least among white, anglophone women) with fairly close relations with the state. In her view, Canadians have a considerable amount of faith in government to meet their needs, and a belief that peaceful pressure will bring about change. She argues that Canadian feminism is *presently* characterized by a synthesis of mainstreaming and disengagement as represented in the national umbrella groups, most notably, the National Action Committee on the Status of Women which brings together women's groups of diverse types and ideologies. She challenges Michel's "iron law of oligarchy" that elected and paid officials in an organization inevitably constitute an oligarchy because of their greater knowledge and expertise. She is critical of a feminist position that assumes that this law necessarily applies to a feminist representative democratic model. Like Briskin, she critiques the radical feminist norms for "feminist process" derived from small group interactions, particularly in the demands that have been made on national umbrella groups to adhere to these norms. Vickers recommends experimentation with feminist-informed organizational strategies and structures in national organizations that will maximize accountability and attainment of feminist aims, as well as reflecting the diversity of positions held by women in the organization.

Miles (Chapter 3) analyzes the activism among rural women in Antigonish, Nova Scotia as representative of the development of an integrative feminist politics. Integrative feminism is a total politics that addresses the whole of society and is grounded in the commonalities and values associated with women's lives and experiences in the work of reproduction — such as nurturing, co-operation, love and mutual service. It is a position that cuts across the liberal, radical and socialist feminist categories, as well as women's experiences in differing social and geographical locations. The rural women whose feminist activism she reports in her chapter, are firmly grounded in a female culture, and their activism can be clearly related to an integrative feminist position. Their activism can also be characterized as an integration of the poles of disengagement-mainstreaming, ranging from local female-centered cultural activities to campaigns designed to change governmental positions in feminist directions.

The concern with "feminist process" is an important issue in feminist activist work. Feminists are, for the most part, eager to avoid the excesses of the abuse of power that have characterized male-centered, hierarchical organizational structures. Women in the consciousness-raising (c-r) movement of the sixties and early seventies, rooted in U. S. radical feminism, devised a number of participatory democratic strategies for equalizing power in small groups, including time and task sharing and consensus decision-making. As noted, Vickers and Briskin critique these strategies for their application to the work of national groups, and suggest they are inappropriate in organizations that are large representative democratic structures, and that include women with diverse aims and needs.

Janice L. Ristock (Chapter 2) further questions these norms for "feminist process" in an examination of the functioning of small social service collectives. These collectives are primarily ones that provide services in the area of violence against women. They are made up of small groups of women who are working towards feminist social change and providing aid to women who have been victims of violence. These collectives are committed to egalitarian and consensus models of organizational functioning. In many respects they are the ideal setting for effective application of such a model: they are fairly small, face-to-face groups; the members generally share the same values and goals, and engage in the same feminist-informed service work. Yet the workers report a number of difficulties with the structurelessness and lack of accountability that are often associated with collective functioning, as well as the sense that the diversity of workers' perspectives are not represented. These were collectives whose functioning was more satisfactory for their members, collectives in which experiments with structural models were being carried out. Like the typical collective, the experimental models are horizontally rather than vertically organized, and avoid the extreme differences of power inherent in a hierarchical organization. But they allow for more accountability, greater efficiency in carrying out tasks, and particularly, allow for the diversity in members' experiences to be expressed and addressed in the functioning of the collective.

These contributions point to the necessity for devising organizational forms and strategies that are appropriate to particular kinds of organizations and particular purposes. They underscore the importance of moving beyond early understandings in the contemporary movement regarding the structures and procedures considered to be feminist, to creative experimentation accompanied by the recognition that there are likely a plurality of feminist organizational forms. In practice, feminists do use a variety of organizational forms to good effect, as is evident in the activist work described throughout this volume.

Feminist Practice

A New Approach To Evaluating Feminist Strategy[1]

Linda Briskin

Lynne Segal in *Is the Future Female?* identifies a growing pessimism among British feminists about the possibilities of making change, a pessimism fuelled both by the limited gains of the last twenty years, and the fragmentation of the women's movement. This pessimism has resulted in a tendency to seek a recreated sisterhood based on "the timeless truths of women's lives";[2] and in a strategic orientation away from economic and social change.

In Canada, women's organizing in the last twenty years has netted some significant gains. Perhaps the 1988 Supreme Court decision declaring the abortion law unconstitutional is the most striking, but a balance sheet would also include other legislative gains in the areas of equal pay, affirmative action, sexual assault, family law and sexual harassment. Increases in women's union activism and the concomitant change in union ideology have begun to reshape the labour movement. Changes in state practices concerning police intervention in cases of wife abuse; in educational practices around sex role stereotypes, career counselling and women's studies; in cultural and media practices around images of women combine to highlight the reconstitution of the sex/gender reality.

Despite these successes, women continue to confront attacks by the new right, conservative economic policies, feminization of poverty, inequality in wages and job opportunities, escalating family and street violence, expansion of the pornography industry, and resistance to change embedded in the structures of unions and political parties. This litany is far from complete. Furthermore, continuing public discomfort with 'feminism,' and more importantly, the on-going invisibility of the more radical vision of women's liberation which would entail major social and economic transformation, remind us of the distance yet to be travelled.

In addition to being driven by the necessity to protect and expand women's rights, feminists in Canada continue to be optimistic about the change process. It is in this context that we need to evaluate feminist strategies and expand our understanding of strategic possibilities. This article approaches this project in a two-fold way. The first section examines the categories through which feminisms have traditionally been explored — the political currents and the politics of identity — and explores both their contribution to, and their limitations in assessing and developing political strategy. The second section introduces a model of feminist practice situated within the activist map of the women's movement. Such a model uncovers the difficulties faced by feminist organizing and highlights the potential resolution that I suggest is embedded in a socialist feminist politic.

Differentiating Between Feminisms

Feminism is not a unitary discourse or a unitary practice. Feminist theorists and activists generally distinguish between feminisms on the basis of long-standing political traditions, out of which emerges what are often called the currents of feminism: liberal feminism, radical feminism, and socialist feminism. Although internationally these particular terms are not used consistently, feminists have categorized feminisms in similar ways. Increasingly, feminists are also identifying themselves through what might be called the "politics of identity": as a woman of colour, a Jewish lesbian etc.[3] Both of these approaches have been significant to the development of feminism; each reflects, however, a weakness in our theorizing of feminist practice.

Political Currents

Organizing our understanding of feminisms through the political currents has been quite useful. Alison Jaggar's *Feminist Politics and Human Nature* has contributed immensely to this discussion in North America. Jaggar systematically locates the roots of contemporary feminism inside the mainstream political traditions. In so doing, she reveals the underlying assumptions about human nature and about the possibilities for change that are imbedded in different currents of feminisms.

This approach, however, is not unproblematic. In the first place, it reifies these categories, implying a rigid separation between them and suggesting an internal coherency to each which is only possible at abstract levels of analysis. It also suggests that each current has a clear institutional base and a practice that can be clearly differentiated from the other.

The sharp-edged clarity possible at an abstract level of analysis often becomes opaque when confronted by the complexities of daily political activity. Decisions to plan a demonstration, to build a certain alliance, or to argue for a specific demand rarely emerge directly from theoretical constructs. In the real world of politics, socialist feminists may disagree with each other as often as they agree, and all feminists certainly agree more than they disagree. Not only do all feminists agree about many basic demands for women, they also actively organize together and build alliances. Analyzing feminisms through the categories of the currents obscures this process of joint political struggle for women's liberation. In practice, then, the threads and currents of feminism blur, shifting and adapting to concrete political conditions, creating complex patterns of alliances and coalitions. It is not surprising that practice conforms only to a degree to theoretical distinctions.

Identity politics.

In contrast to self-identification based on political currents, feminists have increasingly defined themselves with reference to identities based on race, ethnicity and sexual orientation, and particular experiences such as being a black single mother who receives family benefits. This practice must be examined in relation to a central dilemma of feminist practice: dealing with "difference."

The compelling notion of sisterhood — a key component of early feminist ideology — conceptualized woman as a unitary category of analysis around which a somewhat unitary practice could be organized. The inadequacy of this approach rapidly became apparent as the women's movement grew. Through struggle, socialist feminists, in particular, have come to recognize the importance of building sisterhood on the basis of difference — in class, race, ethnicity and sexual orientation. Deconstructing the category of woman through the understanding of difference has inspired a more diverse, responsive and complex feminist practice and created the theoretical space for the articulation of a more differentiated feminist politic.

Despite the importance of the "discovery" of difference, this approach intersects problematically with an over-emphasis on experience inside the women's movement. This has been mediated ideologically through the "personal is political," which challenges the public/private split and the overvaluation of the rational and concomitant devaluation of the affective.[4] It validates experience over expertise and, at the same time, depersonalizes/politicizes women's experience, and provides the basis for a coherent analytical and strategic approach to women's oppression. However liberating, it has often been transformed into an intense validation of personal experience which in turn has translated into both a competitive hierarchy of oppressions and an opposition to any kind of theory.

An anti-theory emphasis on personal experience can individualize difference (each experience as unique) to such a degree that the deep-rooted processes by which experience is socially constructed are concealed. As a result, the complex patterning of women's experiences of class, race, gender, and sexual orientation is masked; even the interconnectedness between different aspects of an individual woman's experience (for example, the links between household and workplace), can be made further inaccessible, thus exacerbating the fragmentation of everyday life within patriarchal capitalism. This tendency to anti-intellectualism and anti-theory in the women's movement which accompanies the emphasis on experience promotes individualism, on the one hand, and on the other, promotes the identification of women, not with reason, but with nature — both of which are ideologies of patriarchal capitalism.

The overemphasis on the personal in the personal/political dialectic also intersects with the politics of identity to establish an exclusionary set of identifications which becomes a competitive hierarchy of oppressions. The strategic positions which flow from this are not problematic, in particular, the assumption that a political strategy and, indeed, often political correctness flow directly from identity. In practice, this can conceal political differences between lesbians, for example, and, at the same time, overemphasize differences, between lesbians and heterosexual women, for example. The competitive identification of certain oppressions as more salient than others promotes bonding on the basis of shared victimization and moralism, and exclusion organized around guilt, both of which undermine the possibility of political alliance and open debate among feminists.[5]

Lynne Segal raises some similar concerns about the emphasis on experience inside the women's movement:

> Women's liberation has always stressed that women use their own feelings, experiences and perceptions to make their analyses ... It was necessary if we were to throw off the mythology of male 'expertise' ... It became a weakness when the emergence of differences and conflicts between women not only produced enormous distress but became immobilising. Either it silenced those who felt guilty for being articulate and privileged or it encouraged the defensive re-assertion of some common oppression, like the experience of male violence ... Within the women's movement the validation of personal experience and talk of 'common oppression' often hides straightforward ignorance of the lives of other women and of the factors beyond gender which determine women's lives ... So resentment and mistrust would seem to be eternal and inevitable

features of feminism were we not able to move beyond individual experience. (Segal 1987, 59-61).

Both the movement from a unitary category of woman through the "discovery" of difference and from a unitary category of feminism through the elaboration of political currents have been important in the development of the politic and practice of contemporary feminisms. However, each, in itself, is inadequate for exploring the complexities of feminist practice.

This suggests the need for an additional framework that is situated more concretely within the activist map of the women's movement and which theorizes feminism in practice. We need to analyze its complexities from the *standpoint of practice* as a counterpoint both to the *standpoint of theory* (generated by the model of political currents) and also to the *standpoint of experience* (within which the politics of identity can be situated). The concept of the standpoint of practice which is developed in the remainder of this chapter is not unproblematic since there can be many forms of practice — moral, sexual, personal etc. — which it does not include. Perhaps it would be more accurate to refer to the 'standpoint of *strategic* practice' in order to highlight, in particular, its collective character and to distinguish it further from the standpoint of experience which is often understood in personal, individualistic ways.

Although this chapter will focus on the standpoint of practice, it is worth emphasizing that an analysis of feminisms and the women's movement must weave together all three standpoints — theory, experience and practice. That the principles of socialist feminism, for example, do not provide a step-by-step blueprint for practical struggle, and in fact, often blur in the context of real political struggle, does not mean that these principles are useless or of concern only to those who debate esoteric issues. On the contrary, these principles establish a framework and a context from which to approach daily politics and within which to situate the myriad of issues, details and decisions which often threaten to overwhelm feminist activists. Nor am I suggesting that the understanding of difference, the validation of experience and the importance of shared identifications are unimportant — just that they are insufficient to understanding the nature of feminist practice and to strategizing about future directions.

To theorize from practice, we begin, not by distinguishing the currents or identities from one another, but by appreciating feminist practice as an intersecting, albeit contradictory, whole. This recognizes the impact that dispersed and diverse forms of feminist practice have on one another, and also highlights the fact that, despite significant local realities, Canadian feminist practice operates within a common sociopolitical, economic and ideological context.

A Model of Feminist Practice

A model which is more firmly situated within, and emergent from, activist feminist experience allows us to highlight a central dilemma of feminist practice, and is suggestive of a new strategic orientation. All feminist practice struggles two poles of attraction — disengagement and mainstreaming. Disengagement, which operates from a critique of the system and a standpoint outside of it, and a desire, therefore, to create alternative structures and ideologies, can provide a vision of social transformation. Mainstreaming operates from a desire to reach out to the majority of the population with popular and practical feminist solutions to particular issues, and therefore references major social institutions, such as the family, the workplace, the educational system and the state.

To some extent these poles of attraction present a tension common to many political situations; however, each pole also contains certain uniquely feminist aspects.[6] The motivation for a standpoint of disengagement rests on the historically specific analysis of the patriarchal character of social institutions and the overwhelming evidence of women's exclusion from power in the public arena. It also draws on an alternative view of institutional mechanisms, often referred to as "feminist process." Implicit in mainstreaming is the feminist commitment to transforming the everyday lives of women. This challenges the public/private split, and conventional notions of agents of change, and draws on the ideology of the personal is political.

Both mainstreaming and disengagement are necessary to the feminist vision. The goal for feminist practice is the maintenance of an effective tension between the two; the dilemma is the tendency for feminist practice to be pulled towards one or other pole. This dilemma is complicated by the fact that each of these poles carries with it a strategic risk. Disengagement can easily lead to marginalization and invisibility; mainstreaming to co-optation and institutionalization. These strategic risks can be countered by an integrated politic which creates a bridge between disengagement and mainstreaming.

The Risks of Disengagement

"The building of alternatives" is one of the concrete expressions of disengagement in the women's movement, one which too frequently suffers from marginalization. Charlotte Bunch (1989) points out that "alternative institutions should not be havens of retreat, but challenges that weaken male power over our lives." Yet the socio-political and personal conditions of patriarchal capitalism, the lack of resources available to the women's movement, combined with an over-emphasis on the 'personal' as a political strategy, most often limit the possibilities of alternatives — in living arrangements, co-operatives and collectives, and in business ventures. In the best of circumstances, they provide safer personal spaces for a few women; rarely are they effective as political strategies.[7]

But even as personal havens, alternatives suffer from serious limitations. The difficulty of establishing any social/political/economic space outside of patriarchal capitalism means that feminist alternative organizations are often forced to reproduce the very norms they have set out to reject, just in order to survive. This has been well documented in relation to feminist co-operatives, businesses and, in particular, in assessing the impact of the funding practices of the state on feminist organizations.[8] Feminist alternatives then are not able necessarily to provide a lived experience or a prefigurative vision of social transformation.

Further, the distinctly feminist process which emerges from an organizational elaboration of the ideology of the 'personal is political' and which is seen to distinguish feminist alternatives from traditional organizations has more often than not been unsuccessful. Notwithstanding the accuracy of the feminist critique of the patriarchal and hierarchical functioning of institutions, feminists have faced serious difficulties in developing alternatives.

Feminist process has suffered from a peculiar counterposition and defense of *personal* over political experience and a paradoxically *abstract* characterization (and rejection) of leadership, voting, organizational structures, etc. as male and patriarchal by definition. Both lead to a depoliticization of feminist organizational strategies, a result of which is that process becomes separated from political analysis, particular strategies and an identifiable set of organizational norms, and further becomes a mechanism of exclusion. The internalized, personal, and often unarticulated character of the norms and practices of feminist alternatives make them inaccessible and uncomfortable to women on the outside. This process of exclusion reinforces a politic of isolation and exacerbates the potential for marginalization inherent in disengagement.

In this regard, it has been fascinating and perhaps discouraging to witness the use and misuse of feminist process at the 1988 annual general meeting of the National Action Committee on the Status of Women (NAC). At this meeting political and strategic differences over the relative importance and nature of an organizational review provoked a divisive and highly charged debate during which feminist process as an ideology and as a practice was invoked. An analysis of the events suggests that feminist process was presented both as a reflection of a homogeneous "woman experience" and as an alternative to politics, seen by definition as patriarchal. Miriam Jones and Jennifer Stephens in their assessment of that meeting said:

> In the discussions which circulated at NAC and since, this process is referred to as though it is apolitical in construction, an appeal to neutrality and homogenity which is intricately linked to the notion of a unified 'sisterhood' (Jones & Stephens 1988).[9]

Despite the difficulty of developing a feminist process, the struggle to articulate alternatives to traditional practices needs to continue; yet at the same time, we need to beware of a process too deeply disengaged from concrete political practice.

Alternatives have not been an effective political strategy for making change largely because they have most often operated as a strategy of disengagement unmediated by a degree of mainstreaming. Although this often results from conditions outside the control of feminists, an uncritical acceptance of the strategy of alternatives or an unelaborated political understanding of their role within the feminist community, also are important contributing factors. The degree of disengagement embedded in alternatives means they are easily marginalized, creating a distance from the larger constituency of women and thereby increasing the inaccessibility and invisibility of the women's movement.

This is not to underestimate the importance to feminists of alternative ways of living our lives. For many of us these have provided support fundamental to our ability to sustain struggle as feminists in workplaces, relationships and even inside the women's movement itself. In this sense, such alternatives have contributed to building the women's movement. However much they may improve the quality of our personal lives, this form of disengagement has not represented a viable political strategy. Space does not permit a detailed exploration of other forms of disengagement, but many exist. For example, the focus on theoretical development amongst socialist feminists in United States and England is a form of disengagement which has exacted a high price given the degree to which it marginalizes and makes inaccessible socialist feminism. Of course, the focus on theory may be the result rather than the cause of this marginalization.

The Risks of Mainstreaming
Mainstreaming is also not unproblematic. Reaching out to the majority of women with popular and practical feminist solutions to concrete problems means engaging with mainstream institutions: the family, the workplace, and in particular, the state and government. Engagement with mainstream institutions often leads to co-optation and institutionalization.

The forms of organization inside patriarchal capitalist institutions such as the state and the school system are hierarchic and bureaucratic. They tend to be inflexible, reinforce patterns of uniformity, regulate and neutralize dissent and difference, and by definition, limit any substantive challenge to their goals and practices. It is difficult for feminists to confront these goals and practices from inside these institutions, in part because of their isolation, and in part because of the power of these practices to subvert the challenge.[10] The process of institutionalization often means that we lose sight of the larger goals of radical social transformation.[11]

Institutionalization does not render an issue invisible however. Once taken up — by the state, for example — the issue is reshaped and reconstituted, its continuing public presence creating a new, and sometimes more difficult task for feminists. For example, in 1987 the Ontario government finally passed Bill 154, a watered-down form of equal value legislation. With the law on the books and the long-term process of implementation under way, it seems almost determined that feminist participation in the process will take a consultative and easily co-opted form. Maintaining a degree of disengagement is increasingly complicated as mainstreaming produces institutionalization. Yet participating in that implementation process as well as mounting a serious critique of and mobilisation around the legislation will be significant in determining its long-term impact on women workers. Institutionalization does not eliminate the possibilities of feminist agency (although feminists have often felt very disempowered by that process), but rather reconstitutes the task.

Understanding the tension between institutionalization and mainstreaming reveals, rather than conceals, our political task. For despite the tendency toward institutionalization and co-optation a central task for socialist feminists, in particular, is to engage with, indeed transform, mainstream institutions. An over-emphasis on the danger of institutionalization can lead to an over-valuation of strategies of disengagement.

The map of practice therefore is shaped by the pulls of disengagement and mainstreaming, and by the dilemmas posed by each: marginalization and invisibility on the one hand and co-optation and institutionalization on the other. The task for feminists is to maintain a complex strategic interplay between disengagement and mainstreaming.

Tensions between Mainstreaming and Disengagement

This model of practice can illuminate the dynamic of particular feminist struggles. Carla Lipsig-Mumme assesses the contribution of feminist strategies to the Montreal garment workers' strike in 1983. In her description, she gives a striking example of the necessity to maintain a balance between disengagement and mainstreaming. In 1980, semi-skilled women operators set up the multi-ethnic Action Committee for Garment Workers (CATV). This committee was influenced by feminism and Québec left-wing socialism. In Lipsig-Mumme's words, it "crystallized a deep-seated rejection of the patriarchal aspirations of typical union elites" and was "profoundly anti-bureaucratic." It focused its energies largely on four tasks:

> First, informing and educating the members as widely as possible; second, using whatever formal protections existed in the contract as militantly as possible; third, exposing the collaboration and cynicism of the union leadership; and fourth, raising . . . the deeper, harder issues about homework and the future of the garment industry (Lipsig-Mumme 1987, 65-66).

It operated from a politic of disengagement in its critique and a politic of mainstreaming in its focus on the particular problems facing women workers on the shop floor. Lipsig-Mumme details many successes of the CATV which I would attribute in part to the delicate balance that was maintained between disengagement and mainstreaming.

During the strike, however, from their fear of institutionalization, the informal feminist leaders of the garment workers (from the CATV) disengaged too deeply and were marginalized. They ran the strike's daycare centre and "refused any formal responsibilities in organizing the strike."

> It was feared that even partial power would corrupt absolutely, would transform feminists into 'apparatchniks' and grind them up in the union machine (Lipsig-Mumme 1987, 66).

Lipsig-Mumme attributes the loss of the strike in large part to their refusal to continue to play a leadership role and points out that the contract was "the worst . . . signed in Quebec since the 1950s."

A second rather dramatic example of the tension around mainstreaming and disengagement can be found in the recent history of the Service Office and Retail Workers Union of Canada (SORWUC), an independent and explicitly feminist union, committed to organizing women workers in what have been seen as unorganizable sectors, like the banks (the Bank Book Collective 1979). In the first instance, SORWUC was extremely successful; it managed to organize 23 bank branches (although not all were certified) and win a Canadian Labour Relations Board (CLRB) decision that overturned a 1959 ruling against branch-by-branch organizing. In the language of this article, I would suggest that this success was rooted in the disengaged stance of SORWUC in its organizing strategy and in its vision of more democratic unions based on feminist principles. But the degree of disengagement was too extensive; SORWUC failed to develop an effective negotiating relation with either the employers or the Canadian Labour Congress. Few of their organized locals were able to negotiate first contracts.

In the first place, it is very important to recognize the powerful forces arrayed against their success — in the banks, in the unions and in the labour law itself. Rosemary Warskett documents, for example, the devastating impact of the legal certification framework of the Canada Labour Code (Warskett 1988). Yet it is equally important to assess the role SORWUC's own decisions played in their marginalization and defeat. Maureen Fitzgerald's conclusion that "an opportunity was lost when the decision was made to keep the UBW [United Bank Workers-SORWUC] out of the CLC [Canadian Labour Congress]..." is significant (Fitzgerald 1981). Entering the CLC would certainly have threatened the degree of disengagement with which SORWUC was operating but it also may have afforded the protection available from a mainstream institution. The model of feminist practice helps make some sense of the tensions faced by SORWUC, in particular the difficulty of maintaining an effective balance between mainstreaming and disengagement.

The Feminist Political Currents and Mainstreaming-disengagement

These applications of the feminist practice model demonstrate an alternative to using the construct of political currents to explore feminism and strategic possibilities. It is also the case, however, that each current of feminism relates to the poles of disengagement and mainstreaming somewhat differently, mediated by its understanding of what kind of change is possible and necessary, and of how change occurs. Radical feminism's tendency to identify, in a trans-historical way, all social institutions with 'the patriarchy' pushes it toward a politic of disengagement unmediated by mainstreaming. This often leads to marginalization and isolation. Liberal feminism's tendency to enter into social institutions with the most limited degree of disengagement and to focus on remedial measures explains its susceptibility to institutionalization.

Socialist feminism is caught in a contradiction. Its politic pulls it simultaneously toward both poles of practice — mainstreaming and disengagement; this sets up, dialectically, both a recurring strategic dilemma, as well as a potential solution that is maintaining a tension between these poles.

The socialist feminist politic is based on a radical critique of the entire society, in particular of existing institutions, ideological practices and the complex relations of power expressed through class, gender, race and sexual orientation. In its opposition to the dominant ideology and institutions, it stands apart from the consciousness of the majority. Socialist feminism is informed by a vision of fundamental transformation and a desire to replace patriarchal capitalism. As such, socialist feminism is pulled toward the pole of disengagement.

At the same time, however, socialist feminism is pulled toward mainstreaming, for a presupposition of its politic is that such a reconstitution of the dominant ideology and social practices depends upon a *public* consensus about and a commitment to a new social vision, and the active support and participation of a significant layer of the population in a mass political movement. Socialist feminists recognize that they cannot organize such a mass movement entirely through the

politics of disengagement because of the risks of marginalization. The socialist feminist task, then, is to take its perspective,
which fundamentally challenges mainstream institutions and
ideology, into those very institutions and out to the public
consciousness.

This tension between disengagement and mainstreaming
poses a dilemma for socialist feminists, and in practice, often
appears irreconcilable. Mainstreaming often leads to institutionalization which may cause socialist feminists to limit the
vision of the change they seek; but disengagement may take
the form of marginalization which results in an inability to
mobilize the large numbers to effect the kind of change that is
necessary. Socialist feminist practice must constantly struggle
to combine and resolve the contradictions of the two poles.

Socialist feminists have had some successes in bridging that
gap. For example, activists in the Ontario Coalition for Abortion Clinics (OCAC), who self identify as socialist feminists,
explicitly attribute their success in establishing free-standing
abortion clinics in Toronto to a strategy which combines mainstreaming and disengagement.[12]

> OCAC has tried to develop a strategy that works at
> two levels simultaneously: transforming immediate
> conditions, and building a consciousness and move-
> ment that could transcend the existing oppressive
> relations of reproduction. We have tried to pose the
> argument for clinics in this double way. The existing
> free-standing clinics have been indispensable in pro-
> viding desperately needed services to thousands of
> women, in dramatizing daily how unfair and un-
> workable the existing law is, and in showing the
> solution in the most concrete and immediate fashion
> possible. At the same time, clinics can be posed as a
> model for the future: centres providing care for the
> full spectrum of women's reproductive lives . . .
> Having a clear and attractive vision of ultimate goals
> is very important, not so much as a blueprint for the
> future, but as an understandable and realizable al-
> ternative that can seize people's imagination and

enthusiasm in the present (Antonyshyn 1988 et al., 149).[13]

Each current of feminism situates itself in a different location on this map of feminist practice; in essence, each evaluates the options for change differently. However, all feminist practice risks institutionalization by organizing for change and involves a degree of disengagement by definition. The relation of the currents to the poles of attraction is more a matter of degree than a rigid separation.

It is worth emphasizing that what is most important about this model of feminist practice is not simply the additional insight into the nature of the feminist currents. This model facilitates the understanding of tactical decisions which may not conform to, or even arise from, abstract ideological principle. It allows us to see the flexibility, mobility and fluidity of feminist political practice; it recognizes that tactical political choices made on a daily basis reflect not only the set of abstract principles which inform feminist currents but also particular historical and conjunctural factors. The map of feminist practice is not shaped within the same parameters as the map of abstract theoretical principle.

Despite what I see to be the usefulness of this framework, there is a danger inherent in this kind of model building. What tends to get lost is the degree to which the choices of feminist practice are constrained and shaped by political, economic and social conditions: the nature of public consciousness, the level of development of the women's movement and other progressive movements, the degree of state repressiveness, the state of the economy etc. I am not suggesting that all strategic choices are available to feminists in any particular instance. The specific conditions we face greatly limit the options. Nevertheless this framework can help us to understand some of the tensions and contradictions of the choices we do make.

It is equally important to stress the other side of the dialectic — agency. In emphasizing the degree to which the political and historical conjuncture shapes our choices, we often lose sight of the very premise of a feminist politic — a belief in our ability to make change. Feminists do exercise agency. Increasing the level of self consciousness about feminist practice should make strategic and tactical choices more effective in the long term.

Conclusion

This chapter presents a framework within which the practice of feminisms can be analyzed and feminist strategies evaluated: disengagement and mainstreaming as poles of attraction, and the risks of each, marginalization and institutionalization. This standpoint of practice not only enriches our understanding of the feminist political currents but also suggests a way of avoiding a strategic and analytic dependence on them. It helps us to focus on the common feminist dilemma — the necessity to bridge these poles of attraction — and allows us to assess strategic choices in terms of their ability to build that bridge.

Feminist Collectives

The Struggles and Contradictions in our Quest for a "Uniquely Feminist Structure"

Janice L. Ristock

Our structure is based on the assumption that hierarchical structures are oppressive to all women. We are attempting to work within a structure that is built on alternative assumptions — feminist ideals; sharing power; women's experiences as valid for social change.

From a collective's basis
of unity statement.

I have been researching the work of Canadian feminist social service collectives for the past four years and have also worked in several of these collectives. My research has included a national survey, an analysis of collective documents and interviews with collective workers. In this chapter I bring forth a reflective and critical analysis of their processes, difficulties and visions. Since feminist social service collectives are continuing to grow and develop throughout Canada, an analysis of their work has implications for feminist community organizing in general.

An Overview of Some of the Issues

Many feminist organizations and groups are organized as non-hierarchical, collective structures because, ideally, working collectively allows for the integration of our feminist theoretical principles with our feminist practices. Yet, the collective organizational structure has also been the site of contradiction, confusion, and frustration for many women. Working collectively can feel like working in a structureless group where consensus is difficult to reach and where organizing efforts remain stuck in a web of conflict. The collectives I explore in this chapter have the additional stress of working within the contradictory context of providing alternative feminist services while receiving government funding and remaining tied to the state. Given the unrelenting demands of this context, on top of the strain of leadership and power issues, the continued existence of these feminist social service collectives (most have been in existence for ten years) is itself a strong political statement.

Unlike the consciousness-raising (c-r) groups of the late sixties and early seventies, from which feminist service organizations first emerged, feminist collectives have not been homogeneous discussion groups. Rather, their membership is usually more diverse — some members have political interests, others have service interests — and always they have a product to deliver. Yet, the self-help groups, counselling centres and shelters, self-defense classes and health-care services that belong to the larger context of alternative services for women have typically been modelled on the early c-r groups. Not surprisingly, critiques challenging the idea of creating organizations based on the consciousness-raising group model (e.g., Freeman 1973) have been around for almost as long as the collectives themselves.

Writing about the early collectives, Freeman urged women's groups to formalize leadership so that those in positions of authority would be made accountable. Her argument was that all groups have leadership, which, if it remains informal, it can become manipulative and undemocratic. Freeman's focus on issues of leadership, authority, and power was prophetic as these remain key issues for feminist collectives into the 1990s.

The particular mandate of the social service collectives in my cross-Canada study falls under the category of services in response to violence against women. These include rape crisis centres, shelters for battered women and transition hostels, to name the most common. In addition to their direct service work, these collectives are also involved in political work such as using pressure tactics to influence opinion and policy on specific issues (e.g., lobbying, demonstrations, letter-writing campaigns) and joining coalitions (such as, the National Action Committee on the Status of Women). Thus they see their work as part of the women's movement and as work for social change (Ristock 1987).

Many researchers have indicated that the dichotomy between the mainstream social service system and work for social change presents an irreconcilable contradiction (Ridington 1982; Macleod 1987). While feminist collective workers are aware of the contradictions in their work that stem from this dichotomy, they have, as indicated by the opening quotation, managed to retain a structure that is consistent with feminist ideology.

Collective practices for the delivery of services, internal processes, and perceptions of work reflect a consistency between their organizational structure and feminist principles. Identifying hierarchical, bureaucratic organizations as perpetuating the power imbalance in our society, they remain committed to consensus decision-making practices. They have adopted the egalitarian principle that each worker is used according to her strengths, and not according to educational background. Attempting to raise the consciousness of women, they bring the community into their work through networking and distributing brochures that clearly depict their services and goals. And foremost, out of their commitment to feminism, specifically in their analysis of violence against women, they sustain a political focus in their work. Feminist social service collectives, then, in their very effort to practise feminism, challenge the notion of a dichotomy between context and aims.

Yet many feminists have continued to criticize the work of government-funded social service agencies for their social control function (Ferguson 1984; Farge 1987) and for the promotion of band-aid solutions to larger social problems. As should be clear by now, I believe that such a harsh assessment of the work of feminist social service collectives not only undermines their effort to develop an internal structure that is consistent with feminism but also misses the substance of the conflicts that they face. My research indicates that collective workers perceive themselves as doing more than providing government-funded services; in fact, they perceive themselves as empowering feminist organizations. If we focus on this we can begin to gain an understanding of the tensions between the individual and the collective, the collective ideal and the internal practices, and possible solutions to internal difficulties.

Empowerment and the Emergence of Power Relations

The ideal of empowerment, of "women helping women to help one another," is usually contrasted to the world of power where women are identified as "other" and experience invalidation, separateness from male norms and powerlessness. The ideal, like the first feminist collectives, took form in the consciousness-raising efforts of the women's movement. In this context, violence against women by men was perceived as one of the most salient and pressing issues, and an analysis of power was acknowledged as central to feminist understanding. Rape received the first focused attention and became the paradigm for understanding other forms of violence against women. Early slogans from the feminist movement such as "porn is the theory, rape is the practice" (Morgan 1980) represented the understanding that rape was not an action of a sick individual but an inevitable consequence of patriarchal culture where women are seen as sexual private property and kept in a subordinate position (Brownmiller 1975).

Andrea Dworkin (1979) wrote specifically of the power of men in our society and male supremacist ideology. She listed seven components of male power: "The power of men is first a metaphysical assertion of self. It expresses intrinsic authority ... Second, power is physical strength used over and against others ... third, power is the capacity to terrorize, to use self and strength to inculcate fear ... fourth, men have power of naming ... fifth, men have power of owning ... sixth the power of money is distinctly male power ... seventh, men have the power of sex" (1-22).

In their ongoing critique of male-supremacist ideology and patriarchal society, feminists have re-conceptualized human relations in a variety of areas in order to eliminate oppressive power relations. The development of feminist therapy over the last ten years is a practical application of the feminist alternative discourse of empowerment. The key assumption of feminist therapy is that it is women's subordinate economic and social position that leads to personal difficulties (Sturdivant 1980). Consequently, feminist therapists argue that women need to understand the profound effects of their social, economic and political oppression as well as work to change the external forces in society which impact so negatively on individual women (Ballou & Gabalac 1985). In practice, feminist therapists challenge the hierarchical nature of the therapist-client relationship, and an egalitarian relationship is sought between them. Reflecting the research insight of community psychologists who have found that individuals who participate actively in community organizations show greater psychological empowerment (Zimmerman & Rappaport 1988), feminist therapists also encourage political activity as a partial solution to individual oppression. Thus empowerment, in the sense of "giving power to," of "authorizing and enabling," is the goal of the therapeutic relationship. Being actively involved on a personal and political level is conceived as an important component in fostering empowerment.

Similarly, social service collectives focus on empowerment as crucial to their work. It is quite literally their goal, as taken from the following basis of unity statement:

> At (name of agency) we attempt to empower both our clients and the women with whom we work. In order to do so we validate each other's feelings, opinions, ideas and experiences. We share knowledge and encourage each other to grow and expand self-awareness.

Yet the work of collectives does not always feel empowering to the workers or to the service recipients. Contradictions arise between the feminist ideal of women helping women to help one another and the day-to-day realities. As a collective worker at a women's hostel some years ago, I spent most of my time distributing and regulating items such as toothpaste, toilet paper, and bus tickets. In other words, in this "homelike" environment filled with diverse groupings of women and children, of all ages and with a variety of needs, I was the "keeper of the keys." My mandate was to make the experience of these many women in need an empowering one. The irony, which I experienced as painful, was that as staff I held the power and I used this power to regulate the tiny details of their lives.

Research indicates that because women working in collectives have a difficult time acknowledging the existence of power relations, they tend to let power issues fester rather than articulating them and working on solutions (Miller 1982; Woolsey & McBain 1987). One explanation given for this kind of tendency is that as women enter adulthood they do not typically take up positions in society which give them a direct, positive contact with power (Farge 1987). Women entering the "helping professions" may have an even more difficult time acknowledging power relations. Those working in feminist social service collectives, while acknowledging the empowerment of women as their goal, disavow power itself as something negative, hurtful and oppressive. The irony is that feminist collective workers do have power, denied or not, and their decisions and actions do affect, positively or negatively, the lives of their co-workers and service recipients.

The first lesson, then, is that in our attempts to create an environment of empowerment, we are mistaken to think that we can get rid of power differentials. Therefore, rather than dichotomizing "empowerment" and "power" and linking power exclusively to negative, oppressive practice, we need to see that power is part of all human interaction. Power relations involve what Foucault (1972) has termed "the microphysics of power" — the tiny, incremental details of daily routine which form the content of our lives. Foucault also suggests that power is productive of all knowledge systems, oppressive and emancipatory, such that to deny the existence of power is also to deny some forms of knowledge.

The Individual and the Collective

When asked whether providing a social service while adhering to feminism posed any contradictions for their collective, the vast majority of respondents in my sample of self-defined feminist social service collectives (25 out of 34) said yes. They listed the following contradictions (these are listed in order of frequency, with the most frequent listed first):

- Social service work is band-aid work that does not address the root of the problem (n=10).
- We are an alternative feminist service embedded within a mainstream oppressive social service system (n=7).
- There is a contradiction between our power as workers and lack of power of service recipients (n=6).
- There is a tension between feminist theory and practice e.g., we use volunteers, and receive government funds (n=6).
- Tensions exist between heterosexual workers and lesbian workers (n=4).
- We are seen as too political by some and not political enough by others (n=2).
- The theory is to work collectively, but there is little time to develop this (n=1).

The responses to this item indicate that the majority of feminist social service collective workers in Canada are aware of contradictions in their work. They also indicate that, overall, the contradictions pertain to power issues in the context of both the wider society and the group dynamics of the collectives themselves.

If we start with the context of the wider society, we can begin to see how some of these tensions are played out in collective work. For example, it is perhaps easier for feminists within collective settings than for any other social group to look outward at the way in which society and the mainstream social service system mistreat women and impose regulations on workers. Unfortunately, with this analysis comes the creation of an "us" versus "them" mentality: the collective versus government funders and other aspects of patriarchal society.

Because in fact the collective is not a unitary domain separate from the rest of society, but a multiplicity of viewpoints,
people, backgrounds, and values, this perception creates dis-
tortions in the collective's internal dynamics. The pressure that
workers feel to present themselves as integral individuals
often makes it difficult to acknowledge that they can feel contradictory feelings and hold contradictory and competing locations in society (e.g., mothers, workers, etc.). One collective
worker that I interviewed commented, "We accommodate superficial differences but what that amounts to is real differences remaining hidden. The accommodation is just to allow
women into the fold to make them become one of 'us' but
differences in feminist analysis, skill and identity remain unacknowledged."

The denial of contradictions and multiple locations within
the collective (e.g., differing feminist analyses; tensions between lesbian women and heterosexual women, white women
and women of colour; differences between service providers
and service recipients, etc.) also serves to mystify the power
relations that operate. There is a gap between the ideal vision
of the collective — the "us" — and the real practices in which
women within the collective engage.

Looking more closely at the internal dynamics, it is helpful
to consider social psychological research which has shown that
highly cohesive groups exert power and control over their
members' behaviour. They want individuals to conform to the
norms of the group. Diversity and difference are seen as
threatening to the larger goal of a collective identity. Thus the
ultimate threat of a non-conforming group member is ostraci-
zation (Brown 1988; Baron & Byrne 1987). In my interviews, a
number of collective workers commented on the effects of
these internal dynamics. One woman described the way in
which "our political ideology (feminism) is often used to hide
truth"and to reinforce the existence of an 'us' and 'them' dichotomy within collectives."

Unfortunately, it appears that feminism as an ideology of
liberation is often seen as the uniting feature of the cohesive
collective. Miller (1977) suggests that the "unwritten" feminist
norm in groups is to suppress the direct expression of differences or anger. My research echoes Miller's findings. Perhaps

one collective worker in my sample put it best, commenting that in her collective, the differences between individuals were not acknowledged. She points to the way in which feminist ideology can be misused: "Factions exist within the collective between lesbians and heterosexual women; between the politically correct and the politically incorrect. Some identities and differences are perceived as having more value — all this does is reinforce a hierarchy of feminism."

Thus some differences in identity are acknowledged, but not all are valued. Another woman commented further on this theme and described the prescriptive mandate or what is required of women in the "in group" in the collective. She commented: "I often feel silenced because I am not a lesbian or a woman of colour. I am a white, middle-class heterosexual who often feels less valued, feels like less of a feminist — because of who I am."

These comments reflect the all too often destructive experiences, alluded to throughout this chapter, which occur within collectives. Individual women are judged as less feminist, or as holding incorrect feminist views or identities, when they are different and when their individual needs are perceived as being different from the needs of the collective. Thus feminist ideology which is inextricably linked to the collective structure is transformed into oppressive rule setting, a prescriber of acceptable attitudes and behaviours. Kathy Ferguson (1984), in *The Feminist Case Against Bureaucracy*, describes the struggles of the individual with the collective as the "tyranny of the collective." She asserts that the maintenance of a dialectical tension between the individual and the collective is necessary to circumvent these struggles.

Janice Raymond (1986), in *A Passion For Friends*, also writes about the way in which feminist theory can be transformed into prescriptive rhetoric within collectives: "Under the rhetoric of 'collective,' 'non-competitive' and 'equal' women who achieve, who are ambitious, and who are successful in what they do are relegated to the status of pariah" (195). She further makes the point that women within collectives often become alienated from their own sense of personal and political power, thus endowing the collective with false power (Raymond 1986). This syndrome of the powerless individual versus the all-powerful collective is built and strengthened by the refusal to acknowledge the "microphysics of power"on the one hand, and the deification of "feminism" as the source of women's empowerment, on the other.

In addition to the questionnaire and interview schedule, I reviewed the internal documents of four collectives — a rape crisis centre, a shelter for battered women, a centre for pregnant teenagers, and a hostel for transient women. The job application forms for example, all stressed a feminist analysis as central to collective work. Questions such as: "What is your definition of feminism?" and "How does feminism inform your work?" were typically raised. In fact, three of these services did not even want to see a resumé of previous work history or educational background. Feminism and the emphasis on certain feminist values were the major criteria for hiring a new collective member and for remaining a part of the collective. The responses to a forced choice item on the questionnaire, which asked women to identify the way in which feminism impacted on their services, similarly identified feminism as the *sine qua non* of collective life. Almost all of the collectives (94 percent) identified feminism as working through their service; 94 percent reported that it sets their organizational goals; 93 percent said it involved them in social change work; 96 percent indicated that it provided them with an approach and analysis for working with their service recipients; and 65 percent reported that it involves them in policy and legal reform work.

Given the overarching emphasis on feminism, it is not surprising that the basis of unity of most collectives becomes a shared ideological commitment. When a woman shows diversity or difference, it is often her feminism that is called into question. She is seen as a deviate, threatening the unity and power of the group. The power bestowed to the collective, however, is not questioned. Thus the analysis which depicts some women as not being "feminist enough" merely individualizes the complexities of collective difficulties and serves to disempower individual women. As Raymond (1986) suggests, it fills the collective with a sense of power that is not based on the strength of its individual members.

The Collective Ideal and Internal Practices

The desire to have a homogeneous collective identity is understandable given the struggles and tensions within the social service context. Women want and need to feel united because their type of service is marginalized within the system. It almost goes without saying that it is desirable to work with women who share your vision of the world, but it is necessary to acknowledge the social construction of the collective identity and the constraints of this construction for women.

In my work as a consultant with feminist organizations, I am often asked what the ideal feminist structure is. In fact, one group of feminist conference organizers entitled a talk I recently gave on collectives "Towards the Development of a Uniquely Feminist Structure" (hence, the subtitle of this chapter). But the construction of a homogeneous collective, or the attempts to develop any so-called unique or ideal model, implies that a static, contextually void construct is desirable and achievable. It is my contention that there is no ideal model. Further, by attempting to construct an "ideal" we run the risk of denying the power relations that operate within any setting. By dichotomizing relations such as empowerment and power and the individual and the collective, the complexities and contradictions within collectives are obscured and mystified. Collectives are also organized to reflect the notion that authority and leadership reside in the collective as a whole, i.e., through consensus decision-making and participatory work practices. But a critical examination of these practices reveals that they are based on assumptions that protect the desire for a homogeneous collective identity.

Eighty-eight percent of the collectives in my sample reported using consensus decision-making practices. In this process everyone has an opportunity to discuss an issue until a decision is reached that everyone can agree with. This is seen as preferable to the majority vote process where a minority voice is oppressed. In addition, this process is used so that authority and leadership can reside with all group members. Nancy Hartsock (1974), writing about the alternative form of leadership and authority within feminist organizations, puts it like this: "To lead is to be at the center of a group rather than in front of others. Authority is based on skill and knowledge and is compelled to demonstrate its force to those concerned in terms which they can grasp, and by dint of being so compelled, is made in some real measure responsible to them" (116).

Decisions by consensus, however, are also based on some false assumptions which challenge such "ideal" notions of authority and leadership. One assumption is that everyone in the group is equal in terms of the personal power and the skills that it takes to be an effective participant in the process. It also assumes that decisions by consensus are empowering because no one is forced by a majority into a decision. Yet, many women claim that in reality it is those who are more articulate, who have been with the collective longer, and who are louder when voicing their opinions, who benefit from the consensus decision-making process (Ristock 1987; Zaremba 1988). As Zaremba explains, "In feminist consensus organizations ... the underlying issue is virtually always control over the organization. Under an overt majority rule structure, the question of control is out front and power can change hands within the accepted process ... But under a consensus system there is no process for control to pass from one group or faction to another" (4).

Traditional small-group theory cannot adequately explain the internal dynamics operating within collectives, for it assumes that all groups are hierarchical in construction and that it is individual leaders who emerge to bring the group through conflict (Corey & Corey 1982). Early social psychological research by Lewin, Lippitt & White (1939) and by Maier (1958) remain the classic model for understanding group dynamics. This research found that the democratic leadership style is the most successful in getting the group to do what the person in authority wants of them. But in collectives, women are struggling with alternative meanings of authority and leadership. The group is consciously attempting to prevent individual leadership from emerging. What I have observed is that it is not so much individual leaders who emerge and struggle for power as it is small factions which form and disagree with one another. Psychological research has not looked at the dynamics of groups within this context of collective leadership. The focus has remained on individuals' behaviour within groups and on positing individualistic solutions for group difficulties. Collectives, therefore, need to understand the emergence of authority and leadership through the development of factions. Explicit discussions of power, rather than assumed equality and denial of power, may be a route for addressing collective difficulties.

Another process used by collectives, which is a powder keg of issues, is the practice of sharing and rotating jobs. Over half of the collectives in my sample (53%) engaged in this practice. The ideal is that responsibility, knowledge, and accountability will be shared equally by all members. No one is placed in the position of being expert, and everyone is assumed to want to engage in all of the tasks equally. Yet this practice denies that certain women have strengths, skills, and preferences for certain areas. It forces a blending of differences. What emerges in practice vis-à-vis job sharing is unacknowledged power struggles between members around issues of accountability.

Some collectives attempt to resolve their internal difficulties by using a model of non-violent communication. In this model women are asked to separate their observation of something they do not like from their evaluation of the action, and to express constructive criticism. The model asserts that mixing evaluation with observation provokes misinterpretation and defensiveness. The goal is to give "empowering" evaluations, where women firstly state their observation of actions they dislike, then state their feelings about this action, followed by a statement of how their personal values are related to their feelings. Finally, they make a request for change in "positive action language" (Rosenberg 1983). But this process has also caused some collective members to be silenced. The process assumes a certain level of rational, verbal, and analytical ability during emotional difficulties. The process also assumes that the difficulties are of an individual nature. Thus even the critique of the underlying processes and assumptions within collectives further reveals the inevitable power relations that exist.

In Search of the Ideal Structure?

Issues of power are evident in the struggles for collective authority and collective leadership. As well, power relations emerge despite the ideal of a homogeneous collective. Often differences have not been named, which further obscures the web of power. This chapter suggests that it is necessary to grapple with power relations in order to build solidarity and foster alliances within collectives.

This chapter has addressed the power relations and contradictions that operate internally within feminist collectives, despite their adherence to an ideology that eschews power and desires empowerment. The findings of my research indicate that a rigid adherence to feminism as a monolithic theory and the belief in an "ideal," homogeneous collective serve to constrain women's abilities to grapple with the contradictions in their work. By challenging the false dichotomies of empowerment and power, of the individual and the collective, collectives will be better able to evolve their organization and foster the development of both the worker and the collective.

Some collectives have begun to take up the challenge of working with differences and acknowledging power relations. Through my research, I have met women who are working on developing new tools for problem solving. These consist of developing mechanisms for on-going evaluations of their work. The emphasis is on seeing the collective as constantly changing and evolving and therefore requiring frequent monitoring of internal processes and individual and collective assumptions. Other collectives are drawing clearer lines of accountability and responsibility for workers through the development of working teams. The creation of teams also allows women to work in specific areas of strength and interest. The working teams regularly meet to share information about each of their complementary components.

Other collectives are working with a model of "group and caucus" for understanding the operations of oppression and dominance within their collective (see Toronto Rape Crisis Centre 1985). Women of various additional oppressions (e.g., women of colour, lesbians) meet in caucus to support one another and to discuss work issues that affect them, while groups of corresponding women (e.g., white women, heterosexual women) also meet to support each other in changing behaviours that arise from their privilege. Each of these attempts is important for the continued development of feminist structures. Collectives cannot remain as static organizational forms if they are to endure.

Although I have been critical of the work of collectives, I view this critique as a necessary reflection that has implications for all of our community organizing work. The efforts of feminist social service collectives reflect women's continued desire to have their organizational structures consistent with feminist ideology. Their efforts have not been in vain but rather, stand as a testimony to the necessity to struggle with developing alternative organizational forms.

Reflections on Integrative Feminism and Rural Women

The Case of Antigonish Town and County

Angela Miles

I have just returned to Toronto after living for seven years in Antigonish, Nova Scotia. While I was there I was involved locally in feminist politics and regionally in feminist networking, and I undertook participatory research into the nature and significance of women's activism in this community.

My intention here is not to present the detailed research findings of this "case study," but to draw on my experience and research in both an urban metropolitan and a small town/rural setting, in two different regions of the country. I will reflect generally on the different needs and concerns of practice in urban and rural settings, and make suggestions for feminist practice grounded in the experience and activism of rural women. I hope this will contribute to the kind of respectful sharing and exchange which will enable us to use our diversity as a resource in broadening our understanding, our vision, and our movement.

While I was still in Toronto I had come to the conclusion, and had argued, that the most significant political division within the women's movement is between a feminism that is a full politics and speaks to the whole of society and a feminism that is essentially a pressure politics which speaks only to the relative position of women. This division cuts across commonly recognized categories. There are radical, socialist, anarchist and lesbian feminists on both sides. So, in order to avoid confusion, I coined the term "integrative feminism" to refer to the former tendency, namely, a full politics.[1]

Both types of feminism are committed to gaining equal status and rights with men for women. Integrative feminism, however, goes beyond this to pose an alternative to the dominant separative, individualist, competitive, materialist rationality of industrial patriarchal society. This alternative rationality is grounded in the special life experience, interests and concerns of women, and as such, expresses the marginalized and subordinated values associated with women and with the work of human reproduction[2] — integrative values, such as nurturing, co-operation, connection, love, and mutual service.

Although the lives of women vary across classes and cultures, and races and nations, there is a sense in which we share subordination and marginalization and, in all its enormous diversity, a responsibility for and experience of paid, and unpaid, work and concerns of individual and social reproduction. The claim that there is a basis in women's lives to develop an alternative rationality and vision is thus not a biological claim of a vision innate in our female essence. It is, rather, a *political* claim that as a social group we have the potential to forge such a perspective consciously in collective practice, as ever wider groups of women gradually win the power to articulate needs and values grounded in the specific needs and concerns of our lives and work.

Building a politics which affirms these female-related values as a frame for our vision, and our practice, involves recognizing women's specificity as a group, as well as our equality with men. Recognizing our difference from, as well as equality with men, as integrative feminism does, allows us not only to insist that women be recognized as human *like men*, but that the activities, characteristics, and concerns that have been associated with women be recognized as *human*. This enables us to go beyond the demand that women be included in the existing definition of humanity to require that this definition be transformed and feminized. It moves feminism from pressure to be "let in" to existing male society and humanity to an immanent critique of that society and all its systems of domination — race and class, as well as gender. It thus provides the basis for a feminist struggle for liberation, rather than simply assimilation.

The time spent in Antigonish confirmed my sense of the importance and "rightness" of an integrative feminist perspective. I learned there, that:

(1) Feminism is present in rural communities even when it has no organized local voice. Our movement has succeeded at least to the extent that feminist questions and redefinitions are "in the air."

(2) Women in rural areas are under tremendous pressure in this period. Rapid social change is leading to the disintegration of rural communities and the undermining of women's work and place in these communities, even as it aggravates their economic dependence and vulnerability, and increases their work load, almost beyond the bearable.

(3) Under these conditions a feminism which affirms women's work and concerns and strength, as well as naming and refusing women's oppression, brings much needed and welcome support to rural women. Feminism which affirms women's specificity as a group, as well as their equality with men, makes sense to rural women whose identity and space is under threat. They recognize themselves in it.

(4) Rural and traditional women do not need feminism to tell them that women are strong and their work is important, that men have the power, that women's lives and work and concerns and characteristics and values are different from men's. These hard-won feminist truths that we have so proudly discovered in our urban practice are the traditional

truths of women's culture. In our struggle to create space for ourselves as women, to identify with other women, to name our experience and our oppression, we 'modern' urban women are reclaiming and re-creating an old knowledge that has been robbed from us.

(5) Although these are not the blinding new truths we thought they were, they *are* important as essential prerequisites for our struggle; and our commitment to collective struggle is something feminists can offer traditional women. Women through the centuries have individually and collectively resisted the conditions of male domination, but a conscious commitment to collective resistance is not part of women's traditional culture. The conviction that men's domination is neither natural nor necessary, the vision of another and better world where women's agenda is the human agenda, and the commitment to build that world, is specific to feminism.

(6) Traditional women can make an important contribution to the development of integrative feminism. Their less problematic sense of women as a specific group can help sustain the complex political project of affirming both women's equality and specificity; their taken-for-granted woman identification can provide an important anchor and check for the less well established, more recently won, woman identification of urban feminists; their deep understanding of their own conditions as women can be a powerful resource in the difficult feminist task of building an ever wider sisterhood across divisions imposed by patriarchy, capitalism and colonialism — for it can help ground connections across class, race, nation, religion, marital status, age and sexual orientation within women's local community and beyond; and traditional women's community-wide role can be an important strength in

our attempts to build a feminism which speaks to the whole of society.

(7) Integrative feminism's recognition and affirmation of women's specificity brings feminism home to women's traditional culture. This allows feminism, wherever even vestiges of this culture remain, to draw strength from women's wisdom and organization. It also provides a ground on which women can unite across rural and urban (and "first" and "third" world) divides,[3] for a feminist critique and vision grounded in values derived from women's specific concerns and experience speaks equally to women who have already suffered the effects of patriarchal and industrial modernization and to those who are just now being subjected to them. It can help make it possible for diverse women to recognize themselves in each other and to struggle together, from both ends of the development process, to impose a new and different, human-centred shape on social change.[4]

Modernization and Women in Rural Communities

It is important not to glorify traditional societies and cultures, most of which are poor and closed and offer very few choices and little but extremely hard work to their members. More important, subsistence and small-commodity production communities in Canada and elsewhere are patriarchal.

Nevertheless, despite women's lack of ownership and control of resources, their lack of protection from physical violence, their unequal work load, and greater vulnerability to insecurity and poverty, women play a central role in community life and development in these societies. It is not simply the importance of their economic contribution that underlies this influence but the fact that women's world and voice is defined clearly and separately from men's in these communities.

Essential reproductive labour and much productive labour is clearly within women's realm. Women are responsible for people's survival and development and the quality of life in both the household and the community. Social services and community support, identity and activity are all traditionally women's responsibility. Health care, education, libraries, churches, community halls, social events, and communication are all public and collective activities of women. Women's organizations in such a context play a large role in community development. A large proportion of the female population belongs to them and they represent important, specifically female, concerns, activities, values and world-view. The point here is not that this important contribution and separate organization gives women equal power or status with men, which it does not, but that it ensures women a specific voice and identity.

The changes that come with modernization have entailed the loss of the collective and public expression of women's culture and identity in urban contexts even while women's separate life pattern has persisted. Urbanization and industrialization have changed the organization of gender roles without lessening their actual difference. In fact, the separation of production from the household clearly exaggerated the division. This new social arrangement was accompanied, originally for upper-class women, and later for all women, by a new ideological emphasis on the difference of women from men — their physical frailty, instinctive (not rational) moral purity, and natural aptitude for mothering, and their particular fitness for "the home" — the sphere that was then declared their own. The pre-industrial recognition of women's strength and competence and economic importance as labourer (for husband) and social support (for the whole community) gave way to a totally individualized ideal of helpmate (still for the husband) emphasizing aesthetic and emotional, rather than economic, services. And the public realm was closed to women.

Liberal and progressive thinkers have in the past and today responded to feminist refusal of this demeaning and limiting definition by simply displacing the feminine. Even though women and men's life experience, activity, concerns, and personal qualities remain deeply different and their power unequal, these thinkers have simply announced that there really is no difference, what is male is female, the term "man" includes women. For the "new woman" of the late nineteenth century, the Flappers of the 1920s and the 'modern' house-wives of the mid-twentieth century, a liberal ideology of same-ness, equality and partnership came to mask the obvious structural difference of men and women's lives, and the in-equality of women and men. Men and women were defined as the best and only companions for each other. Women's (though not men's) shared ideas and activities were displaced by co-education, dating, family activities and a social life built around the heterosexual couple.

'Modern' middle-class women of my mother's generation sought to be included and recognized in male culture — to be broad-minded, to renounce their mothers' suspicion of men and of alcohol, to enjoy being told they thought "like a man" and to prefer male to female company. 'Liberated' women of my generation participated in the male sexual revolution, and added a paying job in the man's world to our full job of work in the home. In these varied ways, both generations of urban women denied our difference from men in favour of an incor-poration in the male world that could not be equal. In the process, our specificity as women was rendered culturally in-visible and we lost our own voice and identity.

It is this claim to a false equality and sameness with men that rural women are so deeply suspicious of. And there are good grounds for this suspicion because this is the ideology that has been used historically to legitimize women's loss of a group identity and organizational base, to hide the specific work modern women continue to do, and to mystify our con-tinued subordination. A feminism which is uncritical of this ideology and poses no alternative may appear to rural women to be in collaboration with forces that are currently eroding their own threatened, but still distinct, culture and identity and space. It will certainly hold little appeal.

Modernization in Antigonish[5]

The process of modernization and erosion is clearly evident in Antigonish. The town of Antigonish is the government, busi-ness, retail, and religious center of this rural Nova Scotia county with 5,000 of the county's total 18,000 population.[6] Over the long term the rural part of the county has seen the gradual encroachment of a cash economy on subsistence forms of living. This has resulted today in the predominance of wage labour followed by farm, fish and forest production for the market, all supplemented by other cash forms such as unemployment insurance, welfare payments, and old age pensions, as well as non-cash rural production.

The pressure on farm operations has been great and has resulted in their drastic decline in numbers, until the farm population now makes up only 6 percent of the county's population compared to the rural non-farm population's 61 percent. Large, highly-mechanized farms, often with a debt load on capital, co-exist with smaller, less-capitalized farms, often supplemented by fishing, forestry, and wage labour. Both these types of family farm operate under uncertain harvest, market and interest rate conditions, and financial worry is a constant source of stress for both the male and female farm population.

However, financial stress is not restricted to the farm population in a county where the average employment income for both men and women is well below the Canadian and even below Nova Scotia levels, and the unemployment rate is high. Both male and female, rural, farm, and town inhabitants of Antigonish County are at economic risk; but women are especially vulnerable. Their economic stress is compounded by an increasing, almost unmanageable work load, and an accompanying reduction in their community involvement and importance.

Increasing capital costs on mechanized farms, the decreasing viability of small farming, fishing, and forestry operations as well as the growing difficulty of maintaining a family on a single wage has led to a marked and continuing increase in married women's participation in the labour force. This is occurring without any significant sharing of housework, by men and with no additional social support services.

For both rural and town women, this has resulted in a substantial net addition to their hours of labour. The triple workload of employed farm women is well documented and consists of paid work, housework and farm responsibilities. Non-farm rural women often have similar additional production responsibilities such as a garden, and many do their housework in primitive conditions. Both groups are forced to spend long hours in transportation for essential errands such as shopping, doctor's appointments, school visits and so on. Even without these additional burdens, employed women in town are putting in a double workday which time budget studies done elsewhere show reaches inhuman proportions for women with young children.

The average income that women receive for an overall work-load well in excess of most men's is little more than half of men's annual average wage. Women's average wage in Antigonish County is lower than the government poverty line for an individual. So women's entry into the paid labour force has not appreciably lessened their economic dependence on men.

This economic inequality contributes to a frighteningly high incidence of poverty among women in general, and especially elderly women, who have very little pension protection. At the same time, women marry men older than they are and have a life expectancy seven or eight years longer, so they are, in Antigonish, almost ten times more likely than men to have an old age alone with only one pension to live on. The uncertainty and insecurity of old age is aggravated for women by the fact that they rarely have ownership rights to the farms or businesses they contribute to.

The incidence of divorce is rising rapidly, even in this largely Catholic county. This leaves a growing number of women responsible for their own support, many of them with dependents; and it adds to the general insecurity of all economically dependent, married women who are increasingly aware that marriage today is not the permanent institution it once was. The lack of support services for women doing an extra job of paid work is doubly damaging for women raising children alone, and the harsh results are easily seen in a small town.

All these changes, taken with the marked long-term trend toward centralization of government services, sales and other activities, are contributing to a major shift in women's role in the local community. Centralization aggravates the impact of other changes on women. Women's work in the clerical, sales, service, teaching and health areas (49 percent of the female labour force in Antigonish) is especially affected. Paid work in these areas becomes inaccessible to some and requires long hours of travel by others. Access to services and stores is harder and this, in turn, adds to women's hours of unpaid work.

The lack of accessibility of services also makes it harder for women to play their traditional role in community activity and support. This is compounded by the increasing work-load that leaves women less time to give to women's organizations and, through them, to the community, or to provide neighbourly and family support to each other. Since more women are leaving home each day for paid work, and both men and women are going further afield for their jobs and to do their daily business, the isolation of people who remain in the home in both town and county has increased enormously to become a problem of major proportions for women and old people. This is compounded in rural areas by the consolidation and abandonment of farms.

Government policies have aggravated the pressures on women and their marginalization. No additional support services are provided for employed women or single mothers; training programs in better paying traditionally male jobs continue to be largely restricted to men; male wage-earning and leisure activities are privileged, and women's loss of control of crucial spheres of influence and community functions is hastened.

In these conditions of change and government androcentrism, the traditional infrastructure of community life and of women's support networks is grievously eroded. The decline in the community role of women, combined with the decreasing recognition of their unpaid individual contribution in the home, along with their integration into the labour force at a dependent, relatively menial (though not unskilled) level, is a major threat to women's dignity and power as a group and women's survival as individuals.

These disintegrating tendencies, however, are not complete. Aspects of women's traditional group identity and community role persist in Antigonish. In the town of Antigonish, and even more so in the county, for instance, women's organizations remain more central in community life than they are in cities, with a larger proportion of the female population as members.

Women still take a more active interest *as women* in community development than in larger centres where active women, apart from feminists, have tended to downplay their femaleness in order to claim the right to speak to "general" issues.

Women in Antigonish who begin to resist the subordination and marginalization of their own interests and values are part of existing and entrenched women's networks which may provide a context for dialogue and activity.

In Antigonish the local radio station, local newspaper, and Continuing Education and Extension departments of the university, all reach a far larger proportion of the population and have closer ties to the community than their counterparts in larger urban centres. The membership of women's organizations includes women who work with and for, and are related to men who control these local institutions and resources.

The same tight channels that often work for one-way top down communication and control, and are noted for doing so in small communities, may also, especially when there are well-developed, all-women's organizations, be opened up to alternative messages and two-way communication. When the alternative messages reflect issues of immediate concern to women in areas that are crucial to their survival or have been women's traditional responsibility, they can be powerful.

It is essential, however, that these messages truly reflect the complexity of women's experience and affirm that experience. The feminist analysis of women's subordination must be presented in a context which recognizes the importance of the work and the human and community values which women (almost alone) have cherished and served. This is a crucial point because women do not recognize themselves in an analysis which is only about subordination and not also about their shared strength and contribution. More important, only a shared value framework will enable women, divided by religion, life situation, and status to discuss issues and come to shared positions. Women's particular work and responsibilities historically — and still today, even though they are rendered more and more invisible — provide a basis for a set of values which are deeply subversive of existing social structures and dominant values, and are more and more essential, not only to women's individual survival but also to the survival of our communities and our planet.

Community concerns have traditionally been the focus of women's organizations. With a new feminist component, these concerns can be developed to include the provision for human and community needs in a hostile environment and a challenge to that environment and its subordination of women and human needs. Without the feminist component these traditional organizations are doomed to lose even their earlier important support role and to witness the continuing disadvantaging and trivialization of women. And with this will go the vestiges of community.

It is hardly surprising, then, that women in Antigonish are open to feminist analysis. Over the last seven years I have participated in and documented the process of interaction between feminism and traditional women's activism there. The encounter is not without some misunderstanding, confusion and distrust, but it can be a fruitful and mutually empowering one.

Women's Activism in Antigonish[7]

In 1974, in anticipation of International Women's Year, Antigonish women, whom one participant described as representing "a solid cross section of the community," organized a group called "Women In Transition." The group had a high profile for the two years of its existence, with a paid-up membership of 54 and attendances of up to 300 at its public meetings. An associated but separate consciousness-raising group persisted longer and had a major impact on the lives of the women involved most of whom were women "from away," who had come to the area as part of a counter-culture movement back to the land. The strong informal support and social network these women had built and maintained through major changes in economic, marital, and parental status was not explicitly feminist, but its women-focused alternative culture has proven to be a rich resource for later feminist activity.

In the following years, a number of women involved in both these groups remained concerned and did what they could as individuals in their trade unions or church groups or political parties, in their private lives, and in their jobs (the town librarian, for instance, maintained a substantial collection of feminist books.) However, the next and most recent women's collective public organizing did not occur until 1982-83 when both the Naomi Society for Battered Women and the Antigonish Women's Association were founded.

Both initiatives benefitted directly from the experience gained and relationships built during the activities of 1974-75. They also benefitted from the fact that even though there was no organized local feminist presence, women's issues were in the air. The women's movement has had a marked influence on people's awareness in rural as well as urban areas, so that women in Antigonish were not only experiencing the pressures outlined earlier, they were hearing them named in the media.

The media tends to downplay the role of feminists and the women's liberation movement in raising "women's issues." It is a rare occurrence to see any acknowledgement that media coverage of these issues results from the power that the movement has won to articulate "social problems" and force attention on them. It is even rarer to see the "experts," whose information and experience is cited, recognized as feminists. Nevertheless, the press, radio, television and popular magazines are full of women's issues (if apparently divorced from the women's movement). Rape, child molestation, property laws, pensions, unequal wages, spousal allowance, women priests, daycare, health issues, educational opportunities, negative images of women in the media, pornography, and wife-beating are frequent topics today.[8]

Four issues in particular seem, by 1982, to have had a strong cumulative impact on women in Nova Scotia. The Supreme Court of Canada's ruling in 1971 that Irene Murdoch had no claim to any of the farm she had helped build up, because she had contributed only what is expected of a wife[9] precipitated large public information meetings across the country, organized and attended by a wide variety of women. Antigonish was a part of this growing pressure for reform of provincial property laws. The issue seems to have played a part in generating interest in founding Women in Transition, for instance, and a number of the group's public information sessions dealt with questions of property rights.

More recently, the government's initial refusal to guarantee equality of sex in the Constitution shocked women in a similar manner. But this was a national as opposed to a provincial matter. Instead of the earlier separate provincial property law campaigns, there was a national response of women focused by the already existing feminist networks and groups, but including responses by traditional women's groups and individual women. Women were deeply incensed at the politicians' gratuitous insult to their dignity and felt able to respond in a situation where women's reaction across the country provided a context in which even a single voice could be heard. This was the first time that many women in Antigonish had any sense that they, as individuals or groups, could be a part of the general defence of women's interests. The women's movement was revealed and created in the constitutional struggle as a national network of women. This reinforced and developed for many women the early sense, initiated by the Report of the Royal Commission on the Status of Women in 1970, and heightened by the debates over property law, that women are a group with potential power.

In 1982, when male members of Parliament were televised laughing at wife-beating and refused to apologize for it, the shock among women already sensitized to the problematic nature of their status activated another immediate and national, though this time uncoordinated, response. The result was an intense period of public education about wife-beating and a growing awareness among ever greater numbers of women not only of the vulnerability of women, but the callousness of men and public bodies in general. In the longer term, federal and provincial governments, in an attempt to save face and to respond to the public outcry and mounting well-organized feminist pressure, voted funds to tackle the "problem." The federal government established a Clearing House on Family Violence and mailed out information about the Clearing House and wife-beating with its Family Benefit cheques. Provincial governments began funding transition houses. Local groups sprang up as a result of people's new awareness and the availability of feminist produced resources. The fact that women are disadvantaged and vulnerable was named more publicly in all areas of the country. In Antigonish it was a day-long public meeting on the issue of wife-beating, organized by the local registered nurses association and attended by 250 people, which provided the initial impetus for the founding of the Naomi Society for Battered Women.

In this period of heightened awareness, the release of the feminist film about pornography entitled Not a Love Story was met with widespread interest. The dismissive and insulting reaction of many male reviewers increased women's concern and the film, available free from the National Film Board, was shown in communities across the country, performing an invaluable educational function, and again reinforcing women's collective awareness of their vulnerability. The threat of pornography on pay TV that emerged in the year after the film was released gave women at large another opportunity to act in a spontaneous and concerted way to defend their own interests and to give political expression to their membership in the group 'women.' As a result the federal government established a Special Committee on Pornography and Prostitution to hold public hearings across the country. These hearings had a large educational impact and gave more women a chance to participate actively around an issue.[10]

These four formative issues all gained popular attention through perceived attacks on women's rights and dignity. They all dramatize women's essential inequality. They graphically illustrate women's poverty, economic dependence, and special vulnerability to violence, and the crying lack of concern among the powers that be. Evidence from interviews, kitchen meetings, conference and classroom discussions in Antigonish indicates that by the fall of 1982, when I offered a course called "Women Today" through the Continuing Education Department of St. Francis Xavier University, women's interest and concern with these and other "women's issues" was high. These issues of economic and physical vulnerability were very real to women in Antigonish not only in the media but in their own lives.

Sixty women participated in the "Women Today" course. They came to "get away," to escape the house and kids, to be with other women, to find out more about the issues, and, (a few) to meet like-minded souls they might organize with.

These women from town and county, from Antigonish and "from away," found a rich diversity of age and background and education and economic and educational and marital and parental status in the class. There were no 'out' lesbians in the class (or indeed in Antigonish), but there were women who were raising children alone on welfare, were widowed, divorced, single, or married; women who were unemployed, employed at the minimum wage, earning a professional salary; isolated in the home, overburdened with paid work and work at home; women who had suffered incest, who were beaten; women who had been savaged by the legal and/or social service system and women who worked in those systems.

They found stimulation and excitement and celebration in each other and an integrative perspective on the issues (housework, history, economics, violence, religion ...) that affirmed the value of the work we do and lives we live as women; they found that rare (perhaps unique in that town at that time) place where each woman could be who she was and not who she was or was not married to; they found consciousness-raising and support for and from each other and the notion that there is worthwhile life after forty and without a man. The autonomous pro-woman message and culture that we created together in the class runs deeply contrary to the dominant culture and was empowering for us all.

In April 1983, when the course ended, twenty women from the class and their friends (some of whom brought their experience of "Women In Transition" and/or the earlier consciousness-raising group), met to find a way to continue meeting. From their initiative the Antigonish Women's Association was founded and by October of that year had received funding for and opened the Antigonish Women's Resource Centre. This grouping, with the Naomi Society and a variety of other, less formal, spin-off feminist discussion and support and social groups, today, constitute a significant feminist presence, and a rich and varied feminist practice in the town and county.

This includes such activity as public information sessions, conferences, outreach activity, support groups, programs with the local Employment Centre, support for striking Canadian

Imperial Bank of Commerce workers, letters and columns in the local paper, information days for students, film series, presentation of briefs to the government, meetings with electoral candidates, study groups, action research, newsletters, production and dissemination of educational materials and pamphlets, exchanges with women from the Third World who, every year, attend the Coady International Institute in town, participation in regional and provincial networking and organizing, dances, parties, picnics, barbecues, pot lucks, and celebrations on International Women's Day, the solstice, or the full moon or any time at all.[11]

The women's movement in Canada is successfully developing the climate for women to become active; and where there are active feminists, the movement's resources and support are enabling them to organize and educate locally. The Antigonish Women's Centre is full of material produced on all aspects of women's lives and activity by movement organizations and individuals. The support and advice available through the centre depends to a large extent on existing feminist networks. The centre's public education and action draws on a wide variety of feminist individuals and groups in the region with experience as advisors and resource people, and is, in turn, providing resources for others.

Conclusion

In Antigonish, in this period of rapid change and pressure on women, the general awareness fostered by the women's movement, and the movement resources available to local feminists, made it possible for rural women to bring their traditional sense of themselves as a group and their traditional role in local communities together with a new feminist resistance to the subordination of women and their concerns. Events elsewhere suggest that this form of organizing is not unique to Antigonish. Reports of feminist or woman-identified activities with a broad community base outside metropolitan areas are more common today at conferences and in feminist publications than they have been in the past. The 1989 Annual Conference of the Canadian Research Institute for the Advancement of Women was held, for instance, in Yellowknife. Also, new women's newspapers such as *Common Ground* in Prince Edward Island and the *Newsmagazine for Alberta Women*, are appearing which combine an inclusive approach to traditional women's news and affairs with new women's issues and clear feminist analysis.[12]

In the process of dealing with "women's issues" as defined by feminists, rural and small town women's organizations are redefining their sense of women as a group in a way that encompasses women's disadvantages without denying their strengths and importance. They are beginning to forge a powerful and compassionate political presence which claims the mainstream for "women's issues" and calls for a transfer of resources and power to women as the key to human and community development. This gradual interaction of feminism with traditional women's community and reform concerns is thus an important factor contributing to a stronger and broader feminism that can presume to speak to social priorities in general and not just women's condition. It is a mutual enrichment and transformation that adds to the possibility of bringing together the principles of equality and specificity in a full politics that moves traditional women's activity out of the political margins and takes feminism beyond protest and pressure.

Theoretical Postscript

In the 1980s feminists have increasingly affirmed women's specificity in urban as well as rural practice. The logic of our politics and the ground we must stand on to make a transformative rather than assimilationist struggle are requiring this of us. So, for instance, feminist activism around peace, development, pornography, and legal reform recognizes women's specificity while insisting that it is a cultural and social, rather than biological fact, which can and must be consciously changed as part of our movement toward a freer and more fully human society. A feminist politics is emerging in these and other areas that integrates a recognition of women's specificity with a refusal of women's subordination, and which presumes to address the whole of society and not simply women's issues, and to challenge not only women's oppression but the dualism underlying all dominations.

More recently, as these presumptions of practice have been noticed, named, and theorized, counter-positions which refuse this integration and insist on women's sameness with men as the basis of feminist politics have been articulated in response. So that today, a theoretical literature is developing around, for instance, issues of:

> (1) whether recognizing women's specificity is necessarily an essentialist position,[13]
>
> (2) whether a feminist politics which addresses the whole of society is necessarily an abandonment of women,[14]
>
> (3) whether feminist law reform which seeks more than formal sameness of treatment for men and women will doom women to "protection" which institutionalizes their inequality (Martin 1984) or will provide the basis for differential treatment which can reduce inequality (Lahey 1989; Miles 1985).

These are crucial questions. The way we answer them depends centrally on whether we see feminist struggle as primarily assimilationist or transformative. In this context of questioning and debate, the experience of Antigonish lends important weight to the case for recognizing women's specificity and illustrates the relevance and importance of the transformative integrative feminism this recognition makes possible.

Bending the Iron Law of Oligarchy

Debates on the Feminization of Organization and Political Process in the English Canadian Women's Movement, 1970-1988

Jill Vickers

In this chapter, I examine recent debates about organization and political process in the English Canadian women's movement.[1] Doris Anderson, previously President of the Advisory Council on the Status of Women and of the National Action Committee on the Status of Women (NAC), has argued that Canadian feminist organizations suffer more from crises caused by differences in political process, strategy and tactics than from issues of substantive policy.[2] Anderson's observations reflect her own experience with English Canadian feminism. Certainly interactions between groups such as NAC and the Fédération des Femmes du Québec (the FFQ) have, in fact, involved conflict over substantive policy. Nonetheless, the recurrence of crises within NAC related to the "how" of politics rather than to "what" has, in general, borne out Anderson's observations.[3]

The question of what causes conflict within groups can be approached by seeing that NAC is a national umbrella organization which brings together women from groups which are very diverse in size, ideology, and political practice. Women bring to NAC diverse experiences of the political process and they come with different views of what feminist politics ought to be like. Women, especially those whose only experience of feminist politics is in a small homogeneous collective, undergo real culture shock when they step into a large political arena with women who have had extensive experience in traditional or union politics. Francophone women face significant culture shock because the Québec movement shares more common assumptions about the nature of the political process than is the case in English Canada.[4] Umbrella structures try to aggregate the views of many diverse groups, including those which see how feminists should "do" politics as part of the agenda. Radical feminist groups, in particular, often challenge the basic norms of liberal, representative democracy, and their critique has had much impact on feminist thought and practice.

In this chapter, I explore the debate over the "feminization" of political process and organization. The argument occurs in four parts. First, I locate feminist concerns with process in the broader framework provided by Robert Michels' "iron law of oligarchy." In this section I critique the goal of an "authentic" politics through which radical feminism challenges the processes of representative democracy that they consider alienating. Second, I explore the political and organizational practices they developed and some responses from liberal and leftist feminists. Third, I contextualize these debates in the English-Canadian movement, focusing on NAC. Finally, I argue that contemporary feminism lacks a developed theory of democratic process and organization and I offer some ideas towards the development of such a theory.

1. Bending The Iron Law of Oligarchy: Radical Feminism and the Goal of an Authentic Politics

Many marginalized people have tried to avoid elitist ways of operating in the groups they form because they have experienced the exclusion, alienation and sense of powerlessness which is the lot of those "on the bottom" (Janeway 1981). One discussion of the possibility of developing genuinely democratic organizations occurred within European working-class movements. Robert Michels developed the proposition that elected leaders and paid officials would always eventually constitute an oligarchy in any organization, regardless of ideological commitments to democratic control, because those at the top (even without any power-hungry intent) develop more knowledge and expertise than those at the grassroots. Michels' "iron law of oligarchy," then, held that the tendency towards top-down control is a characteristic of organizations and not the result of the actions of power-hungry leaders and officials (Michels 1915). It is against this iron law that many contemporary feminists are in rebellion.

Three key aspects of recent efforts to achieve the feminization of political process can be identified. First, the model for a feminist political process is seen in the *authenticity* of small-group processes that allow for *a high degree of comfort* and *recognition of shared experiences*. The origins of this model are in the consciousness-raising groups of the 1960s and the collectives and communes of the 1970s. Second, the model for a feminist political process presumes *the absolute sovereignty of the individual* is central to political decision-making. "The major advantage of consensus over majority rule is that no one becomes committed by others to a decision she cannot live with comfortably" (Hawxhurst & Morrow 1984, 73). Third, the model *rejects representative democracy for direct or participatory democracy*. Things close-to-home are favoured over things far away, and influencing the state is diminished as a goal.

These aspects of the current "feminization" of process debates reflect values developed by radical feminism in the United States where women faced the most powerful state in the world. In this section, I explore the evolution of U. S. radical feminist views in the specific context of U. S. politics. In addition, I outline some of the influences this challenge to liberal values had in Canada, largely because of the movement of U. S. feminists of the "draft dodger" generation to major Canadian cities. I also argue, however, that there was an indigenous political culture associated with the women's movement in English Canada. Some aspects of that political culture were in harmony with the values imported with U.S. radical feminism. The theme of decentralization and local control, for example, was also a feature of the women's political culture developed in the long decades when the ad hoc politics of the community substituted for involvement in the far-from-home politics of the state (Vickers 1988a; Vickers and Tardy 1986). Other values of the U.S. radical feminist tradition, however, were in conflict with the indigenous political culture of the Canadian movement. In this attempt to understand the tensions within Canadian feminist groups, I identify the points of conflict and similarity between the Canadian and U.S. experiences. This is not to suggest that the non-Canadian origin of some political values necessarily discredits them. Rather, we must understand that norms of political culture emerge from specific political experiences. Hence the anti-statism I attributed to U.S. radical feminism emerges from a uniquely American context. Likewise, the sense of Canadian feminists that our state is a less powerful but positive utility which could be successfully influenced shows a uniquely Canadian pro-statism (Andrew 1987).

The contemporary women's movement in Canada is characterized by ideological diversity and a capacity to undertake collaborative actions. As noted earlier, their central institutions, such as NAC and the FFQ, regroup other organizations of diverse ideology, size, purpose and operating style in permanent, if fragile, coalitions for the purpose of interacting with their respective governments. A recent analysis characterizes the contemporary movement[5] as having two "wings", an *institutionalized* wing and a *grassroots* wing (Adamson, Briskin & McPhail 1988). In this account, the institutionalized aspect is characterized as liberal feminist, while the grassroots aspect is seen as containing both socialist-feminist and radical feminist groups. In fact, the umbrella organizations bring together women drawn from many "aspects" into a single political arena and much of the conflict over political process results from this integrative political practice. Difficult though the political experience of the umbrella organizations has been, it has contributed to the development of a uniquely Canadian strain — integrative feminism (Miles 1984 and Chapter 4).

Bonnie Krep's analysis of the women's liberation movement in Canada revealed this tendency as early as 1972. Describing the movement as "a generic term covering a large spectrum of positions," she divided it into the three familiar ideological positions, adding that "all three broad segments have their

own validity, all three are important. One belongs in one segment rather than another because of personal affinity with the
aims being striven for" (Kreps 1972, 74-5). Kreps did not seek
to invalidate other strains of feminism. This tolerance contrasted with the practice in the United States where the word
feminism was rigorously reserved for the ideas of young radical revolutionary women. Liberal feminists included in the
movement by Kreps were defined by U.S. women as "traditional" and excluded because of their reformism and acceptance of ordinary political process and structures (Garretson
1975; Richardson, 1983). In the U.S., therefore, a belief in particular norms of process was integral to the very definition of
feminism:

> "Feminist" here is used to refer to women who
> believe that the inequality of women is the central
> social and political problem; in America, *therefore, it*
> *follows that they would form non-hierarchical organiza-*
> *tions, in which decision is reached by consensus* ... all
> share a belief in the total restructuring of American
> Society (Garretson 1975, 19, italics added).

This tendency to associate feminism with a rejection of representative democracy was less common in Canada than in the
U.S. American anthropologist Joan Richardson, writing about
Montreal in the early 1970s, argues that "the unbridgeable gulf
between women's rights and radical feminist organizations,
such as there is in the United States, has not occurred in
Canada." She attributes this to the characteristics of the
Canadian political culture which, in part, meant that "(t)here
was little fear, as there was in the United States movement, of
the police, of the press, or the accepting of funding from the
government or private sources" (Richardson 1983, 30).

The political culture of the indigenous English Canadian
movement, with century-old roots, can be described as "radical liberalism" (Vickers 1989; Richardson 1983). A commitment
to the ordinary political process is central to its values. Its other
values include: a belief in the efficacy of state action, especially
of the welfare state; a belief that change is possible; a belief that
dialogue with those who differ may be useful; and a belief that

FIGURE 4.1

The Ideological "Lack of Fit"
Between English Canadian Radical Liberalism
and U. S. Radical Feminism

The Political Culture of Radical Liberalism	The Political Culture of U. S. Radical Feminism
A commitment to the ordinary political process	A rejection of the ordinary political process/ rejection of politics in favor of consciousness changes
Pro-statism; a belief in the efficacy of state actions, especially of the welfare state	Anti-statism, a belief in the absolute sovereignty of the individual vs. the state and institutions
Pro-active, a belief that change is possible	Briefly pro-active, mainly politically quietist believing change needed to be total and of individual consciousness
Dialogue with those who differ may be useful	Dialogue with those who differ is not useful — splinter or separate
Helping others, in terms of service, is a valid contribution to change	Assisting others in relation to self-help and aiding the victims of male violence is useful

helping others in service organizations is a valid contribution to change (Vickers 1989). By contrast, the political culture of U.S radical feminism involved: a rejection of the ordinary political process and a rejection of state politics in favour of changes in consciousness; a pessimism about the efficacy of state action; a belief in the absolute sovereignty of the individual versus the state and institutions; a belief that dialogue with those who differ is not useful; and a belief in the value of separatism and a counter-culture. (See Figure 4.1). While these ideas about how to "do" feminist politics have had a significant impact on Canadian women, there was a dialogue here among advocates of the various strains of feminism who had to "do" politics within shared organizations such as NAC and the FFQ. There was, therefore, some "lack of fit" between the generalized political culture which surrounded Canadian feminists and the political values of U.S. radical feminism. In exploring these different values, it is useful to understand their origins.

In the U.S., radical feminism emerged from and in reaction to the largely white New Left — a movement which stressed the theme of *participatory democracy* in which individuals would have control over their own lives (Aronowitz 1984, 21). While the old Left in the U.S. had been pro-statist and valued collective action, the New Left was pessimistic about state action and was radically individualist. There were two distinct counter-cultures in the U.S. in the 1960s that influenced radical feminism. There was the political subculture (the politicos) — "those engaged in the politics of direct democracy, who organized traditional constituencies in new ways" — and there were the cultural radicals who believed that "the struggle within the state and its institutions (was) hopeless and beside the point" (Aronowitz 1984, 24). Believing in an authentic politics centred on the freedom of the individual from restraints, the cultural radicals wanted freedom from the state and from social institutions. The cultural radicals saw conventional politics as "a form of domination infinitely more oppressive than economic exploitation" and challenged the legitimacy of representative government and of majority rule with the belief that the power of "the sovereign individual" had been "systematically undercut by representative government, trade union bureaucracies and large, impersonal institutions" (Tom Hayden, cited in Aronowitz 1984, 32).

The emerging women's liberation movement had both leftist and radical tendencies (Vickers 1989). Its adherents reacted against the sexism of New Left men who exploited women's labour, denied them leadership roles, and denied their grievances status. The movement shared with the U.S. New Left use of an analysis which included the language of liberation from oppression. Its organizational norms, however, developed in reaction to U.S. New Left practice. (The

Canadian New Left — the Waffle — was quite different in its core values (Vickers 1989). Consciousness-raising (c-r) was adopted from the Chinese Maoist "speak bitterness" practice as the method for women to uncover their oppression (Willis 1984, 95). The movement rejected the use of violence and assumed that changes in the consciousness of individuals constituted change.

Some women's groups in Canada shared these views. Certainly the efforts of emigré feminists like Marlene Dixon to import a U.S. style movement had an impact. In Montreal groups, one writer observed, "All value accrued to the individual. The transformation sought was that of the individual, not of the community, or of the society" (Richardson 1983, 411). This put an enormous premium on the achievement of *solidarity* among women. It also resulted in the common process of splintering which affected many early groups because *the emphasis on internal solidarity placed a very high premium on non-conflictual internal processes* (Richardson 1983; Ricks et al., 1972).

These groups developed strategies to overcome tendencies towards internal elitism or leadership, such as issuing speaking tokens to hobble articulate women and empower less articulate women. Tasks were rotated to prevent the development of expertise within the groups; the "shit work" was to be shared by all. Women were reacting to their experiences in other groups in which the articulate dominated, expertise involved control, and the role of women was either "prone" or making the coffee. Out of the process of such groups, a fundamental principle of radical feminism emerged in the proposition that "the personal *is* the political." And an agenda for radical feminist politics was generated out of the experiences of the women in the groups, especially around issues of sexuality and reproduction. Issues of difference, such as racism, while central in most civil rights groups, were submerged in the c-r group's homogeneity and in the concept of a universal sisterhood.

When radical feminists moved on to create counter-culture services for women, they took many of their assumptions about feminist process and organization with them. The c-r groups had tended to be largely homogeneous. Their process was intense, meaningful, and stimulating to self-growth (Allen 1970). An "authentic" politics emerged in which consensus could be reached and decisions made without taking votes and without having winners and losers. This was transferred to the new collectives along with an emphasis on process — "process is our most important product" (Hawxhurst & Morrow 1984, 29). Angela Miles concludes that radical feminists were the first to "work on, and to celebrate, and to establish an enormous variety of grassroots projects which they saw, not in narrow service, cultural or political terms, but as simultaneous consciousness raising, political organizing and theoretical development" (Miles 1984, 60). This collapsing of categories led to a denigration of formal political work, however, which alienated radical feminists in Canada from the more state-oriented organized movement.

2. Political and Organizational Practices Developed by Radical Feminism and Responses from Liberal and Left-wing Feminism

Some practices used by the early radical feminist groups, such as speaking tokens, were not continued beyond their groups of origin. There is, however, sympathy for any mode of operation which will empower the politically inexperienced (Riggs & Tyler 1988). The practices which survive include: (1) rotation of leadership roles, (2) sharing of service roles, (3) consensus decision-making, (4) a commitment to decentralization (small, close-to-home groups), (5) a concern for accessibility in terms of the "costs" of participation, (6) "egalitarianism" — flat pay scales for staff (although rarely voting rights), (7) a rejection of electioneering on the grounds that "money (or being articulate) wins elections." The objective aimed at in each case is *internal egalitarianism*. The rotation of leadership and sharing of work were designed to eliminate the development of powerful expertise and "ego-tripping" leaders (Mitchell 1971). The practices do not reflect efforts to make leadership accountable, to recognize difference, or to manage conflict when it cannot be resolved or transcended.

Radical feminists reject authority structures and hierarchies. They also tend to view leadership in terms of the oppression and exploitation experienced by many women in male-dominated organizations, rejecting the possibility of non-coercive, empowering leadership based on energy, capacity, skill or strength (Vickers 1980; Hartsock 1985). Hence, radical feminists associate exclusively with democracy's *equality* dimension. Only political processes of a direct nature are considered "authentic." Representative structures are rejected as elitist and inauthentic, even if the group is forced by circumstances to adopt them. This tendency to see any form of organizational structure beyond the small grassroots collective as by definition a betrayal of feminist norms limits the capacity of feminist political theory and practice to restructure large groups and to develop feminist institutions which could organize women's power collectively over time.

Arguments against these norms of operation have usually been based on the value of efficiency, such as the argument that we can't afford the time radical feminist process involves. In fact, arguments against also reflect different views of how change can be achieved. On the one hand, most radical feminists believe that societal change occurs when people change their own lives and minds within the local situation (Mitchell 1971, 63). On the other hand, critics of radical feminist process believe that structures maintained by the state and institutions limit the ability of individuals to change their lives and that struggle must occur with the powerful to achieve change.

American commentators critiqued the radical feminist view of political process from several viewpoints. Joyce Rothschild-Witt observed that social control in the small groups fostered by radical feminist norms is often maintained by "personalistic and moralistic appeals" which make it necessary "that the group select members who share their basic values and world view" (Rothschild-Witt 1979, 513). Moreover, early on, critiques appeared of the ideology of structurelessness inherent in the "flat" organizational model. Jo Freeman (1973) argued that all groups involve leadership, informal if not formal, and that informal leadership is more likely to be manipulative and undemocratic. She urged U.S. women's groups to adopt structures to formalize leadership and make it possible to hold those in leadership positions accountable.[6]

Observers in leftist groups also critiqued this view of an "authentic" politics. U.K. socialist Sheila Rowbotham wrote:

> Sisterhood can become a coercive consensus which
> makes it emotionally difficult for individual women
> to say what they feel rather than a source of strength
> ... Our lack of structure can make it difficult for
> women outside particular networks to join. It can
> lead to cliquishness and thus be undemocratic. The
> stress on personal experience makes it hard to com-
> municate ideas which have been gained either from
> the women's movement in the past or from other
> forms of radical politics (Rowbotham 1979, 40).

In Canada, although the relationship has frequently been
stormy, small-group collectives organized along radical feminist norms have operated in state politics under the umbrella
of coalition organizations such as NAC, and Alberta Status of
Women Action Group (ASWAC). Small collectives have also
developed clearing houses, networks and other loose structures of co-ordination.[7] They have also developed techniques
for receiving government and private funding through a networking core, thereby minimizing the steering effects of such
funding on their internal priorities (Cunningham, Findlay, et
al. 1988). Hence it is possible in Canada for such groups to play
a role within the overall women's movement. It is less clear
that they can co-operate effectively with other progressive
forces in coalition activities. Coalition behaviour requires elite
accommodation and the acceptance of instrumental behaviour
such as supporting positions on which not all group members
agree. In groups in which consensus is key, willingness to
suppress disagreements to achieve an instrumental goal is
rare.

The radical feminist goal of a total authentic politics led to
the basic organizational unit of the movement being the small,
homogeneous group in which consensus decision making,
egalitarian role rotation and non-alienating processes could be
sustained. That meant, however, that we rarely encountered
women very different from ourselves in a primary setting. The
goal of integrating into the movement women who are still
very much marginalized in Canadian society cannot be
achieved by using the model of the small group writ large.
Rather, we must look to models emerging from our collabora-

tive structures — the networks, clearing houses and umbrella groups. To this point, feminist views of democracy revolve around the value of egalitarianism and do not address the issues of representation, accountability, majority rule, or the rights of minorities. Hence, it has not been possible to deal with difference in a way which respects the authenticity of the experiences of women with differing points of view.

3. Making a Virtue of Necessity: Contextualizing the Process Debates in the Canadian Movement

The history of the Canadian women's movement is characterized by a propensity to create umbrella structures based on the membership of groups of different sizes, types and orientations and by a succession of effective coalitions based on elite accommodation (Vickers 1988b). Monique Bégin observed that the unique characteristics of Canada's women's movements are the result of the significant revitalization of traditional women's organizations which occurred between 1967 and 1972 because of the cross-country activity of the Royal Commission on the Status of Women. She argues that every existing women's association in the country became, to some extent, feminist, and that the movement was able to build on existing traditions, expertise and membership (Bégin 1988).

In 1971, the National Ad Hoc Committee on the Status of Women sought mechanisms to ensure the implementation of the commission's recommendations (Kome 1985; Appelle 1987). It convened the Strategies for Change Conference which ended in the formation of the more permanent National Action Committee on the Status of Women (Appelle 1987). In the process of NAC's formation, however, the traditional segment of the women's movement found itself engulfed by elements of the women's liberation movement. These women had been active in organizing the cross-Canada Abortion Caravan in 1970 (Collins 1985). Few considered the commission's recommendations very radical. Nonetheless, in Canada in the 1970s quite radical women's liberation groups were willing to work with quite traditional groups (Richardson, 1983).

European and U.S. observers contrast between the two wings of the current women's movements: the older *women's right wing* and the younger *women's liberation wing*. The liberation groups emphasize their radicalism, fear co-optation, see institutional structures as barriers, and reject accommodation with the state (Freeman 1974). The supposition is that each "wing" will inhabit different organizations and assumes women don't have the ability to develop institutions in which groups of all ideological types can be represented. It fails to consider the possibility that women can build successful coalitions and can institutionalize these coalitions in permanent structures. In fact, the Canadian movement sustains such cooperation at the various levels, within NAC and the FFQ as the largest and most inclusive organizations in relation to their respective states.

The founders of NAC were clear that their function was to lobby the federal government until all of the Royal Commission's recommendations had been implemented. NAC began, therefore, as an institution of convenience oriented to state politics. But historically, Canadian women's organizations were also an arena within which women could develop and debate public policy (Strong-Boag 1986). Many enjoyed annual access to the cabinet. It was intended that NAC would build on this tradition both in terms of lobbying and by becoming a "parliament of women." The new elements influenced by U.S. radical thought were philosophically opposed to hierarchy, leadership, and bureaucracy. They emphasized the importance of consciousness-raising and the experiences of "ordinary" women (like themselves) in creating a political agenda. NAC's umbrella structure, based on the membership of groups, was expected to bring together, in a fragile coalition, the major ideological elements evident in the English-Canadian movement, as well as to maintain some relationship between the French-Canadian and English-Canadian movements.[8] But, NAC is a paradox: although it "represents" groups, individuals attend, speak and vote at meetings. Individuals are elected to the executive board and to committees. Their views may or may not mirror the views of others in their groups. Currently, the organized women's movement in Canada is a mass movement with over 2,500 women's groups active. In 1986, over 700 groups were receiving either core or project funding from the Secretary of State Women's Program.

(Emergency Consultation 1986). Over 570 groups were affiliated with NAC in 1988 (NAC Groups/Groupes Membres Du
CCA Brochure 1988). While NAC does not "represent" even
the English-Canada's women's movement in the fullest sense,
it does constitute the most representative body presently in the
movement as the FFQ does in Québec. In each, a feminist
grassroots has been grafted onto an original coalition of more
traditional groups. This has permitted the participation of the
more radical groups within structures which impact their respective governments in a way that has not been achieved in
other liberal democracies.

NAC's role as an umbrella structure has been to organize a
coalition of groups and ideological forces within the Canadian
women's movement. Structurally the groups affiliated include
the following types: (1) pan-Canadian, chapter-based groups
(top-down organizing), (2) pan-Canadian groups based on individual memberships, (3) alliance umbrellas which focus on
the provincial state and which re-group organizations of dis-
parate sizes, (4) national federations of local groups, (5)
national regional/provincial networks of service groups, (6)
single-issue coalitions, (7) local groups, collectives, centers,
services.

This diversity means that there are few shared conceptions
about its proper functioning. On several occasions in the past,
NAC has been rocked by crises about the issues of political
process and organization, but more clearly caused by the sharp
increase in the number of groups demanding representation.
In the early 1980s the crisis was concluded, if not resolved, by
a further "grafting on," this time of a structure for regional
representation onto a Toronto-dominated executive.

In this discussion, I focus on the most recent crisis precipitated apparently by the "feminization of process" approach
presented by the Organizational Review Committee in 1988.
Table 4.1 illustrates the growth pattern for NAC affiliated
groups since 1972.

First, the sheer volume of new groups caused stress. Second,
the new groups were diverse and quite different in character.
Third, the expectations of those newly affiliated groups representing visible minorities, immigrant and disabled women
were high and tinged with suspicion. Fourth, the high cost of

Table 4.1
GROWTH OF NAC: 1972-1986

	1972	1977	1982	1986
Group Membership	31(5)*	120	200	458
Annual Budget	$15,000	$65,000	$296,000	$679,476
Friends of NAC	No Category			900

*4 groups were added during 1972
Source: Appelle, 1987: 55

ensuring genuine participation rather than leadership interaction by francophones, disabled women, poor women and women living at a distance, to note only a few, was staggering.

The relative success of the Canadian movement in organizational terms has probably rested on the shared values of "radical liberalism," outlined in section 1 above, which are unlikely to be shared as fully by women from other political traditions, in particular, newly mobilized groups of immigrant women. Increasingly, many white Canadian feminists, used to seeing ourselves as victimized by men, are being forced to face our own racism, ethno-centrism, able-bodied bigotry, and heterosexist and classist assumptions. Clearly, this will stress organizations like NAC further still. An assessment of the concrete "demands" of those elements expressing their views in the Organizational Review in 1988, however, shows that the concept of "the feminization of process" was blurred into several other concepts which are about the "fairness" of representation in NAC. In fact, they reflect concerns familiar in Canadian politics.

Nicole Lacelle, the Québec consultant, based her report on the premise that an *equal* structural representation of the Québec movement was desirable but not attainable. The possibilities offered were: "two Presidents? equal representation on the Executive Board? different voting procedures? changed numbers and roles of representatives?" (Lacelle 1988, 6) A "federative" or regionalized structure was also considered but apparently not pursued because it could "endanger the autonomy of Québec groups to the extent that such a federation would be one link in a pan-Canadian organization" (Lacelle 1988, 7). These issues speak much more to traditional notions of elite accommodation, concurrent majorities and constraints on claims by NAC to "represent" Québec interests than to "the feminization" of process. Unfortunately, the real issue of equality between national movements was never really raised within NAC generally, perhaps because the norms of radical egalitarianism held symbolic sway in the debate which ensued.

Lacelle's report then proceeded to outline a number of process issues presented as the "minimal requirements to ensure meaningful participation (by Québec women) in NAC." (Lacelle 1988, 8) These requirements focused on improved and expanded translation services, the mandatory wearing of translation devices by anglophones, initiation sessions for new participants, workshops to allow more discussion of issues, clearer and fairer rules of order, anglophone and francophone co-chairs in all sessions. (Lacelle 1988, 9) The core issue was that of feeling excluded and handicapped in participation. Many of the proposed improvements *increased* rather than decreased structure.

The Organizational Review Document produced by the anglophone consultants, Joan Riggs and Lynne Tyler, perhaps for the first time, focused on the need to expand the pool of involved volunteers, on how to effectively utilize the (then) seven-member staff, and how to establish norms of accountability. Five working assumptions were outlined in the Report: (1) "The principle of accessibility and representation of the diversity of women's experience in Canada." The emphasis here was on removing barriers to participation rather than on ensuring representation through, for example, internal affirmative action. (2) "The principle of democracy" conceptualized as everyone having "an equal opportunity to influence and make decisions if they choose regardless of geographic or other factors." This reflects a traditional concern with the inadequate representation within NAC of western, eastern and northern groups. (3) The principle of "accountability" was conceptualized in terms of "Lines of decision-making, implementation and accountability" being clear, rather than any concept of the collective accountability of executives or the holding to account of leaders such as presidents, vice-presidents or committee chairs.[9] (4) The principle of "ownership by member groups" reflected an effort to refocus NAC's efforts towards, for example, the provision of services for member groups in areas such as lobbying. (5) The principle of "empowerment" stressed the sovereignty of individuals "finding their own voices" and "being able to create their lives as they choose" (Riggs & Tyler 1988, 5). Empowerment was to be understood as an individual not as a collective phenomenon.

The underlying conception of the Organizational Review Document was that of a valuable house which must be made accessible to all individuals on as equal a basis as possible. The norms remain those of outsiders wanting to get in. The details of the report, however, reflect glimmers of concern for the development of a political process in which responsibility of leaders and staff will figure more prominently. The initiative represented by this process has, on the surface, failed. Nonetheless, if earlier patterns of NAC continue, some of the concrete changes will be implemented if not the proposed major restructuring.

NAC's most crucial role has been to channel and manage conflict within the women's movement, to permit the building of coalitions. Whether it can incorporate in its processes black feminism, ethnic feminism, disabled women's feminism, lesbian feminism, etc. in the way it brought together traditional social feminism and liberal/reform feminism in the 1970s and further incorporated socialist and radical feminism in the 1980s remains the challenge for the future. It may well be that there is a limit to the number and diversity of groups which can operate under the umbrella structures like NAC.

4. Towards a Feminist Theory of Democratic Process and Organization

Contemporary feminist conceptions of political process and organization evolved within the framework of liberal-democracy, but in opposition to many of its practices. Radical feminists chose the norm of equality as their touchstone, seeing traditional organizations as unacceptable to the extent that they deny absolute equality of participation in decision-making. This emphasis on equality to the exclusion of all other values of importance in liberal-democratic theory and practice poses serious problems for the development of feminist theories of politics.

Taken to its extreme, the egalitarian norm in political process requires the direct involvement of every member or citizen in the making of every decision such that no representative or delegate structures are acceptable. Representative structures are rejected as hierarchical insofar as elite power can develop because the representatives will know more and have more influence over the decision-making process. This rejection means that no rules for controlling leaders or representatives have been developed. For example, no rules that would authorize votes in a network or umbrella organization only on issues pre-decided by the group (instructed delegate) have been developed. Moreover, the egalitarianism reflected in the practice of representation by population has been ignored in favour of a sentimental egalitarianism of one-group-delegate-one-vote. Hence, the theory of representativeness, in terms of ensuring that each of the thousand members of group A has a vote worth the same value as the 10 members of group B also remains unexplored. Indeed, I have heard the desire for representativeness of this sort described as undemocratic on the grounds that the woman with fewer votes to cast would be unequally treated.

If leadership is considered incompatible with egalitarianism and representativeness rejected, devising ways of making leaders and delegates accountable is not a high priority. Although many feminist organizations in Canada designate or elect a president, chair, spokesperson, etc., I know of none with a method for recalling or removing leaders. Also, I know of few feminist organizations with rules specifying the procedures of approval for leaders to speak for or bind the organization.[9] The leadership of the women's movement is little constrained by structures members could use to hold them accountable. In NAC, each president makes her own role and interacts with other groups, the media and government, with very few formal constraints. Hard-working individuals can easily "pirate" committees and the executive member chairing can operate, in much the way the president does, to associate the organization with policies and with other groups without the intrusion of an accountability process. Nor can general assemblies enforce accountability as they are primarily composed of novice delegates whose turn on the rotation principle it is to attend.

Many feminists reject the understanding of democracy as involving majority rule. Their perspective is that the politics of the state and of male-dominated organizations operate on a majority rule principle and that women's interests never seem to get respected in the process. They support consensus as the ideal. There is little appreciation, however, of the fact that the participation costs for most women are too high to make them want to adopt the consensus model in large, instrumental groups. Yet few alternate modes have been explored. Whenever the feminization of process is called for, majority rule and the rules of order are at the top of the list of complaints. To date, however, no experimentation with processes in between consensus and majority rule has been tried.

The principle of democratic theory that the minority must be placated is also little explored. The view is that there should be no minority — no winners or losers. Yet this vision of being able to reach agreement always if only we had the time and the goodwill, which is based on the experience of homogeneity and the ideology of sisterhood, does not realistically accept the fact of difference.[10]

Too often debates concerning political process and organization become reduced to an either/or account. Either we can be efficient and surrender our dream of an authentic politics or we can engage in intimate political debate in impotent isolation from the forces of social change. It is my view that our emerging practice provides the basis for ways of transcending that either/or bind. Few feminists wish to simply replicate the operational modes of male-dominated groups.

We should not surrender our desire for different ways of operating. We should believe that the iron law of oligarchy can be at least bent if not broken. Nonetheless, we must also come to understand that the model of a desirable alternative constructed by radical feminism in the 1960s and 1970s may not be sufficient for the challenges of the current world. In those decades it seemed possible that many of the changes we desired could be achieved in our lifetimes. Now it is apparent that the de-construction of patriarchy is a multi-generational task.

Hence, while there will still be room for small, primary and short-lived groups within which women can experience direct democracy and an intimate involvement in organization, we must also learn how to construct institutions which can survive across time. It is crucial that we construct theories of democratic operation which reflect the experiences of women "at home" in our own organizations to replace those we developed in reaction against male-dominated groups. These theories must modify our dedication to egalitarianism to also include concepts of representation, accountability, norms of decision-making which transcend the consensus/majority rule, and understand power as a collective force.

I am aware that this chapter raises more questions than it answers. Trying to identify the right questions to pose however, can be a valuable contribution. It is my conviction that Michel's iron law of oligarchy can be bent, even in large institutions structured to organize collective power over time and space. I believe that there is much in our political practice that can give substance to this debate. It is to this practice that we should begin to look.

Section II

Feminist Practice

Organizing and Activism

Introduction

This section includes contributions that describe the activism of feminists across Canada, documenting some of the range and breadth, and offering critical reflections that should be helpful to activists in future organizing efforts. The chapters include examples of coalition building, regional organizing, and organizing efforts by women in particular groupings, including farm women, native women, immigrant women, disabled women, and lesbians. Though these chapters vary considerably in style and content, they each explicate the concrete particulars, the "how-to" and "what" of the activist efforts and thus should serve as useful teaching tools. The chapters are presented in an order that represent the mainstreaming-disengaged dynamic described by Briskin (Chapter 1) — from the national coalition organization, NAC, to grassroots feminist activism within particular groupings of women.

Lorraine Greaves (Chapter 5) provides an account of her experiences within the National Action Committee on the Status of Women, and presents a position with regard to structure and process within NAC which contrasts sharply with that of Vickers (Chapter 4), as well as Briskin (Chapter 1). While they consider the representative democratic model utilized in NAC as essentially adequate to the pursuit of the feminist aims of the organization, Greaves sharply questions whether that model is sufficiently feminist in nature, in representing the diversity of women's social and geograhpic locations, and in generally providing a space for women's voices to be heard. NAC is the largest coalition organization in Canada to represent women's concerns and issues; but its growth in size and diversity has often meant, according to Greaves, that a commitment to feminist processes and values is difficult to maintain. She describes the struggles within the organization to work with representation, accountability, decision-making and participatory democracy. She makes a variety of suggestions that she believes would render NAC structure and process more feminist in nature. Her account articulates the challenge of developing feminist structure and process for large, broad-based organizations.

Other contributors to this section take up these themes focusing on the tensions between (1) representing the voices and interests of the diversity of women in an organization, and, on the other hand, building organizations of some durability that achieve goals within reasonable time frames, and (2) operating in a horizontal, rather than a hierarchical structure, in which power and authority are shared, on the other hand, insuring that there is individual accountability as well as expertise for task completion.

For example, Stone (Chapter 13) describes the brief history of a Toronto-based lesbian feminist organization, Lesbians Against the Right. LAR was run on essentially collectivist principles with shared leadership and consensus decision-making. During its brief existence it accomplished a great deal, but Stone states that its structurelessness and lack of individual accountability, as well as the lack of a clear ideology, contributed to its demise. Leah and Ruecker (Chapter 6) discuss the creation of a provincial women's coalition in Saskatchewan, formed in protest of government cutbacks in funding to women's concerns, for which a weekend conference served as the organizing event. Considerable attention was devoted to creating a feminist process that would ensure that the diversity of women at the conference would have an opportunity to express their concerns. The conference itself appears to have been reasonably successful in achieving this goal; but the ongoing coalition structure that was created through volunteers at the conference has since disbanded. Perhaps similar issues regarding accountability and structure bear on its demise.

Doucette (Chapter 12) decribes the early efforts of disabled women in creating a cross-Canada organization, DAWN, the DisAbled Women's Network. Initially, DAWN attempted to function under collectivist principles, but soon moved to a representative democratic structure in which certain individuals are responsible for carrying out leadership. Under the collectivist structure, the group found that one or two individuals were carrying out all of the labour with minimal recognition and resources.

Other contributors discuss the variety of types of organizations that feminists have used to achieve differing purposes. For example, Ontario farm women, as discussed in Haley's brief history (Chapter 9), have participated in both highly-structured, formal organizations, as well as smaller, more loosely structured, informal organizations. Similarly, Reddin describes women's activism in Prince Edward Island. Through interviews, Reddin argues that the use of a variety of organizational forms and processes is necessary to attract and keep active a diversity of women in a small community.

Coalition-building is one common organizational form by which the Canadian women's movement is mobilizing women on a broad range of issues. But geographic distances, harsh climates, few resources and limited support for feminist ideals are some of the challenges facing women in less populated regions. Despite these barriers, many activists have been working to unite the feminists within their provinces. Leah and Ruecker (Chapter 6), as mentioned above, describe the development of a Saskatchewan women's coalition. Graveline, Fitzpatrick and Mark (Chapter 7) discuss the process of establishing the Manitoba Northern Women's Network, as well as some of its successful political actions and projected lobbying efforts. These contributions suggest that the very obstacles to organizing that face women in these provinces provide some commonality in purpose and issues.

In the instance of both of these coalitions, the provincial Status of Women Action Committees played a major role in their organization. The provincial committees have been critiqued as being readily co-opted by the state (e.g., Adamson, et al., 1988); but they can have considerable potential for effecting positive feminist change. Bishop, Manicom and Morissey (Chapter 16) also address the usefulness of the Nova Scotia Status of Women Action Committee in forming a broad-based coalition. Provincial status of women groups are unique to Canada, and these chapters provide some understanding of this specifically Canadian women's movement approach to organizing, and of the links between the movement and the state. They are a source of funding for feminist projects, and frequently are staffed by women who are themselves feminists, and active in the movement. Almost all of the organizational efforts described in this section have relied to some extent on government funding at some stage(s) (with the exception of Lesbians Against the Right), and it's likely that much of this feminist activism would not have occurred otherwise. Yet, the question must be raised regarding the extent to which interaction with state bureaucracy and dependence upon state funding has shaped the nature of Canadian feminism.

Briskin (Chapter 1) has labelled feminist organizing that is centered on the concerns and identities of women who share a particular form of oppression as "identity politics." Identity politics was particularly evident in the Canadian and U. S. women's movements during the late 1970s and the 1980s. The writings and activism of women who have engaged in this kind of politics have been extremely important in educating others about women's diversity, and demanding recognition by the movement of that diversity. Until recently, minority voices have been relatively silent and neglected while white, middle-class women have been more central to the movement.

The last four chapters of Section 2 offer accounts of the efforts of marginalized groups of women to organize around their own issues and needs. Roxanna Ng (Chapter 10) describes the immigrant women's movement in New Brunswick and British Columbia. She comments on the forces that have shaped the immigrant women's movement and examines the impact of organizing efforts on provincial, national and local levels. Shirley Bear, with the help of the Tobique Women's Group (Chapter 11), describes the struggles for equality of the women of Tobique Reserve, and their successful culmination in changes to Canada's misogynous Indian Act. Doucette (Chapter 12) discusses the organizing history of the DisAbled Women's Network (DAWN) as an example of the ability of oppressed people to organize against overwhelming odds — disability, poverty, isolation, and socialized passivity, or internalized oppression. Reddin's (Chapter 8) references to DAWN activities in the P.E.I. women's community indicate DAWN's strength beyond its Ontario roots. Lesbians Against the Right (LAR), the lesbian/feminist political protest organization, is another expression of identity politics.

In sum, the contributions in this section represent many of the major issues that Canadian feminist activists in the 1990s will continue to address. Major themes that arose in the first section are woven through these chapters, including concern with organizational structure and process in feminist activism, recognition and affirmation of Canadian women's diversity, and links between the movement and the state.

Reorganizing the National Action Committee on the Status of Women 1986-1988

Lorraine Greaves[1]

Truthfulness, honor, is not something which springs ablaze of itself; it has to be created between people. This is true in political situations. The quality and depth of the politics evolving from a group depends in very large part on their understanding of honor.

(Rich 1979, 193)

The National Action Committee on the Status of Women (NAC) originated in 1972 as a collection of 32 women's groups, formed largely as a result of the inadequacy of the federal government's response to the recommendations of the 1970 Royal Commission on the Status of Women. By the time it was 14 years old, with 350 members ranging from women's shelters and Zonta clubs to women's caucuses of the three major political parties, NAC was widely known as the largest feminist lobby group in Canada. Funded by government grants from the Women's Program, Secretary of State, membership fees and donations, NAC was regarded as the official voice of the women's movement in Canada, and frequently approached by media for comment on women's issues. Membership in NAC provided access to information on federal government legislation and initiatives, opportunities to join in "actions" lobbying on specific issues, access to briefs prepared by NAC committees, and twice-yearly meetings, one of which, the Annual General Meeting, debated resolutions on NAC policy.

Questions of Feminist Process and Structure

In 1986 I was in my second year as an elected member of the NAC Executive Board, having been a grassroots feminist for years, working mainly in projects creating services for battered women and in various women's health endeavours. At first, I had been puzzled about three characteristics of the NAC executive: the apparent lack of interest, experience in and attention to social and cultural issues affecting women, the dominant emphasis on economic and employment issues, and the rigidity and impersonality of the process used to debate and decide on the business of NAC at both the executive and the annual meeting. It was, in fact, the most "male" organization I had ever participated in. These organizational characteristics did not reflect the interests and operation of the women's movement in Canada, as I knew it.

By 1986 NAC had developed a high public profile, particularly after the 1984 televised Leaders' debate on women's issues. As president from 1984 to 1986, Chaviva Hosek had become very attractive to the media, and consequently NAC, the women's movement, and Canadian feminism had received considerable public attention.

This period marked the beginning of rapid growth in membership, a welcome but challenging and stressful development for NAC. The membership expanded from 350 groups in 1986 to 570 by 1988. As NAC's profile grew, more groups saw the advantage in consolidating feminist lobbying efforts, but the structures and processes that had been in place for years became less adequate in meeting the increasingly diverse interests and demands. The gap between women's expectations and their NAC 's performance led to demands for improvements to allow more participation and more accountability in policy making. It was time for the NAC organizational review project, born at the 1986 Annual General Meeting.

The Political Context and Stresses on NAC

At this time, Canada's political climate was posing serious challenges to NAC, its image, and its funding. The majority Progressive Conservative government, led by Brian Mulroney, now in its second year, had been seen on almost every issue as particularly unresponsive to NAC's positions, demands and actions.

Added to this was the significant challenge to NAC's image and funding being posed by the R.E.A.L. Women of Canada, a right-wing lobby, numbering few members compared to NAC, but with some support in the government. A pressurized campaign to review the funding practices of the Women's Program of the Secretary of State led to nationwide committee hearings. The resulting report, *Fairness in Funding*, (Standing Committee on the Secretary of State 1987) while stressing the need for women's groups to become self-supporting, recommended the continuation of funding for many feminist projects, including NAC. After this politically motivated but thorough review of the Women's Program, NAC and many of its member groups came out relatively well.

The strain of this review process was considerable. Resources of NAC and its member groups were depleted in the effort to affect opinion on the question of funding for women's groups. After a few years of deliberately ignoring the vocal challenge of R.E.A.L. Women, NAC and the women's movement had been forced to reply. In this long process, many Canadians who had been unaware of the Women's Program developed opinions on funding, not all of which were favourable to NAC. Media treatment of the funding issue created a further distortion. Most media considered NAC and R.E.A.L. Women to be 'two sides,' without which no news story, whether on funding or on women's issues, was now complete. This polarization of the ways of thinking about feminism created the erroneous impression that the two groups were equal (in membership, history, organization, and record of achievement), still often reflected in mainstream media.

NAC, by this time, was a large and busy organization, devoted to lobbying the federal government on legislation and policy initiatives. It was variously regarded as the formal women's movement in Canada, the official women's opposition, and the public voice and symbol of feminism in Canada. Its agenda was mainly reactive, based on the federal government's actions and legislative initiatives. Speeches and appearances at committee hearings and commissions were made, briefs were produced, calls to action, and letter writing campaigns organized. The NAC staff, executive and the active members were kept so busy that long-range planning, priority setting, or proaction were rare luxuries. Although the shared goal was equality for Canadian women, a vision of what that would look like was neither articulated nor shared. Until the review began in 1986, the organization itself was left unstudied and unmodified. Retrospectively, this may have been too late.

Need for Organizational Review
Like any Canada-wide political party or organization, NAC experienced the regional, cultural and linguistic divisions and conflicts that make the equal sharing of resources and power very difficult. While appearing at first to be questions of content, the early complaints about NAC's policy-making served, eventually, to focus on aspects of the debating and decision-making process. By 1986, it was clear to me that NAC was a feminist organization without a feminist process. Its executive formed a hierarchy, with the President and a few table officers at the top, Robert's Rules were used routinely in decision-making at the executive and annual meetings, and voting was always the method of resolving conflicts. The importance attributed to the presidential role, while comforting for the public and government, and convenient for the media, was rather a traditional approach for a feminist organization.

Regional Stresses. Feeling their distance from central Canada, and the consequent paucity of information, resources and acknowledgment, the southern British Columbia member groups had been particularly early, active and eloquent in suggesting organizational change. In addition to complaints about the unfairness of NAC's travel subsidy policies for AGM delegates, Megan Ellis, of the Women's Research Centre in Vancouver, raised extensive concerns about the process of policy committee member selection and operation. Having not received satisfactory answers from the NAC executive, Ellis (1985) wrote:

> As NAC endeavours to increase its membership and its public profile it becomes increasingly essential that its internal processes evolve in an attempt to ensure that the women it purports to represent are encouraged to participate. Vague processes are open to abuse.

The southern B.C. groups epitomized the ardent desire of an active group of feminists to become more central to the operation of NAC, and the real need for decentralization. Weaknesses in NAC's regional structure were felt particularly by those most distant from the Toronto-Ottawa axis. With the national office in Toronto, and all annual meetings in Ottawa, some regions, despite executive representation, felt disconnected from the decision making, actions, and media work taking place in central Canada.

The Committees of NAC. Most of the early complaints focused on the structure and process of NAC's committees, where both policy and AGM resolutions were developed. These committees operated with only informal structures, and under no comprehensive plan set by either the membership or the executive. In fact, in the absence of an executive member who had the interest, ability, time or desire to chair a committee in a particular area, no committee would exist.[2] Or, frustration emerged when an executive member with no particular experience or expertise in an area took on the chairing of a committee.

Those with a particular interest and wise to these weaknesses in NAC's organization, could use various methods to get the organization to consider their issue(s).[3] Executive members were often lobbied either before or after election for promises to promote a policy committee. This private activity constituted an informal priority-setting exercise, and contributed to the development of an unofficial NAC agenda. Although certain operational aspects had to be ratified by the Executive Board (participation of non-elected committee members, committee budgets etc.), the choice or number of committees, the size of their budgets, and their internal priorities did not result from an overall priority-setting exercise of the members of NAC or, indeed, of the NAC executive.[4] Instead, executive members would compete, posture, bargain and trade at the first executive meeting of the year to establish as much money as possible for their favourite committee. Inexperienced executive members were often less successful at this, not realizing that co-operation and openness were likely to render them "losers" in the budget allocation process. Consequently, in 1987-88, for example the committee budgets ranged from $500 (disabled women's committee) to $16,000 (employment and economy committee).

Representativeness. The complaints regarding committee structures and policy making in NAC were also about a keenly felt lack of representativeness. NAC did not reflect the full texture of the women's movement in Canada. The issues under scrutiny and the priorities and strategies of the organization were not decided upon collectively by the membership. Those Canadian feminists working and most experienced in the issues that *were* chosen were seldom involved in the committees, even as resource persons, and the committees were usually operating with only informal regional structures, if any. The location of most committee meetings in Toronto (prior to 1987),[5] the use of English in almost all meetings, and the concentration of NAC activity on the Toronto-Ottawa axis prevented effective participation of members outside of Ontario. The vital questions regarding NAC's relationship to the larger Canadian women's movement rarely emerged for consideration by an organization that spent most of its energy meeting short-term goals.

In addition to regional concerns, many different groups such as francophone women, women of colour, lesbians, low-income women, homemakers, immigrant women, women with disabilities, and young women struggled for representation in and by NAC. Some were in member groups, asking for involvement; some were assessing whether joining NAC was advantageous. Simultaneously, other national organizations were developing rapidly, often with government funding, to serve the needs of some of these different constituencies of women.[6] This lack of representativeness was felt acutely by some groups, and led to hurt, lack of trust in NAC, or a sometimes confrontational "we-they" attitude. Some groups countered by nominating a particular person to put forth their interests at the executive meeting, others stayed out of NAC and put their energies elsewhere.

Despite these increasing pressures, the larger question regarding the representativeness of NAC remained unasked. What was NAC's purpose? Was becoming fully representative of the women's movement in Canada an important goal, or was it sufficient to be simply a political organization responding to the strongest and most articulate pressures from various lobbies within the women's movement? Concealed within this question is one of feminist process. Was there really a commitment to accounting for the voices of the women less easily heard or less experienced, and were the opinions of women on the margins of women's politics in Canada to be welcomed? And if there was such a commitment, how were those women going to find their voices? This is really a values question, and values were rarely discussed at NAC.

Accessibility. The practical aspect of increasing representativeness is accessibility. Was every group of women, or kind of woman equally able to consider joining a committee or running for office in NAC? At the 1986 annual meeting, an executive board nominee from the disabled women's network, Pat Israel, was unable to reach any of the microphones from her wheelchair. Although physical accessibility was eventually improved, the more subtle inaccessibilities remained. It was widely perceived, for example, that to run for an executive position required a good education, strong communication skills (in English), personal financial security, and an autonomous job with flexible hours. This belief, coupled with the demanding patterns of executive operation, effectively excluded low-income women, disabled women, unilingual francophone women, non-professional women, women with small children, and those from the regions furthest from central Canada, among others. In addition, the workload, pace and style of NAC executive meetings effectively made NAC inaccessible to the inarticulate, women not formally educated, some disabled women, the "politically incorrect," or the tired. Accessibility, in its widest sense, was to become a clear point of concern emerging from the organizational review consultation process.

The Organizational Review

By 1986, a formal plan for organizational review was established. The first year involved informal consultations and requests for input, carried out by some executive members. The second year was the hiring of outside consultants to carry out a comprehensive regionally-based assessment of the membership's concerns, and the formation of a committee dominated by non-executive members[7] that would present a five-year plan for change to the 1988 meeting.

After the 1987 annual meeting, the Organizational Review committee's positions were filled, and Catalyst Consultants of Ottawa were hired to prepare and present a report on NAC's organizational needs. Simultaneously, the committee began work to develop recommendations and steps for change to be presented at the 1988 AGM.

In September 1987, a parallel Organizational Review Committee was requested by the Quebec francophone member groups to manage a separate consultation, using a different methodology. This effort also explored whether the Quebec francophone groups still wanted to retain NAC membership.[8] No formal communication existed between the two committees, but both final reports were presented to the executive in April, 1988.

The Review Reports

The introduction to the Catalyst report, a "proposed blueprint for the next few years," asserted that "to be a successful lobby, NAC must simultaneously lead and mirror the women's movement in Canada." To accomplish this, organizational changes must "open NAC to more diversity and ground itself more thoroughly in the grassroots women's movement" (Riggs & Tyler 1988, 3). "The decision-making structure of NAC is top-heavy, over utilizes executive members, and under-utilizes its greatest resource, the member groups"

(Riggs & Tyler 1988, 10). These comments brought into focus the reports and impressions of an overworked executive, a generally alienated membership, and a very dissatisfied staff. Eventually the staff, who had long provided the continuity and backbone to the organization, were to attempt to unionize in order to gain contractual definitions for their jobs, a process fraught with dissatisfaction and poor relations between the staff and the executive that culminated in the resignation of all but one staff member at the 1988 annual meeting.

Process and strategy issues. Various process issues were commented upon by the members. It was felt to be ironic that detailed debates and amendments to resolutions that would occupy and often frustrate hundreds of women at the AGM would produce policy on a par with the many remaining resolutions which were referred to the executive with no mechanism for wider debate. Some members questioned the effectiveness and purpose of the annual lobby of the members of Parliament, while others maintained that the traditional face-to-face question and answer session was empowering. The AGM itself was considered by many to be too business oriented, and too short on opportunities for discussion of proposed policy. Some found the AGM alienating as a lack of experience or information rendered them non-participants. Some specified that the adversarial debating style (epitomized by the "yes" and "no" microphones), and Robert's Rules ("rules for civilized war," according to some members) not only disempowered them, but allowed "a misuse of the democratic process" (Riggs & Tyler 1988, 17). In addition, the survey respondents noted the lack of training opportunities for less experienced women, the role of backroom politics in decision making, the incomplete information sharing among executive members and between executive and the member groups, and the generally negative and divisive culture in the executive.

Recommended solutions. To remedy some of these complaints, the entire decision-making process within NAC, which was top-heavy and concentrated in the executive, and had no firm budgetary, policy or priority setting processes was targeted as an area for significant change. Decentralization was recommended, through bolstering the "frail" regional structure, and enabling the member groups to set the priorities and policy.

The Quebec report (Lacelle 1988) endorsed staying within NAC, but only on certain minimum conditions to ensure accessibility to the AGM and the Lobby, including improved interpretation, anglophone and francophone co-chairs for all plenaries, sign language in French, enforced use of earphones by unilingual anglophones, professional simultaneous translation in all workshops and ad hoc meetings, francophone resource persons in each workshop, access to executive candidates for discussions, and bilingual social activities. These particular recommendations were presented to the executive in April, 1988, with the request for immediate changes that would improve the 1988 annual meeting, some of which were made by that time.

Reception of the Review Report
The NAC Executive. When the Catalyst report was presented to the executive in April, 1988, it was not very well received. It was brutally honest about NAC's weaknesses, and consequently created fear and defensiveness among some who felt that NAC would be threatened by its publication.[9] Some felt that the report's conclusions did not fit with their experience of the organization, others questioned the methodology and validity of the report. Some felt that making the report public would create negative media treatment of NAC, with particular fears about keeping NAC's funding secure. And finally, there was continued confusion about the status of the Catalyst's report vis-à-vis the report dealing exclusively with the Québec member groups.

Various approaches to dealing with the Catalyst report were discussed at this meeting, including its suppression. After much deliberation, the report was released as planned, in part because of the prior assurance of the organizational reviews committee's autonomy,[10] and in part because some of us felt that to not release the report in its entirety to the member groups who had directly contributed to its content would be unconscionable. However, this "warts and all" approach to displaying NAC was clearly worrisome to many. Various feelings prevented the acknowledgement of the essence of the report and contributed to a defensive desire for confidentiality. The value placed on the process of NAC, and the value of reflecting and cultivating a healthy women's movement became lost to the value of saving face, maintaining control of the organization's agenda, protecting certain issues, and maintaining the fallacy that NAC indeed had three million involved members fully representing the Canadian women's movement.

The 1988 AGM. "When relationships are determined by manipulation, by the need for control, they may possess a dreary, bickering kind of drama, but they cease to be interesting. They are repetitious, the shock of human possibilities has ceased to reverberate through them" (Rich 1979, 193).

The events of the 1988 AGM, including my resignation from the presidential ballot,[11] and the mass resignation of the staff, brought the need for feminist process into high relief. My action allowed me to use my voice to describe, name, and resist the insidiousness of non-feminist processes in a feminist organization. Releasing myself from the need to maintain solidarity and the façade that all was well within NAC, and being followed by the staff "breaking their silence" on their experience as workers in NAC,[12] allowed others to speak more freely of their experiences with NAC. Newfoundland delegate Dorothy Inglis, on CBC's Morningside following the AGM, stated, "There is great relief. The problem has been named" (Inglis 1988). Beth Brehaut (1988), former executive member from Prince Edward Island, wrote that NAC is "entirely too protective of the 'image' it has built for itself," and that "feminist process is almost non-existent in the workings of this organization." Similar to reactions to revelations of "family" violence, however, some NAC family members preferred continued silence about NAC's internal problems. In her *Toronto Star* column, former NAC President Doris Anderson called the NAC AGM a "débâcle", where "private linen got a very public airing" (Anderson 1988).

The strong and frequently expressed hope of the organizational review committee was to present the report and its recommendations to the annual meeting with a unified voice and the support of the executive. Despite having had eleven weeks to study and react to the committee's report and proposals, some executive members expressed views on the floor of the annual meeting that had never been expressed to me or to the committee in the interim, and that were intended to divert or slow the course of change. This approach resulted in seven hours of discussion, governed by Robert's Rules, on five well-circulated "motherhood" organizational review resolutions.[13] It was futile and contradictory to assume that a creative, open, spiralling discussion, as opposed to an "argument," about the organization could take place using these traditional methods of discourse.

The Organizational Review Committee's operation had been based on a deliberate and evolving feminist process. This eleven-woman group was cohesive, yet able to disagree, representative but devoted to the overall good of the organization, comfortable and empowering. By building consensus, using "process notes," constant agenda amendment, and "check-ins" and "check-outs" at all meetings, the members developed understanding, cohesion and trust. This committee experience, the best I had in three years on the executive, was possibly the first attempt at developing workable feminist process in NAC — an experiment in change from within.

The Future of NAC

Is NAC possible? Can the Canadian women's movement be represented fully and respectfully by one organization? The question rests on the hope that it is indeed possible; the answer depends on the ability of both NAC and the Canadian women's movement to address our collective values and ethics. Do we really want to invite diversity, different opinions, complexity and contradiction into our midst? Or are we content to carry on in a traditional political manner, letting some win and some lose, measuring the worth of a position by the pressure, detail, or articulateness of its lobby?[14]

Feminist Process and the Women's Movement. I am interested in feminist process, not just for NAC, but for the entire women's movement because of its promise to revolutionize not only women's condition, but also the male-dominated institutions that currently control our lives. Feminist process implies inclusivity, increased tolerance and compassion — values notably missing not only from NAC, but mainstream politics and business. Other values needing clarification among feminists include interdependence, trust, supportiveness, and sensitivity.

Feminist process also implies the abandonment of politically correct, unitary positions on issues, the ideological categorization of ourselves and each other, the rigidity and collective defensiveness about our identities or positions, and our attraction and addiction to power. Feminist process would recognize and encourage the organic, ever-evolving nature of the feminist enterprise, invite differences of opinion, and generate opportunities for the empowerment of all women. It could affect the agenda of the women's movement, would certainly slow the pace of the activity undertaken, and change the nature of our membership. It would, one hopes, foster creativity and proaction, and put into perspective our reactive impulses. Most important, it would centre on creating a view of women and women's value that is self and mutually respectful, and demonstrate to the patriarchy that there is a different way of being and doing.

A revised political agenda would draw on, and politicize, the uncharted but very real "women's concerns" in the grassroots. In addition, an emphasis on economic issues as currently defined would probably diminish. Not because economic indicators are not a critical measure of the status of women, but because the very conceptualizations of women's worth that underpin traditional economic thinking are not fully reflective of the condition or worth of women. The gap between NAC's reactive and heavily economic agenda, and the concerns of the women's movement in Canada, particularly the vast violence against women, only widened as NAC concentrated on responding to various legislative initiatives from the government.[15]

The frustration of those women who are uninvolved or uninterested in feminism would not be ignored with feminist process. In NAC, the typical response to those groups who lamented the lack of interest in their issue, or region, or constituency, was a suggestion to elect a representative. Only in retrospect does the complete arrogance and unacceptability of

this response ring out. This reliance on the validity and continued appropriateness of NAC's practices had carried the
organization through many bouts of criticism. The traditions
that had built up within NAC over its first 14 years of operation had become a fixed, unexamined source of comfort, and
for many, a source of identity.

There are not two sides to questions when approached
using a feminist process, but many. Instead of mountains of
policies largely unknown by the NAC membership, there
would be "bottom lines," guidelines, lots of background information, strategies, educational pamphlets, and "how-to"
manuals. Within these limits, women could decide to join and
support NAC if they could at least live with its aims. Feminist
process would abandon the dogged search for a unitary position on issues. NAC's long tradition of clarifying and sharp-
ening for public consumption a singular feminist position on
legislative issues is less appropriate in a more representative,
diverse women's movement facing increasingly complex issues. Singular postions serve the media's interests best in its
search for succinctness, and serve the membership the least, in
ignoring the texture and evolving nature of feminist opinion.

Process Issues and Ideological Streams of Feminism. Feminist
process would probably encourage Charlotte Bunch's "nonaligned" feminism (Bunch 1987, 46-60). Ideological streams of
feminism, although not openly identified, played a part in
NAC. Some suggest that a more open declaration of ideology
would facilitate both decision-making and conflict-resolution,
and that perhaps even the annual elections should be organized along ideological lines, much like "parties within a
party."[16] But Bunch argues that nonaligned feminism allows
for an independent assessment of each issue or situation.
"Such a concept may sound simple, or to some, simpleminded.
It is neither. To be nonaligned is difficult because it requires
careful attention and debate to determine what actions are
appropriate in each situation" (Bunch 1987, 49). Feminist
process may blur ideological lines through recognizing that a
revolutionary feminist politic is in constant evolution, and
draws on many ideological frameworks. Feminist process
would also dignify the many feminists who neither have, nor

desire, nor would find useful an ideological identity, many of whom live outside major metropolitan areas, are not formally educated, or do not describe their approach to feminism as fundamentally "political." Finally, feminist process would give accountability and ownership of the organization to its members if a meaningful, involving regional structure existed. Then, the executive would be truly empowered to represent the membership's positions.

NAC's choices. NAC is at a crossroads. It must equip itself to create accountability in its leadership and membership, by valuing its own health, and creating trust and respect, by dropping its collective defensiveness, vested interests, and ideological barriers. The evolving Canadian women's movement demands a wider embrace of the growing feminist politic and the articulation of a feminist vision that describes a different world, not just a women's version of the same one. Developing a true feminist process would be groundwork for a new social order, and may bring closer the feminist revolution many NAC members often visualize.

Instead of leading the development of a particularly feminist way of doing things, NAC had, as the organization grew, merely appropriated more and more traditional attributes: resolutions, policies, rules of order, and a protective rigidity of opinion. Settling on positions using such traditional techniques was not about to quell passionately held competing points of view on issues as contentious as pornography or the Meech Lake Accord, with the result that NAC was rendered silent on such complex issues.

The resistance to the sharing of power suggested by the organizational review lay in the simplicity of the request: if more women shared the decision making, then a few women may have to give some up. But if more women became true participants in these processes, more women would become empowered. Nothing short of this could be a reasonable goal of a national feminist organization devoted to progressive change, and such empowerment could only strengthen the women's movement as a whole. Only such radical alteration can ensure NAC's survival. Is NAC possible? Is NAC enough?

The politics worth having, the relationships worth having,
demand that we delve still deeper. (Rich, 1979, 193).

Postscript: Between 1988 and 1990, several groups outside of
the NAC executive met to discuss NAC's reorganization. One
of these, the southern B.C. group, created a detailed proposal
for change in preparation for the 1990 NAC AGM. After
months of discussion and compromise, the principles of this
proposal were discussed at the plenary at the 1990 AGM. Late
in the afternoon, after amendments and lengthy debate, and
just before a potentially affirmative vote, a Toronto NAC member called for a quorum. Being a few women short of a
quorum, the matter could not be pursued and was referred to
the NAC Executive, and no formal vote could be held. While
the principles were later passed in the executive, the disre-
spectful process was bitterly received by the southern B.C.
groups. While NAC inches toward meaningful change, amidst
considerable resistance, the need for feminist process appears
more persistent than ever.

Saskatchewan Women Respond to Cutbacks

The Founding of a Provincial Women's Coalition

Ronnie Leah and
Cydney Ruecker

In November 1987, when women in Saskatchewan agreed to build a coalition called Connections, they were ready to voice a strong, united protest against the provincial Progressive Conservative government's funding cutbacks. More than 200 women from across the province gathered at a two-day conference to work towards the goals of networking, support and empowerment of women. During the conference, women expressed their personal despair at the effects of the cutbacks on their lives and became empowered as they strategized political action against the government's destructive policies. They agreed to form a coalition that would enable women in Saskatchewan to develop a province-wide voice, to organize actions supporting women, to develop links among groups of women, and to work more effectively with other coalitions.

Building Connections was an important step in the process of mobilizing women in Saskatchewan. Although limited time, energy, and resources posed obstacles to further development of the coalition after the conference, women in Saskatchewan continued to organize in a variety of ways, sustained by their vision of the future.

This chapter is based on a written report of the Connections conference,[1] which was distributed to all the participants of providing feedback and as an impetus for further organizing. The report was prepared by Ronnie Leah and Cydney Ruecker, who participated in the conference and then continued their involvement on the Connections Steering Committee. In addition to this account of women organizing in Saskatchewan, the authors have also developed an analysis of the strengths and weaknesses of coalition building in Saskatchewan, based on discussion with a number of women active in Connections.[2]

This chapter is intended to reflect the collective experience of the women involved in Connections. It also reflects, to some extent, the specific experiences of its two authors who brought different backgrounds to their involvement in Connections.[3] Through this chapter, we have tried to represent the ongoing debate about structure and process in women's organizing, as it unfolded in Saskatchewan. This debate about an effective and democratic process continues today in many parts of Canada.[4]

Coalition Building against Government Cutbacks

Connections was organized as part of the coalition-building process in Saskatchewan, in reaction to a massive series of provincial budget cuts in 1987. Using deficit reduction as an excuse, the PC government had launched an all out attack on the funding of services to women, seniors, the sick, the disabled, workers, native people, students, rural people, welfare recipients, and the unemployed. The fight-back campaign was on, as groups all over the province began to picket, protest, rally, and organize against the cuts.[5] Then on May 2, 1987, representatives of more than 50 organizations in Saskatchewan came together to discuss the impact of the cuts, to develop a common response, to plan future actions, and to work toward building a broad-based coalition to address common concerns. Groups organizing this historic meeting included the Saskatchewan Action Committee on the Status of Women (SAC), as well as labour, farm, church and Native groups. Representatives were appointed by sectors, designated at the meeting, to sit on the Interim Planning Group (IPG); the women's sector chose Colleen Meyer, President of SAC, and Pat Gallagher, trade union activist and member of Saskatchewan Working Women (SWW). The involvement of SAC and SWW laid the groundwork for women's coalition building. At that time SAC was involved in networking with women's groups, as well as lobbying and political action; it was urging women's groups to work together against the cutbacks and build support among women at the grassroots.[6] SWW included among its membership, union activists and other women already engaged in organizing against the cutbacks; SWW's June 1987 convention focused on the cutbacks issue, and endorsed the call for a provincial women's conference.[7]

The process of coalition building continued over the next few months as local and sectoral coalitions and networks across the province came together over a number of related issues: cutbacks in health, education and social services, privatization, anti-labour legislation, free trade, and the declining rural economy. People were on the move in all major centers — Regina, Saskatoon, Prince Albert — as hundreds marchers and picketed against government cuts. A protest rally organized by the IPG drew 10,000 marched to the provincial legislature. Over the summer the development process continued, and at a provincial meeting on October 17, the Saskatchewan Coalition for Social Justice (SCSJ) was formally organized.[8]

The Provincial Conference

Both SAC and SWW played an integral role in organizing the fight-back campaign. As members of the SCSJ Steering Committee, representatives of SAC and SWW jointly developed a proposal for a provincial meeting of women's groups to address women's concerns about the political agenda in the province, and to enable the women's sector to democratically choose its representatives to the committee. In this way, women would be able to develop their own strategy and also contribute to the development of SCSJ.

Consequently, invitations were issued to women's groups across the province to attend a planning meeting. A core group developed from these planning meetings, including women from SAC, SWW, unions, student groups, community groups and provincial organizations. They determined that a provincial conference of women — to be called "Connections" — would be the most effective way of mobilizing women against the cutbacks.

The provincial conference was seen as the first step in bringing together a large number of women, representing a wide range of groups and sectors, to begin the process of coalition building. While there was little formal discussion about this method of organizing, the core group planning the Connections conference agreed that this was the best way to proceed. Recent organizing efforts in Saskatchewan — and in other parts of Canada — had chosen the coalition approach, and a number of women were already involved in the provincial coalition (SCSJ), organized on the basis of sectoral interests. Most importantly, the Connections conference wanted to reach into the grassroots to mobilize and empower women.[9]

Process of Organizing the Women's Conference

As they organized the conference, the planning committee looked at a number of important issues that were being debated in the women's movement across Canada. They include balancing structure and process; dealing with differences among women; ensuring that women from all backgrounds and classes actively participate. The committee also looked at meeting the three goals of networking, empowerment, and support of women, as well as learning from the experiences of women's coalitions in other provinces; developing and fostering solidarity in order to strategize effectively; and building a structure that would sustain women and continue beyond the conference.[10]

The planning committee hoped that with the wide diversity of women and groups expected to attend the conference, the participants would be able to achieve their goals of networking, mutual support, and empowerment. The conference would also provide an opportunity to choose two representatives for the Steering Committee of SCSJ, thereby strengthening the links between women and the general fightback campaign in Saskatchewan.

Issues of feminist process. Throughout the planning process, women made an effort to recognize and incorporate the principles of democracy, co-operation and egalitarianism into the conference agenda. These important principles of feminist process would be essential for women to truly speak out and voice their concerns on an equal basis.[11] While most of the women involved in the planning committee participated as representatives of groups across the province, they felt that the conference should be directed toward individual women, not groups. To this end, it was planned that the conference agenda would begin with an opportunity for all women to personally express what was happening in their daily lives. The committee felt that this approach would be particularly effective in addressing the needs of aboriginal women, women from rural areas and women from minority groups — women who faced problems of racism and isolation, and who lacked experience speaking out in large groups.

In order to enable women to relate their personal feelings to the overall political situation, to deal with the stress being experienced in women's lives, and to overcome their sense of powerlessness and increasing numbness, the planning committee decided to adopt a "despair and empowerment" model for the conference. A "speak-out" session early in the conference would provide women with a forum to vent their frustration and anger. The strategy workshops and plenaries would provide the means for women to come together, be empowered, and develop a united voice. This two-pronged approach was seen as an important step towards organizing women in Saskatchewan.[12]

The planning committee also decided to invite speakers from women's coalitions in Manitoba and British Columbia to report on similar cutbacks in those provinces. This would assist women in Saskatchewan to develop a balance between their expectations and the everyday realities of coalition building.

The debate in the planning committee about the structure and process of the conference centred around the amount of structure in the agenda that would provide political direction to the participants. Some committee members felt that the issues and strategies should be determined primarily by the women attending the conference. As a result, the planning committee decided to organize only the physical setting of the conference, then serve as a facilitating group to enable the process of the conference to flow smoothly.

This approach had both positive and negative consequences. The open atmosphere contributed to dynamic opening workshops, where, women voiced their many concerns about the effects of provincial cutbacks. However, the great diversity of concerns, combined with the decision not to provide explicit political direction to the conference, made it difficult to focus on a provincial strategy during the closing plenary session on Sunday.

Attendance at the conference. The committee had planned for a target group of 100 women, but in response to the demand, a total of 205 women attended the conference. They were from a wide variety of backgrounds: aboriginal women, immigrant women, trade union women, lesbian women, community health-care workers, students, women on social assistance, and government employees. They represented many regions of Saskatchewan, rural and northern communities as well as urban areas. The planning committee had done its job well; the high attendance reflected more than effective organizing, it also reflected the extent of women's anger and wish to mobilize.

More than thirty women's groups from across the spectrum were represented at the conference — native women's groups, church groups, farm women, labour unions, academics and students, community groups, provincial organizations and other non-governmental organizations (NGO's). With such wide diversity, the conference decision to form a provincial women's coalition was a landmark in building a united voice for women.

Despair and Empowerment:
the Connections Conference

The debates about process that had taken place in the planning committee continued right into the conference. Following the opening remarks on Saturday morning, heated discussion about the format and process took up some time before it was resolved. Debate on this issue was renewed during the afternoon session, following a panel presentation on provincial coalitions. Conference delegates had been addressed by three speakers: Frances Wasserlein, organizer of Women Against the Budget-WAB (B.C. coalition formed in 1984 in reponse to the provincial government's fiscal policies); Tammy Scott, representative of the Manitoba Women's Agenda (provincial group which had lobbied the government about women's concerns); and Pat Gallagher, Saskatchewan trade union activist, member of SWW, and women's sector representative to the Saskatchewan Coalition for Social Justice.

During the question period, a number of issues surfaced regarding the process of coalition building. In response to concerns raised by Wasserlein about the B.C. experience — where women had felt that their power was co-opted in the process — some women expressed reservations about working with organizations such as unions that were formally structured and included men as well as women. In contrast to this approach, Gallagher and other trade union women (who made up a large proportion of conference participants)[13] spoke more positively about their experiences in building alliances with men within the labour movement, as well as building solidarity with women's groups outside the labour movement. These issues could not be resolved in the limited time available for discussion, which led to some continuing tensions among women at the conference.

Participants brought with them different experiences and expectations, a positive factor building a broad-based provincial coalition, also a problem in terms of the divergent approaches and orientations. Such problems are not unique to Saskatchewan women's organizing; they are likely to develop as part of the process of organizing diverse groups of people around common issues.[14] At the Connections conference, there was sufficient unity of purpose to overcome differences for the purpose of building a coalition.

Analysis of women's concerns

As described, on the first day, participants broke into small discussion groups for the purpose of expressing their anger and despair about government cutbacks. The workshops focused on the three-fold effect of the cutbacks — on women's personal lives; on organizations and groups, and on government services. A conscious effort was made to link women's personal experiences with analysis of the political issues. This is an empowering element in the women's movement. The responses of each group, recorded on large sheets,[15] became the basis for organizing the next day's strategy workshops.

Combining women's concerns with the development of strategy, a group of "weavers and gatherers" met with the planning committee that evening and worked on integrating the major issues generated by women in the morning's discussion groups. After reviewing the lists compiled by the groups — focusing on personal, group and provincial concerns — they selected six topics. Several women then continued working long into the night, developing a report for the next morning's conference session.

In line with plans to use the second day for developing strategy, the Sunday morning session began with the planning committee's report, which provided an important bridge from the despair of the first day to the empowerment of the second day. The report, presented by Fiona Bishop, reviewed the effects of the Progressive Conservative government's attacks on women in Saskatchewan, and then challenged conference participants to get on with the task of developing strategies for action.

She addressed the conference, identifying the personal feelings expressed by women in the Saturday morning workshops: anger, fear, apathy, isolation, class separation, loss of security, impact on friendships, division between the 'haves' and the 'have nots,' lack of choices, exhaustion, disenfranchisement, burn-out, intimidation, doom, resentment, illness, demoralization, blaming, no hope for the future, alienation, passivity, stress, and more stress — and above all anger. Bishop praised the women for their understanding of the issues, for the "consistency and wisdom that surfaced" in their discussions, and for their recognition of a consistency in the government's attacks against groups of women:

> The union busting; the constant attacks against native peoples, non-government organizations, advocacy groups, and counselling services; the gay-bashing, the poor-bashing.

On the provincial level, she noted that this was a "political attack by right-wing ideology" that women had not faced before. Bishop pointed out how the government was promoting its policies of "free trade, privatization, contracting out, de-regulation, Meech Lake, cuts and more cuts, all in order to alleviate the provincial deficit." She warned against the efforts being made to divide women. She pointed to the racism being promoted and how the government was "pitting one women's group against another for the precious few dollars that are still being given out for service delivery." This was a deliberate political strategy "to pit services against profits"; it resulted in the "total erosion of human services" that had been identified by women in the workshops.

Having identified the problems, Fiona Bishop then focused on the anger that women had expressed, and their determination to fight back:

> All of you, as a group, were clear about this — we cannot accept the fact that there is nothing to be done to fight back. True, we get demoralized sometimes. But most of all, we get *very angry*. And it is in the anger that we find the strengh to fight back.

Development of strategy

This dramatic presentation set the tone for discussion of strategies and got the conference off to an effective start on Sunday morning.

Conference participants proceeded to strategy workshops organized around the six major areas of concern generated by the Saturday discussion groups: health, poverty, human rights, employment, education, and the rise of the right-wing agenda. The workshops were led by facilitators and assisted by recorders keeping notes. The facilitators were an important key to organizing effective strategy sessions. They met beforehand to plan the sessions; they discussed the role of facilitators and were encouraged to promote the values of democracy, responsibility, co-operation, honesty and egalitarianism in the workshops. Their tasks were two-fold: to encourage discussion, ensuring that each person had an opportunity to speak, and to sum up the contents of the discussion so that a report could be made to the conference plenary. It was felt that the role played by the facilitators contributed a good deal to the success of the strategy workshops.

The time available was limited, but to the extent possible each workshop group was to report on four areas.

1. *Goals.* The workshops on health, poverty, human rights, employment and education had similar goals — to stop the erosion of rights and services; to reinstate funding and programs; and to create a more just system that meets people's needs — for full employment, comprehensive health care, quality education, and an empowering human service system. The three workshops which met to discuss the rise of the right-wing agenda called for grassroots education, actions against the right wing, and the development of an alternative agenda for women.

2. *Strategies.* The workshop reports outlined a number of important stategies to build unity and solidarity among women; educate and empower women; use the media effectively; build a united front and coordinate information with other groups; and work through existing networks and organizations.

Actions were proposed by the workshops, including marches, pickets and creative protests, lobbying, legislative briefs, legal challenges, public forums, International Women's Day action, education campaign on Free Trade and privatization, and women's public strike.

It was proposed that a provincial Steering Committee be formed to continue the work and coordinate proposed actions, and that work be continued within the SCSJ.

3. *Groups.* The workshops listed a broad spectrum of groups and individuals to work with in building a fight-back campaign, suggesting that they include all groups and individuals with whom there is a common goal.

4. *Proposals.* Suggestions ranged from plans for specific actions to proposals for an ongoing provincial women's coalition. These plans, which provided the basis for discussion in the final plenary session, included the following activities:

- organize a provincial women's coalition;
- articulate clear objectives;

- conserve our energy and focus;
- sponsor regular conferences to continue the work;
- continue networking — (a point made by all groups);
- organize a clearing house for information (using SAC as a central resource centre);
- compile a master phone tree of women's organizations;
- ensure the publication of unbiased news reports;
- continue education of the public (especially youth);
- utilize public forums to highlight our vision of society;
- undertake actions which will galvanize the public and force our agenda to the forefront;
- adopt civil disobedience strategies;
- commence fundraising efforts;
- inform all provincial groups about the birth of Connections;
- work towards resolving conflicts between women's groups which may weaken solidarity;
- form a Feminist Socialist political party.

Women now turned their attention to implementing these plans.

Final plenary — debates and accomplishments
There were extreme time constraints during this plenary session, as women raced against the clock to bring the conference to a conclusion. The plenary was badly rushed due to several factors: first, the Sunday sessions had begun late; second, reports from the workshops had taken longer than planned; third, the commitment to democratic principles combined with the decision not to use formal rules of order meant that no-one was prevented from speaking; and finally, the task being undertaken by women at the Connections conference — to transform their "despair" into "empowerment" — was an immense task. As time ran out, conference organizers arranged for an extension of daycare services and postponement of lunch. Major steps were taken by the conference — a provincial women's coalition was established and a steering com-

mittee was selected but the full discussion of alternatives for the coalition was foreshortened.

The issue of racism. Given the importance of the occasion (combined with the pressures of time), intense feelings surfaced as women voiced their concerns at the microphones. Bernice Hammersmith, a member of the Aboriginal Women's Council, addressed the plenary on behalf of aboriginal women. She commented on some of the problems experienced by Native women at the conference and expressed the hope that stronger links would be built between aboriginal women and other women's groups.

Bernice emphasized that Native women had come to the conference to share common concerns as well as common solutions, but they had had problems connecting with other women. She spoke of the racism that tended to downgrade the personal experiences and solutions of Indian people. Bernice pointed out that for the past hundred years, Native people had been experiencing the problems identified by women at the Connections conference — problems such as poverty, unemployment, poor health care, lack of control over their lives, lack of human rights. She reminded women at the conference that "your basic human and civil rights have never been ours."

Bernice issued an invitation to women at the conference on behalf of aboriginal women, "that you come see us in our communities, that you share with us as women what kinds of problems we face." She urged women's groups to come and support aboriginal women in their struggles: "When you ask for our support, please come and support us." She urged the conference to listen carefully to Native concerns: "We're willing to talk if you're willing to listen." Bernice pointed to the aboriginal struggle for self-government, noting that aboriginal women had another set of problems — not only as women but also as Indians.

Bernice promised that if Native women were allowed to participate fully in the women's coalition, "You're going to have the most dedicated women you ever saw — because we know what you're facing now." She emphasized how women would be "really powerful" if they worked together.

Feminist process and the coalition's future. It became apparent that the conference needed to provide a means for women to respond collectively to proposals being made from the floor. As part of the earlier debate on structure and process, there had been a decision by the planning committee not to have formal resolutions brought forward and debated at the plenary session, in order to avoid formal rules of order which might inhibit full discussion and the building of consensus. However important decisions now needed to be taken in a short period of time — and by a large, diverse and vocal gathering of women. To address this problem, a process was devised whereby a number of proposals, based on recommendations from the strategy workshops, would be presented to the final plenary, and women would indicate their endorsement of each proposal by either standing or applauding. This process would enable the plenary to make some plans for the continuing mobilization of women in Saskatchewan.

The proposal that "this conference determines that we are a women's coalition ... called Connections" was endorsed overwhelmingly by conference participants as they stood to indicate their agreement.

The next step was to select a steering committee for the coalition. After some dispute about this process, whether there should be nominations and elections, or whether women should come forward voluntarily to form the group there was general agreement to the latter, to get the coalition going without delay. It was understood that the steering committee could then be confirmed by election at a future meeting.

At this point, 26 women responded to the call to come forward, introduce themselves to the plenary, and sign up as members of the steering committee. While most of the women joined as individuals rather than as representatives of groups — since there was no time for consultation — the new steering committee was broadly representative of a diversity of groups and interests. It was suggested that other women might be added to the steering committee at a later time, in order to ensure that it was representative of all sectors. The conference was then asked for its confirmation of this group of women, and support was indicated by the sustained applause of all gathered there.

Before the plenary adjourned, the conference also confirmed the two women's sector representatives to the steering
committee of SCSJ. This would ensure continuing links between Connections and the SCSJ. However, there had been
little discussion about Connections' relationship to the provincial coalition; this would need to be addressed later on by the
steering committee.[16]

At the very end of the plenary session, the entire conference
linked hands in a circle, accompanied by a song of solidarity.[17]

Coalition Building Continues

The conference was the crucial first step in building a provincial women's coalition. The goal of having a strong, united
voice for women in Saskatchewan had been evoked.

The new Steering Committee turned its attention to the
tasks mandated at the Connections conference: a report was
sent to all the participants, and a draft statement of unity was
prepared, with the aim of presenting it to Connections members at a future conference. For International Women's Day,
Connections organized a strike-support action for Pineland
Co-op workers in northern Saskatchewan, where the workers
— mostly women — had been on strike for three years for
decent wages and protection for part-time workers.

In addition, the committee worked on other related issues
including the consideration of structure for the coalition, discussion of short-term and long-term goals for Connections,
building closer ties with Native women, and ensuring that all
sectors and regions were represented. The Steering Committee
made an effort to begin building links with women throughout
the province and steps were taken to initiate networking by
sector. Connections continued its involvement with SCSJ.[18]

Most important, the Steering Committee turned its attention
to considering how Connections could continue to function as
a provincial women's coalition — given women's very limited
resources of money, time and energy.

Analysis of women's organizing

As part of the process of writing this chapter, the authors
consulted with other activist women in the province and reflected on the future of women's organizing in Saskatchewan.

A number of pressing issues were identified, focusing on three areas of concern: developing effective structures and processes for women's organizing, building strategies for overcoming divisions among women, and finding ways of empowering women in these struggles.

1. *Effective structures and processes.* While the issues affecting women's lives were clearly identified at the first Connections conference, it became apparent that women needed to articulate their goals more clearly in order to be able to strategize effectively. Following through on the debate about structure and process at the conference, there was also concern about building the kind of structure that would make the women's coalition most effective and politically viable. Questions were raised about whether women in Saskatchewan would be served best by a structure that was more definite and better organized, more loosely organized and one that evolved naturally from the process, or, alternatively, a combination of these approaches.

There was a further concern about how women from different groups and organizations — with different experiences and expectations — could work together in building a women's coalition. During the conference, these differences became apparent: on the one hand, some organizations, like unions, tend to be formally organized bodies that utilize a democratic election process, formal resolutions, and decision-making based on majority rule; on the other hand, some women were active in smaller, community-based groups, which tend to be more oriented toward process, with a miminum of structure, and decisions based on consensus building. Coalitions have begun to recognize the importance of developing new methods and strategies which incorporate the strengths of both approaches — in order to be effective in organizing women and inclusive of all women's concerns.

There has also been debate around the issue of how Connections, as a women's coalition, should relate to men, both individually and organizationally. This debate in Connections reflects, in part, the divergent approaches being taken within the women's movement. While the Connections statement of unity has specifically focused on the needs of women and children, members of Connections have been concerned with working to establish a better world for all people — including men. Looking at the ongoing work of Connections, many women are working together on a day-to-day basis with groups that include men (such as women active in trade unions, Connections as an affiliate of SCSJ). At the same time, many women have expressed concern about being co-opted by the male structures which surround women in patriarchal society, wanting to ensure that women's priorities and needs continue to direct organizing activities. Concern has been expressed about how a women's coalition can accommodate these different (but perhaps not contradictory) perspectives.

2. *Strategies for overcoming divisions.* From their experience of coalition building, women in Saskatchewan could see that serious bridge-building had to be undertaken in order to overcome divisions and build a more effective women's movement. In addition to ensuring that women from all regions and all sectors were included in the coalition, it meant that the problem of racism had to be seriously addressed.

Women of colour at the Connections conference emphasized that they face additional problems because of racism and discrimination. Aboriginal women explained how they were struggling long and hard for their rights, both as women and as Indians. This led to the recognition that a strong women's coalition cannot be built without confronting the problem of racism in society, in the women's movement. In response to these concerns, women in Saskatchewan began to recognize the importance of learning from Native women and other women of colour, and to accept the leadership and direction they can provide to women organizing against oppression. Connections has made an effort to be inclusive of all women and all women's concerns in the process of building alliances and offering mutual support.

3. *Empowerment of women.* There has been general concern voiced about how women are coping with the pressure and stress being felt in their lives, as they try to generate energy for the work which lies ahead. Questions have also been raised about how women can incorporate fun and laughter into their organizing and political activity. These concerns need to be addressed in order to maintain women's health and energy

levels; they are also crucial factors in maintaining the momentum of organizing and empowering women for further action.

While there was a deep sense of having achieved something very important at the conclusion of the Connections conference, women were unsure of how to proceed. Most women lack the time, energy, and resources needed to continue the coalition building work (with these problems being caused by the very cutbacks that women are fighting). Since this takes an emotional toll — as articulated by women at the conference — a question must be raised about how women can cope productively with these frustrations and difficulties in order to continue the work.

Women have also reflected on how best to consolidate the work, coordinate actions with other groups, and make full use of limited resources. There has been ongoing discussion about Connections' relationship with other women's groups (such as SAC) and provincial coalitions (such as SCSJ). In addition, when a small group of women are spread thin in the many critical areas of work, how can burn-out be avoided? These concerns have had practical implications for the work of the Connections Steering Committee and activist women in Saskatchewan. Women have raised serious questions about their political activity, asking whether there are more effective ways of coordinating the work, sharing the workload and avoiding duplication in the provincial organizing — all with the goal of empowering women in their struggle for a better life.[19]

As women in Saskatchewan have continued to address these many concerns, they have kept clearly in mind what it is that sustains and empowers women in their struggles: it is essentially a common vision of the future and the strong belief that women can create a better, more humane world for all.

Networking in Northern Manitoba

M. Jean Graveline
Katherine A. Fitzpatrick
and Barbara E. Mark

Northern women in Canada face many challenges in seeking empowerment and liberation, both individually and collectively. Geographic distance, harsh climates, few resources, lack of access to political decision makers, time constraints and limited support for feminist ideals are some of these. The Northern Women's Network is a feminist community organizing project designed with the special needs of northern women in mind. It is based on knowledge of the "herstory" of regional organizing efforts, and the nature of northern experience.

This chapter has been written by three active participants in the development of this project.[1] Together we wrote this descriptive account of the efforts of women to develop an action and support network spanning hundreds of miles, encompassing 10 communities. The salient characteristics of feminist community organizing in a non-metropolitan area are reviewed, along with a description of the developmental process specific to the Northern Women's Network.

Defining Community

Critical to the examination of our organizing efforts is the definition of "community," and an effort to place this definition in a "herstorical" context.

Recognition of the tendency towards the centralization of efforts and services is common to anyone who has lived in a rural area. Service to women in Manitoba's North has usually been delivered out of a centralized location. If "northern" input is sought, provincially or federally, the same few women from the major urban centres are contacted. Several attempts have been made over the years to expand Thompson-based services to other northern locations. These have often failed, primarily due to lack of budget.

When a budget is submitted from the North, including necessary travel and telephone allocations, it is reviewed along with urban budgets for similar projects and often seen as exorbitant. Inevitably, less money is received than requested. Organizations have often chosen to accept the piecemeal dollars and do what they can ... resulting time and time again in centralized development, ignoring the needs of the hinterland (Collier 1984).

Defining community, then, necessarily has become a political issue. We chose to define community as the northern community, with first priority being allocation of resources to development in locations outside of Thompson.The targeted community is women, the work is women oriented, and the goals are the advancement of equality, but those involved are not necessarily self-named feminist women. Feminism is not a well-accepted philosophy, and identification with it can result in ostracism and abuse in some northern communities. We do not target only feminist women, however, involvement in the Northern Women's Network definitely appeals to feminist-thinking women, and once recruited to the network, a woman is provided with information and insight into feminism.

Our community can be defined then, as women of northern Manitoba interested in working to enhance the status of women. Given this definition, an examination of the challenges inherent in organizing a community of this size and diversity is in order.

Geographic Realities
Picture in your mind a region which begins at the 53rd parallel and stretches north to the Manitoba-Northwest Territories border. Populated by a mere 60,000 people, the majority of the

population is concentrated in a handful of well-developed, well-connected centres, while the remainder live in numerous small, isolated settlements.

There are some geographic facts of life worth noting. The first is distance. With few exceptions, all northern communities are separated by at least 100 miles of unpopulated forest land. From Thompson, the largest community, it is a four-hour road trip to most other road accessible communities. Contact between these communities is hampered by unreliable, costly transportation and communication links. For example, a single trip to Gillam for an evening presentation consumed 40 consecutive hours, the equivalent of two paid weeks of half-time work. Funding conditions specify that the cheapest means of transportation must be used, which rules out air-travel. Some of the remote communities are served neither by all-weather roads nor by rail, limiting opportunities for involvement.

Thompson, a city of nearly 15,000, lies at the centre of this geographic network. Because of a broad economic base, Thompson has attracted the most varied population of all communities in the region: Native people, urban professionals from southern Canada, immigrant professionals and labourers from around the world, and Atlantic Canadian miners and their families. The other industrial centres of the region include The Pas, Flin Flon, Snow Lake, Lynn Lake, Leaf Rapids, Gillam and Churchill. Historically located on major water systems are some 20 native communities, differing in size, degree of isolation and development.

The region as a whole lies approximately 500 miles from the nearest metropolitan centre, Winnipeg. It is an eight-hour drive between Thompson and Winnipeg, and the regular return air fare is close to $400. Access to current information, the latest expertise, and goods and services is limited in all northern communities. In fact, the provision of services on par with those available in the South is a political issue.

Political Climate

The North, being a hinterland economy, relies on the good will of the government to return to the people what industry has taken out (Collier 1984). The displacement of native communities due to hydro development and the subsequent flood compensation agreement (Page 1986), and the plight of single-industry towns after the industry goes are two current examples. As women, we are also very concerned about the lack of recognition of the contribution of domestic labour (Luxton 1980), and the resulting lack of consideration of the needs of women in the process of development.

The North has particular difficulties in organizing as a political force. With massive geographic distances and sparse populations, we end up being chronically under represented. The elected members are unable to adequately do their jobs. Federally, the entire North has one member of Parliament; provincially we can boast five out of 57 seats in spite of the fact that we are over 65 percent of the geographic area. Currently, all of the northern provincial and federal representatives are male and all are New Democrats in Conservative governments. While women in northern communities have made recent strides in municipal politics, paralleling the Canadian phenomenon (Brodie & Vickers 1982), equal representation is still a dream of the future.

Under-representation of the region is a significant problem when one reflects on the extent to which many northerners rely on the government for support, either through paid employment or social assistance. This is compounded by overlapping government jurisdiction. The federal government has responsibility for Indian Affairs (including housing, education, and social services on reserves), while the province has responsibility for service delivery off-reserve, including income maintenance, and education. The two levels of government share responsibility for off-reserve housing and multiculturalism. Applying for funds for any northern proposal is confusing, requiring the ability to deal with both levels of government when neither are really accessible.

The concept of "provincialization" (Graveline 1986) dominates our thinking about geographic location. Dollars are critical for political, social, and economic development in the North. Decision-makers, all centralized in the urban south, are inaccessible without funds for travel and long-distance calls. Scarce resources are often utilized to send a few women south to educate and lobby, or to import "expert" help for workshops, with little left for development in the North. Often, urban-based organizations, naming themselves "provincial," use all available dollars in the "best interest" of all women, without consulting women in the North or rural areas. This paternalism is not limited to the South, as Thompson has a tendency to speak for the North.

Northern communities are bound together in a way that southern communities separated by similar distances are not. Northerners depend on whatever tenuous links exist between communities to build social, economic, and political support networks. These networks are essential to achieve what separate communities cannot. Other northern networks include the Northern Crisis Coordinating Committee (NCCC), Northern Association of Community Councils (NACC), and the Manitoba Keewatinowi Okimakanak (MKO). Northern networks are difficult to create and maintain. Whether they are geared to promote economic development, the interests of Native people, or the equality of women, few can survive without funding from outside the region.

The Network Project

The Northern Women's Network was initiated by northern members of the Manitoba Action Committee on the Status of Women (MACSW), a provincial political action group funded through the Secretary of State. The goals of the network are two-fold: to provide research, lobbying and communications support for community-based actions across the North; and to give northern women political voice.

In the fall of 1986, a member of Thompson Action Committee on the Status of Women (TACSW) was contracted to write and submit to the federal Secretary of State a funding proposal charting the initial stages of development. Funding was granted, but immediately, organizers were faced with the same problem which has plagued so many region-wide organizing attempts in the past: less than half of the $44,000 in funds requested were granted. The same amount was granted in the second year of the project, although the budget proposed called for $70,000. Any member of a women's organization deals with the results of chronic under-funding — over-extension of staff. We are no exception.

In preparing the proposal, a survey of northern women was conducted to identify their concerns, and to make initial contact with women who were feminist-minded and potentially interested in participating in the network. The survey strategy was selected in consideration of the geographic and economic realities which placed severe limitations on personal and even phone contact for discussion. We wanted to be able to reach out to a wide number and variety of women to begin the process of networking. We also recognized that government funding rested on justification of need, which could be expressed numerically through use of the survey method.

Written questionnaires appeared to be cost effective, while meeting our objectives of initial contact and information gathering. The questionnaires were sent to women across the North who were identified as feminists, either through their membership in MACSW, or their involvement in work with abused women. They were also sent to women holding positions of leadership or demonstrating influence in their community.

The results of the survey indicated that the three most common concerns among northern women are barriers to equal economic opportunity, lack of access to medical and counselling services, and barriers to participation in community decision-making. We (TACSW) then developed a three-year northern network development plan, designed to respond to these three issues as well as other issues which would arise.

The Network Structure

The network was structured to follow the pattern set by previously established networks, and modelled on informal feminist networking. It is the practice of women who travel across the North to seek out feminist-thinking women in outlying areas for accommodation, conversation, support and information-sharing. As a result of this grassroots networking, some of these women from outlying communities have become members of the network.

We began with at least one woman identified through participation in the survey, and held a series of meetings in nine target communities to attract potential members. Easily accessible communities with larger population bases, which act as secondary service centres, were selected. It was intended that once groups were established in these communities, they could reach out to women in satellite communities.

The results of the initial organizing meetings, held in the spring of 1987, varied widely from community to community. For example, six highly motivated women in Leaf Rapids responded enthusiastically. They requested information, films, and offered several ideas for projects which could be initiated in the community. The women continued to meet informally, but were not in a position to initiate a formal group. Due to many other commitments at work, home and in the community, they lacked the time and energy to pursue many of the project ideas they generated.

In Lynn Lake, the key contact faced extreme isolation, being the only woman in her community publicly committed to feminist action. Organizing efforts in this community focused on public education to create awareness of feminism and issues affecting women. A list of topics for presentation was drafted, ranging from incest to alcohol and prescription drug abuse among women. Her isolation was lessened by active participation in the MACSW provincial executive.

The network contacts in Flin Flon and Snow Lake are committed feminists, but their time and energy was largely taken up with their work of running the local crisis centres. Many staff and board members of crisis centres and shelters are also members of the network. In Snow Lake, the Centre of Family Violence was struggling with town council over the practice of issuing only welfare vouchers. Making payment with vouchers stigmatizes women who depend on social assistance. The lobby, a collaborative effort involving other network members, was successful, and a new policy was instituted.

Network Activities

Although South Indian Lake was not included as a target community, the presence of a MACSW member made it one. Efforts were made through visits and mail-outs to include the member in network activities. The woman there took an unorthodox but imaginative approach to feminist community organizing. She volunteered to drive children to the day-care centre in the morning in exchange for the use of the centre's van in the evening to transport women to meetings. This is an example of resourcefulness which can and should be applied in feminist community organizing whenever the opportunity arises.

Action by TACSW serves as a model for women in other northern communities. The Thompson group successfully lobbied City Council for passage of a bylaw to restrict the display of pornographic magazine covers and videotape jackets (Fitzpatrick 1987a), and to make the welfare by-law more equitable (Fitzpatrick, Graveline, Hughes, Cromwell 1987). A boycott was launched of a local hotel which features strippers as the main attraction in its beverage room. TACSW's record debunked the notion that political action was not possible in a small community. Our action on pornography has inspired other Manitoba communities. The Parklands Status of Women has referred to material from TACSW to plan their own anti-pornography action.

More contacts were made through the MACSW provincial membership drive in January 1988. Recruitment advertisements were placed in several northern newsletters. Women in Flin Flon, Sundance, Gillam, and Churchill became members. Ongoing recruitment is through brochures and by word-of-mouth.

Health-care. In the autumn of 1987, a second round of trips was made to the communities to identify an issue around which a major lobby could be organized. Health-care delivery was the area northern women most wanted to take action on (Fitzpatrick 1988). Complaints about this issue in the North are universal. A Flin Flon woman told of incorrect diagnosis and inappropriate medication. A woman in The Pas related her experiences with the patronizing and presumptuous attitude of southern doctors, and their stereotypical views of northern women. A Lynn Lake woman recalled having to travel a long distance to receive competent care for a common ailment.

A survey on medical issues was drafted, and reviewed and approved by network members. We desired at this time to collect information from which we could have a power base to lobby decision-makers in the area of health. Although individual stories were dramatically moving, they were not getting the political attention we felt was necessary to promote change. Over 100 women in northern Manitoba were surveyed and interviewed. Although some community groups remained unconvinced, other groups were impressed by the magnitude of the problems women in the North face with the health care system. The presentation of the survey results prompted further action by regional organizations and provincial politicians.

Questions focused on: conditions for which northerners have to travel out of their communities and/or the region to receive treatment; the costs of travel for medical treatment which are not covered by the Northern Patient Transport Program (NPTP), such as childcare, food and hotel, and lost wages; problems with the health care system within the communities, such as a high turnover of medical staff or lack of equipment; and the need for policy initiatives, such as additional incentives to attract medical professionals to the North, and the legalization of midwifery.

Inquiries were sent to health-related organizations, such as the Manitoba Health Services Commission, Manitoba Health Organization Inc., and the Manitoba Medical Association, asking if they had conducted any research or established any policy positions on ways to improve the northern health care delivery system. What little work has been done confirms the lack of appropriate services.

A Northern Women's Film Series was made available in 1988, since some members planned to concentrate their efforts on public education and feminist consciousness-raising in their communities. Local network members in the communities of Leaf Rapids, Lynn Lake, Flin Flon, and Churchill selected films, provided facilities and publicized the series.

A network conference was held in Thompson in the fall of 1988. Objectives were: to bring network members together for the first time; to develop lobbying skills; to plan the health-care lobby; and to establish a decentralized process for decision making and political action. Women attended from 11 communities, four of which were previously not targeted communities. Much interesting discussion was had.

Problems in Realizing the Network's Promise

The objectives of bringing women together, developing lobbying skills, and planning the health care lobby met some success. Unfortunately no decentralized process was established for decision-making and political action. Some efforts have been made to avoid the colonizing approach to development that so characterizes centre-hinterland relationships, but this has not been fully achieved. At the time of the workshop, decisions concerning the allocation of resources were made by TACSW, in consultation with network members. Individual women did take responsibility for particular tasks necessary to decentralization, but for a myriad of reasons were not followed up.

Centralization of resources. The power over allocation of resources was left in the hands of Thompson women. In the winter of 1989, TACSW decided that it was in their best interests to have a visible office space in Thompson. No consultation was held between the women involved in TACSW and the Northern Network members outside of Thompson. When budgets were allocated in the spring of 1989 northern development money, which had in the past gone to support the efforts of the Northern Women's Network was reallocated to provide a physical space and a support staff for TACSW in Thompson. Although the paid person has expressed a desire to travel and continue the development, her primary focus is support work for the Thompson branch. The nineteen hours a week allocated is not enough to do both.

Diversion of energy. The energy of many of the Northern Network members has been diverted from development of a political voice through the Action Committee, to the running of the Northern Women's Resource Service, which received funding in the spring of 1989 through the Manitoba government. Although the resource service has personal and political advocacy as part of its mission, the focus is far more on service delivery to individual women and women's groups than development of political strength and unity. Hopefully, we can retain enough "disengagement" and our vision of social transformation while we enter this time of "mainstreaming" with the threat of co-optation as a funded government agency (see Chapter 1).

The development of the network has been a cyclical process. Connecting with women by telephone, mail and in person to identify the issues and activities they want to pursue was the foundation. Accessing resources, including original background research, and the organization of special events is key to initiating local political action. Necessary for our survival is the nurturing of ourselves as women doing battle for equality and freedom. Women across the North are striving for a sense of community, meeting others with whom they can share their opportunities, joys, challenges, and frustrations. All three elements simultaneously combine to form the basis of feminist community organizing.

Geographical distances and isolation. It seems the further women are from the seats of power the less influence they feel they have. Provincial organizations working to enhance women's political voice have been slow to develop in the North, using scarce resources for southern urban development. As a result, there is a lack of political momentum in the northern population. We are often given insufficient notice of decisions pending, or of actions to be taken, so meaningful participation is difficult. Lack of information is noted as a major complaint in our surveys of northern women (Fitzpatrick 1987b), and contributed to the current shift in funding source and focus of the network.

Isolation is a danger faced by all women in the North. Beyond physical distance, isolation refers to lack of "community," and the psycho-social stressors inherent in this. Male domination of industry, of political decision-making, and of northern development as a whole has isolated women through economic dependency. The conservatism of northern attitudes makes the development and sustaining of a feminist identity a challenge. Often, feminist women are closeted (Lester 1984), making networking difficult. Being a lone feminist in a male dominated community means your reality is not accepted.

Isolation is emotionally stressful. Depression is epidemic (Haussman & Halseth 1983) and the prescribing of tranquilizers and anti-depressants is exceptionally high (Evans &

Cooperstock 1983). Appropriate mental health services for women are sadly lacking. Delivery of services is generally more expensive than in urban areas both because of the lower socio-economic status of rural communities, and because of lesser concentration of clients in a given space, meaning less feasibility of fixed service locations (Collier 1984). In short, the services necessary for women suffering from symptoms of oppression are not available in the North.

Severe isolation from other communities and from extended family is compounded by a high turnover of friends. Often it seems a friendship is no sooner established than the woman moves away, leaving a gap to be filled. Turnover has affected the development of the Northern Women's Network. When key women relocate, development in a community is sometimes halted, and the search begins for another contact. Experience has demonstrated that orienting women to the network is an ongoing oft-repeated task.

Women relocating plays a pivotal role in the present and future development of the network. Several of the women with the initial vision are currently residing outside of the northern boundaries. Other women have taken their places and the work continues, but styles of working and priorities have shifted.

Strong personal relationships develop quickly and spontaneously. In network organizing, travel between communities inevitably involves an overnight billet because meetings are usually held in the evenings to accommodate women who work for wages. Thoughts and feelings are shared over meal preparation and child care, intensifying our awareness of personal experiences as political issues.

Women's work. Women often juggle paid work, motherwork, housework, and community work, with little time left for political action. Many small communities offer a large number of associations, but the volunteer workers who develop these groups are few in number, thus the burden is heavier for each individual (Manitoba Advisory Council on the Status of Women 1984). Women are rarely relieved of their other duties to engage in political activism, so add this to their workloads.

Violence against women. Isolation and the high cost of travel has intensified the problems faced by battered women (Claerhout, Elder, Janes 1982). Violence against women is a life and death issue for northern women, often acting as a catalyst for feminist consciousness. Survivors begin to see their experience as a symptom of a wider system of oppression (Schechter 1982). The network provides opportunity for personal analysis that draws these women into other related feminist issues, such as economic self-sufficiency, portrayal of women in the media, and reproductive choice. The staff of local crisis centres are a resource to the network, providing information exchange. They are often over-extended, and their role as front-line organizers may be limited due to the community's negative perception of their work.

Racism and the women's movement. Native women, facing double discrimination, recognize clearly that they must organize themselves. Often a conflict is felt over what level of oppression they should apply themselves to, racism or sexism. Many male leaders stress that to be feminist is to deny tradition, and therefore to be in conflict with the goal of preservation of native identity. The feminist efforts directed towards restructuring family are viewed as anti-family, placing Native women in the position of choosing their cultural belief in the preservation of family (Poitras 1986) or feminism. Access to reserve land is controlled by male-dominated band councils, limiting contact and information exchange. The election of Patsy Turner as chief of Grand Rapids Indian Band, and chair of MKO, a political umbrella organization representing most northern bands, was an indication of the parallel development of a Native women's voice in northern Manitoba. Her attendance at the network conference gives us hope for unity among northern women.

The feminist movement has been organized using non-Native understanding of the world, and we would be wise to recognize the racism inherent in that (Glassco 1986). We in the North must coexist. Government wants all women in Northern Manitoba to have one voice, to submit one proposal, and to all agree. Native women reject this, feeling silenced in non-Native women's organizations. They are developing their own sense of power and belonging. The network supports their right to choose while inviting their participation.

Basis of Unity

We have been asked, "But what do you women in the North want?" Sound familiar? Perhaps a little Freudian?

We want accessibility to politicians at all levels, including those who sit as appointed board members (i.e., Norman Regional Development Corporation, Manitoba Forest Industries, Manitoba Hydro). We want equal representation on decision-making bodies. We want political voice.

We want adequate representation on provincial executives, of women's organizations in particular, and consultation with our urban sisters who represent us at a national level. We want recognition.

We want alternative services provided to women in the north. Life in the North often involves a choice between outdated, patriarchal service or no service. We want quality services.

Many women involved in the Network are actively involved in the struggle to end violence against women. We want safety in our homes, and on the streets.

We want to network across the North so that our voices can reflect the diversity of our experience, with recognition of our commonalities. We want decentralization.

We want distance recognized as a barrier, and geographic discrimination to become as self-evident as other forms of inequality. We want the resources to compensate.

We want to be able to recognize Native women's needs to gather their own strength and resources, to act on their own behalf — and perhaps in the future in concert with us — without government pressure to cooperate/co-opt. We want unity.

Organizing in a Small Community — Prince Edward Island

J. Estelle Reddin

It was around the turn of the century that women in Prince Edward Island began to organize. Like today's feminist activists, their concerns were routed in social justice, and improvement in the everyday lives of women. Their co.*tribution is not forgotten as we start this chapter about women organizing in the 1980s.

International Women's Year, 1975, marked a recent upsurge of feminist organizing in P.E.I. (Conway 1983), while the eighties has been a decade of growth manifested both in the increased number of organizations, including those that have branched off from earlier associations, and a broadened participation base. Some organizations have disappeared while others have survived and evolved; a few have simply remained dormant. Some are beginners, little fledglings or seedlings needing care and nurture.

The material for this chapter is extracted from interviews with five individuals about their work in the women's movement.[1] The organizations that each one represents are examples only, not necessarily representative of type. Throughout this chapter, these interviews illustrate differences and similarities in the organization and development of the groups, the resulting structure of each one, and strategies for coping with inevitable problems and conflicts. The purpose is to raise some questions that need reflection and consideration rather than prescribe solutions. These direct accounts and opinions will facilitate other women's groups in their development and enhance their ability to reach their goals.

The Geographical and Social Context

Prince Edward Island is small both in geographical area and in population. A crescent-shaped island lying in the Gulf of St. Lawrence on the east coast of Canada, separated from the mainland by the Northumberland Strait, with a total area of 2184 square miles, it is spacious for its 126,650 inhabitants while at the same time it is the most densely populated province of Canada. The province is still predominantly rural with only 38% of its population classified by the 1986 census as urban, just half of the 76% urban for Canada as a whole. Its one city, Charlottetown, the capital, has a population of 15,776, while Summerside, the largest town, numbers some 8,000 people.

The Island exerts a strong magnetism for its daughters and sons who leave. Of those who have moved away for economic reasons many return, in retirement if not earlier, adding to the high proportion of elderly in the population. At the same time, it has a slightly higher percentage of children under 15 than Canada as a whole. Of families with children, 10% are single-parent woman-led.[2]

Island women are comparatively well educated: in 1981, 45% with high school, grades 9 to 12, and 32% with some post-secondary education. Although fewer women than men had attained bachelor's degrees in 1981, today women account for a higher percentage of the total enrolment in the Island's university.[3] The number of women in the labour force counted in the 1986 census shows an increase of 86.4% over 1971, with a total female participation rate of 56.4%. Much of this work is seasonal and part time.

Many Island family histories record two centuries of life in the province. After the First World War and again after the Second World War, additional newcomers of various nationalities arrived, but the population remains predominantly anglophone. In the last census only 4% of Islanders listed French as their mother tongue compared with 24% for Canada as a whole, and a mere 1% listed "other" language.

Far from the seats of power, Prince Edward Island's wealth is in agriculture, fisheries, and tourism, all of which are cut short by the long severe winters and late spring. There is relatively little manufacturing and no heavy industry. As elsewhere, service industries are accounting for an increasing proportion of the work force. Wages are low, unemployment is high. The average per capita income for those over 15 years of age is $13,739 for Prince Edward Island, compared with, for example, Ontario's $19,462.

But families are interrelated and extended families are plentiful. Many Islanders seek and find security and satisfaction through the informal economy in providing food, shelter and other necessities. These attributes are "not simply romantic ways of being poor with dignity" (Surette 1989), nor do Islanders consider themselves poor cousins waiting for a handout. Artistic, creative talent and skills are abundant; neighbourly kindness and support still lives on in rural communities. The Island culture could be described as "high context" in an overall "low context" North America: in its language with multi-meanings implicitly understood, its general cultural stability, resistance to change and high value on conformity (Hall 1976). Since many of its values are counter to the prevailing world view of Western industrial capitalism, a certain tension is set up with the reality of the need for federal government support or equalization payments such as unemployment insurance.

Neither the stereotyped romantic society nor quaint rural setting often portrayed in the media, Prince Edward Island nonetheless in its natural environment, traditional culture and ethnography differs from other parts of Canada, providing a milieu for women's activities quite different from that of large urban centres. Women on the Island are by no means immune to the problems of the patriarchal bureaucratic society. Conservatism and repression are common in sexual politics; the prevailing right-wing tendencies of the 1980s coupled with the covert pressures of its high context culture accentuate social ills such as alcoholism, incest, and family violence. Women are vulnerable. The Provincial Advisory Council on the Status of Women recently stated "Equality .... is the only possible position of dignity for human beings" (Brehaut 1989). The women interviewed for this chapter believe that feminist organizing is one type of action to help bring about dignity and justice for women.

Women's Activism

In a small province like Prince Edward Island, emphasis on working together is feasible and appropriate. Many of today's associations have grown out of early cooperative ventures, such as the Women's Travelling Resource Centre, and the Women's Lecture Series. These helped set the tone for future activities and raised awareness of the common issues in women's struggle for equality. The Women's Legal Project led to the formation of the Prince Edward Island Caucus of National Association of Woman and the Law (NAWL) which is rather distinctive on two counts: it includes more lay women than professional lawyers, and it has successfully carried out its purpose in an informal loose structure. Another of the early cooperative ventures on the Island, The Voluntary Resource Council (VRC), although it includes both men and women, is feminist in outlook, and provides space, networking and alternative services to many Island groups.

In 1981 an ad hoc committee with members from the Canadian Congress on Learning Opportunities for Women (CCLOW), Canadian Research Institute for the Advancement of Women/ Institut Canadien de Recherches sur les Femmes (CRIAW/ICREP), Les Femmes Acadiennes, VRC, NAWL, Planned Parenthood, Advisory Council on the Status of Women, and Women's Employment Development set out to "investigate the possibility of women's groups acting together in some cooperative fashion" (Women's Network Project Report 1981). The outcome of this project was Women's Network Inc., an organization that has maintained a strong web of interaction among women's groups across the Island. The formation of the Provincial Advisory Council on the Status of Women in 1975 and the initiation of the Women's Program of the Secretary of State set up a framework and a funding source for women's volunteer activity.

With this brief introduction and description of the context for women's activities in the eighties, we now focus on six associations, each with a specific purpose, and concerned more with those who are in some way disadvantaged in today's society than with the mainstream long-time women's associations.

Six Women's Associations

For the present purpose, the author selected six organizations as case studies of the growth of the women's movement on the Island. Each organization is seen through the eyes of one member or worker. This approach gives a narrow but direct accounting of experience in the field of women's work.

Transition House Association, a provincial association which operates an emergency shelter for abused women and their children, evolved from research on wife assaults in Prince Edward Island. It has recently opened a new second stage housing facility. In the following, Roberta,[4] a former board member, speaks from her experience in Transition House Association.

Les Femmes Acadiennes, involving women in eastern Prince County, the only francophone region in the province, originated in 1979 as an organization for francophone women. Anne Marie, their historian, describes this group.

The East Prince Women's Information Centre provides an information and drop-in center for women in the Summerside region and has sponsored several projects encouraging women's equality. Sally, mother of two who has recently entered the paid labour force as their Assistant Co-ordinator, is their spokesperson.

Women in Support of Agriculture (WSA) and Women in Support of Fishing (WISF) are two groups concerned with women's roles in primary production. Mary is one of the early organizers of WISF.

One goal of Women's Network Inc. is to represent all views that are for the benefit of women. It publishes a bimonthly women's magazine, *Common Ground*, now in its seventh year, discussing issues important to women in a changing society. Women's Network also organizes and conducts an annual Women's Festival, a three-day event in which all kinds of women gather together and take part in activities ranging from workshops to quilting to performing in the annual cabaret.

Betty, a board member, discusses some organizational issues for Women's Network.

DAWN in Prince Edward Island is in the initial stages of organizational development as a branch of the national Dis-Abled Women's Network. I myself, a physically disabled woman, am active in DAWN and a "Dance with Dawn" project which is exploring the possibilities of dance as a component of a women's support group.

Although other members of these groups might have somewhat different perceptions, the reports of these women are nonetheless valid as the personal experience of women participating in the groups.

To see a problem and do something about it has been women's way both yesterday and today (Vickers 1988). What we now consider the "traditional" associations have played a long and continuing role in getting things done for others. The difference in today's feminist groups is expressed by Anne Marie:

> The associations of the past still exist today: the Women's Institute and a French association called "Dames du Sanctuaire," the equivalent of the Catholic Women's League … a lot of their roles were at the service of the community, the church, the school. It was for others — always — while Les Femmes Acadiennes was to be more focused on their own development and women's issues.

Getting Started
Many of the present-day feminist groups had similar beginnings. The East Prince Women's Information Centre, reports Sally,

> started from an ad hoc committee in 1984. A bunch of women got together and talked. They had done a study to see if there was any need for a women's centre. They did find a need and set up the information/resource centre.

Similarly for Acadian women:

> A woman from the Evangeline area ... originally
> from northern New Brunswick — she was perhaps
> more aware and activist — got together with other
> women of the area ... They received a grant in 1982
> to hire someone to do research on the role of
> Acadian women in the Island, and that's where I
> came in. It resulted in a book called *Nous les Femmes*
> (Gallant 1986). And it was to try to describe the
> contribution of women as mothers and in the family
> and in the work place and the community.

Two groups, WSA and WISF, somewhat similar in purpose,
attempted similar initial organizational strategies. Women in
Support of Agriculture in Prince Edward Island grew out of a
"Farm Business for Farm Women" conference sponsored by
the provincial Department of Agriculture. Prince Edward Island farm women who attended the conference decided to
follow the example of farm women in other parts of Canada
and form their own organization.

Mary describes the initiation of Women in Support of
Fishing:

> In the beginning, in 1982, a woman, who now fishes
> herself, came with a Secretary of State representative
> to the ports to see if there was enough interest to
> form a fisherwomen's support group. Secretary of
> State Women's Program sponsored a dinner. We got
> a fairly wide representation from across the Island
> and from that group formed a board of directors.
> The first project was to organize a convention: it had
> a fairly good response with 75 delegates and good
> resource people.

Lack of success beset the initial attempt to organize a Dis-
Abled Women's Network group in Prince Edward Island.
DAWN Canada originated in a national meeting of 17 delegates supported by Secretary of State in 1986. Following this
the Prince Edward Island delegate organized a few meetings

and a workshop supported by the provincial Secretary of State program. However, after this workshop, no one responded to a last call for a meeting. Recently a new group of ten women has come together to learn dance and creative movement for disabled women. As a result of meeting together weekly, with time at each session to discuss their lives as disabled women, a DAWN support group is evolving (Evans 1988).

Obstacles to Growth — Anti-feminist Attitudes

Moving from the originating group to a broader base, even after a successful beginning, is crucial for most women's organizations. Some common obstacles appear and strategies must be devised to deal with them. One of these problems is the constraining influence of a negative stereotype of feminism held by the public. Many, perhaps most, of the initial ad hoc groups would call themselves "feminist"; yet as the organization grew beyond its initial status, perceptions of the group as "feminist" and "radical" frequently caused difficulty. "People say about the Women's Centre," notes Sally, "It's just a bunch of feminists — a *women's* centre. If people would only just come in and see what we do and meet us, their attitude would be different."

Those interested in organizing DAWN find that many disabled women resist being called "feminist" and have difficulty also with the label "disabled." This necessitates an even greater degree of change in acceptance and attitudes for them, and requires patience on the part of the organizers.

For Transition House Association the problem of the public's negative perception of feminism became serious:

> There was a lot of controversy going on at that time about what the philosophy of the house should be and just how feminist it should be. The people who first started the house wished to have a very feminist approach. But to others, a feminist approach is against families. There may have been comments from some in the community and the local churches that Transition House, by giving women a place to go to get away from their husbands, was breaking up their marriage (which basically wasn't a marriage

— if the husband is beating his wife, what kind of a
marriage is it?) But that maybe made people afraid
to say too much openly — Some feminists perceived
the Board as becoming too influenced by these pressures and wanted to get it back to their original
perception — to be for women to be able to live a
decent life.

The annual general meeting when I came on the
board had, so far as I know, the largest attendance
on record. The nominating committee presented a
slate, but in addition to that there were a number of
nominations from the floor which is most unusual.
There was a lot of conflict on the board: not openly
but there were these undercurrents. I came in in the
middle of all this. And I could feel the tension at the
board meetings.

A variety of strategies has been used to deal with the problem of anti-feminism. For Transition House, a board member
proposed a workshop in conflict resolution. At first she was
ignored and didn't get any support, and reports that she "just
felt so awful." However, the executive director thought it a
good idea:

So I proposed it again and somehow it was agreed
that we do a workshop for all the board members to
find out what everybody's perception of feminism
was. It was well attended and a lot of the staff came
... As it turned out most people had a very supportive view of the idea of feminism — especially as we
worked through it and people found it's not this
radical family-breaking-up, bra-burning business.
People's understanding evolved — all people are
human beings and deserve equal respect.

Other groups have dealt with negative views of feminism
through establishing good public relations in the community.
Sally explains how the Women's Information Centre also utilizes women's nurturing abilities: "When people come in we

try to make them feel comfortable — offer them a coffee ... ."
Babies and children are welcome and a play area is provided.

Celebration, having a good time together, has proven effective in building a feeling of acceptance and solidarity.

> On International Women's Day this year we held an
> open house with more than 50 people. We had our
> 3000th visitor — we made a big thing of it — it was
> a man! We invited him to our Open House and he
> cut the cake ... "

Anne Marie reports that Les Femmes Acadiennes also enjoy celebration:

> They held an Acadian women's night recently at
> Étoile de Mer, the Acadian Village. A celebration.
> They had a good time: a meal and after they had
> talent from the area. It was in *La Voix Acadienne* the
> next week that the women had a great time and they
> wanted people to know it.

A Second Obstacle: Fear of Speaking Out

A question that to feminists seems non-debatable, "Should women have a voice?" nonetheless poses difficulties and has tested the patience of the enthusiastic initial small organizing groups. "This woman was saying, 'You can speak out,'" reports Anne Marie:

> It was like a shock. It was not only that this was new,
> but it was from a woman "from away." She was
> more outspoken than the people in the community.
> I think the fact that she was an outsider, even though
> she might have been there for six or seven years,
> people were afraid of her ideas — it was radical ...
> Some of the women who were already more activist
> felt frustrated that it was hard to organize. They'd
> want the women to come and they'd phone and get
> this response: "No. Who will get the meals?" and
> there were children who were really old enough to

do it ... eighteen-year-olds. But she couldn't leave —
she wouldn't go."

Nevertheless, the small group of Acadian women organized
workshops and meetings and they were well attended. Their
historian continues:

> The women would never do this anywhere else —
> they would talk about themselves. The organizers
> were always amazed that a lot did come. They felt
> that they were responding to a need.

Mary also mentions the difficulty for women to speak on
their own behalf:

> Women find it hard to look after their own needs.
> They expect to look after someone else's needs. They
> have given up their autonomy and become depend-
> ent — dependent on someone else needing them.

She describes the problem experienced by WISF:

> Prior to that first convention we had tried to organ-
> ize a few meetings in our own ports. In our port
> there were two or three women who went to the
> meeting only to say how much they disagreed with
> the whole idea of an organization. They talked really
> negatively; they felt strongly that this wasn't going
> to work and that women weren't going to have a
> voice in the fishery because men wouldn't allow it.
> Men had been like this for years, they said. Although
> not stifled in their own lives, these women felt that
> most women are, and are so used to it that they are
> not going to take advantage of the opportunity to
> speak out .... We submitted a proposal to Employ-
> ment and Immigration for resource workers to do a
> simple survey. We wanted some method of meeting
> women at the kitchen table, where they would be
> comfortable and more responsive to the notion that

they could speak up and that they do know about the fishery — but the project was turned down.

Looking back over the experience, she continues:

> If we could have gone to bingo we could have got those women interested. They're prepared to tell you over bingo their opinions. They feel safe. I think they're so used to being active, that it's only when they're doing something that they feel free to talk. If they're playing with the bingo chips, they can talk. They look after the children, and they have a conversation. They talk about fishing while they're cooking the meal. They're always busy at something and maybe they're not comfortable just to sit down and talk.

Kitchen meetings, getting together at Bingo, on the wharf, community schools, dancing together — this, rather than formal meetings, may provide the ambience for some women to find their voice.

Moving On — Issues of Structure and Process

For most groups a second stage of growth follows the projects and activities guided by the original ad hoc group. This usually involves moving towards a structure, which inherently presents new obstacles.

Les Femmes Acadiennes waited for some public acceptance among the women of the community before attempting a structured membership, as Anne Marie reports:

> Now more women are part of it. When they had activities, there always was a high turnout. The numbers kept growing. My feeling now is that it seems they are accepted — it's not radical any more.

A special speaker or special event sometimes marks the passage from the early organization to the more mature. This was the case for the Acadian women:

It might have been in 1986 when they launched the book — it was at a supper and they had a speaker — that you could become a member. There were a lot of women in attendance. Maybe the active group wanted to involve more women and it could be more democratic. They could have their annual meetings and they could elect. Because for a few years — from 1979 to 1986 — it seemed to me it was always the same committee that was in charge. After a while they were ready to [move on] — they had played their role to get it started and do the ground work. Now they were ready to have a constitution. They have annual meetings now, and elections.

By contrast, WISF was unsuccessful at this stage. Its initial organization was in some ways perhaps from the top down. "Government departments were ready to give us dollars very quickly," says Mary "for conferences, mailing, and so on. Also that first conference was going after an organizational structure similar to the Fishermen's Association." She continues:

The first year was the build-up; the second year — what do we do now? The fishery was not good then and women were experiencing stresses similar to those experienced by farm women (Ireland 1983). Just on our Board several were having marital difficulties — keeping a paid job to support the family *and* the fishing, looking after the house and the kids, but with no input into fishing decisions, no access to the higher-ups. They were maybe aware enough to see that the state of the fishery was having quite a lot to do with it — the lack of control they felt. Some marriages did break up ... .

Some Board members thought it was really important to have a constitution and formal structure right away. At that stage a simple statement of philosophy would have done it. I think, if we'd had a more clear definition of our philosophy and our role, then women would have come to our meetings with the feeling, "OK, if I want to go and have a cup of tea and talk about the fishery, I can go to that meeting." And that was the problem with having a big convention right at the beginning. It formalized the whole thing a little too soon. The way the group was most effective was in being a support group — that was to be its role originally .... Eventually, we met one wet night and people were saying this is such a long drive, and we couldn't seem to get together often enough in the winter because of road conditions — so we said this isn't going anywhere. One local group in the western end of the Island did continue.[6]

Transition House Association, after clarifying its philosophy, has settled into the usual board structure. The principal decision-making resides with the board, general membership offers support and volunteers, and staff deal with the realities of battered wives and their children.

"I think originally they tried to make it totally non-hierarchical," explains Roberta.

Totally everybody contributed, both for the board and for running the house. And I think that basically led to chaos. So now the structure that's in place is a traditional board with a president, vice, and secretary; and some decisions are made, when they need to be made quickly, by the executive. But in spite of that structure everybody feels that they have a right to contribute and that they're listened to.

Similarly, for the East Prince Women's Information Centre, within a formal structure, decision-making is largely by consensus, although formal motions are used as needed.

Some feminists debate the relative merits of formal versus informal organizational structures and decision-making, with some maintaining that only the informal is truly feminist. However, as Roberta points out:

I think it depends a lot on the people. You can have a highly traditional structure but with very open people and it can work openly, or you can have it completely open with some very autocratic people and it would end up not working.

Mary's experience with WISF supports this conclusion:

We wanted to make decisions by consensus but sometimes that created a little animosity because it seemed the persons who yelled the loudest got their way. When you have some in the group that are fairly meek and hold back but have very good and worthwhile opinions and you have some very vocal, it's not really consensus. You can't have consensus among people unless they're willing to share authority equally.

The experience of women's organizations suggests that a clear sense of purpose and philosophy as well as an appreciation of the role of the organization are key factors in success, rather than any particular structural forms. Allowing time for appropriate organizational forms to develop is important. As Mary points out: "Women's organizations can't do all this [structure building] at the beginning: often they don't know what they need, or what they can have in the way of staff and so on."

Finding a Voice for the Group

With a clear philosophy in place, the dilemma of who speaks for the organization and when and on what topics is more easily resolved. Transition House Association, having dealt with the problem of feminism, established a statement of philosophy agreed upon by the board. Roberta reports success from the board's point of view in handling the difficult issue of abortion:

After that things were just so much better — it's unbelievable. The original group were much happier. They had been pushing for this over a couple of years and it had been attempted and avoided — started and never finished. Communication had broken down. But now when new members came on the board they were shown the philosophy statement and told, "If you can live with this philosophy, we'd like to have you." The board represents a lot of different viewpoints, but even with an issue like the Supreme Court abortion decision, the board was able to reach agreement on Transition House's public position. Even though some members on the Board were personally more "pro-life," having discussed it in terms of what the aims of the House are, a "pro-choice" point of view was agreed on. That was published in the paper. You figure all hell's going to break loose and the association is going to lose its credibility — but no, one or two phone calls — that was it! The board said what was believed and fine — nobody took away funding or anything. I think, when you've worked together on the philosophy and you're coming from a common thing, to allow diversity from there is easier than when you're starting apart.

Women's Network has moved back and forth from an informal unstructured organization to a structured one, with a resolve to remain feminist. Because it has grown, publishes a magazine for and about Island women, conducts province-wide workshops, and maintains an office with paid staff, it needs an effective structure to accomplish its project goals. In fact, in a 1983 study of women's organizations, Women's Network reported a need for a more formal management structure (Conway 1983). More recently it has had an evaluation of its functions and organization. The reviewer pointed out the necessity for the board to agree on philosophy. However, like Transition House Association in the past, "The board never gets to it." Although its projects have been successful, the lack of clarity in its philosophy and role leads to some confusion for both board and staff members. It now has an orientation packet for new board members, job descriptions for staff. Yet, when issues do come up, without a statement of philosophy, the association has a problem in speaking for all when responding to the media.

Empowerment

Related to the group's philosophy and purposes is the question of empowerment. Anne Marie dealt with that question in her book: "I entitled that part of the book 'Se prendre à main' which means taking control of your life — empowerment is a good word. When they did the workshops they wanted to give the information to the women so they would be able to make their own decisions regarding different issues."

Feminist activists, in the spirit of "se prendre à main," are concerned with associations of people rather than with administration of services for people. Early leaders with commitment and a clear vision can organize workshops, stage demonstrations, carry out monitoring projects in society, form lobbies, etc. The subsequent activities may easily slip into the weakness of many of our present-day women's services. Many of these are in reality done *for* rather than *with* women, although purportedly for their good and benefit (Torjman 1988). If feminist organizations are truly concerned with empowerment, then they must move on to associations of women at whatever level of awareness — economic, political, social, or educational. Empowerment begins with consciousness-raising and the appreciation and acceptance of the dignity of each person (Vanderslice 1984; Morrow 1988). It takes time and patience and persistence and communication.

Under the aegis of the East Prince Women's Information Centre, several projects have been concerned with empowerment; Hurray for Moms, started from the centre, is an example of a group taking things into their own hands.

"It's all the moms getting together and talking about their feelings and things like that," explains Sally. "There are mothers at home with their kids and feel like they're alone — they can't get out."

PAL (Play and Learn), now defunct because of cessation of funding, was another project of the East Prince Women's Information Centre similar to Hurray for Moms. It was an excellent example of an accessible milieu for rural women to "get together and talk." A demonstration project that provided a program for pre-schoolers, with a teacher qualified in early childhood education, and a space for mothers apart from the children, it gave not only respite from the responsibilities of child care, but, like Hurray for Moms, helped overcome mothers' feelings of isolation and lack of worth.

Although DAWN in Prince Edward Island is a mere fledgling organization, nonetheless it is another example of women beginning to empower themselves and take control of their own lives.

As a board member of Transition House, Roberta shows awareness of the difference between doing *for* and doing *with*, consistent with the goal of empowerment, and recognizes the legitimacy of the needs and opinions of workers and users of Transition House:

> I'd like to be more aware of the human aspects of the House — rather than just the financial and political that leave the Board sort of distanced from the reality.

Facilitators

As every woman knows, participation as feminist activists has its costs (Vickers 1988). Coalitions, networking, sharing information and strategies — whether for finding free transportation, devising rituals for the relief of burnout, or planning the best way to storm Parliament — can overcome obstacles and soften the cost.

In Prince Edward Island, in addition to the support given by the Advisory Council on the Status of Women indicated in its recent report, *Diversity, Vitality and Change* (1988), and by the Secretary of State, through both the Women's Program and the Program for the Disabled, certain events have helped balance the stress, hassles and burdens of organizing for empowerment. "Making the Connections," a special weekend of celebration and workshops held a few years ago at a resort hotel after the rush of the summer, infused new energy and was a high point for women participants. Another weekend celebration, an annual highlight of the women's year, is the Women's Festival. For six years Women's Network has organized and produced this event in Charlottetown. Each year it attracts some 200 women (as well as a few men) and each year there are new faces (Gilmore 1988).

Research can make a positive contribution to feminist organizing. In this province, it has been used successfully by several groups to discover women's needs and bring these to public awareness. National associations such as CRIAW/ICREF and special research projects by other groups, both provincial and national, provide further help in building an information base and in developing research projects at the local level.

Universities also play a role. The Women's Studies Group at the University of Prince Edward Island, for example, has originated and carried out a course, "The Family of Women," now in its fifth year, which is open to all students. One of our interviewees has assessed the contribution of this course:

> With its increasing enrolment and bringing mature and younger women together, a blending of young and old, it has been a source of consciousness-raising and empowerment.

Common Ground and newsletters such as *Networking* from the Voluntary Resource Council also facilitate women's organizational activity through publicizing helpful courses, events, conferences and publications.

These are among the many co-operative efforts that encourage and strengthen the web of activity, and keep alive the will and energy that have gone into feminist organizing in the women's movement in Prince Edward Island.

Conclusion

In this chapter we have considered some aspects of women's organizational activity and illustrated some common themes with excerpts from interviews with women active in women's organizations. This glimpse of Prince Edward Island experience shows that there is no simple recipe for successful organizing.

Different timing is appropriate and necessary for women in different situations. The level of consciousness and freedom of the women themselves, as well as the current social, economic and political climate affect the success of organizational moves. Two opposite approaches point out the possible paradoxes in action: initiation from outside but then turning power over to participants so that development is from within; or initiation from within in a horizontal consensus-sharing group that later becomes institutionalized as hierarchical and provides service for its objects. These, of course, are not the only possibilities. The wise move for feminist organizing, according to the representatives of the groups we interviewed, is the flattening of any hierarchical structure and the use of a variety of structural forms and processes appropriate for the immediate project or problem to be solved.

Ad hoc groups are appropriate for some situations and accommodate the complex time patterns of women's lives. On the other hand, for organizations whose purpose requires an ongoing structure, expanding the membership provides more workers to lighten the load and share the burden, and, as well, brings in a fresh perspective. However, for open membership to succeed, a group needs a clear articulation of its philosophy and role, otherwise it may be turned away from its original vision. Even for those ad hoc groups that come together for a particular project and then disband, vigilance is necessary to withstand the storms in the political, economic, and social climate.

Today's challenge is to stretch the women's movement to include all those on the outskirts. Our selection of women's groups for this chapter is biased in favour of those groups concerned with women low on the power scale: battered wives, members of an ethnic minority, wives of fishermen, disabled women.

The question of the place of men in women's organizations seemed of minor importance to these interviewees. None were emphatic about wishing to exclude men totally, but they agree with Ursula Franklin's use of the term "women's world" to mean "the world governed by the values and principles that come out of women's experience but which includes all men and women who subscribe to these values and live accordingly" (Franklin 1984).

Now, many more women are seeking empowerment and social change: no longer do we always see the same faces at every women's meeting. There is an ever widening population participating in women's organizations. The women in the movement no longer are stars, but there is a broader sharing of activity. There are still leaders whose energy and goodwill continually fire the forward movement of women's feminist organizing. As more women possess more confidence and more skills, they are more able to become mentors and share experiences with newcomers.

The goal for the future is not new: to encourage women to think about participation beyond their homes and their kitchens, and beyond individual success in the male dominated market place. Ultimately, if the objective of being open to all is to be reached, we need also to look at the global picture and include marginalized women throughout the world. In searching for a way to think about this worldwide women's movement, I saw, first, a quilt with its many patches placed together as a whole — but a quilt isn't living and changing. Then I rejected also the idea of a web; although it does have the ability to grow and change, it suggests to me the possibility of entrapment. Finally, in agreement with Lewis Thomas (1974) when he answered this question "What is the earth most like?" by saying "It is most like a single cell," I chose the cell as simile: dynamic, able to accommodate change, unified and holistic, its components utilizing information, working symbiotically. The grand vision is not one of millions of women with unquestioned power and wealth, but a single cell, a hologram of the whole of creation.

Getting Our Act Together

The Ontario Farm Women's Movement[1]

Ella Haley

Historically, farm wives have been socialized to "take a back seat" in the farming community. While they pulled a double or triple load, they did not share equally in ownership, decision making, agricultural education or representation in farm organizations. Their domestic role was reinforced by the Women's Institute (WI), which received ongoing funding from provincial and federal governments.

Rural feminism has grown quietly in the form of mutual support and encouragement among farm wives. It has made some advances for farm women despite the conservative nature of rural communities.

The traditional contingent of farm women works to try to win rights and equal opportunities within the existing rural structures. They believe that the system is fair and that they can create change within pre-existing structures. Their strategies include lobbying the government, and encouraging women to gain agricultural knowledge and education so that they can compete for individual power and status in the rural community and even seek office. Those who succeed are viewed as role models, "representing the possibility of equal access for all women" (Adamson, Briskin & McPhail 1988, 175).

This chapter examines four rural organizations in Ontario: the Women's Institute, a long-standing rural women's organization; two of the new farm women's groups (NFWGs) — Women for the Survival of Agriculture and Concerned Farm Women; and the Ontario Federation of Agriculture, a traditionally male-dominated farm organization. Over the past fifteen years, the NFWGs have emerged as grassroots alternatives to the traditional bureaucratic structures of the WI and the Ontario Federation of Agriculture. These new groups are commendable for their efforts and insights. It is hoped that in the future they will go on to address other issues, such as ecofeminism and the inequalities faced by women farm workers.

The Women's Institute

Until 1975, most farm women in Ontario belonged to the Women's Institute, which was formed in 1897 as a rural organization for women that focused on domestic work. Strong-Boag (1986) argues that the focus on home economics had some of the same "consciousness raising and research goals of the modern women's studies programs." She contends that it made women and their work a subject for serious study. Other authors would disagree with Strong-Boag.

> Many farm women were exasperated by the nature of the programs of the WI. Mary Nicolaeff (1919) complained about the narrowness of their program: "Always suggestions about housework, knitting, and the main woman's destination: 'preparing of dainty side-dishes and salads.' Kitchen, kitchen, and again kitchen!" (Cohen 1984, 333).

Sachs (1983) and Cohen (1984) illustrate in their research how government programs in Canada and the United States reinforced women's domestic role, and excluded women from education in farming techniques. Cohen argues that government's view of farming as a male activity reflected the notion that the money-making activities outside the home were rightly the sphere of males. This patriarchal attitude explains why women's contributions to the farm enterprise have consistently been ignored in the official census. It also explains differential child-rearing practices.

> It reflects back on double standards in raising children. Boys are allowed to do 'important' work like driving a tractor. Girls are expected to help mother make something nice for dessert and to learn to do things that look after and please the male members of the household. (Canitz, 1988)

Today, the WI conducts community work, provides social outings for rural women, and cooperates with the NFWGs in a few joint ventures. Due to lobbying by women's groups, the government earmarked funds for rural childcare, and for shelters for battered women. The WI's membership of 50,000 is lower than former years, and it is having difficulty attracting younger members. Some of its members view it as being too bureaucratic, too afraid of taking a stand, and too conservative.

> Trembling, frightened by the idea that we might rock the boat, or anger somebody somewhere, (we modify the wording of our resolutions). If we continue to do this kind of thing, we deserve all the patronizing fun that is made of Institutes. We deserve the dropping membership. (Ruth Hunt, 1988)

The New Farm Women's Groups

The growth of the NFWGs is a bone of contention, and has been the subject of discussion at major meetings of the WI executive. Some members fail to understand or accept the "uppity" behaviour of the members of the NFWGs.

> Grassroots action groups and social movements usually emerge when there is a widening and unbearable gap between desirable circumstances (what ought to be) and the actual situation being experienced (what is). Social action groups, particularly, tend to spring up when this gap is thought to be unjustified and uncalled for. At such times people will get together, first informally, to discuss bother-

some conditions and issues, and later to organize and work more systematically towards solving problems. (Cebotarev & Beattie 1985, 258)

WI members who left to form the NFWGs felt frustrated dealing with its bureaucratic nature, and its failure to address the needs of today's farm women. The NFWGs are action-oriented groups whose members found the decision and policy-making process of the Women's Institute too unwieldy and slow.

Women For the Survival of Agriculture

Orientation. Women for the Survival of Agriculture (WSA) Winchester has been a forerunner for feminism in rural Canada since 1975. As a feminist organization, its focus has been to recognize the contributions of farm women owners or wives of owners, and to equalize their opportunities in agricultural education, representation, bank lending practices, and farm ownership. It further reflects feminist leanings through working to improve the socio-economic situation of farm women, supporting Eritrean women in their peace efforts, and expressing a concern for more ecological farming techniques. Its founder, Dianne Harkin, has written about the health side-effects of herbicides, and in a recent WSA newsletter, the following quotation by David Suzuki appeared.

The future of agriculture lies not with the increased use of chemicals, bio-technology and monoculture, but in taking advantage of the earth's natural genetic diversity. (*WSA Newsletter* Nov.-Dec. 1988)

This questioning of farming techniques reflects ecofeminism with its emphasis on ecological awareness (Sessions 1988). However, to speak out against the dangers of herbicides challenges accepted profit-motivated farming practices. In difficult economic times, farmers are less concerned with ecology than with simply trying "to make ends meet." The farming community has traditionally not given much attention to environment and health protection. Following the advice of experts, it has relied heavily upon the use of herbicides and pesticides, and now is defensive about the questioning of these practices.

WSA's stance on animal rights issues, however, is in contradiction with their growing concern about the use of chemicals. They are adamantly opposed to the animal welfare movement and feel that it is "fueled by emotion rather than facts" (*WSA Newsletter*, Sept.- Oct. 1988, 3). On this issue, WSA members are unable to step out of their entrepreneurial role and question issues such as the implications of the use of drugs and hormones on the quality of food for themselves and consumers. In failing to do so, they are ignoring the fact that when animals are more confined (i.e., chickens in cages), antibiotics become a necessity because of the animals' lowered resistance to infection. Negative attitudes towards animal welfare reflects a position shared by most farmers who raise animals. At commodity producers' meetings, a good deal of time is spent on dealing with the animal welfare issue, which they view as a threat that cuts into their livelihood and profits.

Organization and Action. As a grassroots group, WSA is a community-based group for farm women who farm alone or with their husbands. It focuses on collective organizing within a non-hierarchical framework, publishes a newsletter and helps farm women across Canada to form their own independent groups. At present, there are 1,000 members in various small groups across the country. The members of this informal network share similar goals, and benefit from their joint efforts to support one another. They believe in networking with other farm women (owners and wives of owners) and working in cooperation with other farm and rural organizations. They support the concept of the "family farm" and work as an interest group to educate farm families about important issues affecting the agricultural industry and their lives, and to educate consumers.

WSA's funding comes from both federal and provincial government project-based research grants. These are used to promote women's involvement in farm organizations, and to improve the socio-economic status of farm women. *What Are You Worth?* is a research report based on eastern Ontario farm women, which finally puts a dollar value on their contribution to the farm (Harkin 1986). *Cover Your Assets: A Guide to Farm Partnerships* (1987) is a guide designed to help farm women negotiate formal partnerships with their spouses.

Through lobbying efforts with other farm organizations WSA won legislative changes in capital gains tax exemptions. This means that the husband and wife can now be treated as two separate units if they have a legal partnership. It permits wives who are formal partners with their husbands to contribute to their own pension funds. In addition, WSA lobbied the Farm Credit Corporation on its discriminatory lending practices towards women. This led to the removal of many barriers for women in farming (Harkin 1986), allowing them to borrow money in their own right.

In 1980, WSA Winchester began the first of a series of national conferences, focusing on farm women's socio-economic status, the effect of financial stress on farm women, and the formation of a national farm women's network. Constructive as these conferences were, they did not address the situation of women farm labourers.[2]

The newly formed farm women's network functions like the National Action Committee on the Status of Women. Each member group remains independent, but the groups are united in working together on certain common issues.

Just as the Canadian women's movement has, until recently, ignored racial and ethnic concerns, the farm women's movement fails to adequately address the situation of women farm workers, a minority group who, as yet, have no organized voice in Ontario. They will not be represented in the farm women's networks unless they receive some assistance in organizing. As a support group for a specific class of farm women (farm owners or wives of owners), WSA members may feel that it is beyond their call of duty to address class differences among farm women.

Concerned Farm Women

Orientation. Unlike WSA, Concerned Farm Women (CFW) did not originate as a group with any feminist inclinations, but with time it moved into women's issues. It formed in the Grey and Bruce counties of Ontario in 1981 as a grassroots group reacting to the economic difficulties faced by many farm families in the area. Like WSA, it found the bureaucratic nature of the WI too cumbersome to work with. One member said,

> We felt impatience and a sense of panic. We couldn't wait for the WI resolution to pass through all the channels to get to the top. We thought we could bypass this.

The initial intent of CFW members was to "back up their man" and save the family farm. According to Giselle Ireland, "Our men were working too hard. The men's solution (to economic troubles) was to take on more and more. The women saw that the men didn't have the time (to lobby)."

CFW's focus on the family farm lacks an analysis of the structural inequalities that farm women face. Eighty-seven percent of all Canadian farms are classified as family farms. Yet, the term "family farm" is a misnomer and masks the structured inequalities of the underlying relations of production in farming (Hedley 1981). One person (usually the man) is designated by Census Canada as the "farm operator" (Smith 1987), and the vast majority of farms are owned by one person (usually the man). Yet much of the work done on family farms is by family members and hired help. In the 1981 Census, only 3 percent (8,085) of farm operators were women. In 94 percent of Canadian farms, women are listed as wives of operators (Smith 1987, 147).

CFW's focus on women's concerns emerged partly because of the feminist orientation of their grants. This strategy of pressuring farm women to conduct feminist research is not dissimilar from the government's longstanding history of pressuring the WI to focus on women's domestic role. Says one member, "It wasn't intended to be a women's group or even a women's support group ... (we took that) slant because of our funding source.

Blatant or subtle pressure from government funding sources towards a particular focus must be seriously questioned. The NFWGs are seriously underfunded and therefore vulnerable to manipulation in the quest for funding dollars.

Organization and Action. Whether it is due to the focus of the funding sources, or simply from working together, CFW became a support group for farm women. Using a participatory research method, the group documented the stress faced by 600 farm women in their area. The study showed how farm women have taken on extra roles in attempts to pay the farm bills. Many juggle three jobs: raising children, doing farm work and working off the farm to earn extra money. CFW's research reflects an overall trend for farm women in Canada. Sixty-six percent of farm women do paid work, compared with 56 percent of women in the general population (Bertin 1989, B7).

CFW packaged the results of their study into a book, *The Farmer Takes a Wife.* This was followed by *To Have and to Hold, a Guide to Property and Credit Law for Farm Families in Ontario* (Meanwell & Glover 1985).

Like many grassroots organizations, CFW's membership has suffered from serious burnout. Many of its members have gone bankrupt. It now has a residual group of members and circulates a bi-monthly newsletter.

> The urgency is not there any more. In 1981 we thought the changes would come quickly — they're still not there ... The situation is worse now. Very few people recovered in beef and pork. There's no profit for the crops, and now a drought this year. The economic base is not there for a recovery. (CFW member)

Much of the group's funding was project based, a blessing for some farm women because it provided them with jobs. However, for the unpaid volunteers, these projects were too demanding because of their role overload. "We don't physically have the same time and energy that went into those other projects" (Joy Ward, in Stewart-Kirkby 1988, 8).

Had CFW chosen a different strategy, they would have challenged the marketing practices for their livestock, and advocated a marketing board system. Many farmers in Grey and Bruce counties raise beef and pigs, and "went under" because red meat prices dropped and remained low. This made it impossible for them to financially survive high production costs and bank interest rates. A marketing board system as used by dairy and poultry farmers regulates prices and provides farmers with a more stable income structure. CFW members could have challenged individualistic farming practices and advocated cooperation between farmers in their operations. Free trade, however, has brought serious concerns about the dismantling of marketing boards for farmers.

In actual fact, farmers are a very entrepreneurial group (Giangrande 1985). In farm bankruptcy, other farmers rarely stand behind their distraught neighbours. Instead, many of them blame individual farm families for poor farming practices and eagerly expand their own farms by buying up the bankrupt ones.

The move by CFW members into women's issues was strongly influenced by the funding sources available to them. Yet, basically CFW's philosophy has been more conservative than WSA. Its members are more reluctant to state that they are feminists, and they harbour a number of gender stereotypes. WSA's members set out to improve the socio-economic status of farm women. In contrast, CFW's aim was to act as supportive wives to their men in saving the family farm. Both organizations became support groups for farm women and helped them develop lobbying and research skills. Both are supportive of one another and work together with representatives from the WI and farm organizations within the National and Ontario Farm Women's Networks.

One of CFW's members, Susan Glover (1988), has recently worked within a socio-historical framework to examine the lopsided nature of farm women's domestic work. She compares farm women's disproportionate share of domestic chores today with the situation in the early 1900s, and spells out the need for co-operation between men and women. She illustrates farm men's lack of understanding of the multiple roles that farm women juggle — on the farm, in the house and off the farm.

> You get used to having your meals on time and having your wife truck the grain to the elevator. But now the wife comes home tired and no meal is made and the house is a mess and the kids are neglected.

It causes stress on the marriage. (*WSA Newsletter,* quoting Glover, Nov.-Dec. 1988, 5)

This focus on the lack of recognition of farm women's contributions reflects a new focus for CFW. Glover's work may cause them to join WSA in re-evaluating farm women's position in the family and in the farming community.

The Role of Women in Mainstream Farm Organizations

The Ontario Federation of Agriculture (OFA) represents the majority of family farms in Ontario (20,000 members, mainly men). Bridgid Pyke, its recent President, was the first woman ever elected, and has difficulty understanding why more farm women do not work within its structure. A journalist, who moved to the farm twenty years ago when she married, she is an anomaly to many farm women. Her farm partnership between two brothers and their wives is unique in that it allows the work to be shared between more people and frees Bridgid to work on her OFA duties. Unlike many farm women, Bridgid exudes self-confidence in dealing within the constraints of a male-dominated organization. She questions the emergence of the NFWGs, and feels that women and men simply need to change their attitudes.

> There is no such thing as a woman's issue ... pensions, child care are men's and women's issues ... Women have to get over the hurdle. They have to overcome the power and ego of the [male] farmer. They need a mature enough partner. The men must see that by holding others back, they hold themselves back .... (He) has to stop thinking that the way the farm runs adds up on his scorecard ... Women have to be true to themselves and be assured of their worth. (Interview)

Many people share this belief in individualism — in an individual's ability to change oneself. In assuming that women share an equality of opportunity, they fail to acknowledge the structural inequalities of power, privilege and opportunity that many farm women face. This philosophy implies that if women fail to change their circumstances, it is their own fault.

Many feminists would challenge this belief in individualism and argue that farm women's ability to control their lives is limited by the structure and relations of power within the farm family, the farming community, and Canadian society in general. At first glance, it might appear that farm women belong to one class. Feminists would also illustrate how class, race and sexual orientation differences among farm women enhance or limit their life opportunities. For example, within the farming community, women face structural obstacles as immigrant labourers with no safety regulations, as single women farming on their own and confronting stereotyped attitudes about women's abilities, and as farm wives juggling several roles.

The notion that farm women can transform themselves shifts attention away from the patriarchical and capitalist structures and in doing so, reinforces them. The fact that many farm women are reluctant to speak at public meetings demonstrates the extent to which they have internalized their feelings of powerlessness.

> [Farm organizations] appear to be structured under an "old boys club" mentality ... [But] the fault also lies with many women and their husbands. I have been to meetings regarding farm issues and have seen women that were very reluctant to even come because they had entered a domain reserved for men. They lacked the courage to express their own opinions. (Canitz 1988)

Farm women have traditionally played a passive role with respect to decision-making on farm issues. At meetings, farm women lack

> the courage to express their own opinion. They would look at their husbands to see what they (the women) were expected to be thinking. They vote the same as he does. A neighbour, brother, etc. can vote differently from a farmer, but if his wife does —

society notices and assumes she has done wrong!
(Canitz 1988)

Pyke has difficulty understanding why farm women want
their own organizations. However, she does suggest that perhaps "they don't feel OFA will listen, or perhaps they're intimidated." Other farm women leaders point out the need for
women to work within their own organizations where they
can safely develop their own viewpoints.

> Farm women still feel overpowered by the presence
> of men in meetings, and first need to discover their
> own abilities before they can function in an organi-
> zation for both men and women. (Laura Heuser
> (WSA), in Bongers 1986, 18)

Patriarchy On The Farm

The close personal relationships within farm families has
meant that whatever antagonisms and contradictions arise in
the farmwork pattern are unlikely to be acknowledged as
stemming from women's unequal position in the family farm.
They are more likely to be understood as part of the ordinary
business of getting along in a marriage (Cohen 1984). While
the NFWGs recognize men's disproportionate power, they
have not analyzed this in any depth.

> The men write the cheques as they see fit. The
> women don't assert themselves ... While the
> women handle a lot of the funds for the farm, there's
> no free money for them to do with as they wish.
> (Middleton 1988)

> Historically, males not only owned the means of
> production (farm, machinery, livestock, crops), but
> also decided where capital expenditures would be
> made. The competing demands on women's time
> along with the tendency of farm market activities to
> be dominated by males reinforced the inclination of
> investment decisions to be made in favour of those
> areas where men worked. (Cohen 1984, 334)

The new Ontario NDP majority government is exemplary in its focus on gender equality. It may bring important advancements for farm women.

Government aid traditionally was given to farm men's organizations and education programs were aimed at improving men's agricultural skills (Cohen 1984). This increased the productivity gap between men and women and resulted in male domination in farming.

In the past, the provincial and federal governments provide core funding and, until recently, refused to do the same for the action-oriented NFWGs. Limited to funds based on projects, members of the NFWGs burn out as they juggled their obligations in their own lives and in group activities. The government, however, is being influenced by the farm women's movement, albeit in a token manner. In August 1988, the federal government made available a meagre amount of monies to farm organizations, and to rural and farm women's groups, under its Farm Women's Advancement Program.[3] These monies only equate to approximately $1,000 per group per year over a five-year period. Another change for the NFWGs was the expiry of the government's funding arrangement with the WI in March, 1990. Now, the WI will supposedly compete with the NFWGs for core funding.

The Institute's connection and dependency on government funding helped to explain why its membership was afraid of "rocking the boat." With the government (which historically has fostered women's domestic role), editing WI newletters, the WI's control over its communications was questionable. Its members were limited in the degree that they could question government practices, and brainstorm over alternative solutions. Thus, it is understandable that the NFWGs have operated as grassroots organizations in attempting to lobby for changes, and maintained their autonomy from the WI.

Farm Women's Networks

A solution to the financial worries of the NFWGs may be found in the Ontario Farm Women's Network (OFWN), which hopes to have enough political clout to pursue "no strings attached" funding from the Ontario Ministry of Agriculture and Food (OMAF). "If the network is strong, there's hope.

They (farm women) will work through their politicians to get what they want from OMAF," says a representative from the Department of the Secretary of State.

The OFWN originated in March, 1989, and includes WSA, CFW, 12 other farm women's groups, and other rural organizations which wish to be affiliates. Its present focus is on the quality of life for Ontario farm women (owners and spouses), for example, childcare in a rural setting, education for farm women, and lobbying to change gender inequalities in agricultural policy.

In November 1989, the National Canadian Farm Women's Network was formed. This includes all of the provinces except Quebec, Manitoba and Alberta. Quebec's membership is particularily sought in the future, because the other provinces hope to learn from its organizations and advancements for farm women (Feddema 1989).

Summary and Future Directions

Given the structures of the WI and OFA, farm women had little option but to organize their own grassroots groups in order to act on their concerns. Both WSA and CFW represent the vested interests of farm women who own, co-own or are married to farm owners.

Due to different circumstances, WSA and CFW emerged as NFWGs with different orientations: WSA to improve the socio-economic status of farm women, and CFW to simply help the family farm survive. Without the urgency of financial insolvency, WSA members had more time and energy to address inequities within a male-dominated farming system. CFW began examining women's issues under the guiding influence of funding sources. Both groups have worked together with the WI on issues of joint concern. Both are members of the newly formed Canadian and Ontario Farm Women's Networks.

The Ontario NFWGs are making changes, but they have a good deal to learn from other groups, particularly Quebec and Prairie farm women's organizations. The networks will facilitate a sharing of ideas on the analysis of farm women's concerns, and successful strategies to facilitate change.

Were the farm women's movement to be truly representative it would include farm women labourers in both the Canadian and provincial farm women's networks. At present there is no liaison with this minority group due to their transient nature and lack of organization. Their concerns are very different from those of the NFWGs' members.

Most farm women labourers are immigrants from various ethnic minorities. Often they bring their children to the field with them, exposing them to safety hazards (machinery, animals, herbicides, pesticides, ponds). In fact, between 1981 and 1984, 14 percent of all farm associated deaths in Ontario were of children.

If farm women labourers lobby for farm health and safety standards or better labour laws, they will be challenging the vested interests of members of the NFWGs.

At present farm work is excluded totally or partially from labour legislation regarding hours of work, overtime, vacation pay and safety standards. Ontario, largely due to farm owners' influence, has no health or safety legislation to protect farm employees (Lee 1987). This minority group may have to band together with their male counterparts in order to have some political clout. Just as structural barriers inhibit women's participation in the OFA, similar obstacles in the farm women's movement stifle women's voices. Affirmative action for this minority group within the provincial and national farm women's network is recommended.

Another area that the farm women's movement must address is ecofeminism. Canadian farmers have relied upon agricultural "experts" (government and business) to guide them in their farming practices. These have not necessarily been ecological, but farm women (and their husbands) trusted the "experts" and have not spoken out publicly against them. The current focus on environmental concerns, and the new Ontario Minister of Agriculture's commitments to ecological farming, may lead farm women to reconsider farming practices such as animal confinement, the use of hormones and antibiotics, and the use of biocides. This will challenge many farm women who do not as yet believe in or support sustainable agriculture techniques.

Finding our Voices

Reflections on Immigrant Women's Organizing[1]

Roxana Ng

The International Women's Year, launched in 1975, gave women an official forum to speak out about their oppression and to demand equality in Canada. For women — mainly white middle-class women — years of organizing and agitation had finally resulted in international recognition of their struggle to break the silence surrounding their oppression. Their gains, however, were not automatically extended to their less privileged sisters. Aboriginal women, disabled women, and immigrant women continued to bear the burden of unequal access to the labour market, to child care, to education, and to social services which most Canadians could take for granted.

This did not mean that other women, including immigrant women, were passive victims of a purportedly democratic system which denied certain groups of people their basic rights. Following the momentum gained by the women's movement, immigrant women, too, began to make their needs and concerns known. Since 1975 they have emerged from a silent and neglected minority to a vocal and visible pressure group in Canadian social and political life. In addition to the myriad local groups which have mushroomed to address the diverse needs of immigrant women, most provinces now have at least one provincial network or association representing the collective voice of the local organizations. As well, a national association, National Organization of Immigrant and Visible Minority Women of Canada (NOIVMWC), was formed in 1986 to coordinate immigrant women's organizing efforts and voice their concerns at the national level.

What were the forces which shaped the immigrant women's movement? How did the organizing efforts at the national and provincial levels influence those in local communities, and vice versa? What is the relationship between the growing literature and scholarship on immigrant women and local organizing attempts? These are some of the questions I explore here with reference to the organizing efforts of women in British Columbia and New Brunswick.

This chapter draws on my own involvement in the immigrant women's movement, primarily in these two provinces. In the case of New Brunswick, I also make use of the written records and oral histories by a group of immigrant women in Fredericton, whom I interviewed in the summer of 1988 as a way of documenting the group's history. However, the account here is very much a personal reflection on the rise and development of the immigrant women's movement in terms of the above questions. I make no claim to speak for the women with whom I have worked, or to provide a comprehensive picture of immigrant women's organizing in the two provinces I describe. As yet, we do not have a complete history of immigrant women's organizing on a provincial and national basis.[2]

Much of the work of documenting the different organizing experiences remains to be done.

Beginning in British Columbia

I began working in the immigrant women's movement in Vancouver in the mid-seventies, when the term "immigrant women" was not part of the everyday vocabulary of Canadians. I was working as a community worker in Chinatown in 1976, doing community research and providing direct services to non-English speaking immigrants in an organization funded by a Health and Welfare demonstration grant. The organization was set up to document and demonstrate the needs of specialized services to Chinese immigrants, who could not make use of the regular service delivery system because of language and cultural barriers. The project involved establishing a storefront office to service a variety of needs (such as filling out forms and counselling); networking with and conducting outreach to schools, other immigrant service organizations and government bureaucracies; and documenting the different needs and services required by the Chinese community in Vancouver. This project was carried out during a period when the state was attempting to address the rediscovery of poverty in the western world, including Canada, and to reintegrate dissident voices from the student movement and other minority groups (eg. aboriginal people, women, immigrant) which were becoming increasingly strident.[3]

I joined this three-year demonstration project entitled, "The Chinese Connection," during the last year of its operation. As a community worker and researcher, I came to have first-hand experience in the problems and concerns of working-class immigrants from Chinese and other ethnic backgrounds.

Although I did not consciously identify myself as a feminist at that time, it did not take me long to realize that women's experience of the settlement process is different from that of men's. For example, women are the ones who stay home to look after the children, and therefore feel more isolated; they are the victims of domestic violence. However, these experiences did not appear in the readings on immigration and ethnicity. Theories of ethnic communities and immigrant settlement and adaptation were developed from the perspective of community leaders, who are mostly men. At best, women's experiences were subsumed under those of men's; at worst, their voices were repressed and silenced.[4]

The lack of acknowledgement of immigrant women's experiences, and, by extension, my experience as a community worker dealing with their everyday problems in the Chinese community, made me feel extremely isolated in my work setting. It was partially for this reason that I joined with other women at the Women's Research Centre in Vancouver to explore and analyze the problems of immigrant women in Canada, and to attempt to find a voice for us to talk about our experiences working with immigrant women.[5]

Putting this early organizing effort into context, I should point out that "immigrant women" as a group did not have the clout and legitimacy we have today. While the Women's Research Centre was funded by the Secretary of State Women's Program, immigrant women were not considered a target group, and therefore our activities around immigrant women's issues were mostly conducted by volunteer time and labour; there was minimal state funding of any kind for work concerning immigrant women. Meanwhile, there was pressure from funding programs, such as the Secretary of State, for community groups to design programs for "multicultural women"[6] to fit into the mandate of various government departments, notably the Secretary of State, to implement multiculturalism as state policy. Today, the term "immigrant women" is incorporated into the administrative vernacular of the state, and is thus viewed by many women of colour as a state-owned category. When we began taking up immigrant women's concerns in the mid-seventies, however, it was a category used by immigrant women to resist the state's attempt to make us into "multicultural women." The controversy over the term was very much part of the organizing experience of women in British Columbia in this earlier period.

This, then, was my entry to immigrant women's organizing, which was in its infancy in the mid-seventies in British Columbia. I emphasize that the above account is my recollection of the beginning of the movement in one province. I cannot, and do not, claim to speak for others who have participated in these early efforts. Later, as I travelled across the country to study and to work in Ontario, Saskatchewan, and New Brunswick, it was this earlier experience that became known to other immigrant women and that brought me into contact with them. Subsequently, as I continue to work with immigrant women, and to develop "immigrant women" as a field of scholarly inquiry, they come to know me through my writings.

Working in New Brunswick. My work with immigrant women in New Brunswick evolved naturally from my earlier activities in B.C. When I was offered and accepted a teaching position at the University of New Brunswick, Women Working with Immigrant Women (WWIW) contacted me even before I before I moved there. Many group members already knew of my work, and they invited me to join the group and work with them. I was nominated and elected to the board of directors in February, 1987, and have been working closely with the group ever since.

Although WWIW is a relatively new group, its members became visible in provincial and national social and political life very quickly. When I joined, two members were the provincial representatives of NOIVMWC, and a third was its elected president. In addition, two of these same people sat on various advisory committees of the provincial government, representing the voices of immigrant women at the provincial level. As can be seen, within the short life of the group, its resources were already drained and pulled to the provincial and national levels. There was an acute need to recruit new members to sustain the daily work of the organization.

When I joined the board of WWIW, there were five other new board members. All of us were overwhelmed by the diverse activities the group was carrying out with only a part-time coordinator, who was in charge of direct services to new immigrants and refugees, funded by the federal Department of Employment and Immigration. All other activities were carried out by volunteers. Another difficulty concerned our lack of understanding of the goals and history of the group. As the older members, who founded the group, moved away from its immediate daily operation, there was a real danger that its history would be lost forever.

It was under these circumstances that I initiated a discussion with group members, in the winter of 1987, to document its history. This was supported enthusiastically by the active members. In the summer of 1988, with the help of Jennifer Thompson and funds from the Challenge '88 employment program, I began to interview the founding members and compile the records of the group.[7] It is interesting to note that the group members I interviewed did not make a direct link between their effort and immigrant women's organizing across the country. However, in reviewing its history through oral accounts and documents, it is clear that the group in some sense owes its beginning to the momentum gathered nationally.

Women Working with Immigrant Women in New Brunswick

In 1981, a national conference on immigrant women was held in Toronto.[8] It was originally planned by the federal government for bureaucrats and "experts" to discuss the "problems" of immigrant women; it was not intended for immigrant women themselves. However, as soon as the news about the event reached the immigrant women's community, a wide protest was mounted by immigrant women against their exclusion. Eventually, representatives were invited from each province, and immigrant women from the community in Toronto were allowed to attend the conference. In some ways it can be said that the conference was "captured" by immigrant women, and out of the conference, a follow-up committee was set up to plan another conference for immigrant women in two years' time.[9] After the conference, members of the follow-up committee began to make contacts across the country. It was out of this effort that the women in Fredericton, New Brunswick were brought together initially.

In order to reach out to immigrant women beyond central Canada, the follow-up committee decided to hold a meeting in the Maritimes — in Moncton, in Fall 1983. The meeting's agenda included direct contact with local immigrant women's groups. Since there was no such women's group in New Brunswick, the coordinator of the Multicultural Association of Fredericton (MCAF) undertook to bring together women within the association, and her acquaintances from different ethno-cultural backgrounds, to see if they would be interested in meeting the follow-up committee. Little did this group of eight women, drawn together by coincidence at that time, realize that they would work together very closely for the next few years.

The women who attended the Moncton meeting originated from a very broad geographic base, from different parts of Asia, the Middle East, South America, and Africa. They came to Fredericton for a variety of reasons: as students, as wives of immigrants, and as their husbands obtained paid employment in Fredericton. As well, there were two Canadian-born "white" women among them, one of whom was the MCAF coordinator. What is common among this group of women is that they are highly educated: many of them have graduate degrees. But regardless of their ethnic, religious, and cultural backgrounds, they have all suffered from isolation as women; some have experienced various forms of discrimination as members of visible minority and immigrant groups in Fredericton society. Many of them were active in helping Vietnamese and other refugees to resettle in the area during the refugee crisis in 1978-79. Thus, while they are middle-class women, they all have some experience of what it means to be a newcomer, and are empathetic about the situation of their less privileged sisters.

This group of women came together in the summer of 1983 to discuss their attendance at the Moncton meeting. They still express a sense of wonderment and excitement about this initial gathering. Most of them did not know each other. They didn't know whether they had anything in common. While the meeting with the follow-up committee itself did not leave an impression on these women, the journey to Moncton gave them an opportunity to discover the mutual sense of isolation and loneliness they experienced. They felt keenly the need to continue to talk to each other, to obtain information on immigrant women in other parts of Canada, and to do something on behalf of immigrant women in New Brunswick. The following reminiscence from one member echoed the sentiment of the group:

> The best thing is to ... finally find a niche. For myself, this is where I fit completely ... Because in a [other] women's group, I was always a person from a different culture ... This is the only women's group where my experience totally fits, [is] totally relevant, and I don't have to look at it from another point of view at all.
>
> It was very empowering to find other strong women that were there in the group ... Every woman has done it (peer counselling and support) for other immigrant women ... It's very difficult to find similar women within the mainstream feminist movement.

As early as January, 1984, members began drawing up a constitution, and a committee structure was developed to divide up the multiplicity of activities that group members wanted to carry out.[10] Membership criteria were debated. Group members felt strongly against excluding non-immigrants from working on immigrant women's issues; they felt that it was members' agreement to a set of common goals that was important. As well, it was decided that board membership should not be based on ethno-cultural representation; rather, it should be on the basis of the member's willingness to play an advocacy role for immigrant women. In short, the group was clear about its political objective as an advocacy and lobbying group; members were explicit that it was not a "song and dance" group.

The group became very active in a short period of time. The members wrote to government departments and immigrant women's organizations across the country requesting information on research and other materials. As soon as they were familiar with the issues concerning immigrant women, they monitored government policies closely and wrote letters of recommendation and protest in response to government directives and policies. They wrote to different provincial departments complaining about the lack of representation of immigrant women's perspective in the policy development apparatus. In other words, they quickly made themselves into a visible pressure group in the political landscape of New Brunswick.

While the group had some contact with the national follow-up committee during this formative stage, national organizing efforts had little direct influence on the group. Members were concerned with getting the group off the ground at the local level, and not on networking with other immigrant women's groups elsewhere. In fact, some members expressed feeling alone in their organizing effort, as they struggled to consolidate the group and expand group membership. To make themselves known locally, much energy was spent in introducing themselves to other groups, including other women's groups, and multicultural and human rights associations in the province. As well, plans were developed to hold a mini-workshop to raise the awareness of Frederictonians about immigrant women's issues. Indeed, a one-day workshop was held on April 28, 1984, which successfully put WWIW in the limelight.

As the group consolidated itself and gained visibility, new issues emerged. Some members expressed the need to establish specialized services, which were unavailable in the formal service delivery system, for immigrant women and their families. Others felt that the group should lobby the government to provide these services, rather than providing them through the group. This tension between service provision and lobbying persists to the present time, as group members attempt to define a focus for organizing within the constraints of limited energy and resources.

As the group gained credibility, it was also sought after by different funding programs, such as the Secretary of State and Employment and Immigration Canada (EIC). By this time, "immigrant women" have become a target group in the funding priority of different levels of the government, especially federally. Since WWIW is the only community organization which directly takes up the concerns of immigrant women, it is courted by funding programs in the process of implementing their mandate.

However, the process of seeking state funding has its drawbacks. To begin with, it takes a lot of work. Most members were not familiar with writing applications, which had to be written in a particular format and language. Frequently, in the process of framing the work that group members wish to carry out, the work itself is reframed according to government priorities, rather than the priorities of the group. Furthermore, the process of applying for government funds put WWIW in a competitive relationship with other community groups, notably MCAF, whose major operating budget also comes from EIC and the Secretary of State.[11]

Most importantly, the process of seeking state funding to provide services for immigrant women has created division and tension within the group. One member sums up this dilemma in the following way:

> When we got into action ... that was the same time
> when we got government funding ... That's when

we were fragmented ... First of all, we became very short term, rather than (having a) longer term outlook. We started focusing on ... for example, something like the conference. Everything was about the conference, and all our energy was about the conference ... After that, it was an immediate transformation: now, what about other funding, and what about the short-term projects. For me, that was a problem ... That's why we keep on coming back: we have to have a long-term plan ... There is nothing wrong with having a short-term plan, so long as it fits the overall (goal) ... Perhaps if we look back it's taking us to this thing, but ... if it does it's by chance, not by design.

Although the history of the New Brunswick group is unique, many of the problems it encountered are common to immigrant women's groups in other parts of Canada. The problem of state funding, organizational structure, lack of resources and burn-out are among the recurring issues which confront WWIW and most other immigrant women's organizations. Based on my own participation in and observation of the immigrant women's movement, I would like to conclude by reflecting on the processes which shape immigrant women's organizing efforts.

Reflections

The immigrant women's movement, like other social movements, is continually being transformed in response to changing social, political and economic realities. Free trade is changing many aspects of immigrant women's lives, which will in turn change and reshape the contours of our struggles. On a day-to-day level, changing government priorities and their impact on funding programs will create new possibilities and crises within immigrant women's groups and within the movement. So, what kinds of observations can I make at this point?

From the brief history above, it is clear that immigrant women's organizing must be situated in the context of women's struggles generally in Canada and worldwide. Although most immigrant women did not benefit directly from the second wave of the women's movement, it did make visible the conditions of women's oppression and created a climate which facilitated and legitimized the struggle of immigrant women. This was certainly our experience in British Columbia as we sought to make our voices heard in that province. In general, the women's movement in B.C. was supportive of the efforts made by immigrant women to bring their issues to the attention of the women's movement and to various levels of the state. However, the results of these earlier efforts were slow to bear fruit. When I left B.C. in the fall of 1978, immigrant women's organizing had not attained the clout and autonomy it had in Ontario; much of the work was done by community workers, and was tied to the social service delivery system.

By the eighties, the immigrant women's movement had created its own voice through the formation of provincial and national organizations. In B.C., as well as Ontario, Saskatchewan, Manitoba and Alberta, for example, provincial networks on immigrant and visible minority women were formed to give women a voice independent of service-oriented community groups. Thus, we see that although the women in New Brunswick did not receive direct help from other immigrant women's groups, their organizing was prompted by the momentum gathered by immigrant women's organizing elsewhere in Canada, notably by the follow-up committee from the 1981 conference.

However, the relationship between local, provincial and national organizing is not a simple one. Whereas some provinces have provincial networks which act as a support for local groups, in other provinces local group formation has taken place and has thrived without provincial coordination. As the national organization consolidates itself, there is increasing tension among the national, provincial and local groups with regard to communication, leadership, and allocation of resources, especially human resources. As I mentioned earlier, while national momentum had enabled the local Fredericton group to establish itself rather quickly, its members are also being recruited to provincial and national organizing simultaneously, leaving the local group short of woman power to carry out the daily work of the organization. In provinces where there is a strong provincial network, the three tiers of the organization experience tension about the appropriate mechanisms of communication.

In understanding the political context of immigrant women's organizing, it is important to see that the state has played, and continues to play, a major role in mediating these organizing attempts at the local, provincial and national levels. One notable feature of the immigrant women's movement is its increasing dependence on government funding as groups at various levels struggle to establish themselves. In local groups, there is a tendency to move from lobbying and advocacy work to the provision of services funded through various state programs (such as Immigrant Settlement and Adaptation Program [ISAP] in the case of WWIW). At the provincial and national levels, initiatives launched by immigrant women are closely monitored by state officials, notably from the Secretary of State which provides the bulk of funding for organizations at these two levels. The need to develop an autonomous movement and dependence on state funding are among the many contradictions which are hotly debated within the immigrant women's movement presently.[12]

In particular, the federal government had played a central role in encouraging and facilitating the establishment of a national body through organizing the two national conferences in 1981 and 1986 and through funding. It is clear to me that as immigrant women become a visible interest group, the state is attempting to incorporate them into the electoral process: immigrant women can now be counted upon as a political constituency within the formal political apparatus. While a national body enables immigrant and visible minority women to have a united voice in lobbying government, it also provides a vehicle through which politicians and government departments can consult with this particular constituency without having to respond to the myriad grassroots groups directly. By channelling much of the Secretary of State funding to the national group, the state has also created competition among all immigrant women's groups. It is crucially important for activists to be aware of the contradictory dynamics of our organizing efforts, and how the state mediates these efforts.

Finally, I want to reflect on the burgeoning literature and scholarship on immigrant women and their relationship to immigrant women's organizing. Thirteen years ago, when I entered this field in B.C., we could count the number of works on immigrant women, mostly unpublished, on one hand. The situation has changed dramatically. Today, in addition to studies commissioned by government and pseudo-government departments, there are academic and community studies which reflect the diverse experiences and perspectives of immigrant women. Many of these latter studies and writings treat immigrant women as active agents, rather than as objects.[13]

The relationship between this growing body of literature and immigrant women's organizing is dynamic. While many of the earlier works were prompted by women's organizing experience, once published, they become analytical tools which women in the community make use of in their organizing efforts. As the experience in New Brunswick suggests, print materials serve to link different kinds of organizing activities to local efforts, frequently carried out in isolation; they give women working in isolated areas a sense that there is a larger movement, and that they are not completely alone in their work.

Meanwhile, as the study of "immigrant women" becomes an acceptable field of scholarly enterprise, we face the danger of being transformed into research objects. For example, some researchers are now incorporating female immigrants into their studies, as another "variable," rather than real living individuals. Frequently, the results of these studies tell us little about the needs and experiences of immigrant women. This is another contradiction which confronts the immigrant women's movement as it gains visibility and credibility.

In many ways, this chapter is a work in progress, which doesn't lend itself to a conclusion. We cannot really pinpoint the beginning of the immigrant women's movement; nor is it possible to conjecture what the end would look like. As I write the final words of this chapter, immigrant women are developing new strategies for organizing. They are united and divided by ongoing and emerging social forces which continue to fragment and homogenize the reality of all Canadians. As I reflect on the movement, I am at the same time caught up in its changing contours myself, both as an activist and as an intellectual reflecting on it. It is appropriate to end by emphasizing the struggle continues.

11

"You Can't Change the Indian Act?"

Shirley Bear with the
Tobique Women's Group

In Canada, the Indian Act is federal legislation which governs the day to day lives of more than 350,000 aboriginal people of whom there are approximately 200,000 residing on "Indian Reserves." The Indian Act, legislated in 1869, explicitly defines Canada's original inhabitants, not by blood or familial association, but by marriage. Until 1985, "Indian status" was determined by a patrilineal system; that is, by a person's relationship to " ... a male person who is a direct descendant in the male line of a male person ... " When a woman born of "Indian Status" married a non-status man, even a non-status Native or Métis man, she lost her original status and was never able to regain it even if she was divorced or widowed. Along with losing her status, a woman lost her band membership, her property, inheritance, burial, medical, educational and voting rights on the reserve. However, when a non-status female married a status male, "Indian status" was conferred upon her.

A section of the offending pre-1985 Indian Act reads:

Persons not entitled to be registered

12 (1) The following persons are not entitled to be registered, namely:

(b) a woman who married a person who is not an
Indian, unless that woman is subsequently the wife
or widow of a person described in section 11.

In June 1985, the Canadian Parliament passed Bill C-31,
ending more than 100 years of legislated sexual discrimination
against Native Indian women. The passage of legislation to
amend the Indian Act marked the culmination of a long campaign by Native Women to regain their full Indian status,
rights and identity. This chapter is the story of an extraordi-
nary group of women from Tobique Reserve in New Brunswick who have been in the forefront of that struggle.

These women are uniquely diverse, ideologically, psychol-
ogically and functionally. This is a fairly small group of individuals who came together through their awareness of the
injustices toward women (in particular, aboriginal women) in
Canada. *Enough is Enough: Aboriginal Women Speak Out* (1987),
compiled and introduced by Janet Silman of Winnipeg, chro-
nicles via a series of personal interviews the events that led up
to the now controversial Bill C-31.

My involvement with the Tobique Women's Group started
with my activities on the Big Cove Reserve involving the unjust treatment of single mothers and housing. In late 1980,
members of the Tobique Women's Group invited me to participate in a meeting of aboriginal women interested in establishing a political body that would represent the aboriginal
women of New Brunswick. A provincial conference at Fredericton created a reorganized Native Women's Council, which
remained a daughter organization of the National Native Indian Women's Association of Canada. The women, whose
stories are told in *Enough is Enough*, grew up on the Tobique
Reserve, a community located between the St. John and Tobique rivers in New Brunswick. The community is better
known to its residents as Negoot Gook.

In this chapter I wish to share with the reader my perceptions of who we are and how we developed into "political
activists" as we were later known. This will be done in conjunction with excerpts from *Enough is Enough: Aboriginal
Women Speak Out*.

Activism, social or political, starts when one understands that her deprivation of power stems from an injustice toward her. This growing awareness may take many years to develop, as it did for a small group of women from the Tobique Indian Reserve (Negoot Gook).

Early Recollections

Ida Paul is the eldest of the women featured in Enough is Enough. Her earliest memories recount:

> My father was working in the woods where the men would be gone for two or three months in the winter trapping for furs. When my mother died, they couldn't reach him, and when he got back she was already buried. I was four and my sister Lilly was two. Later my father came back and gave me away to an Indian man and his French wife in Edmundston and Lilly went to a family in Old Town, Maine. We couldn't go to school in the winter time — no shoes. When I was fourteen my grandmother said to me, "Now that you are fourteen, you have to go out and earn your own living." I'd go from one place to another, staying with different people — for a while here, for a while there. I stayed with Madeline for a time, but her husband would say, "I've got kids of my own to feed. I can't afford to keep you." He went down to McPhail's store (McPhail was the Indian agent and owned the store) and asked him for some money for my keep, but McPhail refused, saying, "No, she's got a father. He has to look after her." I met Frank about that time and married him when I was seventeen.

Lilly Harris, Ida Paul's sister, also remembers the hard times as a child without a home. Lilly, unlike her sister, became actively political with the women of the Tobique. Lilly recalls:

> My mother died when I was two so I stayed with my grandmother and shifted around, sometimes with my older sisters. I went to school till about the fourth

grade, but couldn't go to school in winter time — no shoes. One day my girl friend's father left the mother and the children. The mother got some help from the Indian agent, so that my little friend got a pair of rubber boots. She told me to go down and ask the Indian agent. She said, "He gave me a pair so I can go to school. You go down and ask him." I went down early in the morning and sat there. I sat there all day while he was seeing everybody else. I asked him, "I can't go to school. I need a pair of rubbers," and he said, "You've got a father. Let him buy you shoes." So after all that the Indian agent wouldn't give me no shoes. When I was fourteen I left. It was especially hard for orphaned children and for women who didn't have husbands.

Eva (Gookum) Saulis — Gookum, meaning aunt, is the name she's known by in the whole community — grew up in what she calls good old times. Gookum's mother and father had a small farm on the Tobique Reserve. Gookum recalls:

I had nine brothers in all; I was the only girl. The old times were good for my mother, good for us too. By the time I was born, everybody was Roman Catholic. There must have been Indian celebration days and stories of course, but the priests were so against anything traditional, I think they tried to break all those traditions. When people say, "The missionaries christianized the Indians," that means that they tried to take their language, their traditions, their legends, everything. When the missionaries came they told us to bow our heads and pray. When we looked up, our land was gone.

Mavis Goeres grew up on the Tobique Reserve in the 1930s and 1940s and she remembers:

At a very early age my brother quit school and went out working in the woods with my father. They'd be gone all winter long. I don't remember our family ever having a hard time. We had a lot of fun growing up here. We made our own fun and there wasn't any drinking or drugs involved. When I was fifteen years old, I went away to pick potatoes. I was in the eleventh grade and I met a man and got married.

Juanita Perley was the first woman to actively challenge the Reserve administration by taking over a public building. Juanita recalls some early memories and impressions:

The reserve was a really beautiful place to live, for children growing up especially. When people went shopping, they never got money to buy the groceries; the Indian agent would write up a purchase order at his own store — McPhail's store. They'd be making fun of the Indian people that came in — they called us "gimmes" — like "gimme this," "gimme that." I always resented the way the white people treated us and even today resent it — I don't like them one bit, and I don't care if that is printed in the book either!

Glenna Perley is considered by the Tobique Women's Group to be their strength and sustaining courage and is also very respected within the larger community. Her mother died when she was quite young and she recalls living with her grandmother:

When I was living with my grandmother, she would talk to me a lot about religion — but, even though she was a good Catholic, it was her Indian religion she would talk about. Without the ways my grandmother taught me, maybe I would have turned to drinking, but I know I'm strong and that's why, I guess.

Caroline Ennis has devoted a large portion of her time since 1977 to right the unjust attitudes and practices toward women, in particular toward aboriginal women in Canada. When Glenna asked her to arrange media coverage of the first housing

protest on the Tobique Reserve, Caroline's first recollections
are about injustices toward her mother:

> I don't remember much about my father but I know
> my mother left him because he used to drink and
> beat her up. Tobique was a nice place for kids to
> grow up in. You made your own fun. I didn't feel
> poor because everybody else around here was poor
> too.

In 1977, Sandra Lovelace-Sappier, as a woman who had lost
her Indian status through the discriminatory clause, 12 (1)(b),
of the Indian Act, agreed to take her case to the United Nations
Human Rights Committee. Of her early life Sandra remembers:

> We were really poor because my mom brought us
> four girls up by herself. At first we went to school
> on the reserve. The nuns taught us and we couldn't
> talk Indian. They used to tell us we were dirty. They
> made us ashamed we were Indians. After grade six
> we went to school down town and there was a lot of
> "Go back where you came from." The white kids
> would make fun of us, put us down because we
> were Indians, so I quit school about grade eight. I
> figured if this is what the world is like, I don't want
> to be around white people. I left home at about
> seventeen, went with a bunch of girls to work at a
> potato factory in Maine.

Karen Perley, Sandra's sister, is a committed person in community activities. Karen recalls:

> I grew up without my father being around. In this
> little school on the reserve, the nuns used to show
> preference to the light-skinned kids. I was really re-
> ligious and I used to pray every morning, every
> night and sometimes in the afternoon. I would pray
> that I would wake up the next morning and have

blue eyes. In 1966, when Carl and I left for California,
I was fifteen.

A child of the sixties, during the "hippie" movement, Bet-te
Paul is a single mother of two, by choice. Her commitment to
the aboriginal people is definitely radical by any standards.
She doesn't recall much about her early life on the reserve.

Joyce (YC) Sappier, Bet-te's mother, grew up with her
grandmother and was one of the original occupiers of the
public buildings at the Tobique Reserve in 1977.

Cheryl Bear is the youngest member of the Tobique
Women's Group but a seasoned woman activist. Cheryl has a
strong sense of her rights as a person. She has lived through
very difficult relationships. She says of her early life:

> I enjoyed growing up on the reserve — I had a good
> childhood. I was raised by my grandparents. I was
> spoiled, I guess, to put it bluntly. I quit school in
> grade eight. I regret quitting school almost every day
> now — got married when I was fifteen.

My early memories on the Tobique Reserve include the
freedom of movement we had. Children spent much time in
creative play without the worries of physical harm. Being a
typically dark-skinned person, I also recall the different treatment I received from our grade school teachers, the nuns.
Growing up, we all knew that we were different from the time
we started school. Some of us were painfully aware that the
difference was also something to be ashamed of. We didn't
realize that this was in violation of our rights, or that it was
wrong for the religious who were our teachers to exercise these
types of practices and attitudes. We didn't know what it was
called; we just knew that it didn't feel good.

The women grew up experiencing different levels of consciousness, but each one was starting to internalize and intel-
lectualize the various forms of injustices that they were either
experiencing or living. From as early as 1950, some women
were returning to their original home communities only to
realize for the first time that they did not belong. We may have
been told previously that we were no longer Indian but that

had no impact on us until our return. I returned in 1960 after a marriage breakup and my father said that they could not afford to feed me and my two children because we were not Indian or even belonged in Tobique. Because there was no employment on the reserve we were forced to move out.

The Law is the Law

The attitudes at the time that the Tobique women's group came together in the early 1970s reflected the subordination of the aboriginal people. The law was the law, i.e., the Indian Act was considered to be the final arbiter of all matters among aboriginal people, and between aboriginal people and government bureacracy. One exception to this attitude has always been the Six Nations Confederacy, consisting of the Oneida, Tuscarora, Mohawk, Seneca, Cayuga, and Onondaga. They always knew they were sovereign and this has been reflected in their treatment of Six Nations women.

The activism of the Tobique women's group was preceded by the actions of other aboriginal women. Mary Two Axe Early was the first aboriginal woman to speak out publicly against the section of the Indian Act which stripped women of their rights if they married non-status men. In the 1950s, after marrying a non-status man, she moved back to the Mohawk reserve in Quebec that had been her birthplace. She was not refused the right to reside in the community of her birth, since, in accordance with Mohawk culture, the community has always been matrilineal. However, Section 12 (1)(b) did prevent her having access to financial support; it would also have prevented her being buried in the community of her birth. In the seventies, other Native women began to organize across Canada, with the offending section of the Indian Act being one of the major issues they raised. In 1973 the Supreme Court of Canada heard the cases of Jeanette Lavell and Yvonne Bedard against Section 12 (1)(b). In a five-to-four decision, the court ruled that the Indian Act was *exempt* from the Canadian Bill of Rights.

Organizations such as the National Indian Brotherhood (formed in the 1950s to represent status Indians, socially and politically) mounted a lobbying campaign against Lavalle and Bedard. Their argument was that it was necessary for the

Indian Act to be kept intact for use as a bargaining lever with the federal government and any tampering — such as amending Section 12 (1)(b) — would play into the government's 1969 White Paper plan of doing away with special Indian status and assimilating Indians into the mainstream of Canada. It was against this historical background that the women of Tobique began their activism.

An Issue of Housing

In 1976, Juanita Perley's husband threw her and their ten children out of their home and won the legal argument that she had no right to their house. The house was in his name only and only he had any legal right to it. But Juanita, a woman of petite stature, was not going to put up with any nonsense and, more importantly, was not going to see her family be broken up like this and forced to live in the streets. So she occupied a public building. Juanita recounts:

> It was Labour Day weekend when we first got thrown out. When I moved all of the kids up to the band office the RCMP showed up. It was the first time here that anyone had occupied a public building. The police said that I was going to be arrested for breaking and entering. He said, "I'm going to charge you with B and E." I replied, "What's that, bacon and eggs?"

When Cheryl Bear's marriage broke down, she was in need of housing so she moved into the next available house and found that it had been destined for someone else — but she remained strong and stayed. Cheryl's grandfather was encouraging and gave her the spiritual strength needed to maintain her decision.

In 1977, Glenna Perley and Gookum Saulis would no longer put up with housing conditions and the unjust treatment towards women and children in Negoot Gook. They organized women to protest against inadequate housing by occupying the Tobique (Negoot Gook) Band Office. What started out to be an issue of poor housing for women was soon usurped by the media to be an issue of status. One headline in the

Telegraph-Journal in 1977 read, "Women Occupy Band Office — Want Indian Act Changes."

The women in the book identify in their stories where the change began to take place from the Tobique women's original concerns about housing to the media emphasis on the status issue.

Caroline Ennis says:
It was status women who were having trouble with housing. When I got involved in the demonstrations and lobbying, it wasn't for the non-status thing; it was purely a women's thing.

Juanita Perley commented:
This business about women getting kicked out of their homes, it goes way back.

Cheryl Bear says:
See, the woman was supposed to move out with the kids, and it was the man's house.

Karen recalls her mother's situation:
My mother had tried to get some help with the house. She said, "The men are getting helped more than the women are."

The women who had lost their status were moving back to the Tobique Reserve, after marriage breakups, or becoming widowed, and were experiencing difficulties finding housing for themselves and their children. Four of the women tell about their feelings and sudden awareness of their non-status positions:

Lilly Harris:
When we were growing up nobody talked about status and non-status. When I married I lost my status but I didn't know it at the time. I didn't find out until I moved back in the mid-1970s.

Mavis Goeres:
I find out that white women are Indians now, but I'm not! Here, when I came back, men could kick their wife and children

out because the Indian Act made the man sole owner of the house.

Joyce Sappier:
No, I never knew I'd lost it because I didn't sell my rights.

Sandra Lovelace-Sappier:
I had gone to the Band Office before and asked for a house for myself and my child. I'd had to pitch a tent because I couldn't find a place to stay. They'd told me I had no rights, that I was non-status. That was when Dan and Caroline Ennis approached me about taking my case to the United Nations.

The Occupation of the Band Office
In late August women from the Tobique demonstrated in front of the band office over housing. A demonstration was also staged in front of the Indian Affairs office in Fredericton, N.B. At the end of August women of the Tobique began to occupy the band office.

There were frightening instances of verbal and physical harassment toward the women who were protesting, and their children. Some members of the Tobique took the women's action as a personal affront against them and their chief and his supporters; this resulted in a counter-attack. In early September the women were served with an injunction from the chief and council ordering them out of the band office, but they disregarded it. In mid-September the band administration moved all of their equipment and files out of the band office, but the women remained. An election was called on October 3, 1977, and a new chief was declared who supported the women's issue. (Unfortunately, he was pressured to resign within a year.) On October 4, 1977, fire was set to the band office. Fortunately, no one was hurt and the women started to gradually move out though there had been no adequate resolution to the question of adequate housing. The women recall experiences related to the occupation:

Bet-te:
We didn't really move in; we were just going to sit there until we got a meeting with the chief and council. That's actually how the occupation got started.

Glenna:
Really, we went in mainly to try and talk to the chief.

Karen:
The chief treated us like we were invisible, like he couldn't see us. A lot of reserve residents cooked meals and sent them over.

Glenna:
Then they wanted to put us in jail.

Caroline:
The situation got more volatile as the occupation continued.

Bet-te:
We were, "the shit disturbers, radicals, white washed, women's lib" ... we were just women who needed decent homes.

Joyce:
I got evicted because I believed so strongly in what the women were fighting for.

Bet-te:
That's around the time the violence really started. The occupation wasn't only hard on us; it was hard on the other reserve residents, too. When it really got bad, we had guns in the band office.

Glenna:
In interviews (during the occupation), that's when I realized non-status was the main problem I was talking about.

The women discussed the actual violence that they and their children experienced during the three month occupation. All the while they sought help from other political organizations and received very little response from the Native Indian groups, or from the Department of Indian Affairs. The main help came from some reserve residents, namely the elders, and non-Indian women's groups.

On December 29, 1977, Sandra Lovelace (Sappier) filed a complaint against Canada with the United Nations Human Rights Committee in Geneva, Switzerland. For the next four years the main focus was on the discriminatory clause, Section 12 (1)(b), of the Indian Act which dictates a Native woman's loss of Indian status should she marry a non-status man. And, in 1981, the United Nations Human Rights Committee found Canada in breach of the International Covenant on Civil and Political Rights over sexual discrimination.

The 100-Mile Walk

In the meantime, the women never let up on the lobbying momentum. The housing problem did not lessen because the Band Administration had gone through more changes only to find itself with the same leadership that had precipitated the original band office occupations. But by now the women were aware of the power of the political lobby, outside of their own community.

In July 1979, the women who had occupied the Tobique band office saw that the situation was not getting any better so they decided to organize a 100-mile walk from Oka, Quebec (outskirts of Montreal), to Ottawa. This walk by women and children attracted national attention. Native people from British Columbia, the Yukon, Northwest Territories, Ontario and Quebec joined the 100-mile march. During the walk the non-status issue became more focal. Sandra Lovelace, who participated in the walk, gave a number of interviews to the press and the issue of the discriminatory Indian Act Clause 12 (1)(b) received cross-country coverage to the exclusion of the many other concerns of the walkers. The issues that had inspired the walk were not restricted to the sexual discrimination of 12 (1)(b), but included living conditions on the reserves, housing and distribution of resources. The walk received so much attention that government officials had to take notice and start addressing the issues that the women were talking about. The numbers of walkers grew from fifty to more than

200 by the time they reached Parliament Hill in Ottawa. Publicity from the walk precipitated a meeting with Prime Minister Joe Clark, his wife Maureen McTeer, and a number of Cabinet ministers. The women were assured that the government would be making moves to change the Indian Act. Some of the women described their feelings as they made the historic 100-mile walk to Ottawa:

Caroline:
We wanted to raise public consciousness about Native women's problems, and mainly the walk was over housing. I know the RCMP kept an eye on us during the walk, too ... but really, what threat could we be to the country anyway?

Sandra:
When we started out on the walk, getting on the bus here on the reserve, you should have seen the men. They were standing outside laughing at us, saying, "You fools, what are you going to accomplish?"

Lilly:
Oh, it was hot, but most people walked all of the way. I was sixty-two when we made the walk. I think I was the oldest walker.

Caroline:
I'll never forget that hectic first morning at breakfast. We filled the whole restaurant. We had thought we could stay overnight at the Catholic school or some kind of retreat house where they had all kinds of room, but the priest wouldn't let us. We got denied help from the Catholic priests along the route.

Glenna:
When we passed this one reserve, people had sandwiches for us. They knew we would be walking by there around noon hour, so all these women got together and had lunches out along the road. I'll never forget that.

Karen:
We had meetings and meetings. Walking during the day and meetings at night. We'd have meetings to decide whether we should have a meeting.

Caroline:
We got more and more media coverage as we went along.

Karen:
We told people a lot about housing, of course. Then reporters started asking Sandra about 12 (1)(b) and sexual discrimination in the Indian Act.

Sandra:
It all happened on the walk.

Karen:
The last day of the walk before arriving in Ottawa, the women from the NIB (National Indian Brotherhood) offices came and joined us. They were all in their high heels, fancy clothes, the kind of fancy tee-shirts the NIB used to give out, nail polish on their fingers. And here we were, grubby and sweaty.

Sandra:
We really didn't think anybody would listen to us, or that we would accomplish anything. Just getting there was emotional.

Lilly:
There was a big rally when we got to Parliament Hill, speeches, television cameras. People had hot dogs and hamburgers, cold drinks for us.

Gookum:
I looked back to see all them women come walking up. They looked so determined.

Bet-te:
I got chills, seeing that.

Gookum:
I felt like crying.

Karen:
Oh jeeze, it was so emotional. Tears coming down our eyes, crying. I hadn't realized that we had made such an impact, but we did. I'd thought, here we are walking all this way and nobody cares, but they did!

The positive outcomes of the walk were that $300,000 extra housing money was allotted to Tobique Reserve, and the Native Women's Association of Canada received a major increase in funding. But the women had to continue their lobbying after the walk. Unfortunately, Joe Clark's Conservative government was defeated shortly after the walk by the Liberal government of Pierre Trudeau and no action was taken to change the Indian Act. The Tobique women believe that at no point during Trudeau's term of office did he show any interest in the plight of Native women, or a willingness to consider changes in the Indian Act.

The women had continuing problems when they returned to the reserve. Only a fraction of the $300,000 allotted for housing as a result of the Walk was used for housing for single women and their children. Women in desperate need of housing were not getting it and women were still having difficulty getting the other material resources they needed to survive. In spite of efforts to directly pressure the band administration, and another brief occupation of the band office, only token gestures were made by the band council to meet women's needs.

Lobbying to Change the Indian Act

Taking the case of a non-status women to the United Nations had initially been a strategy to put pressure on the Canadian government in order to make officials address the concerns Native women were raising. The Tobique women's strategy of going to the United Nations did exert tremendous pressure on the federal government to change the Indian Act.

On December 29, 1977, the complaint of Sandra Lovelace against the Canadian government was communicated to the

Human Rights Committee in Geneva, Switzerland. Because of delays by the Canadian government in responding to the Human Rights Committee's request for information, the final verdict was not made until July 30, 1981. The U.N. Human Rights Committee ruled in Sandra Lovelace's favour, finding Canada in breach of the International Covenant because the Indian Act denied Sandra the legal right to live in the community of her birth.

The final ruling put additional pressure on the federal government to amend the Indian Act by "embarrassing" Canada — tarnishing the country's image — in the international community. Although the lobbying campaign to amend 12 (1)(b) of the Indian Act seemed on the verge of victory, four more years of concentrated lobbying actually were necessary. During those subsequent years, Tobique women became seasoned lobbyists with an issue that had become a "political football."

The women became involved in a variety of activities that allowed them to exert influence. For example, Sandra Lovelace attended the 1981 U.N. Convention as a Canadian delegate where she spoke about the condition of Indian women in Canada. Caroline Ennis became a member of NAC where her activities strengthened the support of NAC and its member women's groups for the Native women's cause.

My appointment to the New Brunswick Advisory Council on the Status of Women gave us the influence we needed on the provincial level. It also enabled us to take active participation at the five annual First Ministers' conferences on constitutional aboriginal matters because the Province of New Brunswick was willing to assert support on sexual equality.

The Tobique Women's Group has always supported that we, as aboriginal people, should hold a special status in Canada but we did not wish to see it entrenched in the Canadian Constitution, which was repatriated in 1982, without any guarantee that it would apply equally to men and women. It is necessary for this to happen as there is already evidence of continuing discriminatory treatment toward women. It is necessary to have some judicial recourse because Indians negotiating for self-government for Indian communities are making their own membership laws. The same sexual discrimination will happen as in the case of Sandra Lovelace, where women will be denied residence in their mother's and grandmother's birthplaces.

The lobbying continued with the development of a pamphlet identifying the offending law and explaining in detail how it affected women in Indian communities for more than 100 years. This is the time that I became totally committed and involved. It took several political lobbying trips to Ottawa and several more conferences to inform the people of Canada that this offending law had to be eliminated.

Reinstatement

By 1985, when Canada passed legislation to eliminate sexual discrimination from the Indian Act, the women of Tobique had seen how their power was being evidenced within the community. In 1982, it was largely their efforts that finally changed the band administration, by electing a chief who understood the issue of sexual discrimination, and had given his assurance to change similar practices within his administration. The women started seeing a better situation for themselves. When the Indian Act changes came about through Bill C-31, the Tobique Reserve was ready and they hired women who had been in the lobby to change the Indian Act to develop policies to implement the new law.

The first thing that was done was to reinstate to band membership of the Tobique Band all the women who had lost their status through 12 (1)(b) and subsequently, all the first generation children.

There was never any fear that we could not accommodate at the Tobique the numbers of persons being reinstated, or what it would mean in terms of the services we would have to provide. Public statements accompanying the information on Bill C-31 were explicit in their assurances that the Indian reserves would not suffer any hardships from the possible influx of reinstated band members. The impact of Bill C-31 on the Tobique Reserve does not follow in the same pattern as most other Indian reserves.

By the time the government was trying to determine how much money would be allocated for services to the total population increases, the Tobique Reserve already had a large number of non-status residents who were receiving health and welfare benefits. There were also a small number of people receiving education benefits. Concerning the Tobique Reserve, the Indian Affairs department of the federal government assessed the number of persons reinstated against the total required increase of funds, but the actual funding that finally came through was inadequate.

Furthermore, the increase in residency was higher than we anticipated because Tobique had an open-door policy for re-instatement. The Tobique Women's Group would never regress in their political demands and activities. We addressed the injustices and demanded retribution. The issues that we lobbied for were rectified and we celebrated.

The comic but sad situation that has developed, and is causing such confusion within our communities, arises from the fact that the policy developers of the Canadian government, along with the intervention of aboriginal political representatives, produced a compromising Bill C-31. The Tobique Women's Group specifically addressed the reinstatement of the offended women and their first generation children. We did not lobby for the war veterans who had lost their status, nor for persons who for other reasons wanted to enter the Canadian mainstream system. Confusion developed when other lobbying groups saw the momentum we created and insisted on being heard. The resulting Bill C-31 is a weak attempt by the government to appease all factions.

The underlying currents of dissatisfaction towards Indian community leaders, because they cannot meet the demand for proper and satisfying services to every band member, are causing an unhealthy social and psychological backlash in the communities.

Some of the problems are causing hardships for these reasons:

a. The federal government has not lived up to its promised financial support.

b. There is an existing housing shortage.

c. Indian Act policies do not allow for an economic foundation to flourish and encourage a comfortable economic growth.

d. The higher standards of education demanded by residents of the reserve are not being realized, as a result of cutbacks — and, in some instances, denials.

e. Population has increased by 33 percent, resulting from reinstatements.

It's a constant day-to-day negotiation between the reserve administration officers and the Department of Indian Affairs bureaucracy just to make sure that band members on the Tobique are not hungry, cold or uneducated. Misinterpretations of the bill are retarding real progress. Too much energy is being wasted on this process. To the Tobique Women's Group, Bill C-31 meant only the beginning of a real growth of our community.

Many of the women that we grew up with have returned, either alone, widowed, divorced or with their retired husbands. In some cases, their children have decided to return and make their lives at their mother's birthplace. In any case, each person who has returned has brought a new viewpoint, a new energy and a new confidence in the pride of who they are. The grandmothers of this community express the joy that they feel for the return of their daughters who, through no fault of their own, were treated with such disrespect under and over the Canadian law. The book *Enough is Enough — Aboriginal Women Speak Out,* is about struggles; it's about lives and a political progression of this small group of very brave women who cared, and still care as they continue to be involved in the community.

At this writing, two of the women have since passed away — Ida Paul and Lilly Harris. They encouraged us with their humour, common sense and total support through the arduous journeys to Ottawa, fund raising and the battles with band administrations. They are fondly remembered by the group and will continue to remain in our memories through these personal accounts.

The impact of Bill C-31 is being felt throughout Canada in different ways. In 1987, the federal government issued a report on the impact of Bill C-31 which did not involve input by the First Nations. After extensive lobbying from the three national political groups — The Assembly of First Nations, Native Indian Women's Association of Canada, and the Native Council of Canada — an inquiry was developed that established consultation between these three groups and the federal government. The first phase has been realized and some of the points that have been identified in presentations to the inquiry are:

a. Bill C-31 has not improved the lives of Indian people, but has simply created more problems, tensions and splits in communities.

b. DIAND registration process has caused hardship for registrants.

c. Many off-reserve registrants believe that all Indians should enjoy the same rights despite their place of residence.

d. Insufficient information has been provided regarding the registration process and there is a lack of consistency in processing applications.

e. Many registrants indicated that, once registered, they are given no further information as to eligibility to services, etc … Regional organizations felt that they should receive funding to address this informational need of reinstated people.

f. Presenters from Bands and Tribal Councils felt that the federal government has not lived up to its promise to implement Bill C-31 with adequate lands and resources.

g. Band and Tribal Council presenters indicated an increased pressure on program and service delivery coupled with inadequate resources to meet higher demands for these programs and services.

h. Band and Tribal Councils noted that Band staff and councils are not receiving adequate resources to deal with the range of issues brought forward by Bill C-31.

i. Some presenters argued that the social, political and cultural fabric of First Nation communities have been weakened by Bill C-31 while others felt that Bill C-31 has strengthened the community fabric.

j. Organizations stated that, despite Bill C-31, discrimination continues to exist.

This, of course, is only a summary of the positions put forward to date. The inquiry is hearing from small groups, band administrations, provincial organizations and individuals across the country, and those who have been affected by Bill C-31. Extensive reports will be available from the national offices of these three political organizations — The Assembly of First Nations, Native Indian Women's Association of Canada, and the Native Council of Canada — in Ottawa.

The realities of reserve life still reflect colonial influences. The Indian Act perpetuates those attitudes. This is a document that requires massive revision. It does not protect or enhance our Original cultures.

Our land base is painfully small and meagerly supports its residents. Some of our reserves have to accommodate 180 families, a school, a church and possibly a small administration office on a piece of land that is equivalent to the size of a farm in Quebec or Ontario, and definitely smaller than any farm in Saskatchewan.

As it stands, the Indian Act restricts individuals from using their land deeds for collateral for funding purposes, so this restricts individual initiatives in business.

The schooling that our people receive contradicts the philosophies that we are taught at home. When we attempt to form meaningful co-operatives, our CanAmerican-European learned standards get in the way and confuse our innate ideologies.

Self government is a phrase that sounds like a fairy tale when you face the reality of the Indian Act. It can be changed, however. The Tobique Women's Group influenced changes. We hope that the First Nations of Canada will also take a real look at the situation the Original People are in as we enter our 600th year under colonialism.

We can do something about this situation.

We can change the world.

12

The DisAbled Women's Network

A Fragile Success

Joanne Doucette

DAWN is the DisAbled Women's Network, a national organization controlled by and comprised of Canadian disabled women, with local chapters and provincial affiliates across the country. DAWN is a feminist organization (a member of the National Action Committee on the Status of Women), founded in 1985. In this chapter I outline the general status of disabled women in Canada, DAWN's history, its goals and objectives, structure and organizing tactics, as well as discussing organizing problems including DAWN's relationship to the disabled consumer movement (Stone 1988).

DAWN groups and members tend to define disability broadly, using human rights code definitions (such as the Ontario Human Rights Code) or the United Nations' definition: "a person is disabled who 'is unable to do all the things which a person of that age and sex can normally be expected to do'" (Rooney 1985a, 2). Definitions of disability are problematic indeed. More than one million, or 12 to 18 percent of Canadian women are disabled (Vash 1982). About 700,000 Canadians are severely disabled, about half of these are women.

Disabled women consider themselves to be "doubly disadvantaged," or "doubly oppressed," both as women and as disabled people. "Disabled women are more likely to be

employed than disabled men, less likely to be college educated, earn substantially less ... and are less likely to find a job
post disability" (Fine & Asch 1981). This double disadvantage
is reflected in the following statistics taken from a DAWN
Toronto brochure:

- 18 percent of all women are disabled.
- disabled girls are twice as likely to be sexually
  assaulted.
- disabled women are more likely to be the victims of
  violence.
- support and services for disabled mothers are almost
  totally inaccessible [and non-existent].
- the unemployment rate for women with disabilities
  is 74 percent.
- when men become disabled 50 percent of marriages
  break up; for disabled women that figure is 99
  percent.
- the most inescapable reality for women with
  disabilities is poverty.

In general, women earn 60 percent of men's wages; working
women with disabilities earn 64 percent of the wages of non-
disabled women (DAWN Toronto brochure 1986). As Jill
Weiss notes, "The poverty is overwhelming and complete"
(Weiss 1985, 4).

Disabled Women Start to Organize

Disabled women are organizing. Tired of being invisible
women, both within the disabled consumer movement and the
women's movement, we have had enough of being ignored,
patronized and placated. It is men who are, by and large, in
decision-making positions within the disabled consumer
movement. Disabled women are too often seen as helpers.
Even at disabled rights conferences, we have had a hard time
being heard. For example, at the 1985 Disabled People's International (DPI) conference, a scheduled women's plenary was
cancelled at the last minute. Women had to struggle even to
get to the microphone on the DPI conference floor.

Two women from the Coalition of Provincial Organizations of the Handicapped (COPOH) attended the 1983 annual general meeting of Canada's largest feminist organization, the National Action Committee on the Status of Women (NAC) "to establish liaison between NAC and ... COPOH" (Kome 1983b, 78). In 1985, women at the annual COPOH conference met and moved resolutions calling for a workshop on women's issues at the next conference and an investigation of women's role within COPOH.

The Birth of DAWN

In 1985, four disabled women met with representatives of the Canadian government's Women's Program (Secretary of State) to plan a national meeting of disabled women and insure funding support. This national meeting in spring 1985 saw the founding of the DisAbled Women's Network (DAWN), the first national organization of disabled women in Canada.

Having been active in DAWN from its birth, I discuss here some of the difficulties and obstacles we encountered in organizing and some of our strengths. DAWN exemplifies the ability of people to organize and fight for their own rights against overwhelming odds.

The criteria for delegate selection to the founding conference of DAWN were: an ability to empower others, an involvement in disabled women's issues and diversity in terms of geographic, linguistic and ethnic origins and disability. From the beginning, we were looking for organizers and experienced activists.

The meeting brought together 17 women from across Canada for four days in June 1985. The delegates agreed to form the DisAbled Women's Network (DAWN). Because of the difficulty and expense of communicating over the vast geographical distances characteristic of Canada and the uncertainty of funding for executive meetings, a core collective of eight women who had access to computers (with modems allowing them, at least theoretically, to meet over computer) volunteered to coordinate activities nationally. All delegates agreed to return home and set up local and/or provincial networks of disabled women. DAWN was born.

DAWN groups began to form across Canada: in Prince Edward Island in July 1985; in Toronto, Ontario, in September 1985; in Ottawa, the nation's capital; in Halifax on the east coast; in British Columbia, on the west coast; and in Montreal, the largest city in Canada's francophone province, Quebec. In Winnipeg, Manitoba, the Consulting Committee on the Status of Women with Disabilities (CCSWD), one of Canada's first local groups of disabled women, linked promptly with DAWN to share information and work together on common concerns.

Structure and Resources

Yet, except for rare letters between groups and individuals, communication between delegates to the Ottawa meeting broke down. The core collective never functioned. Letters were exchanged between groups, but DAWN Canada was hampered by a lack of funding (no follow-up funding had been provided after the initial meeting) even to do the most minimal mailing and phoning. Of the delegates to the original Ottawa meeting, only 10 actively communicated within DAWN Canada. Several women on the Modem Committee, experienced difficulty using their computers to link up due to unfamiliarity with the technology or lack of the necessary computer components. Meanwhile, the Secretary of State Women's Program staff person, Vera Wall, who organized the initial conference, took a leave of absence from her work, never to be heard from again.

In May 1986, almost a year after the founding meeting, pushed by their concern that unless they acted unilaterally DAWN would never get off the ground, four of the delegates from the founding meeting met during an annual general meeting of the National Action Committee on the Status of Women (NAC), Canada's very large and powerful lobbying coalition for women, to which they were all delegates. Short of material resources, the organizers used every opportunity to piggyback meetings, borrow or beg resources, and even fund mailings out of their own limited finances. At NAC, the urgent need for another national meeting was agreed on and an ad hoc committee volunteered or was recruited to organize the event. Most of the hands-on work was done by paid staff of the CCSWD in Winnipeg. This became significant as it is apparent that the most successful DAWN groups either had paid staff or full-time volunteers who were willing to act as such.

In March 1987, DAWN had its second national meeting in Winnipeg, Manitoba. A board of directors and executive were elected to replace the collective, and a constitution and bylaws drafted and passed. As in the first meeting, delegates agreed to return home and develop local and regional networks.

Issues and Goals

DAWN is working for the full equality of disabled women in Canadian society, while fostering a sense of group identity and pride in its members. This positive sense of self is hard to sustain within male-dominated organizations, or organizations dominated by non-disabled feminists. Disabled women need their own organization, just as non-disabled women have organized their networks. That's why groups run by and for women are so important to us. They are our psychic turf, our place to discover who we are, or could become, as whole independent human beings (Steinem 1986, 231).

Disabled women are doubly oppressed. As disabled people, we are negatively stereotyped because of our disability and, as women, we are kept down by sexism. Those of us who are Native, immigrant women, seniors or poor (and most of us *are poor*) face another, or triple level of oppression. No wonder some of us want to organize and resist.

As women, we have concerns not shared by men. For example, at DAWN's founding meeting the following issues were identified as priorities of concern to disabled women:

1. accessibility to the women's movement and women's services;
2. prevention of violence against disabled women;
3. affirmative action;
4. assertiveness, awareness and self-image;
5. sexuality rights;
6. parenting and child care (see Pelletier 1985, 21-30)

Delegates also produced a list of actions necessary to build DAWN. They needed to build grassroots links between disabled women, raise the consciousness of disabled women, educate the feminist movement and the disabled consumer movement, lobby politicians, develop local groups, reach out to rural and urban women as well as to ethno-cultural minorities, engage in peer support, share skills, gather and distribute information, and undertake their own research projects. (Pelletier 1985, 33-34). The task was large and resources limited.

Implementing the Goals

Feminist Structure and Process

Originally DAWN was to operate as a collective. Rather than a hierarchical organization with formal positions, DAWN was envisioned as a network of equals. In order to function, however, networks require constant communication among members. Communication after the Ottawa meeting soon broke down. In retrospect, an observation from that founding meeting appears ominous: "It is remarkable that often networks fail because members neglect the most basic, elementary factor in the life of a network: feeding information into the system" (Pelletier 1985, 39).

Meanwhile, several local groups discovered that the collective approach did not work for them. At DAWN Toronto and DAWN Montreal, for example, one or two women found themselves doing all of the work of the organization without formal recognition and often in isolation. Members expected a lot, but the degree of personal involvement was low in many groups. This led to frustration and burnout among those active.

It also led to a phenomenon known as "the tyranny of structurelessness" (Freeman 1973). Freeman argues that there is no such thing as a structureless group working for social change. All such groups have leaders, even when leaders are not formally recognized. She argues that hidden leadership is more manipulative and less democratic than formal, visible leadership. She urges groups to adopt formal structures to make leaders accountable, and she called for the distribution of authority.

During DAWN's first year, however, there was effectively no formal leadership. Instead, power was concentrated in the hands of those who did the most work, and those workers were acutely uncomfortable with both the workload and the power. The situation was in opposition to the original intent of empowering other disabled women and sharing responsibilities. DAWN Toronto addressed the problem by electing a board of directors in the fall, 1986, and adopting a constitution and by-laws. DAWN Montreal did the same. DAWN B.C. and DAWN Ontario bypassed the problem by holding elections at their initial meetings. At the second national meeting in Winnipeg, DAWN Canada, the national network, elected a board of directors.

Coming Together

Meetings are obviously necessary to address both organizational issues, formulate goals, boost morale, etc. Whether at the local level (in monthly meetings) or at the provincial and national levels (in semi-annual or annual meetings), meetings are essential. More than anything else, they foster a sense of group pride and identity. They are fundamental for consciousness-raising and empowerment. As remarked after the 1986 DAWN B.C. conference:

> The conference was very powerful. It was the first time that disabled women had a chance to talk with other women about … intimate topics … Several of the women who participated spoke of the importance of having their experiences and feelings validated. (Pollock & Meister 1986)

Another wrote after the 1987 DAWN B.C. conference:

> What happens to a disabled woman attending her first conference of DAWN … ? For me, it was culture shock. Instead of being the only special needs person in my household and immediate neighbourhood, I was just one of many. That at first was scary, but within hours it became liberating as I began to feel

the bonds of unity and the stocks of shared interest.
Now I am a part rather than apart. (Brooks 1987, 4)

Meetings and the ability to meet are often taken for granted,
yet meetings are significant achievements to be celebrated.
Socially, physically and economically isolated, disabled
women have to work hard just to meet. They must consider
the logistics of transportation, attendant care, sign language
interpretation and other special needs, as well as services such
as child care. In a large, sparsely populated country, with a
harsh and extreme climate, transportation and communications are particularly expensive and difficult.

Member Recruitment

At the 1987 DAWN Canada meeting, delegates discussed
membership promotion. Ideally, we wanted every Canadian
disabled woman to know about DAWN. We knew that this
was easier said than done, especially without money.

Recruitment is difficult for a number of reasons. Disabled
women tend not to go to public events where they might hear
about DAWN. Only a very small minority of disabled women,
or disabled men for that matter, are activists and involved in
disabled consumer organizations. Likewise, only a minority of
women are involved in feminist organizations or women's
groups. The existing network that DAWN draws upon is small
and the grapevine is limited. Moreover, disabled women are
often extremely passive. Socialized into positions of learned
helplessness, many are unaware of their rights or afraid to
assert their own concerns and needs. They have learned not to
ask questions or express displeasure with this status quo.
Often raised in institutions or extremely dependent on their
families, they may be very conservative.

Learned passivity means that when women do come to
DAWN, we are likely to sit back and let others do the work.
After all we have always been done *for* and *to*. Self confidence
is so low that it is often hard to even maintain a phone tree.
While wanting to organize and fight for their rights, disabled
women have reported a sense of being overwhelmed at the
prospect. (Pelletier 1985, 36)

Membership recruitment is also hampered by the support of the initial founders of DAWN for minority rights and, specifically, support for the visible presence of lesbian and Native women within DAWN. At the DAWN Ontario Conference, two delegates walked out because of an outspoken lesbian presence. After the event, a large charity challenged DAWN's claim to be role models for disabled girls since lesbians were allowed to be members. The most bitter disappointment for many of the early leaders in DAWN was the decision of the first disabled women's conference in Manitoba not to join DAWN Canada because of the strong support the organizers gave to lesbian and Native rights. As an American feminist has observed:

> Large numbers of women see feminism as synonymous with lesbianism; their homophobia leads them to reject association with any group identified as pro-lesbian. (Hooks 1984, 23)

DAWN is an explicitly feminist group and this scares many women. One delegate to the 1985 Ottawa meeting rejected the term "feminist," calling herself instead "a humanist." Funders also are unnerved by the explicit feminism of DAWN. A federal government official, for example, requested that DAWN Toronto remove the term "feminist" from their literature. Rooney (1985, 66) said of disabled women who do not identify as feminist:

> Their priority is the rights of disabled people, not women's rights or the rights of women within the disabled movement. Several of the women I've talked to seemed to me, and I heard through the grapevine about others, afraid of the term "feminism," even though they live their lives in ways that are very feminist.

Funding

Funding is a severe problem for DAWN. Private donors prefer to donate to established tax exempt charities. While local meetings are relatively cheap, provincial or national meetings are extremely expensive. Disabled women are among the poorest of the poor and are unable to maintain or sustain their own organization financially. Without government funding, DAWN's existence would be in jeopardy. Yet reliance on government funding leaves DAWN very vulnerable to manipulation, both covert and overt. Government priorities and agendas may differ radically from those of the membership of DAWN. While many civil servants are supportive of DAWN some have interfered in ways detrimental to the organization. For example, the Secretary of State was invited to address the second DAWN conference in Winnipeg. He was unable to attend and appointed an official to speak in his stead. That official demanded the right to attend all conference sessions, including in camera policy and funding strategy workshops, on the threat of not speaking and withdrawal of future funding. An appeal directly to the office of the Prime Minister of Canada forestalled such action, but DAWN's vulnerability to political and bureaucratic tampering is evident.

An ability to play political hardball and make decisions under pressure, along with the knowledge of who to contact for support and when, has proved invaluable in such situations. Knowing who our allies were within the bureaucracy, within the governing party as well as the opposition, within feminism and the disabled consumer movement and the media gave us power when others saw us as powerless.

DAWN and Others

Feminists

In the early seventies, feminists largely ignored the oppression of minority women, including disabled women. Even today, feminists are slow to take note of disabled women:

If the National Action Committee on the Status of Women can be seen as representing mainstream feminism in Canada, then the absence of disabled women is almost total. This indicates a critical need for ablebodied Canadian feminists to start examining disability issues and their own prejudices against people with disabilities (Tait 1986, 447).

This ignorance has left a residue of mistrust and resentment. By and large, the women's movement and women's services have been unaware of the need for accessibility and have done little to open their doors. For example, CCSWD (1986) recently surveyed women's organizations in Winnipeg and found that when the needs of hearing, visually, and mobility impaired women were taken into consideration, not one was accessible. Women's groups and services have many excuses for inaccessibility, chiefly centered around funding. "It is a fact that many women's organizations are underfunded but ... statistics very clearly show the LOW priority given to the needs of visually and hearing impaired women" (CCSWD 1986, 10).

The lack of accessibility prompted me to write an open letter on behalf of DAWN Toronto to the women's movement. It says, in part:

> At this point, maybe your heads are shaking and your finance committee is yelling, "IT'S NOT COST EFFECTIVE." (Perhaps the rest of you are simply saying, 'It's too expensive.')
>
> BEING DISABLED HAS NEVER BEEN COST EFFECTIVE AND IT NEVER WILL BE. The same school of non-thought that calmly slaughtered millions of Jews, feminists, socialists, gays and lesbians and other minorities, fed us disabled people to the ovens because we "cost too much." Right here, today, in Canada, disabled women are being sterilized without consent because we "cost too much." The same argument is used to deny us jobs, decent incomes, housing, health care and everything the non-disabled take for granted — because it "costs too much." (Doucette 1986a)

But costs too much to whom? Why?

This letter was reprinted widely by major feminist groups such as the National Action Committee on the Status of Women (NAC) and the Canadian Research Institute for the Advancement of Women (CRIAW), both of which are trying to establish effective liaison with DAWN. While more organizations are making efforts, many disabled women are angry and disillusioned.

Abortion rights has been a rallying cry for feminism and many disabled women actively support freedom of choice. Yet the insensitivity of many abortion rights activists towards disabled people has alienated many disabled women from feminists, reflected in the assumption that a disabled fetus should automatically be aborted. For example, one American disabled activist saw feminists as

> quick to take a knee-jerk stand in opposition to right-wing and anti-abortion forces, without considering it from the perspective of a disabled person. (Anne Finger in McDonnell 1984, 89)

Many disabled women are drawn to the anti-abortion movement because they believe that

> to allow abortion cheapens the value of human life and opens the door to active mercy-killing, infanticide and a general readiness to dispose of "unproductive" or "undesirable" elements in society (McDonnell 1984, 90).

Feminists must address the concerns of disabled women if they wish to involve disabled women in their coalitions as more than token afterthoughts.

It has been suggested that because feminists are very aware of the fragility of their newly-won status, they are less than eager to share privileges with other minorities (Tait 1968, 448-448). Fighting to free themselves from rigid stereotyping, they have yet to expand their own image of woman wide enough to include those who are different from their physical norm. Other feminists, focusing their lives on careers, competition, and achievement are threatened by the presence of disabled women since the existence of disability challenges the premise that all women need is an equal chance to compete in a free market economy.

Disabled Men

While many DAWN members also belong to disabled consumer groups, and DAWN actively seeks to work with the disabled consumer movement, here too there are serious problems.

Traditionally, men have regarded women as extensions or complements to themselves (and women have shared this view). Women's lives were assumed to centre on the domestic sphere of kitchen and children. Many disabled men share this inability to see disabled women as autonomous beings oppressed on the basis of gender.

Some disabled men are acutely uncomfortable with the idea of disabled women acting independently. Within COPOH, for example, a woman's caucus was formed, but men demanded and won the right to belong, thus, defeating the purpose of a woman's caucus. Some see DAWN as splitting the disabled consumer movement, thus reducing its political impact (Watson 1985, 2). Others accuse DAWN of separatism, hostility towards men, comparing the disabled women's movement to "the rightous [sic] anger of the late sixties and early seventies feminist movement" (Elliott 1986). The comparison is apt in that the women who formed DAWN have had a remarkably similar experience to the sixties feminists who became disillusioned with the new Left (see Evans 1979).

It must be stressed that DAWN was not formed to attack the sexism of disabled men, but was formed so that disabled women could focus on issues which concerned them as women. DAWN is not interested in taking over the consumer movement, but complementing it. Advocating female separatism, as Hooks (1984, 70-71) points out, is not necessarily equivalent to taking an anti-male stance.

Disabled Women Helping Themselves

It surprises some that disabled women can organize. After all, it is commonly assumed that we are helpless. The most popular cliché is "confined to a wheelchair." To be confined is to be imprisoned or restricted, and the image is of a pitiful individual whose life revolves around a wheelchair. Yet wheelchair users are no more "confined" to their wheelchairs than drivers are "confined" to their cars. Just as drivers use cars to get around, we use our wheelchairs as vehicles. The concept of women *using* wheelchairs clearly allows for the conception of self-determining action. Women who use wheelchairs can decide to do something other than simply sit in their vehicles. "In fact, humans are nearly infinitely adaptable" (Stone 1984, 189).

Women using wheelchairs are often assumed to be mentally incompetent. We are reminded of a founding DAWN Toronto member who recently died. She had osteogenesis imperfecta and had been raised in an institution, experiencing a great deal of violence and oppression, but this did not prevent her from speaking out publicly. Many of the non-disabled people around her treated her as a precocious child. She was seen as remarkable because she was a *disabled woman* who did not simply sit "confined" to her wheelchair, rather than as a remarkable individual.

A third common assumption is that all disabled women, if they are not using wheelchairs, or crutches, must be either deaf or blind (also grounds for assuming mental incompetence). These are the only valid grounds for claiming the disabled status in the popular mind. Thus, the reality of many women who use canes, have mobility problems not immediately apparent, have chronic pain, or other invisible disabilities such as epilepsy or heart disease is denied (see Charmaz 1986; Koolish 1986; Stone 1984).

Disablement is not seen by disabled activists to be situated in a physical condition or difference per se (the medical model of disability), but socially constructed. Disabled women are excluded from the paid labour force because of prejudice, stereotyping and an unwillingness to accommodate special needs. The unemployment rate among disabled women is estimated to be as high as 93 percent (Doucette 1986b; see also O'Leary 1983).

Disabled women are among the most marginalized people in society. Society devalues women and is designed for able-bodied people only. Given this, it is a tribute to the tenacity of disabled women that we have been able to sustain the momentum necessary for building DAWN.

The creation and maintenance of DAWN, against a great deal of resistance from others, is also an indication of the magnitude of the problems we face in our daily lives. DAWN speaks to and validates our concerns. Social theorists have developed a model which claims to explain the rise of social movements as a function of resources available. This is called resource mobilization theory (see McAdam 1982, 66). It is hard to conceive of how we could have organized DAWN without the pre-existence of both the disabled consumer movement and the feminist movement. Both of these movements initially allowed the founders of DAWN to meet and voice our concerns. We learned organizing and leadership skills in those movements and drew on our extensive network of friends and supporters to provide initial funding, volunteer help, and members to found DAWN.

Without those networks, we would have had a much harder time finding our voice or being heard. Yet the existence of DAWN proves that even the most oppressed people are capable of organizing to challenge and resist their oppressors. DAWN's continued existence will depend on the ability of members to continue to act on their own behalf and use the limited resources available to disabled women without being manipulated by those who control the resources of wealth and power in our society: non-disabled, white, middle-class males. DAWN will reach and perhaps has reached a crisis in growth when the limitations of the networks which fostered DAWN's birth have been reached.

DAWN will have to re-evaluate its goals. Will it become a large organization in the tradition of middle-of-the-road Canadian political tradition and give up its radical edge? Or will it choose to remain a small activist group without a large grassroots membership? DAWN is a fragile success. Will the stress of meeting this challenge fracture and defeat it, as it has so many other feminist and disabled groups, or will the ingenuity and adaptable characteristic of DAWN insure its survival and growth?

Lesbians Against the Right

Sharon D. Stone

Lesbians Against the Right (LAR) was formed in 1981 within the context of an increasingly hostile social climate for lesbians. In this article I discuss LAR's existence, focusing on LAR's basis of unity, goals and strategies, and problems encountered. Although this article emphasizes LAR's first year of existence, I also suggest reasons for LAR's demise in 1983. The article and analysis are based on my own active participation in LAR from beginning to end, as well as interviews with other LAR members.[1]

LAR is presented here as a case study of lesbian-feminist protest. Based on this study, I cannot draw conclusions about lesbian organizing in general. Nevertheless, I offer this in the hope that other feminists, whether lesbian or not, will find reading about how one group of lesbian-feminists went about fighting their oppression to be a useful examination.

The Formation of LAR

The year before LAR's formation, the Lesbian Organization of Toronto (LOOT) had ceased to exist. LOOT had been an important resource for countless lesbians in Toronto, offering a safe, lesbian-positive environment in which to come out and meet other lesbians (see Davies 1988). Shortly thereafter, the popular Fly By Night women's bar also closed its doors. As a result, lesbians were experiencing "a frightening sense of homelessness" (Steiger & Weir 1981).

Then in early 1981, on the heels of a hate campaign mobilized by the New Right against lesbians and gay men, came the infamous bath raids. Although the massive raids on gay baths were not a direct attack on lesbians, a growing number began to feel threatened. The need for their own organization, separate from gay men, appeared urgent.

A day-long forum to address lesbian concerns was organized in spring 1981, attracting approximately one hundred lesbians. Lesbians decided to form their own organization, where their concerns would not be secondary. As one participant expressed it:

> I was disturbed by the collapse of LOOT and the closing of the Fly. Two or three years ago we had lots of dances and cultural events but suddenly we had nothing. It was like we had built something and it had been smashed. So in the May 9 workshop I said, "Look, our movement's being taken out from under us and if we don't want to co-operate we've got to do something."

Another put the need for LAR in the following terms:

> LAR has a very basic ideology which I think is that lesbians are oppressed as women, that heterosexism and homophobia are different from sexism, and because of that there is a need to fight against lesbian oppression autonomously.

LAR was envisioned as a primarily political organization, informed by a lesbian-feminist analysis of oppression. Founders had been active in either the feminist or gay movements (often both) for many years. Prior to joining the feminist movement, many had also been active in left-wing political groups. LAR was founded therefore, by lesbians who had considerable experience in alternative organizations, and were well-versed in the politics of protest. By 1981, they were ready to draw on their experience to fight for their own rights as lesbians.

The catalyst for LAR's formation may have been the particularly repressive social climate of the early eighties, but the desire for a political lesbian group had been growing for a number of years. When asked why she thought a group such as LAR did not appear in earlier years, one said:

> Lesbians have been developing politically in Toronto by going through political experiences together and separately. A certain maturation has taken place. Women are coming to individual decisions and finding that those decisions are the same for other lesbians too.

Another pointed out the significance of the Bi-national Lesbian Conference in Toronto in 1979 (which many, before joining LAR, had helped organize), and noted:

> After the Conference in 1979 there was a growing energy and it took three years to take off. It takes momentum to get these things going.

This is not to say that everyone in LAR had been "out" as lesbians for many years or had political experience. For those who had only recently begun to identify as lesbian, LAR offered the opportunity to meet lesbian-feminists they could talk to and learn about lesbian-feminism.

Nor is this to say that the more experienced lesbians were uninterested in using LAR to meet social needs. As one said:

> I sometimes think that lesbian groups are fated to disintegrate because we all have such incredible needs to be with other lesbians, and to socialize and be accepted. For those of us who don't like the bar too much then the group has to serve that function, and you get so caught up in your own personal needs that, in some ways, it's a lot easier to be active in another group where you don't go to meet your personal lesbian needs, so you are more willing to "serve the cause," so to speak.

Another commented:

> It's a comfortable way to meet other lesbians. I read
> an article where a woman said that when political
> lesbians get lonely they organize a group.

In short, LAR was formed by lesbians who had high expectations for the group. It was to be an activist organization, but
also an organization where lesbian-feminists could get to
know each other and make friends. These ideas were reflected
in LAR's basis of unity which was accepted at the very first
meeting:

> We define ourselves as (1) a lesbian-feminist organi-
> zation; (2) as activists working on social, political,
> and cultural events; (3) as women-identified-women
> who work together to fight the right-wing as lesbi-
> ans from a lesbian perspective.

Goals and Strategies

Although LAR members agreed on the basis of unity, each had
a different conception of what LAR's goals were or should be.
For example, one said:

> From my perspective I saw LAR informing and poli-
> ticizing the lesbian community on one hand, and on
> the other, participating in different things. I think it's
> extremely important not to lose sight of the general
> social movement; I don't think the liberation of lesbi-
> ans will be achieved by lesbians alone.

Another said:

> I think LAR's goal is to make a better world for
> lesbians, whether it's through getting our act to-
> gether so that we can change the external world or
> whether it's just that we can make a little bit of it for
> ourselves better ... One of the problems is that LAR
> hasn't been able to articulate its ideology yet ...

lesbian-feminism is about as hard to define as you can get.

Others said that their goal was to radically change society. A representative comment was:

> The heterosexist assumptions that exist in society are very, very deep. You can see them everywhere. I don't see that we can change just one part of that. I think we have to change the whole thing, the whole way that this society works.

Shortly after LAR first formed, there was a dispute about strategy. The split was over whether LAR should, from the outset, be an action-oriented group, or whether it should concentrate on trying to formulate a clear conception of lesbian-feminist theory.

One side of the debate felt that because LAR was a new group with members who did not know each other well, it was important for theoretical discussions to take place before engaging in collective action. Others argued that if the group began with focusing on formulating theory, disagreements would lessen the possibilities of finding common ground. On this side of the debate, several argued that neither analysis nor strategy could be developed in a vacuum. As one said, "It's only through the concrete, practical application of our ideas that we're going to learn stuff and figure stuff out." Another pointed out that you "learn by doing" and that talking on an abstract level was meaningless. This member believed that "actions speak louder than words."

After much debate, LAR chose to be action oriented, hoping that an articulated politics would evolve through action. Those who strongly disagreed with the strategy left the group.

One of the first actions LAR organized was a lesbian march (Dykes in the Streets on October 17, 1981). As was later written in a pamphlet produced by LAR:

> We organized Toronto's first lesbian pride march so that lesbians could openly declare our pride and power, happily and without fear ... After it was

over, we all knew that it was indeed possible to express ourselves as powerful, visible lesbians, and we were a little less afraid (LAR 1982, 31).

LAR organized a National Day of Action for March 27, 1982, which included cultural events and political discussions. All lesbians were invited to participate in the events of the day, and in fact, a large number did join in.

LAR also participated in the March 8 Coalition to help organize International Women's Day in both 1982 and 1983. In both years, speeches addressed lesbian issues, and large contingents of lesbians marched under LAR's banner. Likewise, lesbians marched under LAR's banner on Lesbian and Gay Pride Day in 1982. For May 1, 1982, LAR worked with a coalition of other local groups to organize a Fight the Right Festival.

During LAR's first year of existence, there were two cases of lesbians being arrested by police. In one case, a lesbian was arrested for "assaulting a police officer" during a demonstration, and in the other, six were arrested by undercover police outside a bar and charged with police assault. In both cases, the lesbians charged maintained that the incidents were provoked by the police. LAR members felt it was important that these arrests be publicized, and produced flyers asking lesbians to support those arrested and attend their trials.

With all of this activity taking place within such a short time, it began to seem to some that LAR was participating in events for their own sake, with no overall direction. Some did not think that enough time was taken to consider in detail the pros and cons of various actions. Nor did they think that enough time was set aside to evaluate and learn from actions. As one expressed it:

> I think ... there always has to be a balance between activism and evaluating what you've done. This is what theorizing is. I'm not sure that I think LAR has actually done enough of that.

In an attempt to remedy this lack of theoretical discussion, LAR organized several afternoon workshops intended to help sort out positions on various topics, away from the pressure of business meetings. The hope was that these discussions would add to LAR's development. One workshop, for example, was held on LAR's relationship with gay men, while another was on LAR's relationship with the feminist movement. There were lively discussions at these workshops, and most of those who attended learned something. Participants, however, were unable to reach firm conclusions about what LAR's policy should be. It became apparent that LAR members came from a variety of backgrounds and had different philosophies. It was not possible to work out a sophisticated theoretical position on anything without alienating someone. For the most part, therefore, members agreed to disagree.

LAR was damaged by the inability of members to reach consensus on direction over the long term, and the general level of commitment suffered. Many remained highly committed to the possibilities of LAR, yet others reconsidered their earlier willingness to invest large amounts of time and energy. As one member pointed out: "How can you be committed to LAR when you don't know what you're committing yourself to? If you don't know what LAR's going to do?"

When I was interviewing members about a year after LAR's formation, almost everyone commented on feeling a sense of aimlessness and confusion. They wondered which direction LAR would take. Yet, openly addressing the confusion continued to be a tactic which was avoided. LAR remained without a clearly defined set of goals, and lacked a unifying political strategy.

LAR and Others — Lesbian Visibility

On one point there was implicit agreement — that LAR needed to maintain strong ties with other organizations. No one believed that LAR could be an effective political voice in isolation. Many LAR members belonged to other groups and when they came to LAR, brought their ties with them. LAR, therefore, had a variety of contacts from the very beginning.

As time went on, LAR began forming links with other organizations. For example, LAR had representatives at meetings of the Gay Community Council, the Ontario Coalition of Abortion Clinics, and a LAR member joined the Board of Directors of the Citizen's Independent Review of Police Activities. All these links with others gave LAR a high profile, at least in "progressive" circles, and helped to establish credibility.

Maintaining a visible lesbian-feminist presence in anti-establishment politics had been a major reason for the formation of LAR in the minds of some members. Those who had previously been active on their own in promoting lesbian visibility were interested in a show of strength. They joined forces in the hope that, together, they would make more of an impact on others. As one explained:

> We wanted one of the important parts of LAR to make people aware of lesbian-feminism and to make a lesbian-feminist intervention into the broader political community ... I saw LAR as the kind of organization that would go into other organizations and ask questions: challenging the progressive community on its positions on women and lesbians.

Unfortunately, the actual logistics of an interventionist strategy were never clearly mapped out. A cynical view was that everyone in LAR seemed to be waiting for someone else to start something. Thus, even though LAR maintained a high level of activity, especially during its first year, very little attention was paid to planning for the long-term.

Actually, a great deal of LAR's time was spent reaching out to other lesbians. This was part of the reason for holding the Dykes in the Streets march, as well as the National Day of Action. In general, LAR members felt that LAR was a group of, by, and for lesbians, and therefore it was important for LAR to be integrated within the lesbian community.

LAR members however, did not see themselves as representing the lesbian community. Nor were they interested in becoming representatives of the lesbian community. Most realized that the community was far too diverse to be able to speak with one voice. Rather than attempt to impose a lesbian-feminist viewpoint on other lesbians — which, in any case, would have been impossible — LAR wanted to be one voice among many lesbian voices.

LAR did, however, want the support of other lesbians. As one member said: "We have to develop a constituency in the lesbian community." Also:

> While it's true that LAR as an organization of twenty-five women could do political work and not really attempt to bring the lesbian community along, I think we have to be careful about that. If we were to sort of go off on our own, there would be a lot of lesbians left behind.

Measured by the numbers of lesbians who attended events organized by LAR, the organization was very successful in gaining the support of lesbians from a variety of backgrounds.

Structure, Leadership and Process

For most feminist organizations, decisions about how to distribute power often prove to be difficult. Many groups simply decide to operate as a collective without really discussing the implications. There is often an assumption that everyone is willing to share information, along with the hope that everyone will take an equal amount of responsibility for the group. In these respects, LAR was no different from many feminist groups seeking to implement non-patriarchal ways of getting things done.[2]

LAR had no formal structure: it was informal and non-hierarchical. No one wanted elected offices such as president or chairperson. Members were in agreement that hierarchy is restrictive and inevitably authoritarian. They were pleased that LAR operated as a collective where, theoretically, everyone's opinion carried equal weight and decisions were not unilateral. As a collective, no one had more power than anyone else.

LAR's distaste for formality was particularly evident when it came to determining who was part of the group. There was no official process for joining LAR. Meetings were not closed, but open to any lesbian who cared to attend. After attending one meeting, one could refer to oneself as part of LAR if so inclined.

A quasi-membership list existed that included names and telephone numbers of lesbians interested in attending meetings or participating in activities. It had been drawn up soon after LAR was first formed. To facilitate intragroup communication, those attending meetings regularly were provided with a copy. The list served to give an idea of the size of LAR, and it was also used to make a telephone tree. There were five contact women, each of whom was supposed to call another five or six women with news and other information. Sometimes women got called, other times they didn't.

The essence of LAR's philosophy regarding power and structure could be seen in the procedure followed for chairing meetings. Members took turns chairing, to ensure that power was not always vested in the same person, and also to give every lesbian a chance to assume responsibility. The practice was based on the assumption that chairing was a skill which could be learned and needed to be practised. No one was forced to chair a meeting, but all were strongly encouraged to periodically take a turn. At the end of each meeting, the chair for the next meeting was chosen. In practice, there were those who never wanted to chair a meeting, and there were those who chaired meetings frequently.

Meetings were semistructured in that the agenda was drawn up beforehand by the predetermined chairperson. Standard procedures regarding agenda items were also followed. For example, meetings always began with announcements, followed by a reading of the last meeting's minutes (minutes were not read for approval, but to provide continuity between meetings). The sequence of items for discussion was predetermined by the chairperson, although that sequence was not necessarily rigid.

Discussions were informal. One did not need the chair's permission to speak, as it was expected that no one would interrupt anyone else. That expectation was not always realized, however. Frequently, the chair was forced to implement a speaker's list as a means of keeping order and ensuring that everyone had a chance to voice their opinions.

Even though LAR theoretically operated on consensus, when decisions had to be made they were often voted on. There was an implicit assumption during discussions that silence meant agreement, so that when a suggestion was made, if no one voiced an objection it was assumed that there was agreement. When decisions were voted on, the count of "yes" versus "no" responses was not necessarily final. After the vote, if those who were outvoted still wished to argue their case, they were free to do so. No decision was considered final until there was no one voicing an objection. In practice, this procedure meant that particularly contentious issues rarely reached a final decision. At other times, such as during the beginning stages of LAR, dissenting members left.

Leadership within LAR came primarily from those who had considerable experience, as lesbians, with the politics of protest. Their past experience helped them to see issues clearly. Not all of them consciously set themselves up as leaders, but they were nevertheless listened to with respect because of their ability to articulate issues and put them in perspective. Some were happy with this situation, while others found it frustrating. Among those who were frustrated, there was the belief that LAR was pretending to be "one big happy family," while avoidance of the issue of leadership was actually creating dissention. One "leader" had the following to say about this situation:

> Leadership operates at the level of social influence. I don't think that's necessarily bad or unnatural. I'm fairly traditional and I like it when women who are older than me and know more things give direction, if it's done in a way that leaves things open for those with less experience to say what's on their minds, to make objections, to have input.

Ideally, all feminist collectives operate such that everyone is free to speak up. The problem is that there are often obstacles which make it difficult for these idealistic visions to become reality. Some of these obstacles were present at LAR.

During the first few months of LAR's existence, it was primarily the "leaders" who contributed to discussions at meetings. There were several reasons for the virtual monopolization of discussion. One was the "leaders," because they were used to speaking up and could articulate their visions, did not hesitate to voice opinions. Meanwhile, less experienced women did not feel confident enough to express an opinion. They often felt intimidated in the presence of forceful personalities who appeared to know what they were talking about. Another factor, and perhaps the more important one, was that the "leaders" had known each other prior to the formation of LAR. Generally speaking, they were already comfortable with each other. They frequently socialized with each other, and discussed issues among themselves. As a result, they sometimes brought "hidden agendas" to LAR meetings. Issues, although presented to the general membership for discussion, had sometimes already been debated. At other times, actions were undertaken without everyone having a clear understanding of their importance, or without a full discussion of alternatives.[3]

During interviews, many said they disliked the way LAR operated. Some felt that they were wrongfully being excluded from discussions. Others thought that the "leaders" were not really interested in hearing the opinions of others.

Some members were in favour of overt leadership. For them, efficiency was important. Without formally recognized leaders vested with decision-making power, it was difficult to respond to emergency situations or otherwise get things done. On many occasions, time was taken up with drawn-out discussions and decisions were postponed. Sometimes, when decisions were made, they were not followed up, and there was a high level of frustration.

As LAR's pace slowed down in the second year, dissatisfaction with structure was addressed, and it was decided to create a coordinating committee. How well this worked, however, is a moot point, because not long after its creation, LAR disbanded.

LAR in Perspective

Despite LAR's problems with structure, and inability to formulate long-term strategy, there were many who believed that LAR's first year was very successful. As one said:

> I think generally that LAR has been much more successful than I ever imagined, in terms of how

> we've managed to hang together in spite of rough
> times, and with a fair amount of integrity.

From my own perspective, I would agree with this statement as a comment on LAR's first year. At the time of LAR's
formation, much was going on in the city to make lesbians feel
threatened and vulnerable, for example, the distribution of
virulently anti-lesbian literature. There were fewer and fewer
spaces left where it was safe to be openly lesbian. These circumstances were the impetus for the formation of LAR.

Almost immediately, LAR became busy with organizing a
march, sending representatives to meetings of other organizations, and other activities. With the attention of most members
focused on making LAR's existence known, there was very
little desire to test the limits of unity. LAR was new, and for
some, its very newness was exciting. At the time, it did indeed
seem like "something" was going to be done to protect and
maybe even expand lesbian space. No one wanted to jeopard-
ize this show of lesbian strength by discussing the philosophical differences between members.

LAR was successful in bringing together lesbians with
different political philosophies to fight a common enemy.
After the first few meetings, when everyone was trying to
figure out what to do with the infant group, there was agreement that LAR should be devoted to political action, and that
agreement never wavered. There was a sense of urgency in the
air — that unless something was done soon, things would get
worse. Among the members, it was understood that whatever
their differences, the fundamental fact of their lesbianism put
them all in the same boat together. It was necessary to present
a united front.

Nevertheless, there were political differences among those
active in LAR. In very simplistic terms, there were lesbians at
LAR who identified with radical feminists, there were socialist
feminists, and there were lesbians who were not sure which
strain of feminism they identified with. All called themselves
lesbian-feminists, but as quoted earlier in this article, "lesbian-
feminism is about as hard to define as you can get." No one
was sure exactly what lesbian-feminism was, or how it differed
from, for example, radical feminism or socialist feminism. I

think it is safe to say that lesbians at LAR recognized their feminist beliefs as intimately tied to their lesbian existence. The problem was figuring out what that implied in terms of changing society. What sort of goals were logical extensions of lesbian-feminism, and what kind of strategy should be used? LAR was unable to come up with answers to these fundamental questions.

As someone keenly aware of what it was like to live as a lesbian in a hostile climate, I had great hopes for LAR. I missed the lesbian spaces which had existed in the city only two years before, and LAR helped to fill that gap in my life. At LAR meetings, I could renew my sense of myself as a lesbian-feminist. It was important to me to be with others, knowing that I was not alone in my fight to make the world a safer place for lesbians. In that sense, I got a lot from LAR, and I was not the only one who felt a little more secure in the knowledge of LAR's existence.

We did a lot at LAR and, especially during the first year, our activities were carried out with a high degree of commitment from almost everyone there. After the first year, though, the numbers committed to making LAR work began to wane. After two years, there was not enough energy left for LAR to continue. What happened to all the dreams for LAR?

In terms of leadership, those with more experience than others were willing to share their knowledge, rather than keep it to themselves. Although the word "empowerment" was not used at the time, there were real attempts to empower the others in the group. This was evident not only in the general willingness to share knowledge, but also in the procedure used for chairing meetings. Anyone interested in taking on responsibility was encouraged and, if she wanted it, given help.

At the same time that those involved with LAR were gaining a sense of power, LAR let other lesbians know that they were not alone. A good example of this was LAR's show of support for lesbians facing what many thought were trumped-up assault charges.

Leadership, however, remained weak. The lack of a clearly defined structure meant that no one was in charge, yet everyone was in charge. Thus, even though there were those at LAR who might have proven to be strong leaders, the structure prevented them from giving any long-term direction. This is not to advocate having someone take over the group and directing it without considering the wishes of others. As one LAR member said,

> I don't want one person doing all the political analysis or organizing ... . The moment someone takes over a group I have to wonder about what she's doing because that means you think the only way it can work is with your leadership and direction.

Yet, as another LAR member pointed out:

> Unfortunately, I think leadership is seen too much in terms of having ideas and speaking about them. But if they don't also take care of the group and make sure it runs, then they're going to be a leader in the bad sense of the word. They're going to be a theoretician who says what's going to be done. Good leaders ... take care of the group.

LAR needed visible leaders to take care of the group. There were lots of ideas about what LAR could or should do, but since no one was in charge, it was difficult to implement ideas. Perhaps a collective structure, where everyone involved has equal commitment to the group, and equal authority, works in very small groups. For the most part, however, an average LAR meeting attracted between fifteen and thirty lesbians. Some of them attended regularly, others only once in a while. In other words, not everyone at a given meeting was equally committed to or took equal responsibility for the group. Furthermore, if getting things done efficiently was important, there were simply too many lesbians involved to make that possible.

In the final analysis, though, LAR's biggest problem was the lack of a clearly articulated ideology — a manifesto. The lack of unifying ideology meant that there were various conceptions of theory, goals and strategy. While LAR's "basis of unity" provided a sense of group identity, it did not go far enough in identifying problems and outlining solutions. The "basis of unity" was far too amorphous to inspire long-term commitment to LAR.

LAR's burst of activity in the first year took its toll on members. The activity was particularly draining because it was not focused. At times, it appeared that actions were initiated simply as ends in themselves. By the end of the first year, exhaustion had begun to set in. LAR had managed to keep a high profile, but was no closer to the realization of goals, because goals had never been concretized in the first place.

As the second year progressed, the lack of a clear focus became more and more of a problem. LAR needed direction. Without direction, it was no longer so easy for LAR to "hang together."

It is always sad, especially for those whose identity is tied to a group, to see a group fall apart. It is not necessarily a bad thing, however, for a group which no longer works to fold. LAR was not a failure and its activities were not in vain. During its short existence, a great deal was accomplished.

Today, there are lesbian caucuses in most feminist organizations and there is a strong lesbian presence in many gay rights organizations, including the national organization EGALE. Across the country, lesbian-feminists are working to create a better world for lesbians. Should lesbians ever feel the need for a unified lesbian-feminist response to political circumstances, we have LAR as a precedent. It was done then and it can be done again.

Section III

Linking Theory and Practice

Organizational Forms, Research,
and Teaching

Introduction

Academe is frequently seen as the primary location for the generation of theory, while the community is seen as the primary location for activist practice. The contributors to this section of the volume make it clear that the divisions between academe and community, theory and practice are frequently bridged by feminists. Feminists have been active in creating organizational forms designed to bridge these divisions, as well as in conducting research and teaching that provides links between academe and the community, and that contribute to feminist praxis—the melding of theory and practice. The chapters are presented in an order from the general to the specific, from a Canada-wide feminist organization representing a coalition of feminist researchers and activists to a specific teaching effort designed to foster student activism in academe.

Two of the chapters (Chapters 14 and 16) that describe feminist organizational forms present somewhat contrasting views of the nature of the division between feminists whose primary locations are academe and the community. Christiansen-Ruffman, in Chapter 14, describes the Canadian Research Institute for the Advancement of Women (CRIAW), a large cross-Canada organization with over 1000 members. The organization was conceived with the explicit aim of linking feminists in the community and in the academy, and has been quite successful in doing so. Christiansen-Ruffman attacks the myth of necessary tension between academics and activists, noting that many feminists are both and that the work of feminist studies academics is itself revolutionary in the academy. She does, of course, recognize structural and language difficulties associated with academic feminists being situated in the hierarchical academic power structure. Yet, she believes that the work and aims of feminists in these two locations are more similar than different and that tensions between them are primarily a result of the masculinist academic bureaucracy and heritage from male practices.

Bishop, Manicom and Morissey (Chapter 16) consider the division between academic and community feminists to be deeper than does Christiansen-Ruffman. They, too, are concerned with the discrepancy in resources , as well as the power available to women in the two locations, as well as with the appropriation of knowledge from women in the community by academic feminists. The university-based organization which they describe has been somewhat successful in bridging the academe-community division, and they make a number of other useful suggestions for such bridging. Christiansen-Ruffman and Bishop, et al., agree that it is necessary for feminists to actively and consciously seek to bridge the separations.

The work that feminists have carried out in seeking to entrench feminism in academe may be described according to Briskin's (Chapter 1) formulation as mainstreaming, while community feminist activism is more likely to fall on the disengaged pole of this dynamic. Drakich and Maticka-Tyndale (Chapter 15) also take up the mainstreaming-disengagement dynamic as a central analytic tool in their examination of the development of feminist activism in the Canadian Sociology and Anthropology Association (CSAA). Academic feminists in every academic discipline in which we have exceeded a minimal critical mass have engaged in more or less successful efforts to organize, to assert our rights as women in the discipline, and to advance the study of women in our own right. Drakich and Maticka-Tyndale's fine-grained analysis makes use of the mainstreaming-disengaged dynamic to clarify tensions and setbacks in the development of feminist activism in the CSAA. The mainstreaming pole is represented by the concerns of female academics in the organization who are primarily concerned with career gains within the academic bureaucracy for women (and themselves as individuals), rather than with the broader aims of the feminist movement. Those whose concerns are on the disengaged pole are more likely to be the activists with strong connections to the women's movement outside academe whose energies and unrecognized labour propel the feminist work of the organization.

In the sole contribution to the volume from the province of Quebec, Karen Messing (Chapter 17) provides an intriguing vision of the melding of theory and practice through a personalized account of her involvement in research on the health effects of women's work. The Université du Québec à Montréal (UQAM) has an agreement with unions that allows university researchers release time and academic credit for carrying out research relevant to union concerns. Though only a small proportion of the university faculty have worked with unions with this agreement, Messing and other members of the Groupe de recherche-action en biologie du travail (GRABIT) have carried out a number of studies. The work is action research; the unions formulate questions of concern to them and researchers do their best to provide data that answer the questions as directly as possible. GRABIT has been particularly responsive to the concerns of women union members, and women employed in ghettos. The researchers have found that their own subjectivity as women and as workers has been invaluable to their work. The model presented by the UQAM union-university agreement is one that could be useful to Canadian academic feminists in other locations.

Another central tool that feminists have used in bridging theory and practice is feminist teaching. Women's studies has been particularly successful in developing feminist consciousness and activism among women fortunate enough to be able to attend universities. Joanne Prindiville (Chapter 18) discusses the more difficult problems posed, as well as the great potential for feminist change, when "the women's studies' classroom is an entire, very large province, and 'the class' never meets face to face." She describes her work in teaching a women's studies distance education course to women across the province of Newfoundland and Labrador. Distance education provides a technology for educational outreach to women in remote communities which have been rarely tapped by feminist academics, as well as an educational approach that involves its own unique set of problems. Through Prindiville's course, women have shared skills and knowledge, have had the opportunity of participating in a feminist forum, and have gained the support of other women. As a result, the course has raised the feminist consciousness and individual activism of the women who have participated.

In our final contribution, Jeri Wine (Chapter 19) describes a graduate level course which she conceived as an explicit effort to bridge theory and practice, in which students formed small collectives and carried out feminist community activist projects. The chapter takes up the theme of the contradictions involved in teaching a course that emphasizes feminist community change in the context of the hierarchical, patriarchal authority structure that is academe. She describes the impact that the course has had on the community through a description of some of the projects carried out by students. Wine provides some analysis of the power relations inherent in the women's studies classroom which is embedded in academe, and suggests that recognition and discussion of these power relations is an important feminist pedagogical strategy.

Bridging the Gap Between Feminist Activism and Academe

The Canadian Research Institute for the Advancement of Women[1]

Linda Christiansen-Ruffman

During the history of the women's movement, considerable attention has focused on overcoming apparent polarities symbolized by the world of academe and the world of political activism. The women's movement has countered these dichotomies with scholarly arguments (see, for example, Christiansen-Ruffman 1989), with political slogans such as "the personal is political" and its corollary, "the intellectual is political," and with feminist organizations and practices such as feminist pedagogy, participatory research, and action research. In the words of a document from the women's movement as reprinted in Adamson, Briskin and McPhail (1988):

> We had lots of arguments in the big meetings about whether we should ACT or THINK. We finally knew we needed both. So we tried to set up some structure. (1970 Montreal Women's Liberation, 272)

This chapter focuses on one such feminist organization, the Canadian Research Institute for the Advancement of Women

(CRIAW). It describes, from my viewpoint,[2] how CRIAW has struggled both at the national level and locally, within Nova Scotia, to deal with and to change features of the inappropriate separation between the world of academe and the world of the activist. In this chapter, features of the context within which CRIAW operates are conceptualized by several models depicting different aspects of the relationship between the world of academe and the world of the activist. The chapter then explores the importance of the relationship and ways in which CRIAW has both attempted to bridge the gap and to mitigate tensions created by contemporary class and elite structures and by patriarchally organized institutions.

The World of Academe and the World of the Activist

The world of academe, or "the academy" as it is sometimes called, is associated with universities and with the production of knowledge. Its relationship with the world, or worlds, of activists may be conceptualized by different models that highlight key features of the inter-relationships between these two spheres.

Dichotomous Model

The world of academe and the world of the activist are often depicted as polar opposites. Division and opposition are often described and experienced between "town and gown," between the university and the community, between the ivory tower and real life, between the academy and the society, between the objective observer and partisan individual, and between the "detached" scholar and the "engaged" citizen. The academy helps to enshrine these dichotomies, in part through distinctions between thought and action, between theory and practice, and between the intellectual and the political.

The dichotomous model depicts the popular conception, or contemporary ideology as it might be called. It pictures unique spheres for the world of academe and the world of the activist as in Figure 1 as distinct, non-overlapping, separate, opposite. Communication seldom flows between them, and they have different bases, are organized around contrasting goals, norms and principles and are seen to have unique memberships. In

FIGURE 14.1

Dichotomous Patriarchal Model of the Gap Between the
World of Academe and the World of the Activist

each sphere, contrasting realities are considered as important, as problems, and as appropriate activities. They each have their own forms of knowledge, orientations to knowledge, ways of using knowledge, and methods of producing and legitimizing knowledge. Participants within each sphere also construct each other as different, as other.

Although ideally activist and scholarly knowledge are equally important and inter-related, in the contemporary patriarchal world, there is a distinct hierarchical relationship between the two. The unequal relationship between the two spheres is manifest, for example, by what might be considered academically sanctioned exploitation of the community by the academic world. In the typical interaction between the academy and the community, the community's knowledge, time and energy are appropriated in the interests of "scholar-ship."

According to the prescriptions of modern social science, interaction or reactivity between the research subject and the researcher should be minimized in the interests of "objectiv-ity" and sound scholarship. In the course of a typical research project, formal contact is made by the researcher for the pur-pose of gathering data that the researcher has identified as important. The researcher makes all decisions in terms of what information to gather, its timing and its use. The researcher appropriates information and produces expert knowledge that then undermines and is often used against its origins in the everyday perceptions and understandings of community members.[3]

In this popular, dichotomous conception of the relationship between the two spheres, there is an inherent gap. The accept-able way to "bridge the gap" is to use the ladder of formal education. It is thought that one must climb the rungs and hurdles of university education, graduate school and univer-sity politics to be considered legitimate in the academic world and thus to hold membership among those who have the right to think, to theorize, to conduct research as well as to be cre-dentialized as intellectuals.

Pyramidal Model

Dichotomies such as the above, and their legitimist, patriarchal education, are powerful ideologies. In a patriarchal and capi-talist world, they create separations, barriers, distinctions and mistrust among people who are potential allies. They under-mine the feminist project and mask the textures, hierarchies, and the structural constraints that are taken-for-granted fea-tures of contemporary society. They delegitimize women's knowledge and the contextualized nature of women's percep-tions and experiences. In fact, Figure 14.1, although consistent with contemporary ideology, is abstracted and does not ade-quately describe the structural power relationships within which the world of academe and the world of the activist are embedded.

The pyramidal model depicts these social structural rela-tionships in contemporary Canadian society. The power and resource relationships between these two worlds and within which these two worlds operate are illustrated by the pyramidal model in Figure 14.1. The diagram shows the two worlds within a larger societal context. It shatters the superficial image of dichotomy by depicting the many other institutions and "worlds" that comprise multi-dimensional contemporary social relations. The diagram shows the academic world and the world of the activist as two of a number of institutions or "worlds" contained within the social structure and partly comprising it. It illustrates how they each reflect the hierarchical structure of the greater society. The structural location of the world of academe means that it speaks for and in the interests of a particular social class and that its research agenda reflects the interests of the powerful in society.[4] Moreover, the diagram implies the interdependence of institutions. For example, the teaching and research agenda are shaped by the activities and priorities of other institutions (e.g., the military, the family, the media, religion, the economy) and social worlds (e.g., activists, the space industry) and by the educational institutions' requirements for resources from other institutional spheres. In turn, the educational institutions manipulate their resources in what are often perceived to be the interests of both the institution and society.

A number of material, organizational and hierarchical differences between academics and feminist activists within the community have been described by Bishop, Manicom, and Morrisey (see Chapter 16).[5] The class structure allocates power, prestige, and resources to academics who are in a relatively privileged position. The organization of work hires, promotes, fires, and rewards in other ways those who perform "correctly," adhering to the patriarchal structure's rules and reproducing its norms and values.

Universities offer their tenured faculty a steady and secure salary and benefits, resources such as typewriters and copying machines, and time needed for research and reflection. Although these resources are minimal compared to those available to other professionals, and especially given the years of training required, academics have more material benefits that would permit their activism than do many community members,

FIGURE 14.2

Social Structural Relationships Between the World of
Academe and the World of the Community Activist

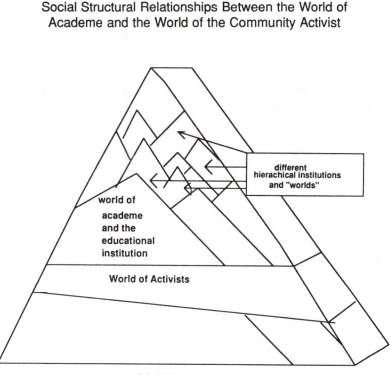

different
hierachical institutions
and "worlds"

world of
academe
and the
educational
institution

World of Activists

SOCIETY

including paid community activists. The institutional structure
of the university and its material resource base thus create
contradictions for the interrelationships between academics
and activists as well as hierarchical class distinctions both at
the individual level and at the collective level.[6] It is not surprising therefore that community workers correctly identify
the academic world as supporting the interests of powerful
elites in society.

Both academe and the bureaucratically ordered institutions
of larger society have egoistic, individualistic, and elitist
norms. Academic norms emphasize specialization, privilege,
expertise, scholarly competition (being the first to prove an
idea), and the exclusivity of "scholarly" knowledge. In academic discourse, knowledge becomes objectified and mystified.

As Arthur Stinchcombe (1984) has pointed out, within scholarly knowledge, the more abstract and depersonalized ideas are considered more important and generate higher prestige. The focus on knowledge for its own sake also has the consequence of appearing objective but is, in fact, being supportive of the structural location that generated it. It implicitly endorses hierarchy. It creates lack of confidence in people's perceptions and glorifies "expert" knowledge. As with any professional paradigm, it fosters distancing statements as: "He must be brilliant because I can't understand a word he says," or "She must be brilliant because I can not understand a word she says." It is organized and maintained to mystify and to discount people's opinions and intelligence in general and women's knowledge in particular.

In contrast, the world of the community activist must be more oriented toward collective, popularist knowledge, with its interconnections with women's everyday experiences, and with its orientation toward activism and change. Rather than abstracted knowledge, it is oriented towards the practical world of women's experiences and strengths, of discrimination and inequality, and of the need for social change.

Feminist Model

The dichotomous model (Figure 14.1) and the pyramidal model (Figure 14.2) are reflections of the contemporary patriarchal and capitalist systems that combine with each other in contemporary society to assert their power over, and to shape, social relationships and discourses, including academic ones. In reaction against the oppressive structure and ideology of contemporary patriarchy, the feminist movement has articulated a feminist alternative.

In the ideal feminist conception of the world, social relationships are not hierarchical or competitive but cooperative, egalitarian, and organic, based on feminist values. One might depict these relationships as a constantly interweaving and overlapping set of spheres that are in process of developing and changing. Picture the lines in Figure 14.3 as dynamic and in flux.

FIGURE 14.3

Feminist Conception of the Relation Between the World
of Academe and the World of the Community Activist

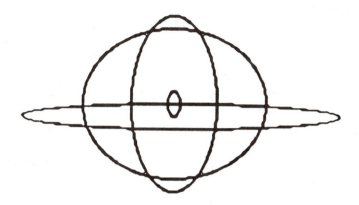

Academe and activism might both be parts of overlapping
and cooperating spheres. Hierarchies would be absent both
within these areas of interest and in relation to one another.

Feminist Realities in Canada and the Development of CRIAW

Although these three models were not part of the conceptual
discourse of academics or activists in Canada in the 1970s, they
focus our attention on popular, structural and ideal feminist
features of the interrelationship between academe and activism that seem to have been important during this period. As
members of the society and the academy, Canadian feminists
experienced the perceived division between activism and
academe, despite the fact that many were both feminists and
academics. Such distinctions, for example, are common in
deciding "what counts" in hiring, promotion, and tenure. Feminists have also faced the sexist, racist, and classist social relations, ideologies, thought processes, and scholarship that have
undermined and confounded feminist ideals, goals, discourses, and activities.[7]

In the late 1960s, the women's liberation movement was relatively strong, and so feminist activism was thriving at a time when feminism in academe was virtually non-existent. Universities in Canada were expanding and a number of junior women scholars were given jobs in academia. The few women scholars who were in universities in the 1970s began to become aware of the discrimination against women that was reflected both in the relative absence of women in academe and in their disproportionate location at the bottom of the steeply pyramidal system. Feminism and feminist organizations helped those in academe to name features of discrimination that they experienced. This historical process displayed one of the fundamental contradictions of feminist scholarship within the academy.

On the one hand, feminist scholars live and operate within the world of the academy that is shaped to some extent by the ideal that universities are supposed to be the source of knowledge and to produce knowledge that is not biased. On the other hand, many feminist scholars in Canada have come to recognize that the scholarly world as we know it falls short of this objective, producing and reproducing knowledge that is sexist, as well as being classist and racist. Many feminist scholars have come to recognize that contemporary discipline-based scholarship has been developed by male theorists, based on male culture, male data and male interpretations of data. Although the academy claims an exclusive monopoly on knowledge, many feminist scholars within the academy have not only come to realize the limits of contemporary academic knowledge but also have come to recognize the significance of knowledge and insights from the activist feminist community.

Feminist activism and feminist theorizing have been important sources of knowledge creation. Feminists, for example, have tended to reject what were once taken-for-granted or popular dichotomies. Early feminists developed conceptualizations that later became key principles of the movement and slogans such as the "personal is political" and its corollaries "the intellectual is political" and "the intellectual is personal." Only after a number of years did feminist scholarship use these movement insights to recognize and reject the dichotomous thought processes of the either/or syndrome and to associate this syndrome with patriarchy itself (e.g., see Christiansen-Ruffman 1989).

Moreover, some feminist scholars have also found in feminism alternative norms and values that are more consistent with scientific colleagiality than those egoistic values that characterize contemporary scholarship. For example, although scientific scholarship is supposed to rest on the basis of openness and mutual availability of knowledge, scholarly norms are often predominant that prevent intellectual ideas from being seen as communal property and prohibit truly collaborative work. In contemporary science there has been erosion of some of the "institutional imperatives" that Merton has identified as part of modern science, especially the feature that "the substantive findings of science are a product of social collaboration and are assigned to the community" (Merton 1957, 536). A feminist version of scholarship is more consistent with this ideal.

In the mid-1970s feminist academics, feminist activists and feminist academics who were also feminist activists had begun to recognize their mutual interconnectedness and the need to develop the feminist potential that comes with bridging the gap between activism and academe. From its inception, CRIAW was, in part, an organizational bridge both based in and dependent upon the strengths of each of the worlds. Gradually the ability of a feminist scholarship to create and to reproduce grew as the intersection between the two worlds expanded. Many feminists within CRIAW increasingly began to recognize themselves not primarily as activists or as intellectuals but as activists *and* intellectuals, as thinkers *and* actors.

We might think about the history of CRIAW as an historical process that has tended to increase the overlap or intersection between feminist activism and academe at the same time as it has reduced the hierarchical relationship. This process over time is illustrated in Figure 14.4. Throughout this historical process, the persistent ideological and structural forces illustrated in Figures 14.1 and 14.2 have attempted and continue to try to undermine the feminist ideals represented in Figure 14.3 and to reassert the power of patriarchy. Thus, there has been a constant struggle within feminist academe and between

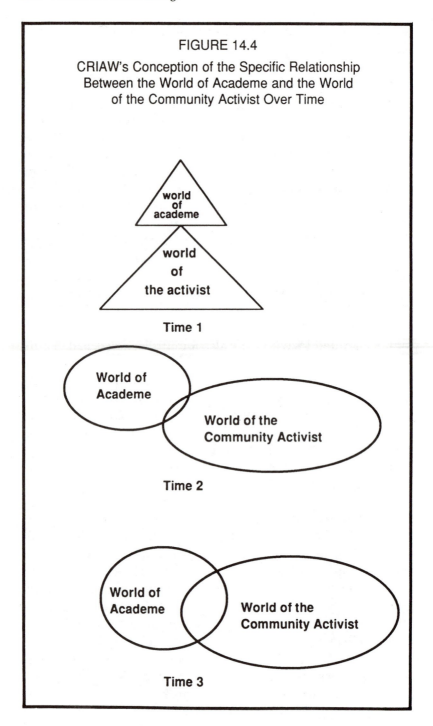

FIGURE 14.4

CRIAW's Conception of the Specific Relationship Between the World of Academe and the World of the Community Activist Over Time

feminist academe and the community to ensure that the bridge is not to be a one way street.

CRIAW's Bridging Mechanisms

CRIAW's organizational work of bridging the gap between academia and activism is reflected in its objectives, its origin, its membership, its policies, and its on-going activities. Meetings, conferences, the newsletter, publications, the bank of researchers, and communication networks, involve both academics and activists as will be elaborated below.

Objectives

CRIAW was founded in 1976 to encourage and to coordinate research into women's experience. CRIAW's objectives include the promotion, the conduct and the dissemination of research as well as two objectives of particular interest to this paper:

> 1. ... to promote the advancement of women through feminist research and ... "

> 2. ... to encourage and facilitate communication and information exchange among academic women, community workers, women's groups and concerned individuals.

Thus from the beginning, the objectives recognized differences among women as well as their shared feminist project — the advancement of women. The objectives also recognized CRIAW as a bridging organization facilitating communication and exchange of ideas among several constituencies, as well as the overlapping participation of these constituencies in the feminist project.

The shared goals are often articulated somewhat differently by activists and academics, and mutuality is reflected in the way that each stresses the contributions of the other. For example, a long-term feminist, CRIAW national president and community activist, Muriel Duckworth, recalls wanting to create CRIAW as a place where academics could present their research, as a place where women who need information might find it, and as a place where scholars in different disciplines might interact and begin to define feminist research activities. I remember, as well, being enthusiastic about CRIAW as a place where researchers could discover the issues in need of research, recognize patriarchally created barriers, and gain feminist insights.

Origins

CRIAW's origins in Halifax and in Ottawa included an orientation to both academic and activist interests in what might be considered three initial organizational efforts. In 1975 in Nova Scotia many initiatives in the aftermath of the Royal Commission on the Status of Women and during International Women's Year signalled that times were ripe for an organization such as CRIAW. From the vantage point of the late 1980s, it is hard to recall what it was like to have virtually no public attention paid to women, no feminist publications available, no feminist explanations, no theoretical or methodological discussions, virtually no feminist organizations. It is now hard to remember the profound public silencing and invisibility of women, to describe the often muted, inexplicable, and unnamed frustrations that feminist activists and academics experienced, and to understand the excitement and liberation generated by and legitimized in the women's liberation movement, in International Women's Year, and in feminist organizations.

In 1975 I was part of the Committee on Women's Research and Publications that was working on a proposal for a negotiated grant with the Canada Council to promote research and writing on women and by women. The focus of this project was the creation of both community and scholarly knowledge. We worked on the project in 1975-76, and when we travelled to Ottawa with endorsements from other feminist scholars throughout Canada, the granting agency was totally discouraging, told us that the field of scholarship was not yet developed enough to support any such effort and that women's studies was not a discipline. Rather than abandon our efforts completely, we decided to end our collaboration with a conference with a similar joint focus. We then organized what turned out to be the first Canadian conference on women and research with the theme, Research on Women: Current Projects and Future Directions. The overwhelming response and interest led us to add additional days, to write more grant proposals and to expand our estimates of participation from 30 to over 300; over 500 attended some part of the Halifax event. The conference was planned with sessions of most interest to local community activists on Saturday, when they were most likely to be able to attend. Papers were presented by feminists, by women academics who had done field work but had never treated women's experiences as theoretically central, and by a few men, either from a feminist perspective or with feminist critiques ensured (see *Atlantis*, 2 (2), part 2, 1977 for selected papers). That conference was in November, 1976, and CRIAW began its annual national meetings in November, 1977.

Pat Saidek, whom CRIAW commissioned to write its history in 1986, describes the Halifax meeting as well as the Ottawa committee of researchers, policy-makers and housewives, initiated by Naomi Griffiths, that met during 1975 and issued invitations to attend a two-day founding conference in Ottawa in April 1976. As Saidek (1986, 1) points out, "Seventy participants from organizations representing Canada's cultural and regional diversities established goals and objectives, adopted a constitution, elected a board of directors and voted (after considerable debate) to name their new organization the Canadian Research Institute for the Advancement of Women." Pauline Jewett, CRIAW's first president, and a number of founding members attended the Halifax conference along with their membership brochure; meetings were held. In Saidek's (1986, 1) words, "It was in this climate of concern ... that CRIAW attracted five hundred members in its first ten months."

In Nova Scotia, Muriel Duckworth, who had been one of the invitees to CRIAW's founding convention and had been elected to its first board as Nova Scotia representative, took her organizational and representational responsibilities seriously and began to organize a provincial chapter. At the first national conference, she organized a caucus of Nova Scotian women. Back in Halifax, she invited women academics and activists within Nova Scotia to a meeting to talk about the new organization and to "report back" on what had happened at the annual conference. She used her persuasive charm to organize meetings and then to form a steering committee of local feminist researchers and activists. As a community activist, Duckworth convinced other activists as well as many academics of the importance of this research organization for feminist research and social change for the advancement of women and soon had women working together on several projects on women and work: (1) video tapes were made for cable television and community use, focusing on women's experiences in different work settings, and (2) a community kit was designed for use by women's groups, trade unions, adult educators, etc. to enable Nova Scotian women to develop effective strategies for achieving equality. Both of these projects involved both academics and activists, and contributed to the community's knowledge, and to creating and sustaining community activists.

Building the Organization

The group meeting in Ottawa and the national board had visions of finding large amounts of money to fund CRIAW as a research institute with a large research staff, located in Ottawa. They and several subsequent CRIAW Boards engaged in major fund-raising quests although the vision later changed to a more decentralized "research institute without walls." In the early stages, CRIAW worked to establish a credible organization with the aid of $5000 in services from the Association of Universities and Colleges in Canada (AUCC), the clerical assistance of the Social Science Federation of Canada (SSFC) and Marion Porter, a volunteer coordinator, subsequently executive director. In 1979, CRIAW was successful in receiving an annual operating grant from the Women's Program of the Secretary of State, that permitted it to hire a small staff.

In the early 1980s, members of CRIAW in Nova Scotia were concerned about what appeared to be top down and hierarchical organizational structures and activities and thought of CRIAW nationally as being rather elitist and centrist, controlled by an academic elite in Ottawa and Ontario. CRIAW Nova Scotia's model emphasizing grassroots connections and local initiatives was at one time discouraged by the members of the national board, but during the 1980s CRIAW began to recog-

nize its networking function and to operate as a research institute "without walls." CRIAW also began to give more priority
to grassroots involvement and to recognize its connection to
the women's movement as essential in accomplishing its objectives — the conduct and dissemination of feminist research
for the advancement of women.

Membership

CRIAW members and project workers have been academic
researchers, applied researchers, community researchers, community activists, members of women's groups and individual
feminists. Many members have been "all" or "most of the
above." Thus CRIAW as an organization bridges the academic
world and the activist world, in part, because a number of its
members are in both worlds. It is also a bridge organization
because its members share a commitment to the importance of
research and to the feminist goals of naming women's experiences, understanding women's oppression, or the discrimination against women, and struggling for feminist social
change or transformation.

Within Nova Scotia, there is a locally based organization
with its own decision-making body or coordinating committee. The important and equal contribution to CRIAW Nova
Scotia's activities of what has elsewhere been called "town and
gown" is one of the criteria informally recognized in the yearly
selection of committee members. Sometimes it is difficult to
categorize women, however, since the categories are not mutually exclusive. For example, since joining the 1988-89 executive, one community-based activist has gotten a part-time job
teaching a course at a local university and two are "mature"
undergraduate students, one a single mother and the other a
senior citizen.

At the national level, CRIAW's board of directors consists
of one representative from each province or territory and six
members at large, at least one of whom must be from Québec.
CRIAW's board has been conscious of representing the diversity of its members and from time to time, it has discussed
constitutional changes to increase the francophone and Québec board membership and to formally represent the diverse
segments of the Canadian feminist movement on its board. In

the 1980s, both in Canada and in Nova Scotia, the governing bodies had a relatively diverse membership in terms of age, employment status (retired, unemployed, underemployed, employed), living situations, sexual orientation, language, ethnicity, race, disability, etc. In 1988 to 1989, most of the board members worked in universities but some also spent their working day in the home, in governments, consulting firms, social agencies, community organizations, unions, and businesses. In the mid-1980s CRIAW elections often selected grassroots feminists to be on the board. In a way, the reverse legitimacy of "community activist concerns" within CRIAW is an important counterbalance to the taken-for-granted hierarchical relationships assumed in the greater community; it is part of the struggle feminists have with patriarchy.

Policies

In order to promote a diverse membership and to ensure CRIAW has roots in and is useful to the women's movement, CRIAW has worked on accessibility policies and their implementation. It has kept membership fees low and encouraged those who could afford more to contribute. Since CRIAW annual conferences are organized by local committees around Canada and there has sometimes been a university-elitist bias as well as a trade-off between the amount of organizing resources and accessibility, the CRIAW Board has established a series of accessibility policies for its conferences. As well, themes of its conferences are designed to attract feminists with different experiences of knowledge creation and consumption (e.g., Women and Well Being; Women and Development; Making Connections). CRIAW's newsletter seeks to make resources accessible to a diverse membership. Recognizing accessibility problems with writing, especially by academics, CRIAW has begun to target its publications towards specific audiences. For example, a research report on women and community politics was written in both a scholarly and popular format, and CRIAW's reproductive technology project has produced two publications; the bilingual collection of essays, abstracts and research resources has a more scholarly tone than the community kit, written in more accessible language and designed for use by women's groups.

These accessibility policies are one of the organizational necessities of having a diverse membership. In addition, CRIAW has needed to adopt feminist decision-making practices that are attentive to strongly held views of minority constituencies. CRIAW has also recognized and tried to promote a variety of types of feminist research and helped to validate the kinds of action-oriented, community-based research that women's groups have been doing and presenting in a variety of formats — briefs, videos, plays, as well as the more traditional research reports. CRIAW's small research grants in aid give priority to community-based research proposals.

Activities Contributing Both to the
Women's Movement and to Scholarship

CRIAW has provided the women's movement with relevant scholarship and information through its quarterly newsletter, its annual conference and conference proceedings, its publication series (Feminist Perspectives and CRIAW Papers), and occasional meetings. For example, in Nova Scotia once every few years CRIAW Nova Scotia has organized a conference or workshop on a special theme high on the feminist community's agenda and defined as in need of special attention. Themes have included: (a) women and health, (b) women and development, (c) women and the environment, (d) reproductive technologies, (e) peace and (f) community action research. Sometimes these events were organized entirely by CRIAW with or without the support of project funding from Secretary of State's Women's Program. They were organized because of both intellectual and activist interests of its members; sometimes the work was done jointly with other women's organizations.

CRIAW's members who are sanctioned as "experts" by the larger society have provided resources and briefs that promote women-centered viewpoints to government and the public. Their recognition of the expertise of local women activists is consistent with feminist principles, although contrary to the hierarchical structures of Figures 14.1 and 14.2. In Nova Scotia, CRIAW has established ad hoc subcommittees of knowledgable women from both the activist and academic communities to work on briefs to governmental commissions on such topics as women and work, status of women, women and occupational health, uranium, pensions, the impact on women of offshore oil, pornography, women and health care in Nova Scotia. CRIAW-Nova Scotia has felt a responsibility to ensure women's points of view are included when the government is addressing such policy questions.

One multi-faceted special CRIAW-Nova Scotia project was initiated at an emergency meeting called by Women Against Violence Against Women, held at the Halifax YWCA as part of a Canada-wide expression of concern in the feminist community about First Choice and about the licensing of cable operators to broadcast American-produced pornography on television. In response to questions about research from activists at the meeting, Sue Shaw, a feminist sociologist, approached other CRIAW members during the coffee break about forming a CRIAW-Nova Scotia task force on pornography. She volunteered to coordinate the task force of interested women in the community and community activists to examine previous research findings. Later in the year, the task force wrote a brief to present to the Canadian government's Fraser Commission on Pornography and Prostitution. The committee went on to develop and conduct a research project focusing on Nova Scotian women's reactions to pornography, the results of which were presented in a report, at a public meeting, and in the press. In a follow-up project, a video tape was produced, designed specifically for use in schools.

Within the academic community, CRIAW's existence, its annual conferences, its publications, its awards, and its bank of researchers along with its sister organization, Canadian Women's Studies, have helped to stretch the boundaries of recognized scholarly research. It has helped to institutionalize theories and methodologies consistent with feminist principles. CRIAW has been in the forefront of identifying and eliminating sexist biases in research.[8] Its existence, strength and community-based skills have provided the support that enables CRIAW members to raise issues of bias against women within other academic and professional arenas and within governments. For example, at the National Ad-Hoc Workshop on Women's Studies in September 1987, CRIAW members were responsible for ensuring that the following resolution was on the agenda and passed: "The workshop reasserts its commitment to women's studies research which is accessible and available to the community it is intended to serve."

CRIAW has been experimenting with alternate types of research methodologies, ones that emphasize collaborative rather than individualistic norms. Rather than starting a research project with one individual following his or her intellectual pursuits and then reviewing the literature and conducting the project, CRIAW has experimented with collaborative and community-based alternatives. For example, CRIAW's research projects have arisen out of urgent concerns of local feminists (e.g., funding and staff cutbacks in British Columbia),[9] out of CRIAW's organizational needs (e.g., computer infrastructure required for CRIAW to become a research institute without walls led to a proposed but unfunded, action research project with Margaret Benston, Ellen Balka and Elaine Bernard), and out of workshops that have brought together various types of expertise and experience on a specific topic.[10] The workshop on feminist ethics that has given rise to the community kit and abstracts has also produced a collaborative project on feminist ethics; the first draft of this interesting methodological process and product was presented at the CRIAW conference in November 1988.

CRIAW has not only begun the process of legitimizing feminist research as distinct from classical discipline-based research, but also has begun to distinguish different types of research. The categorization scheme specifying action research, scholarly research, artistic research, and journalistic research within CRIAW's bank of researchers has begun the process of naming different research approaches and validating different methodologies and forms of presentation. In the short term at least, it has helped to identify both scholarly feminist research and community-based action research as recognizable and as potentially legitimate forms for the purposes of a university career. CRIAW has also been important in helping to institutionalize community-based action research as an important form of feminist research. Action research shares with traditional, academic research the aim of describing, understanding, explaining and predicting. CRIAW's efforts in this direction are by no means complete and face substantial pressures from those opposed to feminist paradigms, and those who find such paradigms too radical or inadequate. For example, CRIAW's northern committee was not successful in its funding proposal for participatory research.

Feminist research and scholarship depend upon the women's movement as a source of inspiration and knowledge, and as a referent to undermine elitist and hierarchical values. Feminist research's grounding within the women's movement prevents the type of decontextualized, irrelevant scholasticism that has characterized the academic establishment and the false certainties of ivory tower, patriarchal arrogance. Working in conjunction with the feminist movement and the women's community helps to prevent new feminist scholarship from becoming obscure and ossified and reproducing the worst features of abstracted patriarchal knowledge. Maintaining and highlighting this interconnection between scholarship and activism is especially important when women's studies and feminist scholarship are being legitimized as new areas of academic pursuit. At this time there is a danger of over-reliance on existing "scientific" paradigms to gain legitimacy for the new discipline as happened historically with the development of home economics and social work. Without the grounded interaction of action and theory, it is easy for academe to get carried away in theoretical rhetoric as have some of the British and American socialist feminists according to Adamson, Briskin and McPhail (1988, 135).

The women's movement and its attempts to rid itself of patriarchal structures, in fact, provide feminist scholars with glimpses of women's culture and feminist culture that are necessary for the development of feminist theory, crucial for the deconstruction of patriarchal knowledge, and fundamental to social changes necessary to end structural discrimination against women and to create a transformed world. Feminist scholars who are increasingly aware of the layered effects of the patricentric and either/or syndromes within contemporary scholarly knowledge and hence, who are genuinely interested in developing new feminist knowledge and understanding, both want to and need to work with the community of feminist activists to develop understanding and insights together. Such collaboration is embodied in CRIAW and is fundamental to the feminist agenda.

Tensions and Their Mitigation

CRIAW's objective of bridging the gap between the world of the activist and the world of the academic has not been easily accomplished. Patriarchal, race and class structures of contemporary society continually impose their values, their evaluations, and their hierarchical "solutions" and create tensions between activists and academics.[11] Although CRIAW was founded as an organization of feminists, and although its name clearly mandates its research activity toward the advancement of women, putting feminist organizational ideals into practice has involved CRIAW in the struggle to overcome the persistent power of patriarchy and structurally generated hierarchy, and there are many times when feminist norms have not been sufficiently strong to overcome social structural forces. Although the feminist membership, policies and principles on which CRIAW is based mitigate these tensions to some extent, and although many find CRIAW meetings fun and tension-free, it is not difficult to think of examples within CRIAW's history where these tensions were evident and led to misunderstandings or resignations.

Tensions between community activists and academics within the feminist community arise from the different institutional orientations to knowledge and to change. They each give different priorities to the need to document in contrast to the need to act. Activists are inclined to become impatient with the academics' tendency to want more information before acting and to wait until they study the potential consequences of each potential action on subsequent social organization and on the organization's "credibility." Academics are considered to be too cautious, conservative, and abstract, while activists are sometimes thought impatient, rash, and shortsighted. Both are occasionally considered by each other to be unreasonable, unrealistic, arrogant, unfeminist, irrelevant, long-winded and to have a misguided or wrong strategy and analysis.

Tensions between community activists and academics within the feminist community come from what might be called the patriarchally generated arrogance of abstracted scholarly knowledge discussed earlier. Not only do the typical, research methodologies give rise to what might be called the academic appropriation of knowledge, but academic women and men are also socialized to consider abstract ideas as important and, even unconsciously, academics "do expertise" over those who are to be impressed with erudition. Scholarly talk is designed for scholarly debate and has the consequence of silencing community women with its million-dollar words or out-arguing women by apparently endless verbal tirades and convoluted logics. Even community-based language and a comment may appear domineering cloaked in the authority of a PhD.

Tensions also come from hierarchical evaluations — that one is better than another, or has more than another — that are generated by social class, race, organizational hierarchies, institutional hierarchies, and social movement norms — and that run counter to feminist egalitarian principles. These social structural evaluations and resource base differentials sometimes reinforce the divisions between academics and community activists. Although feminist activists within CRIAW do not use their PhD status or other signs of prestige oppressively — and some learn to de-emphasize such structural benefits when among other feminists, taken-for-granted language and assumptions often lead to inappropriate words, actions, or unintentional "put-downs." For example, community women with years of "citizen expertise" gained through learning, teaching, and acting were deeply offended when the occupational attribution "suburban housewife" was applied to them by a sociologist, and they considered this term to be an insult. Even when the academic has established extremely good rapport, it is virtually impossible to escape some forms of miscommunication, implicit structural readings of messages — or authority of professorial utterance. For example, in a world of inequality, praise from the academic may be "read" as patronizing and silence, or absence of praise may be taken as failure to recognize one's unique contribution. Moreover, resource differentials such as not having a car, computer, or a modem, may create tensions and prevent equal participation.[12]

Sometimes the workings of the class hierarchy have been even less subtle. In one instance, a community member, without strong feminist identifications, apparently became overly impressed by the credentials of other CRIAW members and decided that anyone lower than her in the class hierarchy was not a potential CRIAW member. A report of this conversation horrified and stunned others, although there was no discussion of its basis in the hierarchal domination of perceived expertise described in Figures 14.1 and 14.2.

These types of contradictions are to be expected as long as patriarchally and structurally generated divisions continue. Thus, it is not surprising that CRIAW in Nova Scotia was called "not activist enough" at one moment, "not academic enough" in the next, and then "too academic." An organization bridging the gap will never completely fulfill society's version of the patriarchal ideal of either side, by definition, and such dichotomous rhetoric masks understanding. Feminists need to recognize the difficulty of even small achievements.

CRIAW has been able to bridge the activist/academic gap as well as it has because of its relatively large number of executive members who identify as both academics and activists, and its increasingly explicit feminist method of operating. Organizationally CRIAW has shown itself to be committed to that objective, and a number of CRIAW practices serve to mitigate structural and hierarchical pressures. One should not minimize the importance of recognizing differences and the potential contribution of each individual, of the complement of agendas, of joint activities and working together, and of accessibility policies that serve to counter hierarchical structures and to equalize resources, at least to some extent.

Conclusion

CRIAW provides an organizational context within which feminists scattered in a variety of institutional contexts may work together, learn from each other and develop new ways to understand and to change societal institutions and to transform patriarchal social structures. In reflecting upon CRIAW's first ten years of growth as a feminist research institute in 1986, Pat Saidek captures three innovative features of CRIAW when she writes: "CRIAW was challenged by feminists to provide a bridge between academic researchers and community activists, to define research and to avoid mimicry of a male institution." These features are interrelated and parts of the feminist agenda.

CRIAW members are learning how to recognize tensions generated both by genuine differences and by patriarchal divisions, and how to use these tensions creatively to build a strong, decentralized research institute without walls. Since our everyday worlds are embedded with patriarchal knowledge, norms, values, and forms of behaviour, focusing our attention on women's collective activities allows us to begin to develop an understanding of women's forms of social organization. That initiates the processes by which feminism, feminist activism, and feminist analysis begin to whittle away patriarchy's defences. Developing new forms of organizations, new knowledge, new forms of research and new interrelationships among diverse groups is a crucial part of our feminist agenda. It is necessary to empower women intellectually, politically, personally and collectively so that our feminist dreams will be fulfilled. The challenge within CRIAW is whether feminist ideals and energies are strong enough to withstand the structural forces of Figures 14.1 and 14.2 that are attempting to transform women's studies into just another abstracted academic discipline like all the others, and to reconstruct barriers between activists and academe.

Feminist Organizing in the Academic Disciplines

The Canadian Sociology and Anthropology Association

Janice Drakich and
Eleanor Maticka-Tyndale

The 1960s were a period of major university expansion and professionalization in academic disciplines. In 1965, sociologists and anthropologists responded to this academic growth by establishing an autonomous national professional association — The Canadian Sociology and Anthropology Association (CSAA). The initial mandate of the association was to encourage research, publication, and teaching sociology and anthropology. Professional interests such as conditions of employment and promotion, professional ethics, discrimination, and public policy issues, among others, evolved over the subsequent years. Women's issues were absent from the earliest agendas; however, questions of women's status in universities and in professional associations were looming in the corridors of Canadian academia.

The Royal Commission on the Status of Women brought the status of academic women to national public attention in 1968. It commissioned the Association of Universities and Colleges of Canada to conduct the first study on the status of women in Canadian universities (Robson & Lapointe 1968) and was presented with a brief prepared by university women (Jewett,

McCrae, Gobeil & Smith 1970). The findings of these studies indicated that women faculty were discriminated against in terms of hiring, promotion, and salary. The publication of these findings and the recommendations of the royal commission prompted universities and professional associations to investigate the status of women in academia,[1] resulting in the publication of more than a dozen studies in the early 1970s. Disconcertingly, each report documented similar trends and realities — women were paid less than their male counterparts and were concentrated in the lowest academic ranks. Academic women within their universities and professional associations began to challenge their male-dominated professions and universities. Not surprisingly, one of the most active groups in mounting such a challenge was women sociologists and anthropologists. The nature of these disciplines uniquely qualified them to examine and understand systemic discrimination against women.

This chapter documents the history of the challenge and demonstrates the activism initiated by academic women within the professional association of sociologists and anthropologists — the CSAA.

The History of Women's Organizing in the CSAA

The history of women's organizing in the CSAA can be separated into four phases. The first phase, 1970-74, was characterized by women on the executive committee of the association initiating actions. It was in response to queries from these women about the effects of nepotism rules on women, that the executive established a Status of Women Committee. Throughout this period, the Status of Women Committee regularly reported to the executive and membership with motions aimed at providing equal access to academic positions, tenure, research funds, and graduate studies for women. These were passed unanimously by the membership,[2] even those which pushed the association to take stands which were fairly revolutionary for the times, such as encouraging universities to establish tenure for part-time faculty, and mechanisms to insure their access to benefits and resources on an equal basis with full-time faculty. What became evident towards the end of this phase was that the association could pass motions, but had no way to guarantee their implementation when they called on bodies outside the organization to act. This posed a serious problem to the advancement of the status of women in the profession, one which continues to this day.

In 1974, in a move to streamline its cumbersome structure, the association replaced virtually all its committees with single members of the executive, appointed to take responsibility for a particular area. In response to this move, Dorothy Smith, the executive appointee in charge of the status of women, alerted women of the need to form ad hoc committees and task forces to deal with issues of particular interest to them. This marked the beginning of the second phase of women's organizing. From 1975 to 1979, in the absence of institutional structures, women's issues had to be addressed by grassroots organizations of women. "Women in Canadian Sociology and Anthropology," one such activist organization, forged ahead with a newsletter, extensive debates on goals, strategies and purposes, and lobbying of the association for action on a variety of issues. Some of the issues of earlier years had to be brought back to the attention of the executive and membership, for, though motions had been passed, the changes called for had not yet been realized. In response, the association established an Equal Rights Review Committee to address male bias in the profession. Reviews of curricula launched by the committee documented both the absence of graduate programs in women's studies, and of faculty to supervise graduate work in this area (Henshel 1976). Consequential to the inaction of universities on motions passed in the early 1970s, members were encouraged to apply pressure to their employers to address the motions of the CSAA.

As it became apparent that little change would occur from within the existing structures, women moved their activism outside the association. From 1977 to 1979, women sociologists and anthropologists directed their energies to the formation of openly feminist groups, to feminist publishing, and to the launching of feminist journals and presses.[3]

Within the CSAA, action to advance the status of women and women's studies came to a standstill. Committees which had been established to address women's concerns were disbanded, their mandates reassigned to more generally oriented standing-committees who, for the most part, did not address those portions of their mandates which addressed women's issues. While activist women were directing energies to establishing strong research, publishing and pedagogical bases for feminist and women's studies outside the association, the association's activism was restricted to passing motions and shunting action to committees.

The third phase, which lasted from 1975 to 1985, saw the new chair of the Social Policy Committee, Linda Christiansen-Ruffman, take up the case of the motions passed, but not implemented, and in the formation of a Women's Caucus. Monitoring of the status of women, the implementation of motions, the presentation of new motions, and the launching of new research, was conducted by members active in the Women's Caucus, who met during the association's annual academic and business meetings, but existed as an unofficial body reporting to the association through the Social Policy Committee. The absence of official status did not prevent the caucus from affecting change on behalf of women, for example, in giving directions to the publications board to review submissions for sexist language and content, revising or refusing publication of offending materials; in the inclusion of a statement on sexual harrassment in the association's Code of Ethics; and in the passage of an affirmative action program.[4]

In 1984 the caucus moved to institutionalize its role through the creation of a formal Status of Women Committee, which in 1985, constituted the opening of the fourth and current phase. The initial task of caucus and committee was to establish a "working relationship." This was articulated in 1986 (Tyndale 1986) with the caucus designated as the body where agendas, priorities and strategies were discussed and set for the committee to then carry out at the association level. The caucus, as a place where the committee's constituents met, took on a monitoring role. From 1985 to 1988 the association passed motions on the representation of women on the CRTC, CBC, and research funding bodies, and has opposed the closure of OISE and its women's studies program.

Problems and Tensions of Organizing

Organizing within the CSAA to challenge and change the status of women within academia, as well as within the disciplines of sociology and anthropology has been characterized by four primary tensions: careerist versus radical goals, mainstreaming versus disengagement strategies, viewing feminist issues as discrete problems versus chronic conditions, engaging in professional versus activist endeavours.

Purposes of Organizing as Professional
Sociologists and Anthropologists

The first tension arises over the very nature and purpose of organizing. Is the organizing careerist, that is, for the purpose of career advancement and improvement of the status of women within this occupation? Or is the organizing radical — for the purpose of applying the knowledge of the discipline to change society?? And are these two goals independent of each other?

Careerist organizing focuses on enabling women to enter and advance in their chosen careers through, for example, affirmative action, redefinition of relevant qualifications, creation of pro-women structures, and associations sensitive to women's position in society. It may lead to the development of structures of power and prestige which parallel men's status hierarchies with "new criteria" compatible with women's position in society.

Radical organizing focuses on changing structures so that they might reflect the different realities of men and women. Advocates of organizing for radical change argue that careerist actions will not significantly alter women's status in their profession since these are entrenched in women's oppressed status in society. In addition, some feminists argue, academic women organizing for their own advancement do so at the expense of other women. In neglecting the plight of other women, academic women eschew the development of critical analyses of structures that oppress and exploit all women.

The division between the two is not always clear. Changing the structures of universities, and the criteria for hiring and advancement gives women greater access to the academy both as faculty and students — both a careerist and a radical effect.

With the availability of new programs, courses, and perspectives brought by these women, radical critiques and actions are promoted and created. Clearly, the two are interdependent or, in creative tension.

Strategies for Affecting Change:
Mainstreaming vs Disengagement

The second tension arises between two strategies for affecting change: (1) whether women should work from within an organization, or (2) separate from the organization to form alternative forums. Briskin in Chapter 1 terms these two strategies mainstreaming and disengagement (also see Adamson, Briskin and McPhail 1988, 176-186). Each strategy has its own strengths, and its own potential pitfalls. Disengagement, in taking feminists outside existing institutions, releases them from the need to comply with organizational requirements. Consequently, all energies may be applied to the development of a clearly and unapologetically *feminist* critique, vision and strategy. However, with disengagement comes the potential for marginalization of feminists, feminist concerns, critiques and actions not only from men and male-dominated institutions, but also from those women who are reluctant to leave these institutions. Thus, in disengagement, is the risk that alternative forums will be separated from the lives and consciousness of non-activist women.

With mainstreaming, feminists remain within existing institutions and structures, thus having greater access to all women, and some men as well. Change is affected through the formation of coalitions between men and women within the institutions and the resources of mainstream organizations may be applied to feminist agendas. However, since feminists must accept the terms of the institution in order to remain within it, they are faced with pressures to conform to institutional expectations, and must expend energies making and convincing others that feminist concerns are compatible with the institution's concerns and goals. There is a potential risk that the feminist vision may be co-opted or sacrificed to the "larger" needs of the institution. In addition, there is the perpetual threat that any gains that are not made intrinsic to the structure of the institution will be lost in times of crisis such as cutbacks, reorganization, etc.

Briskin suggests that to minimize the deficits and maximize the benefits of each strategy, mainstreaming and disengagement should be in a "creative tension" for effective action. Similarly, "Feminist practice must relate to and use mainstreaming, but at the same time confront disengagement, the institutions — and thus the practices and ideas of our society" (Adamson et al. 1988, 187).

Feminist Concerns Represent Acute versus Chronic Conditions

The third tension is between seeing the issues raised by women as acute, though temporary problems, to be resolved with short-term strategies, and seeing them as chronic conditions requiring continual, long-term attention. Those adhering to the former perspective would leave societal structures much as they stand and would work toward guaranteeing women access to these structures. Those adhering to the latter would view this strategy as ineffective for bringing about the necessary changes to effect change in women's position. An example is in the area of assessment of faculty for tenure. Liberal feminists see a need to have women's academic work evaluated on an equal footing with that of men, feeling certain that if women were only given a chance, they would fare well in the existing structures and arenas. Radical and socialist feminists, on the other hand, question the very nature of male-defined assessment levied against women. They raise questions on three fronts: (1) whether women, tied to partners' career paths should be denied access to employment. Restrictive hiring practices, such as rules forbidding the hiring of more than one member of a family in a particular institution, or the hiring of graduate students in a department where they were trained, in both cases without consideration of qualifications, severely limit women's access to academic positions; (2) with regard to advancement in academic employment, whether women, who carry responsibilities for home and family, and are tied to male partners' career paths, should be evaluated with criteria which assume lack of caretaking responsibilities and freedom of geographic mobility; 3) they question whether masculinist determinations of appropriate theory, substance and methodology should be applied to feminist work, which by its very nature, is challenging masculinist criteria in its creation of new approaches to research and pedagogy.[5]

Spending Time in Feminist Activism
versus Professional Activities

The fourth and final tension is between the requirements of feminist community building and action and the requirements of the occupation. For women, this fourth tension is further compounded by women's domestic labour. Women's "double day" of occupation and home/family work has been well documented. When women organize, they add a third drain on their resources, facing a "triple day." The tensions between family and occupation now become tensions between family, occupation, and organizing. At times, devoting time and other resources to one, threatens the continuation of the others. This is particularly true when activities in one area (e.g., child-rearing) are considered antithetical to, in conflict with, or simply not appropriate to, one or both of the others (e.g., occupational demands or time spent in activist organizing).

The Tensions Applied to the History of Women's Organizing

A close examination of women's organizing in the CSAA makes it apparent that of the four tensions — careerist versus radical goals, mainstream versus disengaged strategies, discreet versus chronic problems, and professional versus community activities — the tension between mainstream and disengaged strategies is central. It is around this tension, and the balance struck between its two sides, that the others "fall into place." Let us examine this further. In the CSAA, women have developed separate (disengaged), though connected (mainstream), domains. The separate grassroots organizing of task forces in 1974, a caucus in 1979, and the reaffirmation of the role of the caucus in 1986, connected with the formal institution by funnelling actions through association committees.[6] Women recognized that without women's grassroots, disengaged analysis, strategizing and plans of action, the association would take no action. Conversely, women's plans often required the larger institution to support and take action. Thus a creative tension gradually evolved between disengagement and mainstreaming. In addition, there has been a growing recognition over the years (arising out of the disengaged, grassroots feminist analyses and discussions) of the differences between those problems which could be addressed with specific and discreet actions and those which were more deeply entrenched in the very structures and ideologies of society. The former could easily be dealt with through mainstreaming. For example, in response to complaints of sexism in the publications, the association's publications board was instructed to reject any articles containing sexist language. They required the analyses, deliberations and creation of approaches developed by feminist groups disengaged from the larger institution. For example, women in concert with women disengaged from the mainstream worked both inside and outside of the CSAA to develop feminist theory and methodology to challenge the sexist practices of sociology and anthropology.

In all cases, however, we see that actions embarked on, were limited by women's resources — their triple day. The 1975 Task Force on women was formed by a mere eight women who carried out the bulk of the work. It was the determination of one woman, Linda Christiansen-Ruffman, in 1979, which re-activated the grassroots organizing in the form of the Women's Caucus. More recently, the work of the caucus has been left primarily to its chair.

If we peruse the names of the women involved in feminist organizing, we find the same names appearing over and over. The women who wrote the articles, organized the women and the work of the caucus, and presented motions at association meetings, were most often also sitting on the executive or as members of standing committees of the association.

The activism of disengagement is time-consuming and is also the activity which is *least* likely to be recognized professionally. It is not surprising that women's activism in the association fluctuated. What *is* surprising is that so much was accomplished. Not only did women face their "triple day" but also at times the scorn of their academic colleagues. As Anne-Marie Ambert states in a footnote to her article, "Academic Women: On the Fringe," "This research was initiated for political reasons rather than academic or career reasons — in fact, the time that went into this was detrimental to our more academe concerns" (1977, 6).

The sympathy of the association made the women's work in the CSAA easier. Perhaps because of the sizable representation of women within the association (forming 20 percent of the academic faculty and in the 1980s, 40 percent of the membership of the association), perhaps also because of women's activism, the association has taken stands attempting to raise women to a position equal to that of men within academia, and to correct the male-bias in teaching and research. These sympathetic stands, however, presented problems for the organizing of women to improve their status. The sympathy of male members facilitated the rapid passage of motions dealing with women's concerns. The *ease* with which most issues raised by women received full association support created the illusion of impending, swift action. This illusion often lulled women into relaxing vigilance. When this occurred, no action took place, especially in the early 1970s. In the absence of a woman, or core of women, to make motions, organize and/or sit on task forces, collect, and present information, the association sank into inactivity. It clearly required the women to lobby, caucus, organize, conduct research and present motions in order to advance the status of women in the association. It was activist women who prodded the association to feminist postures.

It is clear that addressing feminist issues remains primarily women's domain. Articles authored by men of the association continue to ignore these concerns. For example, Savage's discussion in "Universities in the Eighties" (Savage 1983) of the impact of recession on the number of academic appointments and the very existence of programs, completely ignored the effect on women academics, or women's studies. The experiences of women sociologists and anthropologists clearly illustrate that women's issues are invisible to men. It is because women's issues are consistently visible only to women that disengagement is necessary. Disengaged organizing makes women's issues visible, and works to establish and maintain the creative tension with mainstream activism. The most recent phase of women's organizing in the association illustrates this balancing of tensions between mainstream and disengaged action.

Status of Women Committee and Women's Caucus: Creative Tension

With the establishment of the Status of Women Committee in 1985, it was necessary to formulate a plan for its relationship with the Women's Caucus. The mechanisms and processes which would enable the enactment of the caucus' role were to evolve over ensuing years.

As in other national organizations,[7] the annual caucus meeting is the only opportunity for members to decide policy, influence decisions, and direct the actions of the Status of Women Committee. However, this once-a-year opportunity is often out of reach for women members. Barriers such as distance, travel costs, and other professional responsibilities preclude the participation of the majority of women. Attendance at caucus meetings may range from 10 to 85 with each year's attendees including a sizable number who have not attended the previous year. The politics, goals and strategies of the caucus in a particular year are dependent on those who attend in that year, and may change from year to year, and likewise its directions to the Status of Women Committee.

The nearly 400 women members of the CSAA are dispersed among 43 academic institutions as well as some government and private organizations. The practical problems in organizing, and communicating to such a large body are enormous. Financial constraints and geography have been the two most obvious problems in effective organizing. In addition, these women are politically, ideologically and strategically diverse, resulting in pushes and pulls from one to the other of the extremes on the four tensions associated with organizing.

What binds women in feminist organizations is that they are feminists. The caucus is viewed by the members of the association as a feminist grouping, yet not all women in either the association or in the caucus are feminists. What binds caucus members is not necessarily their shared feminism, but their shared profession. Among those members who are feminist, all three forms of feminism (radical, socialist and liberal) are represented. Attempts to represent such a diversity of women are often frustrating, and more often than not involve an incredible expenditure of time. Debates that have been put to rest by one group of feminists, or by a caucus meeting in one year, are re-introduced in the next year. These debates cannot be dealt with effectively within the context of a single annual meeting limited to a two-hour time slot embedded in a packed agenda of academic sessions.

The 1988 meeting of the caucus provides a recent example of the problems associated with such organizing. In 1980, the Women's Caucus discussed formulating a series of questions to candidates running for positions on the executive of the association. There were repeated discussions in ensuing years, but with meetings limited to two hours, any item addressed had to be of high priority. It took seven years before the questions became of high enough priority to be addressed. Four questions were formulated at the 1987 caucus meeting and sent to the Status of Women Committee for review.[8] No one queried the questions announced in the report of Status of Women Chair at the association's annual meeting. Later that year, the executive passed a motion to circulate the questions to candidates for office. However, when the questions were sent, some candidates challenged them on the grounds that they violated academic freedom. Heated debate ensued in the sociology and anthropology departments of several universities and in one regional association. There was every indication that these questions would be challenged and debated at the association's 1988 AGM. Women were informed through a newsletter of this potential and were encouraged to attend the Women's Caucus meeting where strategies, in light of the challenge, would be discussed.

Given that there had been unanimous approval of the questions at the 1987 caucus meeting (with over 85 women in attendance), the caucus chair and Status of Women Committee expected the 1988 caucus meeting to begin its discussion from a position of support for the questions.

Attendance at the 1988 meeting was approximately half what it had been in the previous year, despite the need to plan strategy in response to this challenge. A considerable number of the women present at the 1988 meeting had not attended the caucus in 1987. Several women in the caucus challenged the questions, concurring with the concerns that the questions violated academic freedom. Other members of the caucus reacted to the arguments presented in opposition to the questions. The debate pitted women against each other. Those opposing the questions challenged the representativeness of the caucus. They described the caucus as run by a "clique" which worked to further their own interests rather than those of the membership at large. They verbalized their feelings of alienation from the activities of the caucus. Instead of strategies in the face of a challenge to a decision taken unanimously by the caucus, the legitimacy of the decision and the representativeness of the caucus became the central questions of the meeting. The questions were not resolved at this caucus meeting, with the meeting forced to close to make way for an academic session scheduled for the same room.

The debate and events surrounding the questions to the candidates illustrate all four tensions and problems associated with women's organizing within the CSAA. The questions were more radical than careerist, and thus were more threatening and unacceptable to individuals who were not firmly aligned with radical action. The mainstream coalitions were threatened. Women who felt coalitions were important sorely felt this threat. The questions addressed issues embedded deep in the structure and practice of the discipline, not specific problems and injustices. The shifting attendance at caucus meetings, and severely limited time for meeting meant many women party to the debate were never present at the formulation of the original questions.

Women's triple day meant it was a small group who had "gotten the work done." This group was challenged, accused of being a "clique" — a charge not infrequently levied against organizers (Adamson et al. 1988, 238). The geographic distances between committee members, with communication limited to letter writing, meant chairs and members of the committee engaged in solitary work. While attempts are often made to obtain members' feedback or participation, few members, if any, ever respond. In reality, a few women provide the leadership and get the work done.

The lack of participation of the membership places the responsibility for decisions in the hands of the elected members

and renders decision-making informal. This form of leadership often leads to feelings of exclusion and charges of "in
groups." In addition, the fact that neither the chair of the
committee nor the caucus were resident in the area of the
country where members took issue with the questions, meant
those best able to represent and defend the rationales and
procedures involved in formulating and approving the questions, were not present.

The balancing and rebalancing of tensions is evident in this
example, and indeed in the entire history of women's organizing in this professional association. As some women move in
the direction of more radical action, other women feel
threatened. The coalitions between the women supporting
radical and careerist goals are "put on the line."

Women, geographically isolated from each other, of diverse
perspectives, and often with several years between contacts
with their female colleagues, are subjected to pressures, and
fear the loss of allies should their male colleagues, whose support they have carefully nurtured over time, decided to remove their support. The reality accepted by most women
academics is that to succeed in their careers, they must secure
respect and esteem from their colleagues and superiors, usually males, and thus conform to the male models of professional legitimization. For some women, who have endured
a long and often difficult apprenticeship in the profession, the
threat of having their career "put on hold," or, in fact, losing
their career, sufficiently inhibits them from active participation
in areas that are not well respected in academia, such as
women's studies or feminist organizing. Individuals who
"stand to lose," if a given action is taken, are less likely to
support or to take such action.

Adamson, et al. (1988 243) suggest that the creative tensions
are formed from conflict and disagreement, with both necessary to the successful functioning of a group. In the very acts
of disagreement and resolution, not only are differences de-
lineated, but common foundations are discovered, clarified
and reaffirmed. Thus, creative tensions are formulated, and
connections between the diverse sides are reinforced. Such
disagreement and discussion can only take place when women
gather together, reinforcing the need for a caucus which brings

them together. Throughout their history the grassroots women's organizations in the CSAA have allowed and even encouraged the articulation of differences of opinion. The newsletter of the first grassroots organization of women in the CSAA published dissenting views on the purposes of organizing academic women (cf.Henshel 1975, 9).

More recently, dissenting members of the caucus and the Status of Women Committee, after the 1988 Women's Caucus meeting, met together to discuss the issues they had voiced at the meeting. Mainstream activity is critical here as well. Without the mainstream Status of Women Committee, the association would never have faced the issue of the questions — the issue of where it stands on feminism in the discipline. Questions brought by a caucus can be shunted off as reflective of a small group of radicals. Questions posed from within the official structure of the association cannot. It is this which makes us conclude that the tension between disengagement and mainstream organizing is central to the tensions between careerism and radicalism, acute and chronic conditions, activist organizing and professional work.[9]

Future Directions

Women's eighteen-year history of activism in the CSAA has produced research and put motions in place which have advanced the status of women in the profession. These achievements were accomplished through the activism of a few women, often to the detriment of their own academic work, and at times without appreciation from colleagues who, nevertheless, reaped the benefits of their volunteer labours. Strategic grants for research on women, alternative forums for publication, recognition of women's presence in the association, reduction in discrimination against women within the structure of the university, acceptance of women's scholarship, and elimination of some sexist practices are examples of the reforms that have been accomplished which benefit all academic women. By moving women into academic structures and legitimizing a place for feminist analysis within the academy, radical issues are likewise addressed.

The history of women's caucusing and the Status of Women Committees of the CSAA is not unlike the history of other academic women's groups within universities, or university affiliated associations, nor unlike that of national feminist organizations such as NAC or CRIAW. Parallels in experience can be found in the evolution of women's organizing, balancing the four tensions, problems with volunteer participation, representativeness, who does the work, and of course, similarities in objectives.

16

Feminist Academics and Community Activists Working Together

Anne Bishop, Ann Manicom
and Mary Morrissey

While it is often fruitful for feminist academics and community activists to work together, it is also often an uneasy alliance. We cannot overcome the strains by pretending they do not exist. Activists and academics work in settings which, in quite concrete ways, produce stresses and conflicts. It is our view that recognizing and examining how our differences are socially organized is a necessary task to undertake if we are to work together honestly, respectfully and productively.

Our History

The Community Development and Outreach Unit of Henson College, Dalhousie University, has a mandate to bring activists and academics together to work on "issues of substantive public concern," particularly issues of poverty and women's oppression, issues of interest to grassroots activist groups who have traditionally been marginalized in relation to the university's resources.

In the first three years, the Community Development and Outreach Unit has successfully (albeit in a small way) brought feminist academics and feminist community activists together in its own operation and in its community work. The unit's

Advisory Committee consists of feminists working in both spheres; this group acts as a reference and discussion group for all the unit's work.

The unit has come some way in making university resources available to community groups which deal, for example, with single-parenting, with transition houses for battered women, and with women's health-care issues. The kinds of activities have included providing space for meetings, discussing research and evaluation proposals, assisting in conference organization, and providing workshops on leadership development and fund-raising. The unit experienced particular success in sponsoring a public forum on the Nova Scotia government's responsibility to women, which has resulted in the founding of the Women's Action Coalition, an independent, representative lobbying group, with leadership drawn from both academia and community. The coalition is now completing its second very active year, and the unit continues to give the organization support.

The three of us writing this chapter are feminists involved in the unit in different ways, and we come to it with different histories. Anne Bishop became Program Coordinator for the unit during the summer of 1987. Prior to this, she was a community organizer among low-income women in Pictou County, N.S., and worked as a popular educator for a number of years in the area of women and international development. Ann Manicom, a member of the Advisory Committee for the unit, teaches in the School of Education at Dalhousie University and was part of the original group of feminist academics and activists who worked with Henson College to find a structure within which Dalhousie's resources could be linked to the women's community in ways that were more useful to, and responsive to, the needs of particular community groups. Mary Morrissey came to the new unit with a background in social work and evaluation, and with roots in the low-income community of Halifax, established through her work at the North End Community Clinic and Bryony House, a transition shelter for battered women. Originally the unit's only employee, she has fought the battles required by the founding of the unit from the staff level. She is now its director.

The three of us have in common our concern to unite feminist academic and activist work. Yet, with our individual histories, and with the different ways our work is organized and valued at the university, we experience somewhat differing tensions and contradictions. In this chapter, we propose to explore these tensions from each of our perspectives. As we analyze various issues, we will draw on our experiences and efforts to form a bridge between feminist community work and feminist academe.

The Issues: Community, University and Self

The Community

Central to our work has been an awareness of the potential hostility from the community towards the university, and towards researchers in particular, because of class differences and previous experiences of "being ripped off" by academics who have simply used information obtained in the community to advance their own careers. Along with this is a resentment of an academic's relative comfort and wealth, compared to the activist's often insubstantial income, and the even greater struggle of low-income people to survive. Often in the community there is the feeling, "For them it's a hobby; why are they taking up so much of my time?"

Coupled with this is the frustration felt by community groups who have to struggle for meagre resources while the university uses massive resources (some of it taken from taxes paid by the community) to educate an elite and serve business interests. This issue has intensified in the 1980s as universities feel the pressure to forge tighter and tighter links with the corporate sector, both in terms of "training" students to meet the "needs" of the economy, and in terms of securing research funding from the private sector (and being rewarded for so doing).

Further, as many social services are cut back, there is a growing demand from community groups for support, yet within the university we are increasingly constrained in our ability to respond to community requests as the university itself is faced with budgetary crises. We find ourselves in a contradictory position: we are forced to seek external funding, and this often places us in competition with the very groups with whom we are committed to work. This does not lessen the tensions between activism and academe.

The two of us who have spent much of our adult lives working within grassroots organizations know that it is often not easy to work with academics, even when these academics are feminists who feel they are committed to social action, collective work and participatory research. In ventures involving academics and community activists, this difficulty sometimes surfaces as a conflict between the competitiveness and critical response required by an academic career and the non-judgemental support required by community organizing. Other difficulties can surface in the knowledge-sharing models academics are accustomed to use, for example, organizing conferences in ways which exclude or silence the very women who are the "topic" of the conference. Where such conferences do include women from the community, there can emerge the problem that academic attention (invitations to speak on panels, etc.) can create "stars" in community organizations; this can be potentially destructive to the coherence of the community organization.

Conflicts between activists and academics are also visible in the frustration experienced by community organizers when academic feminists are seen to approach problems in an abstract intellectual way. There is a similar frustration felt by academics when activists seem to get too bogged down in practicalities. It is not uncommon, as well, to find that an academic feminist has mastered the language of social action and collective work (the university is, after all, a world created out of language) without really grasping the principles. It is, of course, not easy for a feminist academic to hear these descriptions of academics as merely theoretical, as living comfortable lives, as researching in the community only to produce scholarly chapters. Many women who are feminists and academics are already marginalized within the university; to also be seen as "other" within feminist community work can be painful.

These strains between feminist activists and academics are real in the sense that we feel them, and often strongly. Splits and conflicts are also real in that they arise out of differences in how our everyday lives are put together; they are produced quite concretely, for example, in the ways our workplaces are organized. Analysis of the production of these differences may, in the long run, enable us to work collectively with more understanding and productivity. Since the organization of the university provides the material basis for the work of the three of us, it is to this that we now turn.

Institutional practices and ideologies within the university

Two central problems are addressed here, one for the feminist academic who is trying to accomplish a day-to-day work life within a university setting, the other for community development workers who are employed by the university to carry out its "commitment" to the community. In both instances, we can see that our problems and frustrations are produced through administrative practices (budgetary, planning, and personnel) within the university, practices which are permeated by patriarchal and elitist ideological commitments. These institutional problems are in many ways worsening as the university suffers cutbacks and severe financial constraints.

For the feminist academic, there are well-documented issues, such as the problems for career advancement in a university where feminist methodologies, participatory research and collective products are often undervalued and dismissed as ideological. To be a feminist is to not be "objective." To publish in a feminist journal is considered not to meet the criteria of "established refereed" publications. To do participatory research is suspect, and bound to be "tainted" by lack of objectivity. To engage in sustained community social action is rarely accepted as a way of contributing to the "discipline" (in fact is one of the least valued activities an academic can put on her curriculum vitae). To publish truly collective chapters and research reports means that the publication does not accrue as much "scholarly currency" in an individual faculty member's career. And so on. These are, of course, precisely the kinds of activities valued within feminist community groups. So, for the feminist academic who wishes to root her work in feminist community organizing, and who, at the same time, wants to be able to remain in the academic setting, there are massive contradictions within which she must work.

The second general set of problems revolves around the existence (and maintenance) of a community outreach unit within the university. On the one hand are problems of colleagues not understanding our model of community activism. In the unending struggle for internal resources, we find we constantly have to clarify what it means to make university resources available to marginalized community groups in ways that do not violate the needs, interests, and principles of the groups with whom we want to work. It is difficult to make this understood in an environment where notions of "education" and "research" are elitist, where a commitment to shared power and shared knowledge flies in the face of the authoritarian mode of traditional university/client relationships. It is also difficult to make this understood and supported in a university economic environment where there is an increasing tendency to use business models and serve business interests.

So the community development model itself is problematic within the university. Add to this an explicitly feminist perspective, and the issues are compounded. In the university budget and planning process, we find ourselves dealing constantly with academics and academic administrators for whom the personal and the political are miles apart, and who therefore have negative reactions to our purpose and methodology. We find ourselves being caught between the inability of university administrators to understand a feminist community organizing approach and the horror of what would happen if they did!

Within the university, therefore, particularly for the two of us who are staff members with the Community Development and Outreach Unit, energy and time are massively consumed in the struggle both to maintain the university's commitment to the unit, and to be allocated resources to accomplish our work. For us there is considerable frustration in having to spend so much time fighting the bureaucracy and mysogyny of the university. The frustration is compounded by having to engage in this set of administrative battles which seem futile, petty, and even incomprehensible to the community groups with whom we are working.

Maintaining Community Connections: A Triple Day

For the academic who teaches from a feminist perspective, there is a clear need to be engaged in feminist community struggles in order to bring energy and rootedness to her work within the university. For the community activist who goes to work for a university, there is a danger of losing this rootedness, of losing her community roots, and of becoming a "hit-and-run" activist because she can no longer afford to plug along for months or years on one issue or in one community. The trust *within* the community, which a community activist develops over years of work, can be jeopardized by the ways the structures of the university constrain her work.

Further, there is the need for feminist faculty and staff members in a university to be engaged in struggles *within* the university over women's issues, be these hiring practices, forms of scholarship, criteria for classification and promotion, alternate teaching methods, sexual harassment and collective bargaining.

Finally, we each also have our *own* "communities" where we are active in our "non-work" time, whether for the rights of the hearing impaired, the struggles of incest survivors, the demands for gay and lesbian rights, the work of political organizing. We feel that it is very important (although sometimes difficult) to be engaged in our "personal" community issues along with the work we do on behalf of others.

In all of this, like many activist women, we are faced with the drain of a triple day — work, home, and community work.

Models for Academics and Activists Working Together

Articulating these kinds of problems, sharing them, struggling over them, enables us to keep on going. Through our various involvements over the past few years, both within the community and at the university, we have begun to identify some approaches to links between the university and the community where at least some of the tensions between activism and academe can be resolved, or worked through in ways which are productive. We describe here six models: community extension units, community/academic conferences, consultations involving community, academe, and funders, working committees, and political coalitions. None of these models is magic, of course; we have seen all of them fail to help academic and activist feminists work together. However, with respectful work, honesty, and flexibility, they can be made to bridge the gap between us.

Community extension units, such as our own, have a mandate to make it possible for the community and university to have mutual and useful access. If there are feminists involved, the unit, its projects, its board and advisory committees can become ongoing fora for discussion and strategy in involving women from both sides of "town and gown." The Community and Development Outreach Unit at Henson College described in the introduction to this chapter, is an example. The Advisory Committee of the unit includes three activists from the community and two academic teachers from the university. Together we try to guide and think through the work of the unit so that it will serve the needs and advance the cause of both groups and develop channels of communication between them.

Community/academic conferences work well when the information is provided by people who come from both groups, and when both the research/study expertise and the practical action expertise are seen as equal. Such conferences must, of course, be designed to encourage discussion in small groups with competent facilitators using a methodology that begins with participants' experiences. One example of this method is a series of conferences sponsored by the Continuing Education Department of Saint Mary's University in Halifax. Each year there is a different theme: for example, Atlantic Canada and the Caribbean, Economic Democracy in Atlantic Canada, and the Rural Crisis. The conference has been attended by both activists and academics from all over the region. The early conferences used a purely academic format, a series of panels followed by brief question periods. The activists complained, and over the years the conference has evolved to include small discussion groups and more opportunity to exchange information on an informal basis. The panels are also beginning to include more activists and fewer academics. In the final evaluation of the most recent conference, several participants expressed gratitude for the useful and rare opportunity for exchange between the two realms. These conferences are not defined as feminist, but several of the region's feminist activists and academics have taken part and have used the conferences to exchange experience and information.

A third method is the *consultation of funders, academics and activists*. Some of these have been conferences, some smaller one-time events, and some on-going working committees. All are arranged on an equal and respectful basis to include three quite different perspectives, and to make the actions emerging from the discussion more useful to all three groups. An example here is the consultation on Women and Economic Development held recently by the Halifax office of the Secretary of State Women's Program. The weekend session gathered women involved in economic development projects, representatives of the Women's Program and academic economists representing several different points of view to assess the strategies we are using at the grassroots level.

Working Committees are assembled as reference groups for programs and institutions, planning teams for conferences and events, or in response to particular problems. They include activists and academics, and ensure that the program being planned or advised includes the interests of both. A good example is the Status of Women Committee of Dalhousie's Legal Aid Clinic. This group includes law faculty women, legal aid workers, community workers and representatives of low-income women's organizations. The committee reflects on the problems, particularly the legal problems, of low-income women, coordinates organizations active in this area, and sponsors a project called "The People's Law School," funded by the Secretary of State Women's Program. The "school" is a flexible six-week program which helps women on social assistance understand their rights and the courses of action open to them. It has been given in seven communities over two years, and in each case has resulted in a continuing support group for low-income women. Each "school" year ends with a provincial conference for low-income women. One recent conference resulted in a provincial organization called LINC (Low-income Network Committee) which is rapidly evolving into a lively support and lobbying body. It is completely con-

trolled by its membership; the academic women and community workers act strictly as a resource.

Finally there are *political coalitions*. A coalition forms around
the interests of a group, includes members from across the
community and campus, and works at providing a voice for
that group. One example is the Women's Action Coalition of
Nova Scotia. As mentioned previously, WAC arose from the
Public Forum on Government Responsibility to the Women of
Nova Scotia, sponsored by the Community Development and
Outreach Unit. This forum was organized as a result of the
resignation of the fourth president of the Nova Scotia Advisory Council on the Status of Women. (All four presidents
had resigned in office as a result of the provincial government's on-going record of insensitivity to women's concerns).
The three hundred women who attended the meeting called
for reforms to the provincial Advisory Council, and decided
to form a province-wide women's lobbying body. The
Women's Action Coalition was later constituted as a non-hierarchical, decentralized, cross-partisan political force composed
of member groups from every region of Nova Scotia. The
group which coordinates the work of the Coalition, and particularly its executive, is made up of a mix of women from
community-based women's organizations and the university.

Conclusion

Each of these models is simply a method for organizing
cooperative work among activists and academics. None can
bring about useful and respectful cooperation between campus and community just by nature of its structure. In each case
we know of, there has been a process, often long-term, and
always involving some struggle between the two worlds and
their different approaches, to come eventually to a means of
exchange between equals. Nor do any of these models alter the
organization of our work within the university; the models
merely provide those of us in the university ways of working
from within our institutional constraints.

This struggle is not an artificial thing. The class nature and
true interests of academics and community activists differ and
are often opposed; the pressures on both groups make it easier
to work separately. The path can be stony, paved with defen-

siveness, hurt feelings and stereotypes, but the resulting exchange, if well done, is certainly worth the effort.

Audre Lorde, speaking of differences, captures what we feel:

> As women, we must root out internalized patterns of oppression within ourselves if we are to move beyond the most superficial aspects of social change. Now we must recognize differences among women who are our equals, neither inferior or superior, and devise ways to use each other's difference to enrich our visions and our joint struggles. (Lorde 1984, 122)

17

Putting Our Two Heads Together

A Research Group Uses Subjective Perceptions to Understand Women's Occupational Health

Karen Messing

Recently, Health and Welfare Canada assembled a hundred or so professionals working on women's health, ninety-nine percent of whom were women. We spent several days together, listening to presentations on the causes of women's heart attacks, the best way for a young woman to run her sex life, the advantages and disadvantages of mammary X-rays and so on. Most presenters were health researchers well-respected in academic circles, although some were from women's health clinics and action groups. At the end of the second day, people began to take the microphone to comment on the way the conference was going. Something was lacking, people weren't satisfied. Finally one woman put her finger on the problem: why were we all talking about women in the third person? What did it mean to us to say that "women" should or should not have mammographies or estrogen replacement therapy? How did a group of high-powered women feel about the results of research on stress?

In my work on women's occupational health, I have often felt this sort of call to unsplit my personality. Academics who do research on people must reckon with the context of scientific institutions whose traditions require the researcher to depersonalize and objectify the objects of research. In addition, an academic who wants her research to result in social change must translate human problems into academic terms worthy of grant support, produce information which is at the same time publishable and useful to the people who have the problem, and propose solutions in a comprehensible way. This effort is made more complex when the project involves people of other social classes who are understandably mistrustful of academics, whose use of language is different from that of university professors, and whose lives are constrained in ways that situations are not immediately obvious to academics.

These difficulties are most acute in the case of women academics working on subjects touching women's lives, for several reasons. Pressure to depersonalize women's needs and behaviour comes from scientific institutions with a long tradition of doing misdirected research on women (Messing 1983; Messing et al. 1986a). Women researchers perceive the institutionalized sexism, but are particularly sensitive to accusations of subjectivity or emotionality in treatment of their scientific subjects. However, we also feel pressure to treat women's problems sympathetically, since we frequently share the problems experienced by women under study. Women academics are subject to biological constraints and social oppression, have trouble with child care, menstrual cramps, imbalance in contributions to household tasks, and sexual stereotyping. Like members of any oppressed group, we feel solidarity with our sisters.

As good girls in academia on suffrance, we know we are supposed to separate clearly our experiences as women and our roles as researchers in occupational health. As feminists, we find it difficult. And increasingly, as scientists, we are wondering whether there isn't a way to use our subjectivity creatively as a research tool. Some researchers have recently started to examine the possibility of taking advantage of their own knowledge of the situation of their subjects to create a context for their research results (Gilligan 1982; Lippman 1986).

I have been confronted with these questions in a situation which was particularly favourable to playing out all available roles. During a period of five years, between 1978 and 1983, I held positions which required me to think about women's occupational health as an activist and as a researcher. During this period, I was a member of the national women's committee of my union, the Confédération des syndicats nationaux (CSN), responsible for suggesting union activity in the area of women's occupational health I was part of a group which developed positions on maternity leave, hazards during pregnancy, reproductive rights, protectionism, and physiological requirements of jobs in male and female employment "ghettos." We arrived at certain principles and made suggestions on policy and on union practices which were accepted by the entire union membership.

At the same time, in the context of a union-university agreement (Mergler 1987; Messing 1987), I was and am still part of a research group, almost all women, who have written on women's occupational health. (Messing 1982a; Messing and Reveret 1983; Mergler et al. 1987). I did research on genetic damage in women hospital workers exposed to ionizing radiation, and on the health consequences of work in typical industrial "women's jobs." I eventually resigned from the women's committee, due to overwork, but the experience I gained as a militant has been extremely valuable in orienting our research, and in making us think about problems of subjectivity in academic research and about the proper use of academic resources by women militants.

The context in which I have been working is quite unusual in North America, and I would like to explain about the rather special university in which I work, and the union to which I belong.

Two Contexts: Union and University

The Union Context

The 200,000-member CSN represents a broad spectrum of public and private-sector workers: hospital technicians, print and electronic journalists, assembly-line workers, lumberjacks and secretaries. It offers a great many educational and support services to its members, including four full-time workers in occupational health and two in the women's service. Although it has never supported a political party, the union takes progressive public positions in all debates in the province; for example, it has voted officially to support socialism, Québec independence, free abortion on demand, and disarmament. It has had a very active women's committee for the past twelve years, resulting in great progress in negotiating maternity leave, protection of pregnant women and fœtuses, equal pay for work of equal value, and daycare. Since the CSN represents most of the public service workers, their contract has been a source of advances for women over the past ten years. Many advantages negotiated for women in private-sector union contracts or passed as laws for all women originated as proposals of the CSN women's committee or of its women's service.

The Academic Context: the Université du Québec à Montréal

The Université du Québec was established in 1969 with a mandate to serve the community. Unlike most universities, it did not conceive the community to be adequately represented by bankers and manufacturers. Although these groups have their usual place on the university's board of directors and its money-raising apparati, representatives of women's and community groups serve on the committee which oversees community service.

Because it was a way to link their academic work with their political convictions, many progressive thinkers chose to work on the faculty and staff of the university. In the early years, from 1969 to 1979, the professors' union was among the most active in the province, not only in negotiating for its members (our four and one-half-month strike in 1976 was the longest teachers' strike ever in North America) but also in supporting other workers. The union has moved rightward since that time, but remains affiliated with the CSN.

In 1977, a group of women professors formed the Groupe interdisciplinaire d'enseignement et de recherche sur la condition féminine (group for interdisciplinary research and teaching on women) which developed a series of women's studies courses in various departments, and now has a research centre and an active seminar program. This group has also acted as a lobby for the hiring of women's professors, and has worked closely with the women's committee of the professors' union to write language favourable to women into the collective agreements. As a result, the university had paid maternity leave, a number of daycare centres, affirmative action clauses, and non-discriminatory health insurance before most other universities in North America.

Helped by interest from professors, the university developed its mandate for community service to include formal agreements with community groups. It hired employees specifically to formulate projects with women's groups, community groups and unions. In 1977, an agreement was signed with the two major Québec labour unions, the CSN and the Québec Labour Federation (QLF), which provided that the unions might request the services of professors to do education or research activities described by the unions (Comité conjoint UQAM-CSN-FTQ 1977). In 1982, the university signed a similar agreement with Relais-Femmes, an organization serving as liaison with women's groups (Université du Québec à Montréal 1982).

Subsequent collective agreements provided release time for educational and research activities, and seed money for the research projects. Women's groups have used a professor of biology for health education in collaboration with the women's health centre, and a professor of literature in a reading project in a community centre. Unions have asked professors to do economic analyses, to write histories of union activities, to explain laws and suggest improvements, and to do education and research in occupational health. Each project is followed by a committee from the union or women's group, which eventually does a formal evaluation of the finished project.

In 1985-86 (the last year for which figures are available), professors gave over 500 contact-hours of educational sessions to more than 500 participants in activities sponsored by the union-university agreement. There were 40 research projects in progress, which the university supported with $40,000 and outside funds provided another $100,000 (Comité conjoint UQAM-CSN-FTQ 1988).

The agreement with unions is far from being an integral part of the day-to-day academic life of professors. During the first ten years of its existence, 23 professors from eight departments were involved in educational projects, and roughly the same number in research projects (Comité conjoint 1988). Although the university has shown its approval by financing educational activities in the form of 54 course equivalents, and has put about $35,000 per year into research projects, it is still not as respectable in many departments for research for unions as for granting agencies. Some of the hesitation is due to traditional academic contempt for applied research, but it is considered to be much more desirable for research for companies than with unions.

However, in some cases, union-initiated projects have resulted in posing new questions, leading to grants from traditional granting agencies. The university community has been impressed by the fact that about $100,000 per year comes in as grants for projects initiated through the agreement. This, of course, is a double-edged sword: this kind of support pulls the professor from her original preoccupation with fulfilling the request of the union toward a feeling of responsibility toward the granting agency. In the absence of granting agencies with a specific mandate to fund community-initiated research, the centrifugal force is overwhelming.

Over 30 women's groups have benefitted in some way from an intervention through the agreement with the university (Côté 1988). The number of professors involved, however, is even more limited than for the union agreement; nine professors from seven departments participated in some way in 1986-88, all but one were active feminists. In fact, university resources are not fully available, nor are they fully used through this agreement.

A Granting Institution with Community Participation
In 1981, the Workers' Compensation Commission established a research arm, the Institut de recherche en santé et en sécurité du travail (IRSST), with the mandate to contribute to eliminating risks at the source. The board of directors of IRSST is composed of a 50:50 representation of management and labour. Its regular functioning is assured by a "Scientific Council" composed of 5 scientists from areas fairly removed from occupational health and safety, 4 representatives from the CSN and QLF unions, and 4 representatives from management.

For an academic accustomed to dealing with the usual granting institutions, it is quite strange to deal with IRSST. Decisions are taken by a process very similar to labour-management negotiation of a union contract, although scientists are consulted about the content of specific grant requests. The strong community representation means that the relevance of a proposal is critically important to its funding, but also that criteria for relevance change quite swiftly and unpredictably. For example, in June 1986 the institute decided, without warning, to cut support for all graduate students involved in health rather than safety-related research. Many students who were in second or subsequent years of their programs were left stranded. They had not applied for other support, since there is a tradition of continuing support for students in good standing.

However, the advantage of a research institution whose governing body is composed of representatives of the groups it wishes to support, is that the political character of research is recognized. In fact, the institute has supported research groups with union as well as management perspectives on occupational health. It has given our own research group, the Groupe de recherche-action en biologie du travail (GRABIT, the group for action research on the biology of work), six years of very generous support.

GRABIT and the University-union Agreement

Our research group, GRABIT, includes programs on early detection of genotoxic and neurotoxic damage, as well as on the characteristics of "women's" work and the ergonomic and physiological constraints which restrict access to "men's" jobs. This research is initiated in a formal and an informal context. The formal context originates with the university-union agreement: a union, such as the hospital workers or the poultry slaughterhouse workers, requests assistance in a specific area. University personnel help interpret the union request to a professor doing research in the relevant area, and eventually help the union understand the research results. Funds are initially provided by the university, and eventually, if necessary, through regular granting agencies.

In practice, roles are not so clearly defined. Since union-defined research questions are not necessarily recognized as interesting by academic standards, most professors do not spontaneously involve themselves in such research. Those who do are usually progressive, and thus, interested in the union activity as well as the academic aspects of the research.

The professor may encroach on the formal role of the unions in other ways. Unions do not develop needs as a function of the curricula vitae of university professors. The small number of professors available receive requests on a wide variety of subjects, in very few of which they are likely to be competent at the outset. These researchers have the choice of learning an entirely new discipline every time a request is made, or of re-orienting union requests as a function of their specialty.

Also, granting agencies by and large do not use the same priority scheme as unions in deciding on the interest of research proposals. Many researchers have trouble obtaining funds for union-initiated studies as originally formulated, and are faced with conflict between the needs of the union and the requirements of peer review. They may then feel great pressure to redirect the original union request into something fundable. In the absence of substantial funding for community-based research, there is no way to respond directly to many union needs (Messing 1987).

A great deal of our research comes about through informal contacts with unions, for example, in educational sessions, or in my case, through work with the women's committee. In these cases we become very involved with the union as well as the academic parameters of the research questions.

Mutual Influence of the Union and University Contexts

At the Université du Québec, there is therefore a university context, a union context, a feminist context, and a granting institution, which create an unequalled opportunity for integrating academic research with feminist struggles, within and outside of the union movement. Our research group has grown in this very favourable environment. We are not only women studying women, but also (except for the students) union members studying union members. As such we have sympathized actively with most of the groups we have studied.

Of course, we have been criticized for this attitude. But we have also profited so much from our double identity, both as feminists and as scientists, that we wonder if it is not an important way to gain understanding of our subject matter. Listening sympathetically and empathetically has led us to new scientific and political understanding. And we have eventually been led to develop research methods and statistical tools to organize and profit from our subjective perceptions and those of other women.

As a geneticist, I had a thorough training in embryology and teratology, the sciences which deal with pregnancy and fœtal development. My preparation had shown me that the male reproductive system and that of the female were not so dissimilar that working conditions that were unsafe for pregnant women were safe for everyone else (Messing, 1982b). I was therefore in favour of women working right up to the end of their pregnancy, and taking maternity leave once the child was born so as to rest after childbirth and spend time with the child. Working conditions which made this uncomfortable or risky should be changed.

In Québec, in 1979, a law was passed providing for *retrait préventif*, or precautionary leave, for pregnant women holding jobs which posed a risk for them or the fœtus. Job reassignment or, failing that, fully paid leave was available for such women for the duration of the pregnancy. The women's committee had many discussions on this point, since a pregnant woman leaving a hazardous job would probably be replaced by another women or man who would then be exposed to the hazard. It would be more consistent with our knowledge of occupational risks and my understanding of male and female biology to insist that the employer remove the hazardous condition. And, of course, protectionist policies for women endanger women's jobs, since employers are reluctant to hire women who may take long leaves, when they can hire men who don't get pregnant. Thus, on principle, I was opposed to *retrait préventif*, and should not have encouraged union members to take advantage of it.

However, as a member of the women's committee giving educational sessions on precautionary leave for pregnant women, I had a lot of contact with women for whom "women's rights" were an abstract issue, and uncomfortable working conditions and unreasonable employers were a daily reality. I had, after all, experienced my pregnancies when I was very young, and in a relatively healthful environment, far removed from the solvent fumes of the hockey stick factory, or the violence of the psychiatric hospitals where some of our members worked. It was impossible for me to speak against precautionary leave for very long when so many unionized women regarded it as their only hope for getting through a pregnancy without paying for it in money or permanently impaired health (Bouchard & Turcotte 1986). In fact, I ended up supervising a large research project one of whose aim was to determine grounds for precautionary leave among hospital workers.

On the other hand, the information my colleagues and I could bring up influenced the positions of other feminists in the union, many of whom had very protectionist positions.

Listening to union members has enabled us to pursue lines of investigation we would never have thought of by ourselves. After listening to laundry workers describe the heavy loads they lift, repeatedly, in what is defined as "light" work, in very hot temperatures, Donna Mergler and others began an exploration of the physiological response to this kind of workload (Brabant et al. 1989). Nicole Vezina, another member of our research group, has become involved in the comparison of men's and women's jobs. The usual descriptions of heavy workloads have been developed for men's jobs, and do not include the ergonomic constraints imposed by awkward postures or a fast work speed, typical of women's employment ghettos.

I also changed the focus of a research project after listening to hospital radiology technicians. Their descriptions induced me to put less emphasis on easily-defined risk factors such as radiation exposure and more on lifting heavy patients and on a fast workspeed. In fact, talking to workers has enabled us to understand the great importance of workspeed in determining health symptoms, as revealed by our data.

Effective Subjectivity in Research Methods

When we write grant applications or articles about the use of worker input to generate hypotheses and yield new information, we are often reproached with a lack of objectivity. We are thought to report uncritically the complaints of workers, and we have even been accused of using our academic titles simply to back up workers' grievances.

In some sense this is true. Our research group has depended to a great extent on questionnaires to tap the workers' information on their workplace and their health symptoms (Messing & Reveret 1983; De Grosbois & Mergler 1985, Tierney et al. 1990). These questionnaires are usually developed after a lot of sympathetic listening to worker's descriptions of their workplace and their symptoms. In many cases, this method is the only one available which permits us to learn about the symptoms which may plague workers' lives the most, such as impotence (De Grosbois & Mergler 1987), menstrual pain (Mergler & Vezina 1985), or backache. In addition, some work variables, such as sharing of the domestic workload (Tierney et al. 1990), may only be available through workers' reports.

We think a place should be found in occupational health research for documentation and for statistical description of workers' perceptions. So we find ourselves making such obvious statements as, "Workers report that they work too quickly, and that the more quickly they work, the more they feel exhausted," (Messing & Reveret 1983). We think that when a large number of women are exhausted, scientists should listen to them. We also know that the fact that it's obvious that women shouldn't work so hard because they'll get tired has no influence on work schedules in factories or hospitals. When scientists say the same thing, it may have a greater chance of resulting in a change in working conditions.

We spend a lot of time trying to back up "subjective" with "objective" measures of workplace-induced damage (Bedard et al. 1988 ; Messing et al. 1986b, 1989). Some techniques have been to ask workers to report perceptions of other people ("Has anyone ever told you ... , has a doctor ever prescribed ... ") In some cases we have taken measurements of environmental variables and checked them against workers' perceptions. Other techniques involve correlating worker perceptions with laboratory tests of biological characteristics (Messing et al. 1989), which are regarded, often erroneously, as less subject to variation and interpretation than worker perception. However, we also have to ask ourselves about subjectivity, and see whether using our intuitive identification with women workers is not an excellent research tool.

But it would be a mistake to treat the problem of subject/object as one which only touches women working on women; one of the challenges of science is to learn how to use subjective information appropriately. As scientists, we have been developing this approach in the context of women's occupational health, but it is a problem with a broader constituency.

Conclusion

In our work with women's and union groups in the area of occupational health, we have gained a knowledge of women's working conditions that we could not have had from any source other than working women. This has enabled us to do research on questions of interest to women that are not normally examined by other scientists. With women workers and their representatives, we have developed an approach geared to making the knowledge we gain available to them.

Sometimes we are afraid that our research results are not sufficiently used by the people who have asked for the studies. The wait between the appeal to our group and the response to what seems to the union a simple question, may be too long for the needs of the union. In the present economic context, when unions have all they can do to keep from folding entirely, taking time to work with us may be a luxury that overloaded union leaders cannot afford. But in general, we think (and have been told) that our contribution has helped the union to develop its analysis in many areas involving women's work.

It should be emphasized that we would never have had the energy to do all this without the time given to us in the university-union agreement, which allows course equivalents for educational activites and seed money for research. It seems to us that other universities in Canada could be convinced that they are supported by the money and labour of working people, who therefore have a right to direct access to some of their resources.

Working Together for a Feminist Future

What Can Academics and Activists Accomplish in a Women's Studies Distance Education Course?

Joanne Prindiville

Women's studies courses have the potential to stimulate participants to feminist analysis and activism in their communities, as well as teaching feminist academics about the experiences and needs of women whose lives are different from their own. All too often, though, these courses reach only those women living within a narrow radius of university towns. Distance education, an alternative structure, allows communication with women who are often physically, as well as socially, isolated from the mainstream of feminist activism. While offering special opportunities to bridge the gap between activism and academe, distance education also poses special constraints and challenges and the logistics sometimes enhance and sometimes undercut efforts to practise feminist techniques of teaching and learning, and hence to facilitate feminist activism. The gap between academics and community activists can widen with the addition of all the barriers that separate urban professionals from women living in small, isolated communities. This chapter is about what can happen when a feminist, academic, townie, island-based, "come-from-away" (CFA) offers a women's studies distance education course in Newfoundland and Labrador.[1] It is also about what can happen when "the women's studies classroom" is an entire, very large, province and "the class" never meets face-to-face.

The Setting

Understanding and overcoming the barriers that separate feminist academics from community activists means knowing who we are and understanding our differences and commonalities. For women in Newfoundland and Labrador several features of the physical and social landscape are particularly important. The province covers a vast area, encompassing both island (Newfoundland) and mainland (Labrador) regions. The tiny population, about 560,000, is largely dispersed in small, often isolated, single resource communities. The largest centre of population, St. John's, is a capital city of some 125,000 located on the eastern edge of the island. Populated by "townies," it is the historical and contemporary centre of political and economic power. The rest of the population lives largely "out around the bay" somewhere "beyond the overpass," which is located on the Trans-Canada highway just outside St. John's. The "overpass syndrome" contributes to both the tendency to concentrate wealth, power, and services in St. John's and the widespread resentment toward townies' seeming indifference to the needs of those beyond the overpass.

The population of the island is remarkably homogeneous ethnically and shares a strong collective identity. The population of Labrador is more diverse. St. John's is home to most of the province's CFA's, a category stereotypically characterized not only by its heterogeneous ethnic origins, relatively recent arrival, and ignorance of local culture, but also by its professional status, and political and economic advantages. The only university in the province, Memorial University of Newfoundland, is heavily populated by CFA's.

A poor province in the poorest region of Canada, Newfoundland and Labrador have the highest unemployment and illiteracy rates in the country and an economy highly dependent on natural resources. The fishing, mining, forestry, and petroleum industries account for most local employment. In

Canada, the majority of women work in clerical, service, and sales occupations (Armstrong & Armstrong 1984): in Newfoundland and Labrador, the processing sector is the third largest employer of women. Women have lower incomes and lower labour force participation rates than both Newfoundland and Labrador men and Canadian women (Anger et al. 1986).

This sketch of some important features of the local environment suggests that the barriers separating feminist academics from community activists involve more than the divisions between feminists and non-feminists or academics and activists. Just as important are the factors that physically, politically, and socially separate townies from people beyond the overpass, islanders from Labradorians, and CFA's from locals. Understanding these differences is important in seeking to communicate across the barriers they create and crucial to appreciating the context in which community-based feminist activism takes place.

The Participants

> They (women's studies courses) attract women for whom the mere act of choosing the course demonstrates and highlights the fact they have questions to ask as women and about women. (Mahoney 1988, 103)

> I had a choice between this and physics. I didn't know if I could face a term of physics, so I picked women's studies. I hope it's going to interest me. (Port au Port)[2]

In contrast to the women described in the first quotation above, the women[3] who enroll in this introductory women's studies distance education course do so for a variety of reasons. Some are self-identified feminist activists; others would reject both labels. Some sign up out of either personal or professional interest; others pick women's studies simply for lack of choice. Being selective about one's education is a luxury women in many of these communities do not enjoy. Under these circumstances, the chance to enroll in women's studies can be either an eagerly awaited opportunity or one's last resort.

> I've worked at the Women's Centre here in Labrador City for the past two years and, having worked with women for quite some time, wanted to see if I could get a little more education on the topic. (Labrador City)

> Actually, it's just another credit toward my Bachelor of Education. (Isle aux Morts)

> It just seemed like an appealing course to take — to learn a little bit more and perhaps to contribute a little bit and just hear other people's opinions and views on how they perceive the issues facing women today, and perhaps, what we can do collectively or individually to change things for the better. (Port aux Basques)

> It was about all that was available up here, but I'm sure that I'm going to find it interesting. (Labrador City)

The women's studies students have diverse backgrounds and a relatively high proportion take the course out of interest rather than for the academic credit. Some of these students have never taken a university course; others have already completed degrees. The students come from towns and very small communities, from both Newfoundland and Labrador. The majority are married women with children; most are 35 to 45 years of age. Almost all have some form of paid employment, generally white collar. Although in some ways they are typical Newfoundland and Labrador women, for instance, most were born and raised in the province, in other ways the women's studies students are unusual. For example, their literacy and employment levels are higher than average. In this sense, the social distance between these students and the instructor is less than it might be, making them in some ways ideally situated to mediate between a feminist, CFA, townie academic and the women of their own communities.

In addition to those just mentioned, some other personal characteristics are important in shaping my participation in the course as instructor. Being divorced with no children makes me something of an oddity and, in this sense at least, a role model no one is keen to emulate. One thing I share with many of the students is the experience of living in small, face-to-face communities. Although my experience was gained in Indonesia rather than here, we have a similar sense of both the constraints and the benefits for women of this style of community living. Even more important is the commitment I share with many of the students to understanding and improving women's lives. Although I certainly can be labelled an academic, I am also an activist, a fact of which the students are aware. This self-identification brings me closer to the students who are also feminist activists and causes some uneasiness in those who are uncomfortable with either or both of these labels.

The Course

> However, if WS (Women's Studies) is to keep one of its initial promises — to be the educational arm of the Women's Liberation Movement — then the 'how's' of WS (its teaching practice) are as important as its 'what' (its curriculum). (Klein 1987, 202).

To understand how a women's studies course can stimulate and support feminist activism, it is important to consider both content and process. More attention will be given in this paper to the question of process for two reasons. First, critics such as Klein argue that our reflections on women's studies courses and programs have paid insufficient attention to feminist teaching and learning processes. I believe that our ability to teach and learn from feminist community activists depends less on the specific content of our courses than on the teaching and learning environment we establish. Second, the literature on feminist teaching and learning in women's studies has focused on the joys and problems encountered when participants experience face-to-face interactions.[4] The physical separation of participants in distance education poses additional challenges to feminists as they cope with the logistics of preparing and participating in courses under the temporal and technical constraints imposed by this separation.

Before looking at issues of process, though, it is necessary to briefly summarize the course and to outline some of the prosaic details.

Content and Structure

Women's Studies 2000, An Interdisciplinary Introduction to Women's Studies, has been offered as a distance education course by Memorial University since fall 1986. Women's Studies 2000 is a 13-week, second-year credit course offering an introduction to the subject organized around four themes: Nature versus Nurture, Language and Symbolism, Work, and Power, and one special topic, Feminist Perspectives on Sexuality. The case material is drawn wherever possible from women's experiences in Canada generally and Newfoundland and Labrador particularly. Course assignments, drawing on resources readily available to the students, ask them to apply the concepts introduced by the course to the understanding of their own and other women's experiences. The emphasis throughout the course is on learning ways of thinking rather than on absorbing information. Students should leave the course with a tool-kit of feminist frameworks for analyzing women's experiences, responding to critics, and devising strategies for action.

The quality of the teaching and learning environment in a distance women's studies course depends heavily on the form the course takes. Current technology provides a number of options. Women's Studies 2000 is a multi-media course including print, in the form of readings and a course manual, videotape, in the form of both original programs and films transferred to videotape, and teleconferences. Memorial University's teleconference network is a two-way audio communication system linking 55 centres across the province and accessible to most communities.

Students do some course work at home and some at the teleconference centres. This aspect of the course contributes to significant differences among students. Some are alone in their centres, relying solely on the teleconferences for regular contact with other students and the instructor. Others have the support and stimulation of at least weekly contact with a face-to-face group.

> In the other centres where there's more than one person doing the course I think they have the advantage of being able to discuss the different terms, concepts, etc. I find myself at a loss; like it's just my single opinion that I have on certain matters. (St. Anthony)

Not surprisingly, it is students in smaller, more remote communities who tend to be isolated in this way, and students in larger, more accessible population centres who tend to have support groups. These larger centres are also more likely to offer feminist support services such as women's centres. (The instructor is alone in St. John's.)

In discussing the processes through which the course stimulates and supports feminist community activism, it is important to keep in mind the constraints imposed by distance; the "class," diverse in terms of background and expectations, is also scattered across the province. Nevertheless, as we will see below, this factor is a strength as well as a limitation.

Facilitating Feminist Activism[5]

> If WS is to be more than just another discipline or "just" feminist scholarship integrated in conventional disciplines, the distribution of knowledge requires a teaching practice which fulfills its original promises to the Women's Liberation Movement to empower women intellectually, politically and personally. (Klein 1987, 202)

Given the dispersed makeup of the participating group at any given time, as well as the number and relative isolation of their different communities, it is not practical to think in terms of engendering collective feminist community action by the course participants. There are three things we can expect of the course, however. First, it should, in the long run, contribute to creating a social environment that generates and supports feminist activism. Second, in the short run, it should develop and enhance the feminist consciousness and commitment of the participants, and give them the confidence and skills to engage in feminist action in their personal lives and their communities. Third, it should, as far as possible, provide an experience of feminist community for the participants. There are, of course, many limitations on our ability to achieve these ambitious goals, but rather than focusing on failures, I want to consider our successes. If we accept that the task we have set ourselves is enormous and that progress is certain to be slow, we can value and learn from the small steps we take towards our goals.

> If WS claims to be feminist then it has to be committed to change. Maybe it is over-ambitious to set as our target the world, tomorrow, but at least we could be thinking about ways to organize our courses so that we can become aware of some of the changes we want as individuals and collectively to make. To bring about change requires women to take the initiative, to take charge, if not control, and to have the confidence to do so. (Mahoney 1988, 105)

> Women should become involved at the community level in economic development. Who better to become involved than women? (Burnt Islands)

> A couple of weeks ago I was included in the labour force survey for the first time and the woman asked me if I worked. I said, "Yes, I do a double shift; I work 16 hours a day." She said, "Oh my, girl, that's slave labour; we don't count that." I said to her that she should count it, that it wouldn't cost Statistics Canada any more to record that kind of domestic labour than to ignore it. It's something I'm going to take up with them and see what their answer is. (Labrador City)

> We have to stop being the influencers and become
> the leaders, stop being the props that carry the poli-
> ticians in power and become the politicians in
> power. We have to support women and get them
> elected so they can have some voice in policy
> making, and we have to become advocates on the
> outside bringing pressure to bear on politicians who
> are in the power positions. We have to make issues
> important to us known by becoming and remaining
> politically active. (Colliers)[6]

The woman who made this last statement telephoned me
before our first teleconference meeting to express her reservations about taking the course. She was not a feminist, she said,
and she did not feel there were any problems or inequalities
in her personal or professional life. Her interest in the course
was that of a mildly curious, unengaged observer. By the end
of the course she had developed a passionate commitment to
working for women's well-being. She still considered her own
situation unproblematic, but rather than accepting this state of
affairs as normal, she now felt that she was exceptionally lucky
and privileged. She had developed a sense of responsibility for
other women's well-being. What had been "other women's
problems" had become "our problems." What happened
during the course to cause this transformation? The process
can be summed up in three terms: empassionment, empowerment, and legitimation.

1. Empassionment

At its best, the course engages the participants' minds and
spirits in a commitment to feminist principles and feminist
action. The aim is, as Klein citing Janice Raymond says, "not
to enforce feminist ideology but rather to *empassion* students
with feminist knowledge" (Raymond 1980/85, 57-8, cited in
Klein 1987, 210). This process proceeds in stages that vary
somewhat depending on the starting point of each participant.
Our first task is to define feminism, reclaiming the label from
those who distort and misrepresent it. Many of the students
live in communities where direct access to feminist information is limited or non-existent. Most are familiar with the term,

but reject it as a label for themselves. When asked if they can define feminism or whether they would call themselves feminists, they reply with varying degrees of suspicion and reluctance.

> I think a lot of women would like you to define "feminist" before they commit themselves. (Stephenville)

> The stereotypes about what feminists are usually come down to a man-hater, one who is anti-family and is pro-abortion. These are the things that come across in the media; these are the things that people pick up on. (Port aux Basques)

Despite some reservations, most students are prepared to learn more about feminism. Bringing an accurate sense of the meaning of feminism to women who otherwise would not have access to this information and, through them, to communities isolated from the mainstream of feminist activism is by itself an important contribution to building an environment that accepts and supports feminist goals. This is one reason why I find it useful, rather than problematic, that many women come to the course with little knowledge of, or commitment to, feminism. These are women we need to reach. Preaching to the converted is not only a luxury for feminists in Newfoundland and Labrador; it makes for a very small audience. The women this course reaches have the potential to become articulate spokeswomen for feminism in their communities; the credit course format allows us 13 weeks in which to make our case and engage their sympathies.

> I'm definitely not a family-hater and I don't believe in abortion; I'm not a lesbian, obviously, but I guess the reason that I've chosen this course is that I do want to find out what feminism is and to be able to explain it and to define it to other people around me. (Hawkes Bay)

Some participants, often those from communities with Status of Women councils, come to the course as self-identified feminists with a good sense of what this means.

> I regard feminism as a matter of having choices, and that's what it basically boils down to for me. I believe that women and men should be able to make the choices that they would like to make without feeling any pressure or any compulsion to do it because of society, or a husband, or a father, or another woman — just the right to make the choices that you feel are right for you. (Port aux Basques)

The course provides an opportunity for women who have both an understanding of feminism and experience with feminist action to deepen their understanding.

> Most of what I have learned is very valuable in my work with battered women and children (Corner Brook).[7]

> What really bothers me is that I always considered myself pretty much a feminist and it's not until I'd taken this course that I've considered the implications of what really goes on. It's pointed out a lot of new things to me. (Labrador City)

This woman, who works full time in the home, talked about the agreement she has with her husband, who works in the paid labour force. Each works an eight-hour day at their separate tasks. After that time all work must be divided equally. The principle underlying their agreement is that both partners' work should be equally valued and each should have an equal opportunity for leisure. Taking the course helped this student to see that her husband's private recognition of the value of her work, positive though it is, is not enough if society does not also recognize and monetarily value the work she does in the home.

Empassionment, of course, means more than simply understanding what feminism is. It involves a personal identification with feminist principles and a commitment to action. This process entails an examination of the participants' own lives as well as their communities and society at large; it involves rethinking and reassessing familiar situations. They may recognize the fundamental inequity of situations they previously considered fair, or they may realize that they are already engaged in feminist activism without recognizing it. For instance, many women who have started the course insisting that the division of labour in their homes is completely equal have realised that, while their husbands and children may help out a bit, they themselves do most of the domestic work. This has led them to renegotiate this division of labour. One woman who successfully complained about an instance of gender discrimination in the armed forces years ago now sees her actions as feminist advocacy benefitting military women generally.

While readings facilitate this process of rethinking and reevaluation, I believe that the video programs, films, and teleconference discussions have much more impact, largely because they have a personalizing effect. These media allow us to take abstract ideas and attach them to known persons and familiar situations, making these principles easier to understand and identify with. Seeing Canadian and local feminists on the video programs talking about what feminism means to them and the strategies for change they pursue, seeing women confronting and dealing with inequalities in the films, and talking to the other women during the teleconferences develops participants' awareness of feminist issues and the urgent need to address them.

> A lot of women aren't aware of these issues. (Labrador City)

> If they're content, why upset them. (Stephenville Crossing)

> I think it's a myth that they're all content. (Port aux Basques)

How do you reach the thousands of women out there and try to get these things across to them? (Labrador City)

2. Empowerment

Another goal of the course is developing in the participants the feeling that action is possible, the confidence that they are capable of acting, and the knowledge that support is available. Many aspects of course process and content contribute to the empowerment of participants. Three of these are: (1) sharing skills and knowledge, (2) decentralizing, and (3) creating a supportive environment.

Sharing Skills and Knowledge. While the participants learn a great deal about feminist action from the video programs and films, and derive considerable encouragement from "meeting" the women appearing in them, the teleconference is probably the most important forum for empowerment offered by the course. The differences we bring to the teleconference discussions contribute to the process of mutual learning and mutual empowerment. They teach us about the range of women's experiences, about the "normalcy" of the problems we experience, about the ways we can cope with oppressive situations. Feminists and non-feminists learn about problems they both face and how they deal with them. Women of different generations learn from each other about what has and has not changed. Women from urban areas learn about the problems confronting women from small, isolated communities.

I could see why she [a battered wife] stayed. I think if you're told you're stupid, the blame's put on you enough, you're going to believe it after a while, and she was particularly isolated. She had no support groups. (Labrador City)

Where was she going to go? How was she going to get there? I think that the physical impossibilities were there as well. (St. Anthony)

We discuss familiar issues such as family politics and "forbidden" topics such as lesbianism, which are seldom or never discussed openly in the participants' communities.

> We discussed the film for a few minutes afterward and I think the majority of us felt that the film was very enlightening. I hadn't thought about lesbian mothers as such, but my own views were rather narrow-minded ... and I think it made me a little more broad-minded after seeing the film. (Stephenville)

Again and again, as we discuss different issues, we reiterate women's right to make choices and the ways we can help to make this possible, for ourselves and for other women.

Decentralization. In this empowering process of sharing and learning it is important that everyone take part and that the group does not focus on the instructor as the authoritative voice. Our attempts to decentralize are not always successful, but as the course progresses, students increasingly talk to each other and challenge the authority of the instructor.[8] Students begin to offer comments on each other's contributions.

> No, I'm a classroom teacher, nothing special. (Port au Port)

> I'm a classroom teacher, somebody special. She said she wasn't special. That's not nice to say that about yourself. (Channel)

To facilitate the process of decentralization, from time to time I leave the students to have discussions on their own.

> She asks us to discuss the questions and leaves us alone. This is the blind leading the blind, as far as I'm concerned. (Channel)

> Yeah, but at least you got more blind people up there. One blind person's really desperately lost. (St. Anthony)

While being left on their own is somewhat disconcerting at first, students soon recognize the value of this "time alone." The first time the course was offered, we tried this technique only once. The response convinced me that it should become a regular feature of the course.

> I think we should have been talking like this all through the course. (Port aux Basques)

> I just said the same thing, and we would have learned so much more. (Port au Port)

> I wouldn't be so depressed up here in St. Anthony. (St. Anthony)

Given the nature of distance education, there are very few opportunities for students either individually or collectively to influence the structure and direction of their courses, which are generally pre-packaged. The teleconferences provide at least some opportunity for flexibility and responsiveness to the women's studies students' needs. This does not give students control over the course, but it does allow me at least to share control.

Support. In the course we work very hard at collectively creating a supportive environment for discussion and developing strategies to broaden support for feminist action in the community at large. At the suggestion of one of the students, each term I compile and circulate a list of the participants' addresses and telephone numbers, which allows them to keep in touch with each other outside the weekly teleconferences and after the course ends. Students also keep in touch with me after the course is over, extending invitations to speak to local groups, asking for advice about projects they are pursuing, telling me about their ongoing problems and successes.

Participants are very supportive of each other during tele-conferences and particularly sensitive to the needs of their most isolated colleagues.

> I just wondered if anyone else found it like that, or was it just me. (St. Anthony)

> No, it's not just you. We in Stephenville felt the same way. (Stephenville)

We all work to make the teleconference discussions a "safe" forum for discussing experiences, ideas, and reactions to feminist perspectives. There are limits on the trust we have been able to develop so far; some women have been willing to discuss being victims of batterers, but others have not been willing to share their experiences as lesbians. I am not sure that we will ever succeed in empowering all the women in the course to participate freely in discussions, but I think, because of the feminist commitments of many participants, we have achieved more than many face-to-face groups. Even when individual women do not feel able to speak about their personal concerns, I believe our collective willingness to discuss these issues can have an empowering effect.

3. Legitimization

Another way the course empowers women is by legitimization, in various senses. The fact that a dominant institution such as the university offers a women's studies course bringing feminist perspectives to students "beyond the overpass" serves to legitimize both concerns with women's issues and feminist approaches to dealing with them. This legitimization is important to women not only for themselves, but also in their efforts to legitimize these concerns to others.

> My husband asked if I was getting credit for it, and I said, "Of course!" (Labrador City)

> I tend to get myself into the occasional argument about women's issues, and, being a feminist in a small community, any time women's issues are

brought up you're usually in the middle of it, so I thought this might be a good opportunity to pick up a bit more ammunition. (Port aux Basques)

What Have We Accomplished?

I think I could almost write a book now myself on my own feelings. (Goose Bay)

This course has been the most difficult thing I have ever done, but it has also proven to be the most rewarding. (Glovertown)[9]

Given the nature of distance education and this particular course, it is not realistic to expect collective feminist action by the participants. It is fair, though, to ask if the course is at all successful in introducing feminist ideas, encouraging and supporting feminist activism, and providing an experience of feminist community. We have both negative and positive evidence that the course is at least partly successful. A negative indicator of the degree to which the course increases feminist awareness and impels participants to action is their expressed sense of risk and danger. At times, ambivalent about what this feminist knowledge means to them, they discuss their fears and concerns, as well as their commitment and excitement.

I don't know if I can handle this knowledge, and I don't think I'm doing a very good job of it, to tell you the truth … All this program is pointing out to me is how much I'm doing as a human being — a full time job, and a hard job at that, raising three children. I don't know if it's a good course for me to have done. I mean, it is a good course for me to have done, but is it going to make me dissatisfied? (Goose Bay)

These aspects indicate the degree to which the course touches their minds and hearts, transforming their perceptions and feelings. This reaction also reflects the real risks involved in developing feminist consciousness and initiating feminist activism in isolation from feminist support networks. Physical isolation compounds the constraints on feminist activism posed by women's social and emotional isolation. What impresses me is the degree to which these women, knowing the risks and still somewhat unsure of their own capacities, are prepared to struggle for changes in their personal lives and their communities.

> It's pointing out things that I know are right, yet when I delve into it myself I don't know how you would change it; I don't even know how to change it myself in my own family. (Goose Bay)

While she was taking the course, the woman who made this statement frequently expressed ambivalence about her developing awareness of feminist issues. Two years later she sought me out when I visited her community to engage me in an intense discussion about her continuing efforts to achieve an equitable division of labour within her family. Although discouraged at times, she was determined to continue the struggle. This is one example of the positive way the course encourages and supports various types of feminist activism, sometimes in diffuse, indirect forms.

> You may never know all the personal changes as a result of a student taking your course ... The course made me consider what was happening in my own life on a broader scale. Everything I studied could be applied to my work, my relationship, or my personal life. (Labrador City)[10]

This woman used her new knowledge to lobby for and manage a job-training project teaching feminist research methods to women in her community. One woman reconsidered her decision to give up her job and follow to another province the man with whom she was involved. A woman who had previously believed that women must hold their marriages together at whatever cost supported her daughter's decision to take her two children and leave an abusive husband. A crisis intervention worker showed the course tapes to women at the transition house where she worked. They discussed not just their personal situations but also the general inequities women face and the need for collective action. A community college teacher reported:

> I have shown two tapes from Women's Studies 2000 to my stenography class to get them thinking about equality, because I'm sure some of the younger students don't realize that they are sometimes discriminated against because they are female. After each film, we had a class discussion about it. I was never hesitant to talk to them about women's studies. (Clarenville)[11]

On the principle that it is sometimes more effective to have an outside "expert" present feminist ideas, former students have invited me to speak to community groups, professional associations, and women's groups. Since taking the course some women have become involved in collective forms of feminist activism such as anti-pornography campaigns in their communities. As these examples indicate, the women's studies course has generated, or supported, diverse forms of feminist activism, from community mobilization to small but significant changes at home.

> I took part of my husband's gas money and dart money and part of the kids' allowance and paid someone to come in and do the house once a week. (Labrador City)

Participating in this distance education course has taught me a great deal about Newfoundland and Labrador women's lives. In particular, the other participants have given me an appreciation for the realities of feminist activism in their communities, the priorities they have set, the strategies they find effective, and the obstacles they confront. They have taught me how privileged I am in many ways; they have pointed out changes I need to make in my feminist analysis, strategies, and style if I am to work with them effectively.

Looking Back, Looking Ahead

Internal Politics Creating a Feminist Forum

Our success in linking women's studies courses to feminist community activism depends on our ability to create a feminist environment within these courses. Commentaries on the internal politics of women's studies courses generally point to the potential for feminist practice, while also recognizing the constraints on our ability to create feminist environments in our classes, mainly arising from the authoritarian nature of our educational institutions. The additional constraints imposed by the logistics of distance education might make women's studies distance education courses seem particularly improbable venues for feminist consciousness-raising and feminist action. Our experience has been that the collective struggle to overcome the constraints of time, distance, personal and regional differences, and institutional hierarchy and inflexibility can itself be a worthwhile exercise in feminist consciousness raising and feminist practice. Our successes may seem modest, but they are disproportionately significant to the women involved, given the conditions under which they are achieved.

External Politics: Fighting for Survival

Women's studies distance education courses can make valuable contributions to feminist activism in isolated communities, but they are very vulnerable creatures. In the "pay-as-you-go" environment of university continuing education, they serve a clientele with limited financial resources. In provinces such as Newfoundland and Labrador, the clientele is even more limited by low literacy levels.

From the time it was first proposed, the course described here has been under attack by administrators. The grounds for criticism are political and philosophical as much as economic. The course owes its development and survival to the continuing support of feminist community activists across the province, many of whom have not taken and do not intend to take the course themselves. The survival of the course is a testimony to the co-operation of feminist activists and academics and to their shared conviction that this course can and does make a contribution to feminist community activism in Newfoundland and Labrador.

Feminist Activism and the Feminist Studies Classroom

Jeri Dawn Wine

Feminists who have reflected on feminism in academia are deeply cognizant of women's studies' activist roots and its highly political orientation to change (e.g., Bunch & Pollack 1983; Howe 1975, 1983; Rich 1975; Schniedewind 1985; Treichler 1986). Women's studies' happy, if somewhat precarious, position would not exist without activism in the women's movement. Indeed, the very existence of women's studies is one of the movement's major triumphs, perhaps the premier accomplishment that differentiates between this and earlier waves of feminism.

In my feminist teaching over the years I have increasingly wished to foster the activist efforts of the women in my classes. I believe that the oft-mentioned gulf between academic and activist feminists is a false one, as do many other writers in this volume. There is danger, of course, of academic feminists becoming overly committed to the development of theory, or too focused on a narrow slice of feminist scholarship and thereby neglecting the work of women seeking social change. As well, activists can become too focused on immediate goals without developing a broader framework for understanding change. But women's studies would not exist without the women's movement; many feminists are both academics and activists; feminist academics must be activists in order to establish and maintain women's studies programs; many activist feminists come to academic feminist studies programs to ground their community work in the feminist literature and to gain credentials; and most Canadian feminist academics are activists in areas beyond their academic work (Eichler, 1990).

The present chapter describes my three years of experience in teaching a graduate course entitled "Feminist Organizing and Community Psychology." The course is part of a doctoral program in Community Psychology at the Ontario Institute for Studies in Education (OISE), but is open to masters level students and to students in other programs and departments in the institute. It is a course that I conceived as an explicit effort to bridge academia and activism, and in many respects it has been successful in doing so. Though it has been a highly rewarding course, it has also been the most difficult course I have taught in my 19 year teaching career in terms of tension and conflict between students and myself as instructor, far more so than any other feminist studies course that I have taught.

In the chapter I take up two themes: (1) the contradictions involved in teaching a course that emphasizes feminist collective process and focuses on fostering feminist community change in the context of the hierarchical, patriarchal authority structure that is academe, and (2) the impact of the course on feminism in the community, presented through a description of some of the projects carried out by students in the course. Prior to launching into the themes, it is necessary to provide some description of the course and its context.

The setting

OISE is an institution affiliated with the University of Toronto; through that affiliation agreement it is the Graduate Department of Education at the university, and offers MA, MEd, PhD, and EdD programs. Within the institute, which has its own administration and governing structure, there are eight sub-departments that essentially operate as university departments.

OISE is well known for its feminist scholarship, but it does not offer a unified feminist studies program. Rather, feminist studies is housed in differing ways in various departments; of eight departments, four offer some opportunity to do feminist studies. In the Department of Applied Psychology, feminist studies is offered under the rubric of the program in Community Psychology, which is a program staffed by left-wing men and feminist women. The students attracted to the program tend also to represent these differing perspectives. It is the sole program in the Department of Applied Psychology to eschew the individual as the unit of analysis and the individual change model and to focus on more macro analyses and on social change.

The differing analyses and resulting models for social change held by the left-wing faculty and students and the feminist faculty and students has been a source of some tension; but we have managed to maintain a vision of community psychology as the program with radical content and purpose in the department, and an appropriate site for dissension. In the debate between autonomous feminist studies and the integration of women's studies in mainstream academia I strongly favour the former.[1] But failing that, in my view, community psychology is a highly appropriate home for feminism in psychology because of its identification with oppressed groups, its focus on empowerment of the oppressed, the socio-politico-historical nature of its analyses, and an explicit attention to the dialectic between the individual and society.

The community psychology program has been in existence for six years, and since its inception it has included a strong feminist component; indeed, feminist studies is formally described as a core component of the program. I was the sole feminist faculty member for the first four years but I've recently been joined, to my delight, by two feminist colleagues. A number of the feminist students attracted to the program have been activists and women who have done front-line service work in a variety of feminist helping services, such as shelters for battered women and rape crisis centres, or have been radicalized through working with women in mainstream social service agencies. These students have exerted some pressure on the faculty to accommodate their vision and concerns. My course on Feminist Organizing and Community Psychology was the first course I designed explicitly for the Community Psychology program, partly in response to student requests. In designing courses appropriate for the program, I believed it was important to foster feminist activism and to address student needs to develop the individual-social change dialectic.

The Feminist Organizing Course

My vision for the course

In my conception, the course was to be focused on praxis, on a synthesis of thought and action, theory and practice. The focus was reflected in the nature of course requirements, with readings on feminist theory and strategy, combined with activist projects. It was a single term in length, or 13 weeks, with one three-hour class per week. A massive amount of work was carried out in that short time. The students did a considerable amount of reading and analysis of literature on feminist community organizing and related theory; but the major course requirement was that students form small collectives and carry out feminist community organizing projects. We defined "community" broadly so that some projects have been carried out in the community outside academia, others in the academic environment. The size of the class has ranged from 12 to 20 students, while the number and size of the collectives in each class have varied considerably, with five, three and two collectives in the classes over the three years. In practice, we have devoted one half of each three-hour weekly class to general course readings, the second half to collective meetings; though each of the collectives has met for many more hours outside of class time.

Students have been encouraged to avoid "reinventing the wheel" (Spender 1982) by linking with activist organizations in the community, by seeking knowledgeable activists as informants in the area of their projects, by learning from each others' experience and by doing what reading they could to inform themselves. The published feminist literature is rather sparse regarding the strategy and practice of feminist organizing and is largely American; much of the Canadian literature that exists is unpublished and difficult to obtain, or in feminist movement publications that may also be difficult to obtain. We are fortunate to have in the OISE Women's Educational Resources Center and the Toronto Women's Movement Archives the largest collections in Canada of unpublished women's movement materials, and Canadian movement periodicals.

I encouraged collectives to carry out time-limited projects encompassed by the length of the class, e.g., single events such as a forum, a small local conference, a workshop, a rally or a march, a lobbying or petition or fund-raising campaign regarding some particular feminist issue. If engaging in long-term projects, I suggested that these be an aspect of the ongoing work of an existing feminist group. Students were encouraged to maintain awareness of the theoretical grounding for the work of their collectives, in order to avoid the experience of feminist activism being carried out without a clear understanding of the theoretical bases and implications of the work. We found Charlotte Bunch's work especially useful for demystifying feminist theory and clarifying links between theory and practice. Her article entitled "Not by Degrees: Feminist Theory and Education" (1983), in which she presents a straightforward model that links theory and action was especially helpful.

The organizing projects were carried out in collectives, partly because the collective organizational form has been quite characteristic of the feminist movement, though other organizational forms have been used by feminists and were described in course readings and discussions. It is also the case that there are a variety of issues and problems that arise with regularity in collective work, and I considered it useful that students anticipate and mindfully work through these issues in preparation for further collective work in the community. I've used a number of different readings on collectives through the years I've taught the course; the most useful being a booklet produced by the B.C. Women's Self-Help Network, *Working Collectively* (1984). They describe the horizontal, power-sharing nature of collective structure and process, and provide trouble-shooting suggestions for many of the issues that tend to arise in collective functioning, such as conflict resolution and delivering critical feedback constructively.

The evaluation scheme that I proposed to each class had an equal weighting for the work and readings of the class as a whole and for the collective work. Though I insisted on maintaining these weightings, the specific criteria for evaluation were generated in discussion between the class and myself, and in each class included criteria judged by me, by the members of each student's collective, as well as through self-evaluation.

I described myself as a resource person for the collectives, and rotated among them during their meeting times in the class. I encouraged them to bounce ideas off me, to check on the feasibility or appropriateness of their planned activities, to ask me for resources. I was, in fact, able to supply each collective with a tiny amount of funding (up to $50 for each project) for duplicating advertising material, or other appropriate expenditures. Beyond conceptualizing myself as a resource person and as a catalyst for the projects, I had some commitment to the basic features of feminist pedagogy in terms of wishing to foster student ideas and self-initiated activism, and to share power to the extent possible in a graduate classroom. Feminists have discussed the difficulties that are involved in such attempts at feminist pedagogy or gynagogy[2] in the context of the hierarchical authority structure that is academia (e.g., Duelli-Klein 1987). Schniedewind (1983 & 1985) has made some of the most useful specific suggestions for reducing power differentials between students and instructor, and among students. For example, her co-operatively structured learning groups are quite similar in nature and purpose to the collectives in my course. However, it simply is the case that none of these approaches can completely eliminate the instructor's power and authority relative to that of students.

My hopes for the course were that students would emerge from it with some useful feminist activist experience, a clearer understanding of the joys, difficulties and means of improving the functioning of collectives, as better informed feminist activists with a clearer understanding of the links between theory and practice; and, of course, I hoped that the course projects themselves would have a positive impact on the community. I also hoped that the students and I would see ourselves jointly as furthering the feminist project of transforming society through our work in the course.

The experience of the course

As is often the case in teaching, my vision and hopes for the class were somewhat different than the actual experience of students and of myself as instructor. I'll discuss these differences from the perspective of the first theme noted in the introduction, i.e., the contradictions involved in teaching a course that emphasizes feminist collective process and focuses on fostering feminist community change in the context of the hierarchical, patriarchal authority structure that is academia.

The students attracted to the course, perhaps understandably and to my relief, have all been women. As is true of the OISE student body in general, the students were mature, ranging in age from approximately 25 to 45, most of them white and middle-class, with a mix of heterosexual and lesbian women. I had required as a prerequisite either previous feminist course work or some involvement in feminist activism. As I had hoped, the prerequisite insured that most of the students who came into the course were self-defined feminists, many of them with some activist experience.

I required students to sort out their collective projects, in a general sense in terms of area, as well as the membership in each collective, within the first three weeks of the class. This was a tumultuous period during which a variety of ideas were proposed, rejected or revised, and women considered and reconsidered their project commitments and collective memberships; and during which two or three students in each class dropped out, reportedly overwhelmed by the prospect of carrying out an activist project in the context of academia. Though we spent part of each class discussing readings, it became clear early on that the students' energy, anxiety, and interest were primarily invested in the formation of the collectives, and shaping of projects — an impression that I had no reason to change as the course progressed.

The collectives took on a more powerful reality than the course as a whole; students' commitments were very much to their collective and its project. The second and third years I taught the course, I was aware of the tension between the collectives and the class as a whole, with the accompanying likelihood that students would be more invested in the collectives. However, I stubbornly continued to believe that it was possible to learn something as a class from reading and discussing the relevant feminist literature, and after my first experience with the course, that collectives should be able to learn from each others' process and planning. After the first year, I built in more class time for collectives to communicate with each other about their work; and I invited students to select literature related to each collective's project for the entire class to read and discuss in the latter half of the term. These efforts were partially successful; but it was the collectives that continued to have the most concrete reality for the women. This was not, of course, necessarily negative; indeed, it is evidence of the success of the major structural feature of the course.

The collectives, for the most part, attempted to work toward an equal sharing of power and equality in decision making. The usual characteristics of individuals that determine leadership and task differentiation in small groups, such as knowledge, articulateness, energy, and available time, were operative in these groups. However, they were at least aware that egalitarianism was the appropriate mode of functioning for collectives, and most of the groups made an effort toward equalizing power to the extent possible. The collective process, in other words, rendered the women highly cognizant of power dynamics and quite committed to an horizontal power structure.

In contrast, in spite of my commitment to sharing power in the class, there were tasks and roles that I, as a paid representative of academia, was required to carry out, involving certain requirements and limits imposed on the students associated with the demands of academia that I as instructor had to voice and enforce. These included my role as the individual responsible for submitting student grades, for monitoring students' reading and attendance, however informally, and for enforcing the end of term time-limit.

Attempts to equalize power between instructors and students can only be partial in success given the very real power differential that does exist between them, and the differences in responsibilities. Students are essentially responsible only for themselves and their own learning — in the case of this class that responsibility extended to members of their collective — while the instructor is responsible for shaping the curriculum, preparing resources, setting or helping students to set growth-enhancing assignments in short, for insuring the best possible learning experiences for everyone, as well as for collecting evidence that learning has occurred, and seeing that the class is terminated at the "proper" time.

It became clear that the usual difficulties of carrying out a genuinely feminist pedagogy within the hierarchical academic authority structure were exacerbated greatly by the contrast between the process of the collectives and features of the graduate classroom. The contrast and my academic roles ensured that I became seen as a representative of the power structure, to be viewed suspiciously and negotiated with warily. In addition, there were the tiny amounts of funding for which collectives had to apply, while adhering to certain rudimentary guidelines. In essence, I became a representative of bureaucracy, whether one conceives such bureaucracy as academic or as a funding agency. As such a representative, I was imposing certain conditions — evaluation, time constraints, criteria for funding — which were experienced by the students as foreign to or infringing on the collective process.

The kinds of problems that ensued as a result of the contradiction between collective process and the requirements of academia included conflict over evaluation, which wasn't entirely alleviated by including students in the creation of the evaluation scheme and as evaluators. Indeed, some of the students moved to resenting evaluation of any sort, and vocally resented being involved in evaluating each other or themselves, sometimes to their own surprise. Students who had most enthusiastically built themselves into the evaluation scheme earlier in the term were often those most appalled by their involvement when the time for evaluation arrived. The kind of process they were experiencing in their collectives which, ideally, valued each member equally was experienced as antithetical to evaluation. Yet, evaluative feedback to members is one of the most difficult problems faced by feminist collectives, one that has blown many collectives apart. Typically this occurs because feedback is neglected altogether until problems become impossible to ignore, then criticism erupts angrily and non-constructively. Though I had not insisted that students provide academic grades for each other, I did express my belief that it was very important that the women learn to provide feedback to each other for their future functioning in feminist activist groups. It was also the case, of course, that they had more knowledge of each others' work in the collectives than I could possibly have, and so could more accurately evaluate each other.

An additional source of conflict was that some of the women saw the requirement of writing up their projects for submission to me as competing with the demands of the projects themselves, though the paper requirement could be interpreted very differently, depending on the nature of the project. Again, I was seen as an agent of the authority structure making demands that interfered with the collectives and their goals.

Collectives also tended to see themselves in competition with each other for carrying out the "best" project, and for my positive evaluation. The information-sharing in class about each collective's work was as likely to be anxiety-provoking as it was helpful, because the collectives moved through their work at very different paces and in differing ways. Apparently, as a combined result of seeing me as a powerful source of evaluation and of the shared strength gained through the collective process, as the term progressed some collectives occasionally asked me to not attend certain meetings, or showed a reluctance to use me as a resource or for feedback. The money I was able to provide for collective activities was occasionally another source of resentment, with some students chafing against the requirements for receipts and a rationale for expenditures.

These tensions and resentments were not always expressed in open conflict with me, perhaps because of the danger of doing so in the context of my professorial authority and the associated power I wielded. Occasionally, they were expressed indirectly; for example, on one occasion in the second year of the course, the entire class "forgot" an end-of-term party to be held after the last class of the year. I arrived on the appointed day with the sole contribution to a "pot luck" celebratory meal. The incident may be partially explained by the fact that the party hadn't been mentioned during the preceding two classes, and that the last class was not really the end of term. Rather it was a very midstream and unfinished time for the collectives which almost invariably continued their work up to the deadline for grade submissions, about six weeks after the last class. Even so, I suspect this incident was another piece of evidence of rebellion against academia and me as its representative.

After teaching the class the first time, I became convinced through reflection, and through speaking to other feminist academics and to students who had experienced the class, that the problems were primarily structural in their source, rather than a result of poor teaching, though I certainly made mistakes. In the next two years, I included in the course description, and in class discussion, reference to the academic-feminist collective conflict and the likelihood of students coming to see me as a powerful, and thus untrustworthy, representative of bureaucracy; and I attempted to discuss the associated power issues as they arose in the course of the class. As Constance Penley (1986) has noted, attempts to eliminate authority in the feminist classroom may simply disguise the hierarchical distribution of power inherent in the university's institutional structure. "The risk in aiming toward or claiming the eradication of power relations, is that the force and pervasiveness of those relations may be overlooked, 'out of sight, out of mind'" (138). By defining these power issues as legitimate for discussion, I attempted to render them relevant and central to our work as feminists. These efforts served to only partly ameliorate the problems, since they did not, in and of themselves, eliminate the structural and power issues. They were, however, useful in terms of students becoming cognizant of the kinds of issues to be faced in an activist movement like the Canadian feminist movement which is largely funded by the state, as well as the conflicts and contradictions involved in academic feminism being embedded in academic hierarchical power relations.

In short, then, the feminist organizing course has been a difficult one, particularly for me as instructor, with certain problems arising predictably from year to year, issues that arise largely from the conflict between the values and practices associated with collective process and those associated with academic bureaucracy. Another way of conceptualizing these problems is in terms of the power differential that exists between professor and student, and the potential of the students' experience in the collectives to empower them to challenge me and my power. Viewed from this perspective these recurring problems were evidence that the course was "working" in a very basic sense. Indeed, many of the problems that I've detailed can be defined as evidence of the course's success. The extent to which students became committed to the women in their collective and to its project was impressive. Their commitment was reflected in the amount of time that the women were willing to invest which, in most cases, was at least one meeting each week outside of class, usually two or three hours in length, as well as the practical and academic research involved in preparing for the project, and the various tasks associated with carrying it out.

In spite of the recurring problems and my discomfort with my own role in the class, most of my hopes for the course were realized. Students did, indeed, emerge from it with some useful feminist activist experience.

In the following section, I describe briefly some of the projects that were carried out. Though collectives varied, most of them did approach collective work reflectively with a commitment to "doing it right." In doing so, they developed a clearer understanding of the positive and negative features of collectives, as well as means of improving their functioning. However, I should note that the collectives were so short-lived that they still tended to be in the positive glow of the first stage of group formation by the end of the term. So many of the problems longer established collectives face with some consistency simply did not appear for these women. I had also hoped that students would emerge as better informed feminist activists, with a clearer understanding of the links between theory and practice. I feel less confident that this happened for many of the women, largely because the students were caught up in the time and energy-consuming practical work toward carrying out their projects, and a number of them did not generate a clear theoretical analysis of that work. My vision that the course organizing projects themselves would have a positive effect on the community, and concommitantly would further the feminist transformation of society, was one of the most clearly realized of all of the aspirations I initally had for the course, as will become clear in the following section. I do feel that the students at the closing of each class saw me as an outsider to that process. However, each year several students have come to talk with me weeks or months later to express their understanding that this was a unique course in fostering activist work, and their gratitude that they had been able to do such work for academic credit. I also should note that formal course evaluations at the end of each class were quite positive.

The work of the collectives

The students were highly inventive in their choice of organizing projects. The projects carried out over the years included a forum on violence against women, a series of writing workshops for women in OISE, a feminist issue of an anarchist publication, preparation of a manual for childcare workers in battered women's shelters, a one-day conference on race, class and therapy, work toward a sexual harassment policy for OISE, a body work workshop for academic women, a fundraising campaign for a lesbian mother on trial for kidnapping her sexually and physically abused children, a workshop on homophobia and heterosexism, and a workshop on violence against women. All of these projects have had lasting effects in terms of the ongoing work of at least some of the women involved in them.

The forum on violence against women was one that immediately attracted the attention of the women involved in it from the first day of class, many of them activists and/or service workers in the area, and therefore, already linked with professionals and activists in the community. They were able to connect with the work of a local organization that had funding to carry out conferences or meetings on violence against women, but no personnel to do the organizing. The goal of the collective from the beginning was to create a network of feminists working in this area, and the forum, which was itself highly successful, was only a step in that direction. In the following year, the network that grew out of the collective's work became the third reincarnation of the Toronto Women Against Violence Against Women (WAVAW).

Another project that had ongoing organized impact on the community was the conference on race, class and therapy. A number of feminist therapists at the conference expressed a need to develop an organization that would continue beyond the conference and address the issues it raised, and others. The resulting organization is the Toronto Feminist Therapists Association. I don't wish to over-emphasize the role of the course in the initiation of these organizations. Clearly, the need existed among women in the community quite independently of the class, but I do believe that the work of the collectives served as a catalyst for their creation.

Other projects were equally successful, but because of their time-limited nature were not ongoing. A case in point was the fundraising campaign for the lesbian mother. Her trial took place very near the end of the course, so in a sense, the project was tailor-made for the class. The students were able to raise in that short time about twelve hundred dollars, using a variety of inventive approaches, including approaching strangers on the street, making pleas at social services conferences, circulating among marchers at the International Women's Day parade, passing buckets at gay and lesbian dances, underwriting the expenses for a national appeal by mail to female lawyers. The project was a very powerful learning experience for both the lesbian and heterosexual women in the collective, which was equally comprised of both. Approaching perfect strangers with requests for funding for a lesbian required them to articulate their rationale for that request and to wrestle with their own internalized homophobia. Their discomfort and strategies for overcoming it were shared in the collective meetings.

Another project with a similar outcome was the workshop on homophobia and heterosexism; the collective was comprised of three lesbians in quite differing stages of coming out and one heterosexual woman. To hold a workshop addressing homophobia and heterosexism was a very public and frightening statement for all of these women, with differing implications for the lesbian and heterosexual women. All were confronted with their own homophobia, the lesbians with their terror of rejection and stigmatization and an acceleration of their coming out process, the heterosexual woman with the difficulty of working with lesbians on issues so tied to lesbian experience, occasionally in danger of being perceived as the enemy, and occasionally recognizing in herself the very homophobic attitudes that made her the enemy. All of these issues were addressed directly in their meetings. In practice, the workshop was rendered more effective by the presence of all of these women with their differing sexual identities. At least one of the lesbian women has made a commitment to continue on a long-term basis carrying out workshops and educational outreach on the issues of homophobia and heterosexism.

Certainly not all of the projects have been as successful as those I've described, though none was a total failure. I think that some of the variables that pointed to their relative success were: (1) a mixture of women in the collective, including those with activist experience, as well as novices; (2) links with or ability to negotiate those links with the feminist activist community, e.g., an inventive project, the creation of the manual for childcare workers in battered women's shelters had no immediate community impact as none of the women had experience in, or prior connections with, shelters. However, one of the women has, since the class, become quite active in shelter work; including providing workshops for mothers based on the collective's manual. Often, inexperienced women were exceedingly good at negotiating community links through sheer chutzpah and commitment, though, in the case mentioned, shelter workers were understandably offended by inexperienced women implying that they had greater knowledge of the needs of children in shelters than did the shelter workers themselves; (3) the appropriateness or readiness of the political context for the project, e.g., the collective that worked on a sexual harassment policy for OISE found a surprisingly unreceptive unenvironment. One of the students has continued working in this area, completing sexual harassment surveys of staff and students; her research is feeding into current work on an institute sexual harassment policy; (4) personal commitment of the collective members to the collective project and to its goals. Occasionally, women came together on the basis of a commitment to a general area of feminist concern but had considerable difficulty agreeing on a particular project; usually, these differences were worked out early enough in the course for a reasonable project to be carried out; (5) the sheer "do-ability" or feasibility of the project within the time frame of the course. Occasionally, the collectives were over-ambitious, in spite of my efforts; and (6) the ease or difficulty of a particular mix of women working together as a group, their compatibility, similarity of interests and analyses, as well as their individual and collective commitment to the ideals of collective process.

Summary

Teaching the Feminist Organizing and Community Psychology course has been an important learning experience for me as a feminist academic who, with other women's studies teachers, attempts simultaneously to represent the academic establishment and the revolutionary ideals of feminism. I've learned that, in spite of my desires and efforts to share power and my commitment to the egalitarian ideals of feminist pedagogy that I do, as a result of being a representative of academe, indeed, have very real power. I've learned to treat that power with some respect and delicacy, and to view opportunities to discuss power relations in the classroom as important learning experiences for both me and for my students. I consider these power relations important for us to understand and useful to our feminist growth as activists and academics.

The collective structure and process provided very powerful learning experiences for the women in my feminist organizing classes. In two of the rare articles on strategies of feminist pedagogy, Nancy Schniedewind (1983, 1985), as noted earlier, has described a similar approach toward co-operatively structured learning as being highly useful to the egalitarian ideals of the feminist classroom, though the label she uses is cooperative learning groups. In these groups as in the collectives in my classes, students work toward a common goal, and they "sink or swim together"; the students become accountable to each other and committed to the common group goal(s). Her model is quite comparable to the experience of the students in my classes, who, almost uniformly, became absorbed in their collectives and projects to an extent that initially was surprising to me. Their experience in their collectives often empowered them enough to confront me as the visible representative of the power structure.

Evaluation was, and remains, a thorny issue, especially at the graduate level in which academic marks must be submitted and high marks are quite important to students for funding decisions and program advancement. Early in each term most of the women were at least willing to participate in an evaluation scheme. However, by the end of the term their collective experience and accompanying commitment to cooperation and egalitarianism rendered them resentful of such participation because of the contradiction between these collective values and differential evaluation. My own discomfort with the contradiction between my feminist ideals and the requirements of academic bureaucracy is exemplified by this issue, one which I have not satisfactorily resolved.

Teaching the feminist organizing course has had a lasting impact on me; I've learned a good deal about power and hierarchy in the feminist studies classroom which is embedded in academe. The recognition that equalizing power between students and professor is not fully possible can provide opportunities for learning about the dynamics of power and the nature of hierarchical power structures. I've also learned that, despite the difficulty of carrying out activist work in an academic environment, the effort is worth taking and can be quite successful. The course has had a lasting impact on many, perhaps most, of the students who have participated in it, as well as on the community as a result of the many fine feminist action projects that have been carried out.

Endnotes

Section I

Chapter 1, Briskin

1. The first draft of this paper was presented at the Third International Interdisciplinary Congress on Women in Dublin in July, 1987. It also draws on material from *Feminist Organizing for Change: The Contemporary Women's Movement in Canada*, co-authored with Nancy Adamson and Margaret McPhail (1988). This version is part of a larger piece previously published in *Studies in Political Economy* (1989). Isa Bakker, Mariana Valverde, and Lorna Weir read an earlier draft of this paper and provided helpful comments and criticisms; thanks also to Roberta Hamilton for her skilful editing.

2. "The cultural politics of ... the early seventies (were) extraordinarily, if naïvely optimistic that as women we could change our lives and those of others once we saw through 'male lies.' Many feminists were eagerly attempting to change every aspect of their lives: how we lived with and related to other adults and children, how we worked and developed new skills, how we saw ourselves ... Much of the cultural feminism of today, in contrast, is less concerned with change: it calls upon the timeless truths of women's lives, sufficient in themselves, but threatened by the perpetual and invasive danger of men. It suggests that women do not need to change their lives, other than to separate themselves from the lives of men, and that there is little hope of men themselves changing." (Segal 1987, 68-9)

3. Mariana Valverde pointed out the importance of this kind of self-labelling in the women's movement and suggested the term the "politics of identity." Later, I came across the following comment in an early statement from black feminists: "This focusing upon our own oppression is embodied in the concept of identity politics. We believe that the most profound and potentially the most radical politics come directly out of our own identity, as opposed to working to end somebody else's oppression". (Combahee River Collective, in Eisenstein 1979, 364)

4. For an extended discussion of the contradictory contribution of "the personal is political," see "The ideology of the women's movement," Chapter 6, in *Feminist Organizing for Change*.

5. In her analysis of sisterhood, Bell Hooks makes the point that bonding based on shared victimization reflects male supremacist thinking since "sexist ideology teaches women that to be female is to be a victim." Further, Hooks points out that by "identifying as 'victims,' they (white women) could abdicate responsibility for their role in the maintenance and perpetuation of sexism, racism and classism, which they did by

insisting that men were the only enemy." Hooks goes on to argue for bonding on the basis of "shared strengths and resources." (Hooks 1986, 128)

6. Although beyond the scope of this article to develop, it seems to me that this paradigm transcends some of the theoretical and strategic limitations of the perceived opposition between reform and revolution.

7. It is interesting to note that Jaggar uses the quote from Bunch cited in the text to distinguish between radical feminist and socialist feminist alternatives: "Radical feminists intend their alternative institutions should enable women to withdraw as far as possible from the dominant culture by facilitating women's independence from that culture ... Socialist feminists, by contrast ... build alternative institutions as a way of partially satisfying existing needs and also as a way of experimenting with new forms of working together." She herself points out that these distinctions are not "clear cut." (Jaggar 1983, 336)

8. For a recent rather damning discussion of feminist organizations, see Ruth Latta, "Working for Feminist Organizations," *Breaking the Silence*, VI/4 (June 1988). For a discussion of the impact of government funding on the practice and organization of rape crisis centres, see Toronto Rape Crisis Centre, "Rape," in Guberman and Wolfe (1985). See also Hunter (1977), Smith (1984) and Bouvier (1986).

9. For further discussion of feminist process in relation to this AGM, see Backhouse (1988), Zaremba (1988), and Adamson and Molgat (1988).

10. See Findlay (1987) for a description of the process of the Canadian state integrating the representation of women's issues into the policy-making process, and a discussion of the difficulties faced by feminists working as civil servants in attempting to intervene in that process.

11. Smith (1979) discusses a process she calls "institutional absorption," which occurs as the women's movement interacts with the social institutions, a process not dissimilar to what I have called institutionalization. She says: "A major danger is the process of institutional absorption. I imagine it to be like a starfish eating a clam, sucking the living tissues from the shell. Institutional structures are set up to organize and control and they do it well. When critical positions and action emerge related to an institutional focus, processes are set in motion which bring things back in line, which absorb the anomaly, and keep things stabilized ... Each new way of absorbing women's movement initiatives into the institutional structure isolates them from the movement and depoliticizes them ... as the work is absorbed by the ruling apparatus it is withdrawn from the general struggle ... " (13-14). She goes on to argue that the problem is that much of feminist organizing has been "in relation to the institutional structure of the ruling apparatus. To do something about rape it seems that we should work in relation to the police, the courts and the law." (14)

12. "But it was from socialist-feminist politics that we drew our guiding principles on how to build a campaign and movement in support of clinics and women's right to choose." (Antonyshyn, et al. 1988, 132)

13. It is also interesting to note that Adamson and Prentice (1985) criticize OCAC for inadequate "disengagement," in particular, for an underlying acceptance of the medical model.

Chapter 3, Miles

1. I have made this case in some detail in a number of places. See, for instance Miles (1982, 1984 and 1985).

2. The term "reproduction" is used here in its broadest sense, to refer to all the human-centred activity involved in serving people's needs and making and sustaining people as full and active human beings.

3. The growing international interchange and co-operation among women that the United Nations Decade for Women has witnessed and encouraged is another extremely significant factor contributing to feminism's broadening self-definition and increasing focus on society and community as a whole. For Third World women also bring to the exchange the strength of more intact women's cultures and traditions of community involvement and development than urban North American women have been able to call on. For discussion of this see Antrobus (1982), Bunch (1985), Feminist Workshop at Stony Point (1980), Sen & Grown (1985). In fact, not only rural and Third World women, but native women, old women, disabled women, working-class women, black women, lesbian women, Jewish women, immigrant women, young women all bring important concerns and strengths to their activism which continue to add to the richness and diversity, depth and breadth of feminism's vision and practice.

4. Recent studies documenting the negative relative impact on Third World women of "development" involving the growth of market economies in which men have privileged access to wages and technology have thrown new light on the earlier process in our own societies — the process that continues today in rural areas. For early treatments of this question see Tinker, Bramsen, Buvinie (1976), Danber and Cain, D'Onofrio-Flores and Pfafflin (1982), Rogers (1980), special issues in *Signs* on Women in Development (Winter, 1977 and Autumn, 1981).

   Other writers have documented women's continuing increasing relative disadvantage in advanced industrial nations (As 1978; Larsson, 1979) Numberless studies of women's double workload, criminally low wages, extreme vulnerability to poverty and violence, isolation and lack of social support in industrial societies support their case.

5. For a recent thought-provoking analysis of rural change see Sim (1988). Antigonish town and county are reflected with eerie accuracy in the particular model of rural community Alex Sim calls "Fairview" in this book. His discussion provides a richer human sense of this type of rural community than I have been able to do here.

6. The demographic and the statistical information in this article is taken from the 1981 census and the Antigonish *County Statistical Report*, Nova Scotia Department of Development, September, 1983.

7. My reflections on women's activism in Antigonish in this article are based on research which has consisted mainly of interviews and meetings with women from Antigonish town and county, conducted, until recently, in

a context of, and as a supplement to my observations as an active feminist in the area.

8. Abortion has been omitted from this list as an issue with a very special resonance in a county whose population is 82 percent Roman Catholic. Women's right to abortion is a prominent issue in the media and is central to women's dignity and independence as well as the creation of a caring and humane society. Women are the ones who suffer abortion and are faced with the terrible decisions involved. Feminists, in demanding control over this decision for women, are demanding that the question be left in the hands of the group that has most consistently proven itself "pro-life," even at great personal expense, over countless generations.

This is never acknowledged in a public debate, whose terms feminists have so far been unable to define even as we participate in it. Women (or "other women") who suffer abortion are presented as murderesses — shallow, amoral, self-indulgent destroyers of life. This calumny bears no relation to reality, but a marked relation to the misogynist misrepresentation of women so central to patriarchal western culture.

In a context of mutual respect and caring among women that departs radically from dominant misogynist images we might be able to initiate a mass dialogue among women which challenges the core of the existing debate and communicates a new articulation of the issue that is life affirming and compassionate. But we have not done this yet and so remain locked in a male-defined debate that leaves women deeply divided.

9. Irene Murdoch left her husband of 25 years when he locked her out of the house after assaulting her. At the time of their marriage her mother had contributed to the down-payment for the farm and the purchase of furnishings. Irene Murdoch had also contributed at least half the work involved in building up the farm valued at $300,000. She ran the ranch herself during five months of the year when her husband was away working elsewhere. Irene Murdoch fought for two years through the Alberta Supreme Court and the Supreme Court of Canada arguing that she was entitled to a half interest in the farm properties by virtue of her contribuiton of labour and money. In 1972, with only one dissenting voice, the Court granted Mrs. Murdoch $200 a month in alimony. The judges commented that her contribution was part of the "normal duties of a wife." They noted also that "It cannot be said that there was any common intention that the beneficial interest in the property in issue was not to belong solely to the respondent" and that to declare that Mrs. Murdoch had an interest in the property itself "would be tantamount to establishing a precedent that would give any farm wife a claim in partnerships."

10. Antigonish Women's Association presented a brief to the committee that was printed almost in full in the local newspaper, undertook a series of educational meetings, and had a letter to the editor of the local newspaper condemning Penthouse magazine's printing of violent pornographic images endorsed by a wide variety of other local groups.

11. The detailed story of this activity, its tensions and difficulties, as well as its sisterhood and its triumphs is, of course, complex and can't begin to

be told here. The list of activities included here is merely meant to give some idea of their extent and diversity and should not be read to imply that moving beyond our first and exciting discovery of sisterhood and each other has been simple or without tensions.

12. The mutual transforming interaction between feminism and established women's organizations in this period is also seen in the active response of groups like the Women's Institutes and University Women's Clubs to issues defined by feminism, and in the willingness of women profession-als such as nurses, teachers and social workers to make public statements *as women,* and to challenge the hierarchical organization and other basic principles of their professions. In trade unions and the churches, as well, ever larger numbers of women are becoming aware of their specific interests as women. They are founding caucuses, and links between and beyond their organizations, and are bringing pressure to bear on the structures, the definition of the work, the distribution of resources and the establishment of priorities in their institutions. In all of these cases, women are recognizing their special interests and concerns and dis-advantages even as they speak from and build their strength in ways that bring power to all women.

13. In some recent feminist literature feminist theoretical positions that rec-ognize gender differences have recently been attacked as essentialist, i.e., they have been accused as implying that such differences are immutable and grounded in biology. See Segal (1987) and Snitow (1989). I do not agree that the integrative feminist position I have presented here is an essentialist one.

14. See Terry Mehlman, Debbie Swanner & Midge Quant, "Pure but power-less: A woman's peace movement," *Broadside,* July 1984, and the letters replying in the following issue for an idea of the issues in this debate.

Chapter 4, Vickers

1. Primary sources consulted in preparation of this chapter were:
Emergency Consultation of Women's Groups Funded by the Women's Program, Secretary of State. *Final Report.* CRIAW, Ottawa.
National Action Committee on the Status of Women:
1986-88 Membership Brochures
1973-77 *Status of Women News*
1978-84 *Status*
1985-88 *Feminist Action*
1988 *Consultant's Report. Organizational Review*
1988 *Report of the Québec Consultation, Organizational Review*
Report of the Royal Commission on the Status of Women. 1970. Queen's Printer, Ottawa, Canada.

2. Anderson was interviewed as part of the hour-long video "The Politics of the Women's Movement" created by Jill Vickers as part of the Carleton Video Series, "Through Her Eyes."

3. The FFQ withdrew from NAC for a period because of NAC's constitu-tional stands which permitted Constitutional repatriation without Qué-bec's concurrence. Native women's groups were also alienated because "the" women's movement grabbed "the brass ring" of women's rights

and did not support, to the limit, the constitutional protection of Native rights. The Meech Lake debates have provoked similar conflicts.

4. This is largely induced by the movement's cohesion. Like the Scandinavian movements, it has a linguistically homogeneous population in a geographically compact area within a single state.

5. It deals almost exclusively with the anglophone movement, in fact.

6. Although lip service is paid to her notion that structureless organizations are impossible and her article has often been reprinted, few feminist groups took up her challenge to develop practices which clarified feminism's conception of democracy and ensured the accountability of those who acted in the name of other women.

7. Women's Centers, Rape Crisis Centers, Incest Survivor Groups, Battered Women's Shelters have all formed umbrella-type networks to interact with governments in Canada. These groups, however, are service providers primarily and their need for funding provides a shared goal.

8. An Annual General Meeting survey in 1984, when NAC had 458 member groups, seventy of which were national organizations, revealed the following ideological profile:

Factor 1	Factor 2	Factor 3	Factor 4
10.2%*	9%	7.2%	5.7%
Strong Feminist Force	Traditional Force Force	Economic Force Force	Liberal/Reform Force

*of a 32.1% variance resolved by factor analysis
(from Appelle 1987).

9. Indeed, the 1988 Organizational Review saw it as an advantage that each occupant of the presidency could create her own role. This was presented to legitimize the idea of choosing presidents from outside of Toronto or Ottawa. The fact that traditional liberal-democratic theory justifies the geographic rotation of leadership roles seems unfamiliar to the authors.

10. In recent years, what I have called the lure of "the Icelandic Solution" has persuaded many anglophone feminists in Canada that an intense, authentic politics in large groups is not a dream. Speakers from the Icelandic Women's Party have described their use of feminist process norms in state politics. The homogeneity of Icelandic society, its small size and population are ignored.

Section II

Chapter 5 Greaves

1. The author acknowledges valuable insight and assistance from Sandi Kirby, Gillian Michell, Mary Lou Murray, Jan Richardson and the London Feminist Process Group.

2. This led to the unsettling situation in 1986 and 1987 where there was no pornography committee, even though important federal legislation was pending during that period, and a large portion of the membership of NAC appeared to be vitally concerned with this issue.

3. One unusual method was demonstrated at the 1988 annual meeting, where a group of housing activists (who actually described themselves as non-members of NAC) requested that each of the Executive Board

candidates visit their booth in the display area in order to have their positions and commitment to the housing issue assessed.

4. Official priority setting had usually been avoided or resisted at the NAC executive, but eventually the first priority setting attempt occurred in Spring, 1988, when a short-term subcommittee of the executive brought a report to the Annual General Meeting. Although the development of an inclusive priority-setting process was directed by the members at the 1988 AGM, the 1989 AGM received a list of priorities suggested by the Executive, *before* the policy resolutions had been dealt with.

5. In 1987, teleconferencing and corresponding committee memberships were introduced to try and reduce member group alienation. The Health Committee in 1987 was the first committee to meet exclusively by conference call, and the Lesbian Issues Committee was one of the first to become Canada-wide through the use of corresponding memberships.

6. For example, DAWN (DisAbled Women's Network), National Organization of Immigrant and Visible Minority women, National Lesbian Forum etc.

7. Megan Ellis, a delegate from B.C., led the move at the 1988 AGM to amend the recommendation regarding the makeup of the committee by increasing its non-executive membership. The strong support for this was also a reflection of the level of alienation of the membership on the issues of reorganization, particularly the level of trust in which the executive was held, and the determination of the membership to have more decision-making power. One of the Organizational Review Committee's resolutions eventually approved at the 1988 AGM directed that all committees have a non-executive co-chair. Despite this, the 1988-89 Organizational Review Committee had two executive co-chairs, again concentrating the decision-making power within the executive, and against the spirit and direction of both the 1987 and 1988 annual meetings.

8. The Fédération des Fémmes du Québec (FFQ) a federation of 98 Quebec groups eventually withdrew their NAC membership in May 1989.

9. One executive member observed that it would indeed be ironic if a report commissioned by NAC to improve itself were to destroy NAC.

10. This motion was reraised by the Quebec representative at a later executive meeting on the grounds that not many executive members had been present for the initial discussion. This was indicative not only of the growing unease with the distance that the committee purposefully took from the executive, but also the tendency, noted in the consultant's report, of the executive to remake decisions, long after the initial delegation or decision had been made. (Similar autonomy was not granted to the 1988-89 Organizational Review Committee).

11. For the text of this speech, see Greaves (1988a).

12. The resolutions under consideration included; an endorsement of the organizational review committee's report, a continuation of the review process by a committee dominated by non-executive members, the design of a member-inclusive priority-setting process, directives for one regional meeting per year, and various democratic reforms to committee operation

and member selection processes, including the introduction of non-executive co-chairs.

13. For the text of the speech by Marylou Murray, on behalf of the NAC staff, see Murray (1988).

14. See the following post AGM articles on feminist process and NAC: Michell, Greaves & the London Feminist Process Group (1989), Riggs & Tyler (1988), Greaves (1988a), Backhouse (1988), Costigan (1988).

15. Women involved in single-interest member groups often lamented the absence of apparent interest or support within NAC for their particular issue. One distinct and important example is the participation (or non-participation) of the feminists in Canada concerned with violence against women. This large section of the women's movement, and indeed of NAC's membership, devoted to issues of wife battering, sexual assault, pornography, incest, and related issues, was, during 1986-1988, consistently underrepresented both on the executive and in the planning and priorities of NAC.

16. At the 1987 AGM considerable discussion was held in the plenary on the acceptability of advertising a "left caucus" meeting, for the purposes of discussing candidates and issues.

Chapter 6, Leah and Ruecker

1. Connections Conference Report, "The Founding of a Provincial Women's Coalition," is available from SAC, 2149 Albert St., Regina S4P 2V1.

2. A number of women involved in Connections have discussed this article and contributed their insights and analysis, in particular, Fiona Bishop, Marj Brown, Jan Joel, and members of the Connections Steering Committee. The chapter was written collaboratively by Ronnie Leah and Cydney Rueker; however, additional revisions have been made by Ronnie Leah who takes sole responsibility for the final version of the chapter.

3. Ronnie Leah, a political activist for the past 20 years, has been involved in both the women's movement and the labour movement. Cydney Ruecker became active around issues of women's health and culture, and has been active in community based women's groups for the past several years.

4. See, for example, the discussion of feminist process in Adamson, et al. (1988, Chapter 7) and the discussion of coalition building in the March 8th Coalition (Egan, et al. 1988, 25).

5. For analysis of the effects of government cutbacks in Saskatchewan, and early organizing activities, see *Briarpatch*, "Down the cutbacks road," Special Issue (Spring 1987) for a report on SAC's role in the fightback campaign.

6. SAC is a provincial organization of women, working to promote the social, political and economic equality of women in Saskatchewan. SAC was in a good position to help mobilize women in the province, given its ties to many women's groups, its elected board members from across the province, its full-time coordinator and other paid staff, and its publication of *Network* six times a year. See SAC's *Network of Saskatchewan Women*, 4 (6) (Spring 1987), for a report on SAC's role in the fightback campaign.

7. SWW, an organization of working women in Saskatchewan (union and non-union members, paid and unpaid workers), grew out of the union movement in 1978; it has had a history of building solidarity with women workers and focusing on issues of concern to working women. With its close ties to union women in the public sector unions, which had been hard hit by the government's cutbacks in public services, SWW was well situated to coordinate with labour and other activists in Saskatchewan.

8. For a detailed report on early activities of the Saskatchewan Coalition for Social Justice, see SCSJ Newsletter, January/February, 1988, published in *Briarpatch*, 17 (1): 15-18.

9. As noted by Egan, et al. (1988, 25), coalition politics enables oppressed groups to develop alliances, to link and integrate their struggles, and to build a broader political movement for social change. Through coalition politics, we can "develop the strategy and theory of working in common in practical and concrete ways." Similar issues were addressed during a panel discussion on "Coalition Building: Organizing the Popular Sectors" (Leah 1989).

10. Some of these debates are outlined in Adamson, et al., (1988) Part III.

11. For a discussion of feminist process (as it has been practised in the labour movement), see Edelson, 1987. Edelson explains that "process" refers to "an interest in *how* we work together in addition to a concern regarding *what* we work at" (4). This concern for process, which arose out of the women's movement, focuses on issues of democratic leadership, consensus decision-making, and resolution of conflict.

12. Women organizing a 1981 conference in Alberta used a similar model for linking women's personal experience with political action (see "Women Organize Alberta," cited in Adamson, et al. 1988, 235). Other feminists have also made use of small group consciousness-raising as the essential basis for women's organizing.

13. It is estimated that trade union women constituted one-third of conference participants (conference organizers did not keep precise records of attendance by affiliation). Union women included staff representatives, elected leaders and rank and file members.

14. For example, Adamson, et al. (1988, 12, 231 ff.) have also focused on the diversity and heterogeneity of the women's movement, noting the different approaches taken by grassroots feminists and those working within formal institutions such as unions.

15. These lists of women's concerns were then compiled and typed up following the conference and made available, as promised, to conference participants. This "Supplementary Report" of the Connections Conference is available from NAC.

16. These questions were taken up by the newly formed Connections Steering Commmittee. As the previous representatives to SCSJ (from SWW and SAC) were no longer able to fulfill their commitments as women's sector representatives, new representatives were chosen from the Connections steering committee.

17. For further details of the Connections conference, see J. Joel, et al., "Making Connections ... ," In *Network*, 5, (1): 6-11.

18. As one of the groups affiliated with SCSJ, Connections was involved in planning for a Saskatchewan People's Congress, held April 9-10, 1988. For a detailed report of the People's Congress, see *SCSJ Newsletter*, May/June, 1988, published in *Briarpatch*, 17 (3): 9-12; see also J. Joel, "Social Solidarity," in *Network*, 5 (2): 14-15.

19. Since the time of writing this chapter, in the summer of 1988, Connections has ceased to function as a women's coalition. Activists in Saskatchewan concluded that it was no longer practical or possible to sustain a separate women's coalition. Women have directed their energies to the Saskatchewan Coalition for Social Justice (SCSJ) in organizing against cutbacks and the Saskatchewan Action Committee, Staus of Women (SAC) has continued to coordinate women's activities in the provice.

For further information about women's organizing in Saskatchewan, contact SAC at 2149 Albert St., Regina S4P 2V1. For information on the provincial organizing, contact SCSJ at 2138 McIntyre St., Regina S4P 2R7.

Chapter 7, Graveline, Fitzpatrick and Mark

1. Jean Graveline, a long-time resident of the North and a member of the Coordinating Committee of the Manitoba Action Committee on the Status of Women, actively lobbied MACSW to contribute resources to northern development. She and other northern members provided vision to the project. Katherine Fitzpatrick was hired as a private consultant to do the initial research to support the network's bid for continued funding. Her contract was extended to assist in developing the Northern Women's Network in targeted communities. Barbara Mark was one of the first women contacted through the network, due to her volunteer work in Churchill in the area of abuse of women.

Chapter 8, Reddin

1. I wish to thank especially, among the many women who have participated in feminist community organizing in Prince Edward Island, those who provided descriptive materials and contributed their time and thought in interviews reporting on the progress, problems and strategies of women's groups in P.E.I.: Ellie Conway, Marion Copleston, Cecile Gallant, Vicki Gauthier, Heather Orford, Sheila Perry, and Nancy Reddin.

2. Applicable 1986 Census Reports, e.g., Statistics Canada Catalogue, Nos. 94-103, and 93-114, Table 5.

3. From Women's Division, Province of Prince Edward Island, Fact Sheet 1 (March 15, 1988): Women and Education in Prince Edward Island. Charlottetown.

4. Pseudonyms have been used for the women interviewed.

5. The final draft of this chapter was read by each of the women interviewed for their comments. All concurred that their perceptions were fairly presented. For a discussion of trustworthiness in naturalistic inquiry see Lincoln and Guba (1985).

6. Several women in a recent study of the role of women in the P.E.I. fishery have expressed support for the concept of an organization for women in the fishery, but cite the barriers of transportation, long distance, winter snowstorms, child care, etc.

Chapter 9, Haley

1. Special thanks to Richard Tunstall for assistance with editing, and to Dianne Harkin, Dorothy Middleton, Kay Canitz, Marion Meredith, Rennie Feddema, and the many other farm women and funding agents whom I interviewed.

2. The term "farm labourer" refers to a woman or man who works on a farm for wages, and who has no ownership of the farm. For the purpose of this chapter, farm labourers do not include children of owners.

3. The monies are used to fund "thirteen types of eligible projects:
   1) action oriented research,
   2) information exchange,
   3) resource material for farm women, issues education,
   4) projects for development of farm women's participation skills,
   5) advocacy projects,
   6) policy development,
   7) delegate exchange and membership debriefing,
   8) public relations projects,
   9) farm women's conferences
   10) seed money for project planning, conferences, action oriented research,
   11) membership drive
   12) planning and organizational development,
   13) colloquia and workshops for farm women" (Marion Meredith, Farm Women's Bureau, Agriculture Canada).

Chapter 10, Ng

1. This is an abbreviated version of a longer paper bearing the same title. Due to space limitation, I have omitted many details and endnotes in this version. I want to take this opportunity to thank members of WWIW in New Brunswick for their encouragement and support, and to Jennifer Thompson for helping me to transcribe and compile interviews and other WWIW materials in the summer of 1988.

2. The exception is Tania Das Gupta's book on immigrant women's organizations in Ontario. Her book is a useful assessment and summary of grassroots organizing in Ontario. See Das Gupta (1986).

3. For a succinct review of the rediscovery of poverty in the western world, see Edwards and Batley (1978). For a discussion of the rise and politics of citizen participation in the 1960s and 1970s, see Loney (1977) and Ng (1988, Chapter 2).

4. For a discussion of the invisibility of immigrant women's experiences in research, see Jacobson (1979).

5. One outcome of our work through the Women's Research Centre was the organization of a workshop series for female community workers to share our experiences in the summer of 1977. See Ng and Sprout (1977).

6. Indeed, there was a group called "The Multicultural Women's Association of B.C." formed under the auspices of the field officer of the Secretary of State around 1976. I was a member of this group and attended meetings of the group as a representative of the community organization where I

worked. Also see Carty and Brand (1988) for a discussion of the term "visible minority."

7. The details of how I went about doing this research appear in the longer version of this paper. I also discussed the methodology in a presentation I made to the 1989 annual meeting of the Atlantic Association of Sociologists and Anthropologists (AASA). The presentation is entitled "Immigrant Women's Organizing in New Brunswick."

8. See the two-volume proceedings of the conference entitled *The Immigrant Woman in Canada — A Right to Recognition*: Part I: Report of the Proceedings of the Conference; Part II: Recommendations from the Conference: Toronto, Ontario, March 20-22, 1981. Available from the Ministry of Supply and Services, Canada.

9. In fact, the follow-up conference, which became the founding conference of NOIVMWC, did not take place until 1986. But that is another story which cannot be told here.

10. According to the minutes of the February 19, 1984 meeting, six committees were established. They were: Health, Social Services, and Culture; Immigration and Employment; Education; Public Relations and Liaison; Research; and National Affairs. Most of the time the group did not operate along committee lines. Members simply carried out what had to be done. There were some subsequent attempts to revamp this structure by combining and renaming the committees, but this didn't seem to work satisfactorily either.

11. For a detailed discussion of the possibilities and limits of state funding as it pertains to WWIW, see Ng, Kwan and Mediema (1989).

12. The problems of state funding have been a subject of numerous discussions recently. See, for example, my discussion in *The Politics of Community Services* (Ng 1988, Chapter 6), and Carty and Brand (1988). However, I disagree with Carty and Brand's assertion that the national and Ontario immigrant women's networks were completely initiated by the state. It is important to bear in mind that these organizations are products of struggles between immigrant women and the state.

13. See my discussion in "Immigrant housewives in Canada: A methodological note" (Ng, 1982).

Chapter 13, Stone

1. I am grateful to the LAR members who took the time to share their views with me, and make this article possible.

2. Recently, controversy over how to organize and run the National Action Committee on the Status of Women has sparked a debate in the Canadian feminist press on this very issue. See, for example, arguments made by Greaves (1988), Backhouse (1988), Cameron (1988) and Adamson and Molgat (1988). Also relevant are Zaremba's (1988a; 1988b) comments on running a feminist collective.

3. These concerns with regards to the functioning of groups by collective principles are similar to those raised by Freeman (1973) and Ristock, Chapter 2.

Section III

Chapter 14, Christiansen-Ruffman

1. My thanks to the women with whom I have worked over the past years. Without having learned from them in discussions and action, this paper could not have been written. A specific thanks to CRIAW members Muriel Duckworth, Stella Lord and Angela Miles and to anonymous reviewers who read an earlier draft of this paper and made a number of helpful suggestions. I wish there had been time to have written it in a more interactive way, and I am particularly grateful to Stella Lord for her careful and helpful reading of successive drafts, each of which led to improvements and forced me to clarify my own thinking.

2. In setting out to write a brief article about CRIAW I knew, and the reader should remember, that there are many possible histories and descriptions of CRIAW. I have been involved with CRIAW in some way for most of its history, including as a past president, both nationally and in Nova Scotia. This article is too short to capture the collage of recalled events that constitute CRIAW's activities and history, and the focus of this chapter also limits its scope. The specific analysis developed here has not been part of CRIAW discussions and was not explicitly part of my own thinking until asked to write this paper on bridging the gap between activism and academe.

3. Feminists have proposed a collaborative model of research that shatters the rigid division of labour between researcher and the researched. Feminist methodologies have challenged the purposes, norms, structures, and relationships underlying this classical model of research interaction as well as the legitimized exploitation (see, for example, Kirby & McKenna 1989; Maguire 1987).

4. In some historic periods intellectuals act as critics of the larger society. In contemporary Canadian society, however, in part as a result of the worsening work and economic conditions, academics increasingly see themselves as dependent on the resources of government and industry, and academics and the Canadian elite may increasingly be seen as having the same agenda. This process is encouraged because of the societal undervaluing of scholars. The relatively low salaries of academics, especially given their years of training and specialized expertise, gives rise to the possibilities and probabilities that knowledge and expertise may be bought by those with money and that knowledge will be shaped very explicitly to serve the agenda of the powerful. Increasingly we are seeing the commodification of knowledge and training — as something that may be bought and sold.

   At the same time, it is important to recognize that part of the depiction of scholars as "eccentric," "ivory tower," and impractical is to undermine the "findings" and analyses of scholars from the academy whose findings challenge those in authority. As the community of scholars strives to gain prestige, legitimacy, and "relevance," and to counter these negative stereotypes, there is a danger that scholarship will increasingly come to see the world from the position of the powerful.

5. Their analysis and most feminist experience involve academics who have more money and prestige in the social structure than do community members. The concept "community" as used within the activist community and in the community development literature refers mainly to working-class and oppressed members and implicitly excludes the upper classes. Such a concept has a number of politically important uses, but its generalized connotation and the similar practice of naming all high-status women as academics, may obscure analysis and mask common interests and agendas. This apparent confusion also illustrates the power of elitism and classism in our society.

Academics are not always in different social classes from community members — both because of the unfortunate frequency of unemployed academics and the possibility of high-status feminist non-academic professionals or practitioners in the community. Moreover, historically intellectuals have supported popular movements and class divisions may seem to cross-cut rather than reinforce the division between academics and community members.

6. Many university professors also see it as creating a moral obligation to policy formulation and community involvement, but their discipline's narrow and abstract focus is often not as useful as the more strategic and broadly based perceptions of community members. One of the contradictions is that community members often have more sensitive analyses of the political situation than do academics.

7. The contradictions created by patriarchal and contemporary structural forces continue to challenge and to undermine feminist values and practices. Even some feminist books such as *Women's Ways of Knowing* (Belenky et al., 1986) are based on an implicit hierarchy of knowledge and of worth that reflects contemporary society's educational and stratification systems more that they do a world based on feminist principles and values.

8. CRIAW national conferences in the early 1980s focused on Sex Bias in Research. A selection of papers from the Ottawa conference was published in Vickers (1984). Margrit Eichler participated in that conference, and her *Sexism in Research and Its Policy Implications* was published by CRIAW (Eichler 1983). Meanwhile Naomi Black on the Social Sciences and Humanities Research Council, Canada's major granting agency, headed a committee that facilitated the publication and free distribution of Eichler and Lapointe (1985). Another attempt to raise awareness of sex bias in research was carried out through the Social Science Federation of Canada's Task Force on the Elimination of Sexist Bias in Research (see Christiansen-Ruffman 1986).

9. As an incorporated educational body with charitable tax-exempt status, however, there have been restraints on CRIAW's activism. As an organization, for example, CRIAW was advised by its board and its lawyers against taking a political stand against cutbacks in British Columbia or acting directly as an organization. Instead, conference participants launched the protest and CRIAW authorized a study monitoring the effect of these cutbacks. Four volumes reporting this research, done under

the direction of Mary Lynn Stewart, are now available through CRIAW, 151 Slater Street, Ottawa.

10. For example CRIAW received money from UNESCO to conduct a study on women and politics in Canada. CRIAW used its bank of researchers and newsletter to identify CRIAW members who had already done research on this topic. Approximately eight researchers — from the academic community and from the francophone and anglophone communities — came together with the aid of simultaneous translation to discuss their past research, their current research questions and a possible methodology. In retrospect, the day-and-a-half meeting was probably not long enough for researchers who differed greatly in their analytic approaches and in their orientation to, and experience with, participatory research. Nevertheless, under the coordination of Jill Vickers, the research was carried out in several communities across Canada and the results published as CRIAW (1986) and Vickers (1988).

11. In my experience, those most vocally critical of academic elitism, often without apparent provocation, seem to be recruits to new professions such as community activists, community employment trainers, community consultants, and graduate students, rather than individuals located centrally within the community realm. Perhaps the community versus academic tension may be partly generated by territorial demands of new professional identities; as these new professions need to establish their own legitimacy, and their own right to speak with authority, they use common rhetorical devices within patriarchal structures, such as putting down all adjacent potential claims and expecting authoritative recognition. These new professionals also fulfil the very important function of reminding academics — and all of us — of the taken-for-granted hierarchies that must be confronted and challenged continually — and that frequently confuse our well-intentioned attempts at sisterhood.

12. Discussions about tensions between academe and activism are reminiscent of tensions that have classically plagued struggles of the left where socialist academics tried to identify with, but could never actually "be" the oppressed workers in whose interests they were working. Some of these debates and associated "guilt trips" have been inappropriately transferred to feminists without recognizing a crucial difference. Whereas historically, leftist academics and workers were not the same person and did not share the same oppression, feminist academics and activist women often are the same person; the types of discrimination faced in many different institutional spheres are different forms and expressions of patriarchy. Because many leftist male academics cannot be part of the oppressed proletariat because of their class position, while feminist academics are part of the oppressed category of women, the relationship of feminist academics to our struggle, our activism and the people with whom we are active can be different.

Chapter 15, Drakich and Maticka-Tyndale

1. The 1970 reports on the status of women are listed in the references. See also Hitchman (1974), Eichler (1975), and Symons and Page (1984).

2. All references to motions passed, committees and task forces struck, are taken from minutes of the Executive Committee and Annual General Meetings located in the CSAA office at Concordia University, Montreal.

3. Sociologists and anthropologists were active in the formation of organizations such as the Canadian Research Institute for the Advancement of Women (CRIAW), the Canadian Women's Studies Association (CWSA), and the National Action Committee (NAC). In addition, research and publication on women's issues was moving forward with work on the *Canadian Newsletter of Research on Women* (later renamed *Resources For Feminist Research*), *Atlantis*, the first Canadian Women's Studies journal, and the publication of the first two books on women in Canada by sociologists Marylee Stephenson (*Women in Canada*) and Anne-Marie Henshel (*Sex Structure*).

4. For more detailed accounts of women's action, see Christiansen-Ruffman (1979); Tyndale (1981); Maxwell (1981).

5. See Adamson, Briskin and McPhail (1988, 9-12) for a brief summary of the differences between liberal, radical and socialist feminists.

6. Executive Committee in 1974, Social Policy Committee in 1979 and Status of Women Committee in 1985.

7. For example, CRIAW, NAC and virtually all the academic associations.

8. The candidates were instructed:
   "The Women's Caucus and the Status of Women Committee invite you to respond to the following:
   1. Please comment on your use of a feminist perspective and women's studies materials in your teaching and research.
   2. What have you done to ensure the growth of women's studies in your department, faculty, and university?
   3. Describe your activities relating to the status of women inside or outside the university.
   4. What do you think are the critical issues for the status of women in the CSAA?"

9. The questions were challenged but not struck down by the Annual General Meeting and continue to be sent to candidates.

Chapter 18, Prindiville

1. This paper was conceived as a joint effort with Cathryn Boak of the Division of Education Technology, Memorial University of Newfoundland, the producer of the distance women's studies course discussed here. Although other commitments prevented her collaboration, the discussions we have had about feminism, women's studies, and community activism are reflected in this paper.

2. Unless otherwise identified, all students' comments are drawn from audiotapes of the teleconferences. The names of their communities follow the comments in parentheses.

3. Since, to date, only one man has enrolled in this course, I will discuss the experience only from the perspective of female students and instructors.

4. See, for example, Bunch and Pollack (1983), Culley and Portugues (1985), Devor (1988), Klein (1987), and Mahoney (1988).

5. Assessing the literature on women's studies teaching and learning, Klein notes that most accounts are from the perspective of instructors, while " ... the students' views of their experiences have yet to be made public (1987, 188)." While this paper suffers from the same flaw, I have attempted to include students' voices, mainly in the form of comments made during teleconference discussion.

6. Course evaluation, 1987.

7. Course evaluation, 1987.

8. An analysis of teleconference interactions in courses from subject areas as diverse as English, Business Administration, Physiotherapy, and Women's Studies, found that the levels of student-initiated and student-to-student interactions were particularly high in the Women's Studies course (Boak, 1988).

9. Course evaluation, 1987.

10. Letter, 1987.

11. Course evaluation, 1987.

Chapter 19, Wine

1. See Aiken, Anderson, Dinnerstein, Bowles & Duelli-Klein (1983), Raymond (1985), Lensink & MacCorquodale (1988), and Dubois, Kelly, Kennedy, Korssmeyer & Robinson (1985) for discussion of both sides of this debate

2. Gynagogy is a term coined by Culley & Portugues (1985), which substitutes the Greek "gyn," woman, for "ped," child; thus, pedagogy becomes gynagogy.

References

Acadia University Committee on the Status of Women. 1978. *Report*. Wolfville, N.S.

Adam, June. 1971. *A Profile of Women in Canadian Universities*. Ottawa: Association of Universities and Colleges of Canada.

Adamson, Nancy, & Molgat, Anne. 1988. The mystique of feminist process: A report from the NAC AGM. *Cayenne: A Socialist Feminist Bulletin*.

Adamson, Nancy & Prentice, Susan. 1985. Toward a broader strategy for choice. *Cayenne: A Socialist Feminist Bulletin*. (3 May-June).

Adamson, Nancy, Briskin, Linda & McPhail, Margaret. 1988. *Feminist Organizing for Change: The Contemporary Women's Movement in Canada*. Toronto, Ont.: Oxford.

Aiken, Susan Hardy, Anderson, Karen, Dinnerstein, Myra, Lensink, Judy Nolte, & MacCorquodale, Patricia. 1983. *Changing Our Minds: Feminist Transformations of Knowledge*. Albany, N.Y.: State University of New York Press.

Allen, Pamela. 1970. Free space: A perspective on the small group in women's liberation. *Notes from the Third Year: Women's Liberation*. New York: n.p. pp. 93-98.

Ambert, Anne-Marie & Hitchman, G. Symons. 1976. "A case study of status differential: Women in academia." In A.-M. Ambert, ed., *Sex Structure* 2nd rev. ed. Don Mills, Ont.: Longman.

Ambert, Anne-Marie. 1976. Personal addendum to the Report on the Status of Women's Studies at the Graduate Level, *The Canadian Sociology and Anthropology Association Bulletin*, 39: pp. 3-4.

Ambert, Anne-Marie. 1977. Academic women: On the fringe? *Society/Société*. 1 (1): pp. 6-8, 11-13.

Andersen, Margret. 1975. Economics and sex Roles in academe, *CAUT/ACPU Bulletin*, 24: pp. 6-8.

Anderson, Doris. 1988, July 30. [Column] *The Toronto Star*.

Andrew, Carolyn. 1987. Women and the welfare state. *Canadian Journal of Political Science*, 14: p. 4.

Anger, D. et al. 1986. *Women and Work in Newfoundland*. Background Report to the Royal Commission on Employment and Unemployment. Government of Newfoundland and Labrador, St. John's, Nfld.

Antonyshyn, Patricia, Lee, B. & Merrill, Alex. 1988. Marching for women's lives: The campaign for free-standing abortion clinics in Ontario. In Frank Cunningham, et al., eds., *Social Movements, Social Change*. Toronto, Ont.: Between the Lines.

Antrobus, Peggy. 1982. Equality, development and peace: A second look at the goals of the U.N. Decade for Women. Barbados: The Women and Development Unit, Extramural Department, University of the West Indies.

Appelle, Chris. 1987. *The "New Parliament of Women,"* M.A. Thesis. Ottawa, Ont.: Carleton University, Institute of Canadian Studies.

Armstrong, Pat & Armstrong, Hugh. 1984. *The Double Ghetto: Canadian Women and Their Segregated Work*. Toronto, Ont.: McClelland and Stewart.

Aronowitz, Stanley. 1984. When the New Left was new. *The 60s Without Apology, Social Text*, 3, (3) & 4, (1)

As, Berit. 1978. A five-dimensional model for change: contradictions and feminist consciousness. *Women's Studies International Quarterly*, 4, (1): pp. 101-114.

Association of Universities and Colleges of Canada. 1975. *Status of Women in Canadian Universities*. Ottawa, Ont.: AUCC.

Association of Universities and Colleges of Canada. 1977. *Second Report of the Committee on the Status of Women in the Universities on the Progress Made by AUCC Member Institutions Regarding the Status of Women*. Ottawa: AUCC.

B.C. Women's Self-Help Network. 1984. *Working Collectively*. London: Ptarmigan Press.

Backhouse, Constance B. 1988. If I can't dance..., *Broadside*, 9, (9, July): p. 4.

Baker, M. 1988. Teacher or scholar?? The part-time academic, *Society/Société*, 9 (1): pp. 3-7.

Ballou, Mary & Gabalac, Nancy. 1985. *A Feminist Position on Mental Health*. Springfield, Ill: Charles C. Thomas.

Bank Book Collective. 1979. *An Account to Settle*. Vancouver, B.C.: Press Gang.

Bannerji, Himani. 1987. Introducing racism: Notes towards an anti-racist feminism. *Immigrant Women*. Special issue of *Resources for Feminist Research*, 16 (1): pp. 5-9.

Baron, Robert & Byrne, David. 1987. *Social Psychology: Understanding Human Interaction*. Boston, Mass.: Allyn and Bacon, Inc.

Bedard, Sylvie, Brabant, Carole & Mergler, Donna. 1987. Thermal discomfort and seasonal/ambiant temperature in an industrial laundry. Presentation to the American Industrial Hygiene Association, Montreal, May, 1987.

Bertin, Oliver. 1989. Family tradition dies as revolution alters life down on the farm. *Globe and Mail*. (January 23).

Bégin, Monique. 1988. Silences and debates in Canada, in *Daedalus*. (Fall).

Bill C-127 Working Group. 1983. Lobby logistics: Bill C-127. *Broadside*, 4 (3): 4.

Boak, Cathryn. 1988. Delineation of instructional approaches in teleconference classes. Paper presented at the 14th Conference of the Canadian Society for Studies in Education, Windsor, Ont.

Boivin, Michelle. 1987. Farm women: Obtaining legal and economic recognition of their work. In *Growing Strong, Women in Agriculture*. Ottawa, Ont.: Canadian Advisory on the Status of Women.

Bongers, Agnes. 1986. Slaying dragons and 'sass and grit'. *Ontario Farmer*, Western Edition. (April 9).

Bouchard, Pierre & Turcotte Geneviéve. 1986 La maternité en milieu du travail, ou pourquoi les québécoises sont-elles si nombreuses à demander un retrait préventif? *Sociologie et sociétés* 18 (2): pp. 113-128.

Bouvier, Isabelle. 1986. Women's groups and their relations with the state. *Communiqu'elles*, 12 (1).

Bowles, Gloria & Klein, Renate Duelli. 1983. Introduction: Theories of women's studies and the autonomy/integration debate. In Gloria Bowles & Renate Duelli Klein, eds., *Theories of Women's Studies*. London: Routledge & Kegan Paul.

Boyd, Monica. 1979. *Rank and Salary Differentials in the 1970s: A Comparison of Male and Female Full-Time Teachers in Canadian Universities and Colleges*. Rev. Ed. Ottawa, Ont.: Association of Universities and Colleges of Canada.

Brabant, Carole, Bédard, Sylvie, Mergler, Donna. 1989. Cardiac strain among women workers in an industrial laundry. *Ergonomics*, 32: pp. 615-628.

Brabant, Carole, Ferraris, Jocelyne, Latour, Alain & Mergler, Donna 1988. Application de différentes techniques de modélisation à l'étude de l'évolution de la fréquence cardiaque. *Comptes-rendus du Colloque "Méthodes et domaines d'application de la statistique"* 56e Congrès de l'ACFAS, Moncton. Montréal, Qué.: Université du Québec à Montréal.

Brehaut, Beth. 1988. Is NAC in Crisis? An urgent need for change, *Womanist*, 1, (1, September).

Brehaut, Lyle. (1989). *Believe Her: A Report on Sexual Assault and Sexual Abuse of Women and Children.* Charlottetown, P.E.I.: Advisory Council on the Status of Women.

Briarpatch Magazine. 1988. Down the Cutbacks Road: Special Issue. *Briarpatch,* 16 (4): 2-17.

Brodie, Jean & Vickers, Jill. 1982. *Canadian Women in Politics: An Overview.* Ottawa, Ont.: Canadian Research Institute for the Advancement of Women.

Brodribb, Somer. 1988. *Women's Studies in Canada,* Special Supplement of *Resources for Feminist Research.*

Brooks, Eunice. 1987. Culture shock at DAWN. *Kinesis.* (April): p. 4.

Brown, Rupert. 1988. *Group Processes: Dynamics Within and Between Groups.* New York: Basil Blackwell.

Brownmiller, Susan. 1975. *Against Our Will: Men, Women and Rape.* New York: Simon and Schuster.

Bunch, Charlotte. 1981. The reform tool kit, in Quest staff, ed., *Building Feminist Theory: Essays from Quest.* New York: Longman.

Bunch, Charlotte. 1983. Not by degrees: Feminist theory and education. In Charlotte Bunch & Sandra Pollack, eds., *Learning Our Way: Essays in Feminist Education.* Trumansberg, N.Y.: The Crossing Press.

Bunch, Charlotte. 1985. U. N. World Conference in Nairobi. *Ms.* (June): pp. 79-82

Bunch, Charlotte. 1987. *Passionate Politics.* New York: St. Martin's Press.

Bunch, Charlotte & Pollack, Sandra, eds. 1983. *Learning Our Way: Essays in Feminist Education.* Trumansberg, N.Y.: The Crossing Press.

Cameron, Nancy. 1988. NAC AGM: Growing up and outward. *Kinesis.* (June): p. 3.

Canadian Association of Women Deans and Advisors. 1974. *Report on a Survey Taken in 1973 of Women Deans, Counsellors and Advisors in Canadian Univesities and Colleges.* n.p.

Canadian Federation of University Women. 1976. *The Potential Participation of Women in University Affairs.* [s.l.].

Canitz, Kay. 1988. Commentary, Unpublished document.

Carty, Linda and Brand, Dionne. 1988. Visible Minority Women—A Creation of the Canadian State. *Resources for Feminist Research,* 17, (3, September): pp. 39-42.

Cebotarev, Nora & Beattie, Kathleen. 1985. Women strengthening the farm community: The case of the "Concerned Farm Women" group in Ontario. In A. Fuller, ed., *Farming and the Rural Community in Ontario: An Introduction.* Toronto, Ont.: Foundation for Rural Living.

Charmaz, Kathy. 1986. *Living with invisible disabilities.* Paper presented to the American Sociological Association Annual Meeting, New York.

Christiansen-Ruffman, Linda. 1979. Positions for women in Canadian sociology and anthropology, *Society/Société,* 3 (3): pp. 9-12.

Christiansen-Ruffman, Linda. 1981. Social policy report, *Society/Société,* 5 (1): pp. 10-11.

Christiansen-Ruffman, Linda et al. 1986. *Sex Bias in Research: Current Awareness and Strategies to Eliminate Bias Within Canadian Social Science.* Report of the Task Force on the Elimination of Sexist Bias in Research to the Social Science Federation of Canada (SSFC), Ottawa.

Christiansen-Ruffman, Linda. 1989. Inherited biases within feminism: The patricentric syndrome and the either/or syndrome in sociology. In Angela Miles & Geraldine Finn, eds. *Feminism: From Pressure to Politics.* Montréal, Qué.: Black Rose Press. pp. 123-145.

Claerhout, S., Elder, J., & Janes, C. 1982. Problem-solving skills of rural women. *American Journal of Community Psychology,* 10: pp. 605-612.

Cohen, Marjorie. 1984. The decline of women in Canadian dairying. *Social History*, 17 (34, November): pp. 307-34.

Cole, Susan. 1987. Incest: Conflicting Interests. *Broadside*, 8 (4): pp. 8-9.

Collier, K. 1984. *Social Work With Rural Peoples: Theory and Practice*. Vancouver, B.C.: New Star Books.

Collins, Anne. 1985. *The Big Evasion*. Toronto, Ont.: Lester & Orpen Dennys.

Comité conjoint UQAM-CSN-FTQ. 1977. *Le protocole d'entente UQAM-CSN-FTQ: sur la formation syndicale*. Montréal, Qué.: Université du Québec à Montréal.

Comité conjoint UQAM-CSN-FTQ, 1988. *Le protocole UQAM-CSN-FTQ: 1976-1986. Bilan et perspectives*. Montréal, Qué.: Université du Québec à Montréal.

Confédération des syndicats nationaux (CSN). 1982, *Les femmes à la CSN n'ont pas les moyens de reculer*. 4th annual report of the Comité de la condition féminine de la CSN. Montréal, Qué.: Confédération des syndicats nationaux.

Confédération des syndicats nationaux (CSN). 1984, *Dix ans de luttes: les femmes à la CSN continuent d'avancer*. 5th annual report of the Comité de la condition féminine de la CSN. Montréal, Qué.: Confédération des syndicats nationaux.

Consulting Committee on the Status of Women with Disabilities (CCSWD). 1986. *Equal Access and Equal Opportunities for Women with Disabilities*, Winnipeg, Man.: [author].

Conway, Eleanor, E. 1983. *Study of Women's Organizations and Issues on Prince Edward Island*. Report prepared for Women's Programme, Department of the Secretary of State. Charlottetown, P.E.I.: Department of the Secretary of State.

Corey, Gerald. & Corey, Marianne. S. 1982. *Groups: Process and Practice*. Monterey, California: Brooks/Cole.

Costigan, Annette. 1988. Is NAC in crisis: The straw that broke this feminist's back, or a plea for consciousness-raising groups. *Womanist*, 1 (1, September).

Côté, Marie-Hélène. 1988. *Bilan des activités 1987-88 et perspectives pour la prochaine année*. Montréal, Qué.: Université du Québec à Montréal.

Culley, Margo & Portugues, Catherine. 1985. *Gendered Subjects: The Dynamics of Feminist Teaching*. London and Boston, Mass.: Routledge and Kegan Paul.

Cunningham, Frank, Findlay, Sue, Kadar, Marlene, Lennon, Alan & Lennon, Sylvia, eds. 1988. *Social Movement and Social Change: The Politics and Practice of Organizing*. Toronto, Ont.: Between the Lines.

D'Onofrio-Flores, P. & Pfafflin, S.M. eds. 1982. *Scientific-Technological Change and the Role of Women in Development*. Westview Press (for UNITAR).

Danber, R. & Cain, M. L., eds. *Women and Technological Change in Developing Countries*.

Das Gupta, Tania. 1986. *Learning from Our History. Community Development by Immigrant Women in Ontario. 1958-1986. A tool for action*. Toronto, Ont.: Cross-Cultural Communication Centre.

Davies, Megan. 1988. Culture is politics is unity: LOOT and the growth of lesbian feminist consciousness. *Rites*, 4 (9, March): pp. 12-18.

DAWN Toronto. 1986. *DAWN Toronto Brochure*.

De Grosbois, Sylvie, & Mergler, Donna, 1985, L'exposition aux solvants organiques en milieu de travail et la santé mentale. *Santé mentale au Québec*, 10 (2): pp. 99-113.

Devereaux, M.S. & Rechnitzer, E. 1980. *Higher Education-hired? Sex Differences in Employment Characteristics of 1976 Postsecondary Graduates*. Ottawa, Ont.: Statistics Canada and the Women's Bureau.

Devor, Holly. 1988. Teaching women's studies to male inmates. *Women's Studies International Forum*, 11 (3): pp. 235-244.

Dixon, Marlene. 1975. The sisterhood rip-off: the destruction of the left in the professional women's caucuses. *Women in Canadian Sociology and Anthropology Newsletter*, 2 (2): pp. 3-7.

Doucette, Joanne. 1986a. Open letter from DAWN Toronto to the women's movement. Toronto.

Doucette, Joanne. 1986b. Disability, women and unemployment. Defining the scrap heap. Unpublished manuscript.

Dubois, Ellen Carol, Kelly, Gail Paradise, Kennedy, Elizabeth Lapovsky, Korssmeyer, Carolyn W., & Robinson, Lillian S. 1985. *Feminist Scholarship: A Kindling in the Groves of Academe.* Urbana and Chicago, Ill.: University of Illinois Press.

Dworkin, Andrea 1979. *Pornography.* New York, N.Y.: Perigee Books.

Edelson, Miriam. 1987. *Challenging Unions: Feminist Process and Democracy in the Labour Movement.* CRIAW Feminist Perspectives No. 8. Ottawa, Ont.: Canadian Research Institute for the Advancement of Women.

Edwards, John and Batley, Richard. 1978. *The Politics of Positive Discrimination: An Evaluation of the Urban Programme. 1967-77.* London: Tavistock Publications.

Egan, Carolyn. 1987. Toronto's International Women's Day Committee: Socialist feminist politics. In Heather Jon Maroney & Meg Luxton, eds., *Feminism and Political Economy: Women's Work, Women's Struggles.* Toronto, Ont.: Methuen.

Egan, Carolyn, Gardner, Linda Lee & Persad, Judy Vashti. 1988. The politics of transformation: Struggles with race, class and sexuality in the March 8 coalition. In Frank Cunningham, Sue Findlay, Marlene Kadar, Alan & Sylvia Lennon, eds., *Social Movements Social Change: The Politics and Practice of Organizing.* Toronto, Ont.: Between the Lines.

Eichler, Margrit. 1975. Sociological research on women in Canada. *Canadian Review of Sociology and Anthropology,* 12 (4): pp. 474-481.

Eichler, Margrit. 1985. And the work never ends: Feminist contributions. *Canadian Review of Sociology and Anthropology,* 22 (5): pp. 619-644.

Eichler, Margrit & Lapointe, Jean. 1985. *On the Treatment of the Sexes in Research.* Ottawa, Ont.: Social Science and Humanities Research Council of Canada.

Eichler, Margrit. 1983. *Sexism in Research and Its Policy Implications.* Ottawa, Ont.: Canadian Research Institute for the Advancement of Women.

Eichler, Margrit. 1990. *Not always an easy alliance: The relationship between women's studies and the women's movement in Canada.* Report #4 of the Canadian Women's Studies Project, OISE, Toronto. To appear in Constance Backhouse and David H. Flaherty, eds., *The Contemporary Women's Movement in Canada.*

Eisenstein, Zillah, ed. 1979. *Capitalist Patriarchy and the Case for Socialist Feminism.* New York: Monthly Review Press.

Elliott, Bob. 1986. Letter to the editor. *Transition* (July-August): pp. 5-6.

Ellis, Megan. August 30, 1985. Letter to the Executive of the National Action Committee on the Status of Women.

Evans, J. & Cooperstock, Ruth. 1983. Psycho-social problems of women in primary resource communities. *Canadian Journal of Community Mental Health,* 1: pp. 59-66.

Evans, Linda. 1988. Dancing with DAWN. *Common Ground: The News and Views of PEI Women,* 7 (3-4): pp. 29-30.

Evans, Sara. 1979. *Personal Politics: The Roots of Women's Liberation in the Civil Rights Movement and the New Left.* New York, N.Y.: Vintage Books.

Fairness in Funding. 1987. Report on the Women's Program. House of Commons, Ottawa. The Standing Committee on the Secretary of State.

Farge, Brenda. D. 1987. Hostels for women and "the Microphysics of Power." *Resources for Feminist Research,* 16 (4): pp. 35-37.

Feddema, Rennie. Interview, 1989.

Feminist Workshop at Stony Point, N.Y. April 20-25, 1980. *Developing Strategies for the Future, Feminist Perspectives.* New York, N.Y.: International Women's Tribune Center.

Ferguson, Kathy. 1984. *The Feminist Case Against Bureaucracy*. Philadelphia, Pa.: Temple University Press.

Findlay, Sue. 1988. Feminist struggles with the Canadian state, 1966-88. *Resources for Feminist Research*, 17, (3): pp. 5-9.

Fine, Michelle & Asch, Adrienne. 1981. Sexism without the pedestal. *Journal of Sociology and Social Welfare*, 8 (2): pp. 233-248.

Fink, Deborah. 1986. *Open Country, Iowa: Rural Women, Tradition and Change*. Albany, N.Y.: State University of New York.

Fitzgerald, Maureen. 1981. Whither the feminist unions: SORWVC, AUCE, and the CLC. *Resources for Feminist Research*, 10, (20).

Fitzpatrick, Kathy A. 1987a. Brief to City Council, City of Thompson re: Bylaw to control the display of adult magazines, books and videotapes in retail stores. Thompson Action Committee on the Status of Women.

Fitzpatrick, Kathy A. 1987b. The northern women's resource service; A proposal. Thompson Action Committee on the Status of Women.

Fitzpatrick, Kathy A. 1988. Analysis of health survey. Thompson Action Committee on the Status of Women.

Fitzpatrick, Kathy A., & Hughes, J. 1987. Brief to the task force on affirmative action in Manitoba. Thompson Action Committee on the Status of Women.

Fitzpatrick, Kathy A., Graveline, M. Jean, Hughes, J., & Cromwell, C. 1987. Brief to the Mayor and Council, City of Thompson re: Bylaw 1237, to provide for the granting of municipal assistance to persons in need. Thompson Action Committee on the Status of Women.

Foucault, Michel. 1972. *Power/Knowledge: Selected Interviews and Other Writings*. New York, N.Y.: Pantheon Books.

Franklin, Ursula. 1984. Will women change technology or will technology change women? *Knowledge Reconsidered: A Feminist Overview*. Ottawa, Ont.: Canadian Research Institute for the Advancement of Women.

Freeman, Jo. 1973. The tyranny of structurelessness. In Anne Koedt, et al., *Radical Feminism*. New York, N.Y.: Quadrangle.

Freeman, Jo. 1974. *The Politics of Women's Liberation*. New York.

Gallant, Cecile. 1986. Nous les Femmes...Temoignages des Acadiennes de l'Ile-du-Prince-Edouard. Abram-Village, P.E.I.: L'Association des Acadiennes de la région Evangéline. (Out of print; available on inter-library loan from Robertson Library, University of Prince Edward Island)

Garretson, Lucy. 1975. American women in politics: Culture, structure and ideology. In Dana Raphael, ed., *Being Female*. The Hague: Monton.

Giangrande, Carol. 1985. *Down to Earth, The Crisis in Canadian Farming*. Toronto: Anansi.

Gillett, Margaret. 1978, The majority minority: Women in Canadian universities. *Canadian and International Education*, 7: pp. 42-50.

Gilligan, Carol. 1982. *In a Different Voice: Psychological Theory and Women's Development*. Cambridge, Mass: Harvard University Press.

Gilmore, Rachna. 1988. Celebrating our diversity. *Common Ground: The News and Views of PEI Women*, 7 (3-4): pp. 4-6.

Glassco, M. 1986. Women of colour: The issues of concern and their involvement in the women's movement. Manitoba Action Committee on the Status of Women.

Glover, Susan. 1988. Nellie, we've got washing machines — Working out on the family farm. *This Magazine*, (December).

Graveline, M. Jean. 1985. Support groups for rural women: Decreasing invisibility and isolation. Unpublished Masters Thesis, University of Manitoba.

Graveline, M. Jean 1986. Equality is more than principle.*Action*. (October).

Greaves, Lorraine. 1988. A presidential candidate withdraws. *Womanist*, 1 (1, September): p. 36.

Greaves, Lorraine. 1988b. NAC '88: Split resolve. *Broadside,* 9 (8) (June): p. 3.

Greaves, Lorraine. 1988. Upon reflection. *Womanist,* 1 (1, September): p. 40.

Grose, R.E. 1973. *Prospects for Development.* Charlottetown, P.E.I.: The Atlantic Development Council.

Haley, Ella. 1988. *Against the grain: Farm women and the current economic crisis.* Paper presented in the Canadian Association of Rural Studies session, at the Learned Societies Meeting, Windsor, Ont.

Hall, Edward T. 1976. *Beyond Culture.* New York, N.Y.: Anchor Press/Doubleday.

Harkin, Dianne. 1986a. Farm women—A new dimension. Unpublished paper.

Harkin, Dianne. 1986b. *What Are You Worth?* Winchester: Women for the Survival of Agriculture.

Hartsock, Nancy. 1974. Political change: Two perspectives on power. *Quest,* 1: pp. 3-19.

Hartsock, Nancy. 1985. *Money, Sex and Power.* New York.

Haussman, M. & Halseth, J. 1983. Re-examining women's roles: A feminist approach to decreasing depression in women. *Social Work With Groups,* (Fall/Winter): pp. 105-115.

Hawxhurst, Donna & Morrow, Sue. 1984. *Living Our Visions: Building Feminist Community.* Temple, Ariz.: Fourth World Publisher.

Health and Welfare Canada, Statistics Canada. 1981. *The Health of Canadians: Report of the Canada Health Survey.* Ottawa, Ont: Statistics Canada.

Health and Welfare Canada. 1985. *The Active Health Report—Perspectives on Canada's Health Promotion Survey.* Ottawa, Ont.: Health and Welfare Canada.

Hedley, Max. 1981. Relations of production on the "family farm": Canadian Prairies. *Journal of Peasant Studies,* 9: pp. 71-85.

Henshel, Anne-Marie. 1973, *Sex Structure.* Don Mills, Ontario: Longman Canada.

Henshel, Anne Marie. 1975. Letter. *Women in Canadian Sociology and Anthropology Newsletter,* 2 (1): pp. 1, 8-9.

Henshel, Anne-Marie. 1976a. Report on women's studies in graduate departments of anthropology and sociology. *The Canadian Sociology and Anthropology Association Bulletin,* 39: pp. 4-5.

Hitchman Symons, G. 1974. A report on the reports: The status of women in Canadian universities. *Canadian Sociology and Anthropology Association Bulletin,* 34: pp. 11-13.

Hooks, Bell. 1984. *Feminist Theory: From Margin to Center.* Boston, Mass: South End Press.

Hooks, Bell. 1986. Sisterhood: Political solidarity between women. *Feminist Review,* No. 23 (June).

Howe, Florence, ed. 1975. *Women and the Power to Change.* New York, N.Y.: McGraw-Hill.

Howe, Florence. 1983. Feminist scholarship: The extent of the revolution. In Charlotte Bunch & Sandra Pollack, eds. 1983. *Learning Our Way.* Trumansberg, N.Y.: The Crossing Press.

Hunter, Sally. 1977. Government strategies. *Priorities,* 9 (May).

Inglis, Dorothy. May 19, 1988. On *Morningside,* CBC Radio.

Ireland, Gisele. 1983. *The Farmer Takes a Wife, A Study by Concerned Farm Women.* Chesley, Ontario.

Jacobson, Helga E. 1979. Immigrant women and the community: A perspective for research. *Resources for Feminist Research,* 8, (3 November): pp. 17-21.

Jaggar, Alison. 1983. *Feminist Politics and Human Nature.* Totowa, N.J.: Rowman and Allanheld.

Janeway, Elizabeth. 1981. Powers of the Weak. New York, N.Y.: Morrow Quill.

Jewett, Pauline, H., McCrae, M. Gobeil & M. Smith. 1970. Brief No. 443, presented to the Royal Commission on the Status of Women in Canada. Cited in

Florence Bird, Chair, *Report of the Royal Commission on the Status of Women in Canada.* Ottawa, Ont.: Supply and Services Canada.

Joel, Jan. 1988. Social solidarity: People shaping a new agenda. *Network of Saskatchewan Women,* 5 (2): pp. 14-15. Regina, Sask.: Saskatchewan Action Committee, Status of Women.

Joel, Jan, et.al. 1988. Making connections...Setting the agenda...Are you listening? *Network,* 5 (1): pp. 6-11. Regina, Sask.: Saskatchewan Action Committee.

Jones, Miriam & Stephens, Jennifer. 1988. Tempest in a Teapot: NAC Annual General Meeting. *Rebel Girls Rag,* II/4 (July, August).

Kirby, Sandra L. & McKenna, Kate. 1989. *Experience, Research, Social Change: Methods from the Margins.* Toronto, Ont: Garamond Press.

Klein, Renate Duelli. 1987. The dynamics of the women's studies classroom: A review essay of the teaching practice of women's studies in higher education. *Women's Studies International Forum,* 10 (2): pp. 187-206.

Kome, Penny. 1983a. *The Taking of Twenty-Eight: Women Challenge the Constitution.* Toronto, Ont.: Women's Press.

Kome, Penny. 1983b. Women and disabilities. *Homemaker's Magazine,* (September): pp. 78-85.

Kome, Penny. 1985. *Women of Influence: Canadian Women and Politics.* Toronto.

Koolish, Lynda. 1986. *We are the canaries: Women, disability and coalition building.* Paper presented to the National Women's Studies Association Conference, University of Illinois at Urbana-Champaign.

Kopinak, K. & Tannenbaum, D. 1975. Letter. *Women in Canadian Sociology Newsletter,* 2 (1).

Kreps, Bonnie. 1972. Radical Feminism. In *Women Unite.* Toronto, Ont.: Women's Press.

Lacelle, Nicole. April, 1988. *The NAC Consultation in Quebec.* Toronto, Ont.: National Action Committee on the Status of Women.

Lahey, Kathleen A. 1989. Celebration and struggle: Feminism and law. In Angela Miles & Geraldine Finn, eds., *Feminism from Pressure to Politics.* Montreal, Que.: Black Rose Books.

Larsson, Maria Bergon. 1979. *Women in Technology in Industrialized Countries* Science and Technology Working Papers Series; UNITAR.

Leah, Ronnie and Ruecker, Cydney. 1988. Connections Conference Supplementary Report. Unpublished report. Saskatchewan Action Committee.

Leah, Ronnie and Ruecker, Cydney. 1988. The Founding of a Provincial Women's Coalition: Connections Conference Report. Unpublished report. Saskatchewan Action Committee.

Leah, Ronnie. 1989. Session Coordinator. *Coalition Building: Organizing the Popular Sectors* Society for Socialist Studies, 1989 Learned Societies Conference, Quebec City, June, 1989.

Lee, J. 1987. Women as non-family farm workers. In *Growing Strong.* Ottawa, Ont.: Canadian Advisory Council on the Status of Women.

Lefflet, A. D.L. & Gillespie, E. Lerner Ratner. 1973. Academic feminists and the women's movement. *The Insurgent Sociologist,* 5 (1): pp. 44-55.

Lesbians Against the Right. 1982. *Lesbians are Everywhere Fighting the Right.* Pamphlet produced by LAR.

Lester, T. 1984. Rural conference unifies women. *HERizons,* 1: p. 16.

Lewin, Kurt, Lippitt, Roger & White, Robert. 1939. Patterns of aggressive behaviour in experimentally created social climates. *Journal of Social Psychology,* 10: 271-279.

Leyton, E. 1984. Universities' positions on the employment of Canadian women. *Society/Société,* 8 (2): p. 7-8.

Lincoln, Yvonna S. & Guba, Egon G. 1985. *Naturalistic Inquiry.* Beverly Hills, Calif.: Sage Publications, Inc.

Lippman, Abby. 1986. Prenatal diagnosis: A chance for action-research. *Resources for Feminist Research/Documentation sur la Recherche Féministe*, 15 (3): pp. 65-66.

Lipsig-Mumme, Carla. 1987. Organizing women in the clothing trades: Homework and the 1983 garment strike in Canada. *Studies in Political Economy*, No. 22. (Spring).

Loney, Martin. 1977. A Political Economy of Citizen Participation. In Leo Panitch, ed., *The Canadian State: Political Economy and Political Power*. Toronto, Ont.: University of Toronto Press.

Lorde, Audre. 1984. *Sister Outsider*. Trumansberg, N.Y.: The Crossing Press.

Luxton, Meg. 1980. More Than a Labour of Love. Toronto, Ont.: Women's Press.

Mackie, Marlene. 1986. Women in the profession: Collegiality and productivity. *Society/Société*, 10 (3).

MacLeod, Linda. 1980. *Wife Battering in Canada: The Vicious Circle*. Ottawa, Ont.: The Canadian Advisory Council on the Status of Women, Ottawa.

MacLeod, Linda. 1987. *Battered but not Beaten: Preventing Wife Battering in Canada*. Ottawa, Ont.: The Canadian Advisory Council on the Status of Women.

Maguire, Patricia. 1987. *Doing Participatory Research: A Feminist Approach*. Amherst, Mass.: University of Massachusetts Press.

Mahoney, Pat. 1988. Oppressive pedagogy: The importance of process in women's studies. *Women's Studies International Forum*, 11 (2): pp. 103-108.

Maier, N.R.F. 1958. Three types of appraisal interviews. *Personnel*, (March-April): pp. 27-40.

Manitoba Advisory Council on the Status of Women. 1984. Some concerns of rural women.

Maroney, Heather Jon & Luxton, Meg, eds.. 1987. *Feminism and Political Economy*. Toronto, Ont.: Methuen.

Martin, Diane. 1984. Women as victims. *Status of Women News*, August, 2.

Maxwell, M. Percival. 1981. Report on survey of progress toward the elimination of sexist language in printed materials of departments of sociology and anthropology. *Society/Société*, 5 (3): pp. 9-11

McAdam, Doug. 1982. *Political Process and the Development of Black Insurgency, 1930-1970*. Chicago, Ill.: University of Chicago Press.

McDonnell, Kathleen. 1984. *Not an Easy Choice: A Feminist Re-examines Abortion*. Toronto, Ont.: The Women's Press.

Meanwell, Catherine and Glover, Susan. 1985. *To Have and To Hold, A Guide to Property and Credit Law for Farm Families in Ontario*. Chesley, Ont.: Concerned Farm Women.

Mergler, Donna. 1984. Les effets des conditions de travail sur la santé des travailleuses: rapport-synthèse. In *Les effets des conditions de travail sur la santé des travailleuses*: pp. 215-228. Montreal, Que.: Confédération des syndicats nationaux.

Mergler, Donna. 1987. Worker Participation in Occupational Health Research: Theory and Practice. *Int. Journal of. Health Services*, 17: pp. 151-167.

Mergler, Donna, Brabant, Carole, Vezina, Nicole, and Messing, Karen. 1987. The weaker sex? Men in women's jobs report similar health symptoms. *Journal of Occupational. Medicine.*, 29: pp. 417-421.

Mergler, Donna & Vézina, Nicole. 1985. Dysmennorrhea and cold exposure. *Journal of Reproductive Medicine*, 30: pp. 106-111.

Merton, Robert. 1957. *Social Theory and Social Structure*. Glenco: The Free Press.

Messing, Karen. 1982a. Do men and women have different jobs because of their biologicaldifferences??*Int. Journal of Health Services*, 12: pp. 43-52.

Messing, Karen. 1982b. Est-ce que les travailleuses enceintes sont protégées au Québec?? Union médicale, 111: pp. 1-6.

Messing, Karen. 1983. The scientific mystique: Can a white lab coat guarantee objectivity in the pursuit of knowledge about the nature of women? In Ruth

Hubbard and Marian E. Lowe, eds., *Women's Nature: Rationalizations of Inequality*. New York, N.Y.: Pergamon Press: pp. 75-88.

Messing, Karen. 1987. Union-initiated research on genetic effects of workplace agents. *Alternatives: Perspectives on technology, environment and society*, 15 (1): pp. 15-18.

Messing, Karen, & Reveret, Jean-Pierre. 1983. Are women in female jobs for their health? Working conditions and health symptoms in the fish processing industry in Quebec. *Int. Journal of Health Services*, 13: pp. 635-647.

Messing, Karen, De Koninck, Maria and Lee, Lesley. 1986a. Femmes et/Women and Sciences. Issue of *Resources for Feminist Research/Documentation sur la Recherche Féministe*, 15.

Messing, Karen, Seifert, Ana Maria, Bradley, W.E.C. 1986b. *In vivo* mutant frequency among technicians professionally exposed to ionizing radiation. In M. Sorssa and H. Norppa (Eds.): *Monitoring of Occupational Genotoxicants*. New York, N.Y.: Alan R. Liss.

Messing, Karen, Seifert, Ana Maria, Bradley, W. E. C., Ferraris, Jocelyne, Swarz, Joel. 1989. Mutant frequency among radiotherapy technicians appears to be related to recent dose of ionizing radiation. *Health Physics*, 57: pp. 539-544.

Michell, Gillian & Greaves Lorraine & the London Feminist Process Group. 1988. The future of NAC: Some questions of feminist process. *Kinesis* (April): p. 15.

Michels, Robert. 1915. *Political Parties: A Sociological Study of the Oligarctic Tendencies of Modern Democracy*. (Collier Edition, 1962).

Middleton, Dorothy. 1980. Interview. Women for the Survival of Agriculture.

Miles, Angela. 1982. Ideological hegemony in political discourse: Women's specificity and equality. In Angela Miles & Geraldine Finn, eds. *Feminism: From Pressure to Politics*. Montreal, Que.: Black Rose Books.

Miles, Angela. 1984. Integrative feminism. *Fireweed: A Feminist Quarterly*, 19, (Summer/Fall).

Miles, Angela. 1985a. Feminism, equality and the law. *Canadian Journal of Women and the Law*, 1, (1): pp. 42-68.

Miles, Angela. 1985b. *Feminist Radicalism in the 1980s*. Culture Texts. Montreal, Que.: New World Perspectives.

Miles, Angela. 1989. Ideological hegemony in political discourse: Women's specificity and equality. In Angela Miles and Geraldine Finn, eds., *Feminism: From Pressure to Politics*. Montreal, Que.: Black Rose Books.

Miller, Jean Baker. 1982. Women and power. Stone Center for Developmental Services and Studies, Wellesley, Massachusetts.

Ministy of Colleges and Universities. 1975. *Women and Ontario Universities: A Report to the Ministry of Colleges and Universities*. MCU, Toronto.

Mitchell, D. 1984. Banking on the family farm. *Briarpatch*, 13 (10).

Mitchell, Juliet. 1971. *Woman's Estate*. New York, N.Y.: Pantheon.

Moffat, Linda K. 1980. *Room at the Bottom: Job Mobility Opportunities for Ontario Academics in the Mid-seventies*. , Toronto, Ont.: Ministry of Colleges and Universities.

Morgan, Robin. 1980. Theory and practice: Pornography and rape. In Laura Lederer, ed. *Take Back the Night*. New York, N.Y.: Bantam Books.

Morris, Cerise. 1980. Determination of thoroughness: The movement for a Royal Commission on the Status of Women in Canada. *Atlantis*, 5 (2).

Morrow, Dianne. 1988. Power for women. *Common Ground: The News and Views of PEI Women*, 7, (3-4): pp. 8-10.

Murray, Marylou. 1988. The NAC Staff, except one, resign at the AGM, *The Womanist*, 1 (1, September).

National Council on Welfare. 1988. *Poverty Profile*. Ottawa, Ont.: Ministry of Supply and Services.

Ng, Roxana and Sprout, Janet. 1978. *Services for Immigrant Women*. Report and Evaluation of a Series of Four Workshops conducted in the Summer, 1977. Women's Research Centre, Vancouver.

Ng, Roxana, Kwan, Liz and Miedema, Baukje. 1989. *State Funding and Immigrant Services — The Experience of an Immigrant Women's Group in the Maritimes*. Paper presented at the 1989 Society for Socialist Studies annual meeting, Quebec City, June 1-4.

Ng, Roxana, Walker, Gillian, Muller, Jacob, eds. 1990. *Community Organization and the Canadian State*. Toronto, Ont.: Garamond.

Ng, Roxana. 1982. Immigrant Housewives in Canada: A Methodological Note, *Atlantis*, 8 (1, Fall): pp. 111-118.

Ng, Roxana. 1988. *The Politics of Community Services. Immigrant Women, Class and State*. Toronto, Ont.: Garamond.

Ng, Roxana. 1989. *Immigrant Women's Organizing in New Brunswick*. Paper presented at the Atlantic Association of Sociologists and Anthropologists (AASA) annual meeting. Cape Breton, March 16-19.

O'Leary, Judith M. 1983. Disabled women and employment. *Rehabilitation Digest*, 14 (5): pp. 7-10.

Page, R. 1986. *Northern Development: The Canadian Dilemma*. Toronto, Ont.: McClelland and Stewart.

Parlby, Irene. 1927. Co-operation in the rural home. *Annual Report of the U.F.W.A.*: pp. 6-9.

Payton, L.C. 1975. *The Status of Women in Ontario Universities: A Report of the Council of Ontario Universities*. Toronto, Ont.: COU.

Pelletier, Jacqueline. 1985. *Report: Women with Disabilities Networking Meeting*. Convergence Consultants, Ottawa.

Penley, Constance. 1986. Feminism and psychoanalysis. In Cary Nelson, ed., *Theory in the Classroom*. Urbana, Ill.:.University of Illinois Press.

Poitras, E. 1986. The philosophy of native women: A regional commentary. *Saskatchewan Indian Federated College*, 2: pp. 11-18.

Pollock, Marion & Meister, Joan. 1986. DAWN BC conference a success. *Kinesis*, (April): pp. 16-17.

Potter, C. & Dustan, L. 1983. Data analysis with respect to a survey of members of the Manitoba Action Committee on the Status of Women and other women in areas outside Brandon and Winnipeg.

Prince Edward Island Advisory Council on the Status of Women. 1988. *Diversity, Vitality and Change: A Three Year Report*. Charlottetown, P.E.I.

Profile of Women in Canadian Universities. 1972. *University Affairs*, 13 (January): pp. 6-7.

Rauhala, Ann. 1988. *Globe and Mail*, May 16.

Raymond, Janice. 1985. Women's studies: A knowledge of one's own. In Gloria Bowles & Renate Duelli-Klein, eds., *Gendered Subjects: The Dynamics of Feminist Teaching*. London, Ont.: Routledge & Kegan Paul.

Raymond, Janice. 1986. *A Passion for Friends*. Boston, Mass.: Beacon Press.

Report of the Royal Commission on the Status of Women. 1970. Queen's Printer, Ottawa, Canada.

Rich, Adrienne. 1975. Toward a woman-centered university. In Howe, Florence, ed., *Women and the Power to Change*. New York, N.Y.: McGraw-Hill.

Rich, Adrienne. 1979. Women and honor: Some notes on lying, in *Lies, Secrets, and Silence*. New York, N.Y.: Norton.

Richardson, Joan. 1983. *The Structure of Organizational Instability: The Women's Movement in Montreal, 1974-1977*. Ph.D. Dissertation. New York, New School for Social Research. (Copyright 1984 University Microfilms International, Ann Arbor, Michigan).

Ricks, Francie, Matheson, George and Pyke, Sandra. 1972. Women's liberation: A case study of organizations for social change. *Canadian Psychologist*, 13 (1).

Ridington, Jill. 1982. Providing services the feminist way. In Maureen Fitzgerald, Connie Guberman & Margie Wolfe, eds., *Still Ain't Satisfied: Canadian Feminism Today*. Toronto, Ont.: Women's Press.

Riger, Stephanie. 1984. Vehicles for empowerment: The case of feminist movement organizations. In J. Rappaport, C. Swift & R. Hess, eds., *Studies in Empowerment*. New York, N.Y.: Hawthorne Press.

Riggs Joan & Tyler, Lynne. 1988. *NAC Organizational Review: The Next Steps*. Ottawa, Ont.: Catalyst Research.

Riggs, Joan & Lynne Tyler. 1988. What is feminist process? *Womanist*, 1 (1, September): pp. 42-3.

Ristock, Janice. 1987. Working together for empowerment. *Canadian Women's Studies*, 8 (4): pp. 74-76.

Robson, Reginald & Lapointe, Mireille. 1970. *A Comparison of Men's and Women's Salaries and Employment Fringe Benefits in the Academic profession*. Report to the Royal Commission on the Status of Women in Canada. Information Canada, Ottawa.

Rogers, Barbara. 1980. *The Domestication of Women: Discrimination in Developing Societies*, Tavistock.

Rooney, Frances. 1985a. Editorial. *Resources for Feminist Research*, 14 (1, March).

Rooney, Frances. 1985b. The issue is ability. *Resources for Feminist Research*, 14 (1, March): pp. 64-68.

Rooney, Frances & Israel, Pat, eds. 1985. Women and Disability (special issue). *Resources for Feminist Research*, 14 (1, March).

Rosenberg, Marshall. 1983. *A Model for Non-Violent Communication*. Philadelphia, Pa.: New Society Publishers.

Rothschild-Witt, Joyce. 1979. The collectivist organization: An alternative to rational-bureaucratic models. *The American Sociological Review*, 44 (August).

Rowbotham, Sheila, Segal, Lynne & Wainwright, Hilary. 1979. *Beyond the Fragments: Feminism and the Making of Socialism*. London: Islington Community Press.

Sachs, Carolyn. 1983. *The Invisible Farmers, Women in Agricultural Production*. Totowa, N.J.: Rowman and Allanheld.

Sagon, Jean & Ted. 1987. Staying on the Land, In T. Pugh, ed., *Fighting the Farm Crisis*. Saskatoon, Sask.: Fifth House.

Saidek, Pat. 1986. *CRIAW Celebrates 10 Years of Growth as a Feminist Research Institute*. Ottawa, Ont.: Canadian Research Institute for the Advancement of Women.

Saskatchewan Coalition for Social Justice. Newsletter, January/February 1988. *Briarpatch*, 17 (1): pp. 15-18.

Schechter, Susan. 1982. *Women and Male Violence: The Visions and Struggles of the Battered Women's Movement*. Boston, Mass.: South End Press.

Schniedewind, Nancy. 1983. Feminist values: guidelines for a teaching methodology in women's studies. In Charlotte Bunch and Sandra Pollack, eds., *Learning Our Way*. Trumansberg, N.Y.: The Crossing Press.

Schniedewind, Nancy. 1985. Cooperatively structured learning: Implications for feminist pedagogy. *Journal of Thought: An Interdisciplinary Quarterly*. Special issue on feminist education, 2 (3): pp. 74-87.

Schreader, Alicia. 1990. The state-funded women's movement: A case of two political agendas. In Roxana Ng, Gillian Walker & Jacob Muller, eds., *Community Organization and the Canadian State*. Toronto, Ont.: Garamond Press.

Secretary of State. 1984/85. The Women's Program, Minister of Supply and Services, Cat. No. S78-3.

Segal, Lynn. 1987. *Is the Future Female? Troubled Thoughts on Contemporary Feminism*. London: Virago.

Sen, Gita & Grown. 1985. *Development, Crisis, and Alternatives: Third World Women's Perspectives*. DAWN, Toronto, Ont.

Sessions, G. 1988. The deep ecology movement: A review. *Environmental Review*, (Summer): pp. 105-125.

Signs. Special Issues on Women in Development, Winter 1977 and Autumn, 1981.

Silman, Janet and the women of Tobique Reserve. 1987. *Enough is Enough: Native Women's Rights*. Toronto, Ont.: Women's Press.

Sim, R. Alex. 1988. *Land and Community: The Crisis in Canada's Countryside*. Guelph, Ont.: University of Guelph.

Slumskie, Beth. 1986. Concerned Farm Women. *The Observer* (Winter).

Smith, D. 1975. An analysis of ideological structures and how women are excluded: considerations for academic women. *Canadian Review of Sociology and Anthropology*, 12, (4): pp. 353-369.

Smith, Dorothy. 1979. Where there is oppression, there is resistance. *Branching Out*, 6 (1).

Smith, Dorothy. 1984. Does government funding co-opt? *Kinesis*. (June).

Smith, Dorothy, Cohen, A., Burt, G., Drakich, Janet, Rayside, David & Staton, Pat. 1986. A future for women at the University of Toronto. OISE Center for Women's Studies in Education Occasional Paper Series #13.

Smith, Marion, Jewett, Pauline, McCrae, J. & Gobeil, M. 1969. *Women in Canadian Universities*. Graduate Students' Union, Toronto.

Smith, Pamela. 1987. What lies within and behind the statistics?, In *Growing Strong*. Ottawa, Ont.: Canadian Advisory Council on the Status of Women.

Snitow, Ann. 1989. Pages from a gender diary: Basic divisions within feminism. *Dissent*, Spring: pp. 205-244.

Social Science Federation of Canada. 1986. Report of Task Force on Elimination of Sexist Bias in Research. Linda Christiansen-Ruffman, chair.

Sousi-Roubi, B. 1983. *Women in Agriculture*, Supplement No. 13 to *Women of Europe* Session of The European Communities, Brussels.

Spender, Dale. 1981. *Men's Studies Modified: The Impact of Feminism on the Academic Disciplines*. Oxford: Pergamon.

Spender, Dale. 1982. Re-inventing the wheel. We've been here before. *The Leveller*, 16: pp. 12-13.

Stasiulis, Daivia A. 1987. Rainbow feminism: Perspectives on minority women in Canada. *Immigrant Women*. Special issue of *Resources for Feminist Research*, 16 (1): pp. 5-9.

Steiger, Brenda and Weir, Lorna. 1981. Lesbian movement: Coming together in a hot gym. *Broadside*, 2 (10, August/September).

Steinem, Gloria. 1986. *Outrageous Acts and Everyday Rebellions*. New York, N.Y.: New American Library.

Stephenson, Marylee, ed. 1973. *Women in Canada*. Don Mills, Ont.: General Publishing.

Stewart-Kirkby, Carol. 1988. Concerned Farm Women amid self-evaluation. *Home and Country*, (April, May).

Stinchcombe, Arthur. 1984. The origins of sociology as a discipline. *Acta Sociologica*, 27 (1): pp. 51-61.

Stone, Sharon D. & Doucette, Joanne. 1988. Organizing the marginalized. *The DisAbled Women's Network, Social Movements and Social Change. Socialist Studies* 4. Toronto, Ont.: Between the Lines.

Stone, Sharon D. & Doucette, Joanne. In press. Diane Driedger & Susan Gray Dueck, eds., *The International Disabled Women's Anthology*.

Strong-Boag, Veronica. 1986. Pulling a double harness or hauling a double load: Women, work and feminism on the Canadian prairie. *Journal of Canadian Studies*, 21 (3, Autumn).

Strong-Boag, Veronica. 1988. *The New Day Recalled: Lives of Girls and Women in English Canada, 1919-1939*. Toronto.

Sturdivant, Susan. 1980. *Therapy with Women: A Feminist Philosophy of Treatment*. New York, N.Y.: Springer Publishing Company.

Surette, Ralph. 1989. In pursuit of alternatives. *Atlantic Insight*, 11: pp. 9-43.

Symons, T.H.B. & Page, J. 1984. The status of women in Canadian academic life. In T.H.B. Symons & J.M. Page, eds., *Some Questions of Balance: Human Resources, Higher Education and Canadian Studies*. Ottawa, Ont.: Association of Universities and Colleges of Canada: pp. 187-214.

Tait, Janice J. 1986. Reproductive technology and rights of disabled persons. *Canadian Journal of Women and the Law*, 1 (2): pp. 446-455.

Thomas, Lewis. 1974. *The Lives of a Cell: Notes of a Biology Watcher*. Toronto, Ont.: Bantam.

Tierney, Daniel, Romito, Patricia, Seifert, Ana Maria & Messing Karen. 1990. She ate not the bread of idleness: Exhaustion is related to domestic and salaried workload among Québec hospital workers. *Women and Health*, 16: pp. 21-42.

Tinker, Irene, Bramsen, Michele Bo, Buvinie, Mayra, eds. 1976. *Women and World Development*. Praeger.

Torjman, Sherri. 1988. *The Reality Gap: Closing the Gap Between Women's Needs and Available Programs and Services*. Ottawa, Ont.: Canadian Advisory Council on the Status of Women.

Toronto Rape Crisis Centre. 1985. Rape. In Connie Guberman & Margie Wolfe, eds., *No Safe Place*. Toronto, Ont.: Women's Press.

The Toronto Rape Crisis Centre (working class caucus). 1988. Around the kitchen table. *Fireweed* (Winter/Spring): pp. 69-81.

Treichler, Paula. 1986. Teaching feminist theory. In Cary Nelson, ed., *Theory in the Classroom*. Urbana, Ill.: University of Illinois Press.

Tyndale, Eleanor. 1981. Women in Canadian Colleges. *Society/Société*, 5 (2): pp. 11-13.

Tyndale, E. 1987. Status of Women Committee and Women's Caucus, *Society/Société*, 1 (3): 29-30.

Université du Québec à Montréal. 1982. Le protocole UQAM-Relais-femmes. UQAM.

University of Toronto Faculty Association. 1982. *Final Report of the Committee on Academic Appointments*. Toronto, Ont.

Van Wagner, Vicki. 1988. Take the state out of gestation. *Broadside*, 9 (6): p. 4.

Vanderslice, Virginia J. 1984. Empowerment: A definition in process. *Human Ecology Forum*, 14, (1): p. 2-3.

Vash, Carolyn. 1982. Employment issues for women with disabilities. *Rehabilitation Literature*, 43 (7-8, July-August): pp. 198-207.

Veillette, Huguette. 1988. Bureau de la repondante à la condition féminine, Government of Quebec, MAPAC, (conversation), November.

Vickers, Jill. *But Can You Type? Canadian Universities and the Status of Women*. Ottawa: Clarke-Irwin and Canadian Association of University Teachers. CAUT monograph series, no. 1.

Vickers, Jill McCalla. 1980. Coming up for air: Feminist views of power reconsidered. *Canadian Women's Studies*, 2 (4): pp. 66-69.

Vickers, Jill McCalla. 1984. *Taking Sex Into Account: The Policy Consequences of Sexist Research*. Ottawa, Ont.: Carleton University Press.

Vickers, Jill McCalla. 1988a. *Getting Things Done: Women's Views of Their Involvement in Political Life*. Ottawa, Ont.: Joint publication of UNESCO, Division of Human Rights and Peace, and the Canadian Research Institute for the Advancement of Women.

Vickers, Jill McCalla. 1988b. *Politics as if women mattered: The institutionalization of the Canadian women's movement and its impact on federal politics, 1965-88.* ANS-CANZ '88, Canberra, June.

Vickers, Jill McCalla. 1989, May. *The intellectual origins of women's movements in Canada.* Institute for American Studies Conference on the Canadian and American Women's Movements, London, Ontario.

Vickers, Jill & Tardy E. et al. 1986. *Women's participation in political life.* CRIAW papers 16/17. Ottawa, Ont.: Canadian Research Institute for the Advancement of Women.

Vogeler, I. 1981. *The Myth of the Family Farm: Agribusiness Dominance of U.S. Agriculture.* Boulder, Colo.: Westview Press.

Warskett, Rosemary. 1988. Bank worker unionization and the law. *Studies in Political Economy,* No. 25 (Spring).

Weiss, Jill. 1985. Disabled women. *Resources for Feminist Research,* 14 (1, March): pp. 4-6.

Wells, Kennedy. 1988. *The Fishery of Prince Edward Island.* Charlottetown, P.E.I.: Ragweed Press.

Willis, Ellen. 1984. Radical feminism and feminist radicalism. *The 60s Without Apology, Social Text,* 3 (3) and (4) (1), (Spring and Summer). New York.

Wilson, Barry. 1988. Federal funds expand farm womens roles. *Western Producer,* (August 11): p. 3.

Woolsey, Lorraine & McBain, Linda. 1987. Issues of power and powerlessness in all-woman groups. *Women's Studies International Forum,* 10 (6): pp. 579-588.

Women for the Survival of Agriculture. 1987. *Cover Your Assets: A Guide to Farm Partnerships.* Winchester: WSA.

Women's Network Project Report. 1981. Charlottetown, P.E.I.: Women's Network Project.

WSA Newsletter, September-October, November-December, 1988.

Zaremba, Eve. 1988a. Collective crisis, Broadside, 9 (10) (August/ September), p. 4.

Zaremba, Eve. 1988b. Collective trouble, Broadside, 10 (1) (October): p.5.

Zimmerman, Michael A. & Rappaport, Julian. 1988. Psychological empowerment. *American Journal of Community Psychology,* 16: pp. 745-750.

Zur-Muehlen, von, Max. 1982. *Past and Present Graduation Trends at Canadian Universities and Implications for the Eighties, with Special Emphasis on Women and on Science Graduates.* Ottawa, Ont.: Statistics Canada.

Contributors

Shirley Bear was born into the Wolostukwiik (Maliseet) Nation at Tobique, New Brunswick, Canada. She was schooled in St. Basile, New Brunswick, at College Maillet, and through several workshops or evening courses in various parts of the United States and Canada. She has been educated through creation, travelling and people involvement. She has served on several women's committees for the advancement of women's rights to health, education, spirituality, economics and basic choices. Her main interest is art and its origins with all the different disciplines. "I enjoy whatever I'm doing, at the time I'm doing it."

Anne Bishop became Program Coordinator for the Community Development and Outreach Unit of Henson College, Dalhousie University during the summer of 1987. Prior to that time, she was a community organizer among low income women in Pictou County, Nova Scotia, and worked as a popular educator for a number of years in the area of women and international development.

Linda Briskin teaches women's studies at York University and has been an activist in the women's movement since 1969. She co-edited *Union Sisters: Women in the Labour Movement*, an anthology of articles by union activists; co-authored *The Day the Fairies Went on Strike*, a non-sexist pro-union children's story, which has been translated into French under the title *Quand les fées font la grève*; co-authored *Feminist Organizing for Change: The Contemporary Women's Movement in Canada*; and co-directed *Rising up Strong*, a one-hour long documentary on the women's movement in Ontario. Many of these projects were motivated by a desire to document the struggle of women to make change.

Linda Christiansen-Ruffman is a feminist scholar and activist in Nova Scotia. She is a professor of sociology at Saint Mary's University and has a Ph.D. from Columbia University. She has been the president of CRIAW (the Canadian Research Institute for the Advancement of Women) both at the local and national levels. Her research has focused on contemporary women's organizations and on women's politics—the ways in which women have defined what is important, and the ways they seek to accomplish these defined tasks. She has used participant observation and action research methodologies and has been actively involved in women's action caucuses and groups in the community and academic spheres.

Joanne Doucette is a co-founder of DAWN (DisAbled Women's Network) Toronto and DAWN Canada. She was born in a small village in Ontario and lives in Toronto. Her roots are in Cape Breton—Acadian, English, French and more, probably. She has a hereditary muscle disorder and stubborn pugnacity, reputedly also an hereditary "Doucette" trait. She fights for access to women's services and the women's movement, for the right to live free from the threat of violence, for enough money for social assistance recipients (like herself) and working poor people to live in dignity. She is a feminist, environmentalist, an artist, a public speaker, a disabled rights activist and definitely a nuisance to some. Power to the pesky!

Janice Drakich is an assistant professor in the Department of Sociology and Anthropology at the University of Windsor. She has been an active member of numerous status of women committees at the University of Toronto, University of Windsor and within the Canadian Sociology and Anthropology Association. She is currently working on the Status of Women in Ontario Universities Project funded by the Ministry of Colleges and Universities.

Katherine A. Fitzpatrick works as a private communications consultant based in Thompson and has been closely involved in the development of the Northern Women's Network. Her formal involvement in the women's movement began in 1986, when she joined the Manitoba Action Committee on the Status of Women.

M. Jean Graveline is currently an assistant professor for St. Thomas University in Fredericton. She originally comes from northern Manitoba and has been active in working with the feminist community there for the last three years. She has been active in the women's movement, primarily in rural and northern areas for fifteen years.

Lorraine Greaves is a sociologist teaching in London, Ontario. A long time activist on women's health and violence against women issues, she is a co-founder of the London Battered Women's Advocacy Clinic. She is also involved in several research projects on women's tobacco use. She is a former vice-president of NAC (the National Action Committee on the Status of Women), and co-chaired the 1987-88 organizational review committee.

Ella Haley is a doctoral candidate in sociology at the University of Toronto, and a lecturer at Wilfrid Laurier University. She comes from a family farm background in southwestern Ontario, and has trained in both the biological and social sciences. She is active in protecting women's choices in health care, and supporting the continued regulation of naturopathic medicine in Ontario. Other areas of interest include women and aging, the graduate school milieu, environmental health, community action, and creative writing.

Ronnie Leah is Assistant Professor in the Department of Sociology, at the University of Lethbridge, where she teaches Women's Studies courses. She has written on women's trade union organizing, racism, and coalition building. Ronnie has been involved in the women's movement and labour movement for many years. While living in

Regina, she was active with Saskatchewan Working Women, Connections and the Saskatchewan Coalition for Social Justice.

Ann Manicom is a member of the advisory committee for the Community Development and Outreach Unit of Henson College, Dalhousie University. She teaches in the School of Education at Dalhousie University and was part of the original group of feminist academics who worked with Henson College to create a structure within Dalhousie that would respond to community needs.

Barbara E. Mark is a lesbian feminist and an original Northern Network member from Churchill. She has recently left her work as a counsellor/advocate for battered women to work as an educator in the Native child welfare field.

Eleanor Maticka-Tyndale has been a professor of sociology at Vanier College, St. Laurent, Quebec since 1974. She has been actively involved in feminist organizations and organizing since the early 1970s. She was a founding member of the West Island Women's Centre in Montreal and of the first women's studies program in Quebec. She chaired the Women's Caucus of the Canadian Sociology and Anthropology Association, 1986-87. Her research interests are primarily in the area of women's sexuality, leading to publications on women's control of their reproductive capabilities. Her current research is on the impact of AIDS on heterosexual adolescents.

Karen Messing is Professor of Genetics at the Université du Québec à Montréal, and co-director of the *Groupe de recherche-action en biologie du travail*. She does research on the health effects of jobs in women's employment "ghettos," and on ways to adapt "men's" jobs to a wider range of physical capacities. She has been a feminist since 1963, and was a member of the Front de libération des femmes, the women's committee of her union, and is still a member of the *Groupe interdisciplinaire d'enseignement et de recherche sur les femmes* (GIERF) and the Canadian Research Institute for the Advancement of Women (CRIAW). GIERF received the CRIAW Muriel Duckworth Prize in 1990 for having contributed through its research to improvement in the status of women. With Maria de Koninck and Lesley Lee, she edited an issue of *Resources for Feminist Research* on women and the sciences. She has served as a token feminist on many government and university committees, and has always tried to do her best.

Angela Miles has a PhD in political science from the University of Toronto and teaches adult education at the Ontario Institute for Studies in Education. She was a founding member of such organizations as the Feminist Party of Canada, WAVAW in Toronto, and the Antigonish Women's Association in Nova Scotia, and is involved in women's studies and feminist community activities. She has a research interest in popular female culture in general and romance novels in particular, but her main work is concerned with the theory and practice of feminism as an international and grassroots politics, its theory, its place in history, its current roots in post-industrial developments and its relation to class politics and to traditional women's culture(s).

Mary Morrissey is Director of the Community Development and Outreach Unit of Henson College, Dalhousie University. She came to the Unit with a background in social work and evaluation, and with roots in the low-income community of Halifax, established through her work at the North End Community Clinic and Bryony House, a transition shelter for battered women. Originally the Unit's only employee, she fought the battles required by the founding of the Unit from the staff level.

Roxana Ng came to Canada as a landed immigrant in 1970. She has been active in the immigrant community since 1976, and has worked with immigrant women's groups in Vancouver, Saskatoon, Regina, Toronto, Kingston and Fredericton. Her research since 1976 has been concerned with immigrant women's experiences in Canadian society, and to bridge the gap between community groups and the academy. She now teaches sociology at the Ontario Institute for Studies in Education.

Joanne Prindiville has taught women's studies and anthropology at various Canadian universities. She is currently employed as a consultant on women's issues in Canada and Southeast Asia. As a member of the Newfoundland and Labrador branch of the Canadian Research Institute for the Advancement of Women she has organized and facilitated workshops for women community activists on topics such as group process, goal setting, research skills, development and computer communications. She is also a founding member of the 52% Solution: Women for Equality, Justice and Peace whose goal is enhancing women's participation and decision-making institutions in Newfoundland and Labrador.

J. Estelle Reddin teaches in the Home Economics Department at the University of Prince Edward Island. She is presently actively involved in DAWN (DisAbled Women's Network), is the P.E.I. board member in CRIAW/ICREF, has contributed to seminars and publications on low-visibility women's work and women's needs, and is doing research with wives of fishermen in Prince Edward Island.

Janice L. Ristock completed her doctorate in community psychology at the Ontario Institute for Studies in Education. She has taught women's studies at Trent University, and is presently Assistant Professor of Women's Studies at the University of Manitoba. She has been active in many feminist organizations in Toronto, Guelph and Winnipeg. She also does facilitating, workshops and consulting for feminist organizations. Her research interests include feminist organizations, burn-out and violence against women.

Cydney Ruecker is the mother of three children, working on a bachelor of education degree at the University of Regina. She has been actively involved in the feminist community for several years especially in the areas of women's health, daycare and education. Cydney has been an active member of Connections, Regina Healthsharing, Inc. and the Saskatchewan Association for Safe Alternatives in Childbirth.

Sharon D. Stone is invisibly disabled and a feminist activist with a particular interest in lesbian visibility. She is editor of *Lesbians in Canada* (Toronto: between the lines, 1990). She left Toronto for rural life in her native Quebec, where she is completing her PhD dissertation (Sociology, York University), a study of how feminist issues are treated in newspapers. She also teaches part-time at Bishops University and at Concordia University, and "Lesbians in Society" in the 1990 winter term.

Jill Vickers is Professor of Political Science at Carleton University in Ottawa and Director of the Institute of Canadian Studies which "houses" Carleton's Graduate Women's Studies Program. A past president of the Canadian Association of University Teachers and of the Canadian Research Institute for the Advancement of Women, she served as Parliamentarian of the National Action Committee on the Status of Women from 1983-1988. Co-author of *But Can You Type? Canadian Universities and the Status of Women* and Editor of *Taking Sex Into Account: The Policy Consequences of Sexist Research*, she has written extensively in the areas of women in politics, feminist theory and epistemology and the structure of women's movements.

Jeri Dawn Wine is Professor in the Department of Applied Psychology, Ontario Institute for Studies in Education where she teaches feminist studies, community psychology and counselling psychology. She was active in the Feminist Party of Canada, and is presently active in the Canadian Research Institute for the Advancement of Women, the Canadian Women's Studies Association, and the National Lesbian Forum. She is concerned with helping to foster an inclusive feminism that reflects women's diversity. Her research interests are in lesbian studies, feminist activism in Canada and violence against women.

Printed by
Ateliers Graphiques Marc Veilleux Inc.
Cap-Saint-Ignace, Québec
in August 1993.